The Phoenix of Philosophy

The Phoenix of Philosophy

*Russian Thought of the Late Soviet Period
(1953–1991)*

Mikhail Epstein

BLOOMSBURY ACADEMIC
NEW YORK • LONDON • OXFORD • NEW DELHI • SYDNEY

BLOOMSBURY ACADEMIC
Bloomsbury Publishing Inc
1385 Broadway, New York, NY 10018, USA
50 Bedford Square, London, WC1B 3DP, UK

BLOOMSBURY, BLOOMSBURY ACADEMIC and the Diana logo are trademarks of
Bloomsbury Publishing Plc

First published in the United States of America 2019
Paperback edition published 2021

Copyright © Mikhail Epstein, 2019

For legal purposes the Acknowledgments on p. vii constitute an extension
of this copyright page.

Cover design by Eleanor Rose
Cover illustrations: Sergei Rozhin, St. Petersburg, 2018 (Clockwise from top left: Mikhail Bakhtin, Aleksei Losev, Lidiia Ginzburg, Grigorii Pomerants, Merab Mamardasvili, Sergei Averintsev, Iuri Lotman) © Sergeu Rizhin; Background image © Getty Images

All rights reserved. No part of this publication may be reproduced or
transmitted in any form or by any means, electronic or mechanical,
including photocopying, recording, or any information storage or retrieval
system, without prior permission in writing from the publishers.

Bloomsbury Publishing Inc does not have any control over, or responsibility for, any third-party websites referred to or in this book. All internet addresses given in this book were correct at the time of going to press. The author and publisher regret any inconvenience caused if addresses have changed or sites have ceased to exist, but can accept no responsibility for any such changes.

Whilst every effort has been made to locate copyright holders the publishers would be grateful to hear from any person(s) not here acknowledged.

A catalog record for this book is available from the Library of Congress.

Library of Congress Cataloging-in-Publication Data
Names: Epstein, Mikhail, author.
Title: The phoenix of philosophy : Russian thought of the late
Soviet period (1953–1991) / Mikhail Epstein.
Description: New York, NY : Bloomsbury Academic, 2019. |
Includes bibliographical references and index.
Identifiers: LCCN 2019007931 (print) | LCCN 2019015924 (ebook) |
ISBN 9781501316425 (ePub) | ISBN 9781501316432 (ePDF) |
ISBN 9781501316395 (hardback : alk. paper) |
Subjects: LCSH: Philosophy, Russian–20th century. | Philosophy–Soviet
Union–History. | Soviet Union–Intellectual life.
Classification: LCC B4231 (ebook) | LCC B4231 .E67 2019 (print) | DDC 197–dc23
LC record available at https://lccn.loc.gov/201900793

ISBN: HB: 978-1-5013-1639-5
PB: 978-1-5013-7624-5
ePDF: 978-1-5013-1643-2
eBook: 978-1-5013-1642-5

Typeset by Newgen KnowledgeWorks Pvt. Ltd., Chennai, India

To find out more about our authors and books visit www.bloomsbury.com
and sign up for our newsletters.

Contents

List of Figures	vi
Acknowledgments	vii
Introduction	1
I Vicissitudes of Soviet Marxism	17
II Neo-Rationalism, Structuralism, and General Methodology	77
III The Philosophy of Personality and of Freedom	113
IV Culturology, or, the Philosophy of Culture	175
Conclusion	231
Notes	237
Bibliography	261
Appendix: Original Russian and Other Foreign-Language Titles	271
Name Index	283
Subject Index	288

Figures

1.1	Evald Ilyenkov	27
2.1	Iurii Lotman	84
2.2	Georgii Shchedrovitsky	93
2.3	Vasilii Nalimov	99
2.4	Merab Mamardashvili	104
3.1	Mikhail Prishvin	115
3.2	Iakov Druskin	119
3.3	Lidiia Ginzburg	124
3.4	Grigorii Pomerants	127
3.5	Andrei Sakharov	163
4.1	Mikhail Bakhtin	178
4.2	Aleksei Losev	186
4.3	Iakov Golosovker	194
4.4	Vladimir Bibler	204
4.5	Sergei Averintsev	211
4.6	Georgii Gachev	223

Acknowledgments

My work on this book took place over a period of twenty-seven years, most intensively in 1992–5 and in 2016–18. It incorporated significant input from a number of institutions and individuals, and I am deeply grateful to all of them.

In 1992–4, this research, initially titled "Russian Philosophical and Humanistic Thought after 1950," was generously supported by funding provided by the National Council for Soviet and East European Research (Washington, DC). In the spring semester of 2018, an Emory University Research Committee award enabled me to concentrate on completion of the manuscript by releasing me from teaching. I am deeply indebted to these organizations. (The opinions expressed in this book are mine alone and do not necessarily reflect their views.)

I would like to express my sincere gratitude to my former research assistant Thomas Stuart, who in the early 1990s helped me to type and edit the first version of this study, and to Dr. Anesa Miller, whose scrupulous comments helped me in editing the second version in the mid-1990s and led to its substantial revision.

I would like to express my deepest appreciation to the editor of the final version, Dr. A. S. Brown, who has played the most significant role in the preparation of this book. I am extremely grateful to Dr. Brown for his most dedicated, responsible, and intellectually generous help. Dr. Brown has made a thorough editing of the entire final draft, offering his invaluable advice in stylistic, terminological, and technical aspects. His devotion to the project was amazing, and he was extremely open and responsive to my queries and opinions and initiated many productive discussions that led to the significant improvement of the manuscript. Overall, we exchanged about 1200 emails while consulting on all aspects of this work, including the organization of the textual material and modes of expression for certain concepts. There was no issue regarding which Dr. Brown did not provide his most thoughtful, illuminating, and timely input.

I want to thank Dr. Igor Klyukanov for his considerable assistance in editing Part I, "Vicissitudes of Soviet Marxism," and Dr. Alyssa DeBlasio for her input in editing the chapters on Sergei Averintsev, Vladimir Bibler, Iakov Druskin, and Iurii Lotman.

My special thanks to Sergei Rozhin, an illustrator based in St. Petersburg, who designed sixteen excellent graphic portraits of philosophers for the book.

I would like to extend my sincere thanks to Haaris Naqvi, editorial director at Bloomsbury, who was instrumental in making the publication of this book possible. I am deeply grateful to him for his interest in the proposed manuscript and his patient guidance and generous advice throughout my work on it. My thanks also to Bloomsbury editorial assistant Amy Martin, who kindly helped me at various stages of the editing process.

My colleagues and friends at Emory University, Drs. Juliette Stapanian-Apkarian, Julia Bullock, Elena Glazov-Corrigan, and Vera Proskurina, were generous in providing the necessary creative atmosphere in my department and helping me to obtain the funding and release time necessary for my work on the project.

My wife, Marianna Taymanova, is a permanent source of support and encouragement, and her advice has been most valuable and formative throughout all my work.

Introduction

The fact that one can annihilate a philosophy ... or that one can prove that a philosophy annihilates itself is of little consequence. If it's really philosophy, then, like the phoenix, it will always rise again from its own ashes.
Friedrich Schlegel, Athenaeum Fragments (trans. Peter Firchow)

The more total society becomes, the greater the reification of the mind and the more paradoxical its effort to escape reification on its own.
Theodor Adorno, Prisms (trans. Samuel and Shierry Weber)

The Role of Philosophy in Russian and Soviet History

The Karamazovs are not scoundrels, but philosophers, because all real Russians are philosophers.
Dmitrii Karamazov, in Fedor Dostoevsky, The Brothers Karamazov (trans. Richard Pevear and Larissa Volokhonsky)

It is characteristic of the Russian people to philosophize.... The fate of the philosopher in Russia is painful and tragic.
Nikolai Berdiaev, The Russian Idea

Historians of philosophy do not usually regard Russia as a great philosophical nation, and many have pointed to its excessive susceptibility to Western intellectual influences. But while it may be true that Russia has not produced an abundance of original philosophical ideas, she is a philosophical nation in a deeper and more comprehensive sense. Perhaps no other country in the world has so totally surrendered its social, cultural, and even economic life to the demands of philosophical concepts.

It is difficult to trace the origin of this disposition, but if we trust the testament of the most ancient Russian chronicle, *The Tale of Bygone Years*, Russia adopted its religious faith from a "philosopher," a missionary sent by Byzantium in AD 986. This is the figure credited with unfolding before Prince Vladimir the mysteries of the Old and New

Testaments and persuading him of the superiority of Orthodox Christianity to all other faiths and denominations.[1] A few small Christian communities did exist in Kiev at that time, but it was not Vladimir's intention to adopt Orthodoxy because it corresponded to the way of life of the still overwhelmingly "heathen" Russian population. Rather, this was an act of embracing an imported heritage—one that predetermined the identity of the Russian nation for the next millennium. An entire new civilization evolved, not through the gradual, indigenous development of society, but from the adoption of a set of foreign philosophical and theological precepts.

Similarly, many subsequent turning points in Russian history have hinged on ideas enthusiastically embraced by the country's rulers rather than engendered by organic national evolution. Thus, in the eighteenth century, despite the meagerness of Russian society's educated sector and the recency of its apprehension of the spirit of the Enlightenment, Catherine the Great became the most thorough personification of the "philosopher on the throne" in all Europe, following—at least in her intentions—the intellectual guidance of such European thinkers as Voltaire and Diderot. Philosophically, Russia has been a "naïve" nation, a sort of *tabula rasa* that time and again sought from abroad the kind of philosophical instruction that could organize the diverse aspects of its existence into one self-conscious whole.

The nineteenth-century tsars, from the closing years of Alexander I's reign onward (he died in 1825), clung to the policies of conservative synthesis expressed by the famous formula "autocracy—Orthodoxy—nationality" (*narodnost'*), and failed to provide the state with effective intellectual leadership. Thus the task of establishing a philosophical orientation for society increasingly fell to the intelligentsia, beginning in the 1820s with revolutionaries from the nobility (the Decembrists), and continuing in the 1840s, with offspring of the middle and bourgeois classes known as *raznochintsy*. In considering the Russian intelligentsia as a social class, we should bear in mind the original meaning of the word, which is derived from the Latin *intelligentia*, signifying the speculative capacity of the human mind, the ability to perceive logical relationships and general concepts. Only in Russia (along with Poland, which was at that time part of the Russian Empire) could this abstract notion of *intelligentsia*, nurtured on the speculative philosophy of Kant and Hegel, have come to signify a specific social group. The cognitive capacity of the mind, its ability to grasp and then beget general ideas, became the preoccupation not of professional thinkers, but of a peculiar class whose ambition was to change, through the power of thought itself, the entire society and, ultimately, all of humanity. Succeeding generations of the Russian intelligentsia differed in terms of their particular political goals and methods (liberals, conservatives, radicals, revolutionaries), but what remained constant was the attempt to intellectualize the very substance of social life and the course of history. In the early twentieth century, the influence of the intelligentsia, of both leftist and rightist orientations, became ever more prominent in the life of an increasingly turbulent Russian society.

After the October Revolution, the intelligentsia as the bearer of ideology became politically dominant for the first time, as members of this class formed the ruling elite of what was, ironically, called "the dictatorship of the proletariat." In a certain sense, the revolution constituted the transformation of a living historical society into a philosophical entity, one that would henceforth develop according to the laws of the mind as embodied in the ideocratic State and the ideological activity of the Party.

The Bolsheviks' usurpation of Marxist ideas took full advantage of the Russian people's inclination to "philosophize," but the fate of the philosopher in Russia proved, as Berdiaev put it, "painful and tragic." Immediately after the Civil War, when the Bolsheviks had mastered the country they intended to "rationalize," many Russian philosophers were forcibly exiled to the West, while those who failed to emigrate were either persecuted or silenced. This was not because philosophy was no longer needed; on the contrary, the entire country had to be brought under a uniform set of philosophical concepts. Ironically, the intelligentsia in general, and philosophy in particular, became the first victims of this ascendancy of ideas in the new power structure. The obvious paucity of properly philosophical systems in the Soviet epoch is due precisely to the fact that the entire political system was based on one specific philosophy. To the extent that philosophy heads for power, power beheads philosophers.

Another paradox concerns so-called "dialectical materialism." Marx famously claimed he had found Hegel's system standing on its head (idealism) and set it right side up, on its feet (materialism). But the version of Marxism established in the Soviet state immediately commenced lapsing back toward the supremacy of ideas. Materialism, though nominally an official doctrine, became nothing more than an expression of materialistic *ideology*, a new tool of the intelligentsia for conquering the material world. Boris Pasternak in *Doctor Zhivago* describes the winter of 1917–18, which saw the first glaring appearance of the revolution's tendency to erase reality itself, leaving ideas in its stead: "They had to prepare for the cold, stock up on food, firewood. But in the days of the triumph of materialism, matter turned into a concept, food and firewood were replaced by the provision and fuel question."[2] And so it continued till the very end of the Soviet period: in 1982, the year Leonid Brezhnev died, and at the very height of so-called "developed socialism," the country was in fact incapable of feeding itself and featured a state-sponsored "Provision Program." Soviet society thus "dematerialized" as a historical body in order to become fully transparent to ideocratic rule. Reality proved to be a substance of pure thought, its visible and tangible embodiment.

In the Soviet period, it became a typical Russian trait to deduce all practical and theoretical issues from the "highest" philosophical considerations. The violence of the October Revolution could easily be justified as "a qualitative leap in quantitative social change," while the extermination of the kulaks as a class was dictated by the necessity to sharpen "the struggle of opposites" in the construction of a socialist society. Indeed, nothing could be more sacred to an exemplary Soviet citizen than "the unity and struggle of opposites" or "history as a form of the movement of matter" (philosophical postulates and idioms of Soviet Marxism). Neither worker nor peasant, scientist nor politician, writer nor artist, could succeed in their respective fields without special preparation in "the dialectical forms of the movement of matter" or "the ABCs of historical materialism," which were taught at all institutions of higher education, including engineering, medical, and agricultural schools. The philosophy of "dialectical materialism" was the core of all practical decision-making: it guided the political and economic course of the country and determined even the rules of everyday behavior.

Thus, the argument in favor of communal apartments, shared by several families, was that they implemented the philosophy of "collectivism" and the conditioning of "social consciousness by social being." Even such questions as the ratio of epic and lyric components in literary works, or decisions regarding the hybridization of vegetables, were treated as, ultimately, philosophical problems. For example, the prominent agricultural scientist and plant breeder Ivan Michurin (1855–1935) enjoyed enormous practical and ideological support on the part of the Soviet government because his experiments asserted the insignificance of inborn qualities of plants as compared with outside influences (nurturism versus naturism), which admirably conformed to the philosophy of Marxism. According to a Soviet philosophical dictionary, "Michurin's theory is based on a dialectical understanding of living nature, the recognition of the unity of the organism and external environment, and the dependence of embryonic cells and the entire process of fertilization on the organism's conditions of life."[3] For his part, Michurin himself claimed to have conducted his experiments under the "truly scientific" guidance of dialectical materialism; he urged his colleagues "to raise the elaboration of philosophical problems of biology to the highest level on the firm, unshakable foundation of Marxist-Leninist methodology."[4]

In the Soviet state, more than ever before in history, philosophy became a supreme legal and political institution, acquiring the power of a suprapersonal, universal "Reason." It was typical in the USSR to speak of the party as "the collective reason [*razum*] of the people," of the Politburo as "the collective reason of the party." In other societies, the supreme value and highest authority resided in religious beliefs, or economic profit, or dynastic interests, but in communist Russia, it was philosophy that served as the ultimate criterion of truth and the foundation of all social and economic transformations. The Soviet Union was the only great power in world history to be ruled by philosophical ambitions and assumptions, as distinct from the religious and occult preoccupations of even those regimes that can also be called "ideocracies," such as Orthodox Byzantium or Nazi Germany. Loyalty to the teachings of dialectical and historical materialism was the prerequisite of civic loyalty and professional success. Russia has suffered not from a lack, but from an excess of philosophy.

Thus, in the twentieth century, Russian thought found itself at the crossroads of two major historical tendencies of Western philosophy, one calling for the "practical implementation" of philosophy and its synthesis with the state, the other warning that such a union would be disastrous and give birth to totalitarian monsters. No other national philosophy has been so agonizingly divided between these tendencies, and so well qualified to testify to the meaning and outcome of this conflict.[5]

Philosophy and *filosofiia*: The Scope of the Concept

In the Soviet Union, the term "philosophy" was reserved for orthodox Marxism-Leninism. Officially the philosophy was regarded as a "party discipline": only members of the Communist Party and Komsomol leaders and activists were eligible for enrollment in the philosophy departments of top Soviet universities. Many original

Russian thinkers thus emerged from or retreated into different fields of the humanities that were relatively more free from ideological pressure: literary studies, aesthetics, linguistics, ethnology, and psychology. As Gary Morson and Caryl Emerson remark in their study of Bakhtin, it often happens that, "in Russia, criticism and theory become the practice of philosophy by other means."[6] In Russia, philosophy is less a noun, a self-sufficient entity (a field, a discipline, a profession), and more an *adjective*, an attribute or a property of various *philosophical* activities: the philosophically oriented humanities, or philosophically inspired cultural creativity, or philosophical aims of sociopolitical undertakings.

Even in the context of prerevolutionary Russia, the term "philosophy" usually covered a broad range of social, religious, ethical, and literary thought, and cannot be reduced to an academic discipline. The most visible and influential Russian thinkers of the nineteenth century, including Petr Chaadaev, Aleksandr Herzen, Mikhail Bakunin, Fedor Dostoevsky, Lev Tolstoy, Nikolai Fedorov, Konstantin Leontiev, and Vladimir Solovyov, were writers, journalists, critics, politicians, and librarians, not university professors or academic scholars.[7] This lack of academic affiliation is characteristic of many twentieth-century thinkers as well. Hence my preference for the term "philosophical thought," or even simply the Russian word *filosofiia* (as opposed to its English equivalent), to designate the broad conceptual scope of these intellectual practices, as distinct from the more specialized field of academic *philosophy*.

Filosofiia, an outcome of the Russian intellectual tradition, encompasses various fields of the humanities and cultural theories insofar as they contribute to universal conceptual systems and respond to the most general and "absolute" demands of the human mind and spirit. *Filosofiia* also signals the diversity of genres, ideas, and movements within Russian philosophical thought, which has historically included everything from academic scholarship, journalism, political and social theory, ideology, and the very idea of "thinking" as a philosophical act. *Filosofiia*, in this context, is defined not as a scholarly discipline or a language of argument, but as a broadly construed and often holistic relationship to the act of philosophizing—a relationship that may be exercised through any of the human avenues for creative and rational thinking. As the Russian philosopher and theologian Pavel Florensky described the position of Russia's philosophers:

> Philosophy in the sense of work performed in a private study, the work of "the mind," did not take root in our country, just as it did not in [Greek] antiquity. Our philosophers strive to be not so much clever as wise, not so much thinkers as sages. Moral pursuits, religious consciousness, and the activity not just of the head, but of all the organs of the spirit—in a word, we believe that life outside the private study is of the ultimate seriousness and is wholly dignified.[8]

Few Russian thinkers have made their way into the canon of Western philosophical inquiry. Perhaps this is due to the Russian tradition's diversity of philosophical genres and discourses and its creative interplay between *filosofiia* and philosophy proper. This investigation encompasses a broad range of problems and interests not normally treated in specialized philosophical speculation. It has often been noted that Russian philosophy has been inspired and even created by writers of fiction, such as Dostoevsky and Tolstoy. This tradition of blending philosophy and literature in one synthetic discourse was preserved in the period under consideration, in the philosophical prose, poetry, and criticism of Boris Pasternak, Mikhail Prishvin, Daniil Andreev, Aleksandr Solzhenitsyn, Andrei Siniavsky, Aleksandr Zinoviev, and Joseph Brodsky. Russian philosophy has never isolated itself from neighboring social, religious, ethical, and literary areas. For this reason, the study of Russian thought may prove equally valuable to specialists in philosophy and to those with broader interests in the history of ideas.

Three Philosophical Awakenings

The final period of the Soviet ideocracy, from approximately the late 1960s through the 1980s, can be characterized as a period of "philosophical awakening," to appropriate a felicitous expression of the theologian Georgii Florovsky (1893–1979):

> Such awakening is usually preceded by a more or less complicated historical fate, an abundant and long historical experience and ordeal, which now becomes the object of interpretation and discussion. Philosophical life begins as a new mode or a new stage of national existence.... One can sense in the generation of that epoch some irresistible attraction to philosophy, a philosophical passion and thirst, a kind of magical gravitation toward philosophical themes and issues.[9]

Florovsky refers here to Russia's *first* "philosophical awakening," which occurred in the 1830s and the 1840s and affected the generation of Chaadaev as well as the early Westernizers and Slavophiles, such as Vissarion Belinsky, Aleksandr Herzen, Nikolai Stankevich, Mikhail Bakunin, Aleksei Khomiakov, Ivan Kireevsky, and the brothers Ivan and Konstantin Aksakov.

Russia's *second* philosophical awakening occurred in the first two decades of the twentieth century, in particular, following the failed Revolution of 1905 and the intellectual elite's disenchantment with populism, Marxism, and other socialist theories marked by what it viewed as a primitive materialism and positivism. This intellectual renaissance is associated with the philosophical collection *Landmarks* (1909) and the writings of Dmitrii Merezhkovsky, Vasilii Rozanov, Nikolai Berdiaev, Sergei Bulgakov, Semyon Frank, Pavel Florensky, Lev Shestov, and other prominent figures of the so-called Silver Age.

Finally, after the soporific years of Soviet materialist scholasticism, the period of the 1960s–80s saw a *third* philosophical awakening. This latest renaissance had its origins in the period of the Thaw (the mid-1950s through the early 1960s), which engendered new trends of thought implicitly independent of, or even opposed to, official Marxism, leading to the latter's radical transformation. In the 1960s–80s, forbidden philosophical works made the rounds in various forms: "samizdat" ("self-publishing"), "tamizdat" (publishing them "there," i.e., in the West), and "togdaizdat" ("then-publishing," i.e., the circulation of materials printed in prerevolutionary Russia). These conveyed a profound charm that could not be explained in terms of mere "truth or falsity." Even simply touching these books, by Berdiaev, Rozanov, Shestov, and others, instilled in the reader a sense of joy at the mystery of self-reflective existence.

According to Florovsky, in the 1810s and the 1820s, prior to the first philosophical awakening, it had been poetry—that of Vasilii Zhukovsky, Konstantin Batiushkov, Aleksandr Pushkin, Aleksandr Griboedov—that formed the pinnacle of cultural priorities and played the role of spiritual magnet for educated society. The same could be said of the Soviet intelligentsia's infatuation in the late 1950s and the early 1960s with the poetry of Evgenii Evtushenko, Andrei Voznesensky, Bella Akhmadulina, and Bulat Okudzhava. By the late 1960s and the early 1970s, however, poets' influence waned, and in their stead such thinkers and scholars as Mikhail Bakhtin, Aleksei Losev, Iurii Lotman, Sergei Averintsev, and Merab Mamardashvili came to the fore. Florovsky had coined a formula for the earlier instance of this maturation process: "From the *poetical* stage, Russian cultural-creative consciousness passes into the *philosophical* stage."[10]

Existing Scholarship and Its Limitations

Our focus in this book will be on the period from the apex of the Soviet empire—a *philosophical* empire that by the mid-twentieth century, the time of Stalin's death in 1953, included a full third of the global population and had established itself as "the world system of socialism"—to its downfall in 1991. These dates are not just political signposts, but demarcate an important stage of Russian philosophical development, and one that remains almost uncharted in the West.

Russian philosophy of the first half of the twentieth century has been explored more or less systematically in the extensive historical surveys of Nikolai Lossky, Vasilii Zenkovsky, Sergei Levitsky, and Frederick Copleston.[11] Regardless of the time of their completion, these narratives end abruptly in the middle of the twentieth century, as if to imply that nothing significant could have occurred thereafter. The names mentioned last in these four most comprehensive surveys are those of Sergei Bulgakov (1871–1944), Vladimir Lossky (1903–1958), Lev Shestov (1866–1938), and Boris Vysheslavtsev (1877–1954), respectively.

Typically, discussions of postrevolutionary Russian philosophy focus on two mainstreams: (1) Marxism-Leninism in the Soviet Union, and (2) the religious and idealistic thought of émigré authors. The third major constituent, non-Marxist thought within the Soviet Union, remains mostly ignored. It is true that official Marxism strived to subsume all independent philosophical thought in the domestic arena. Nevertheless, even in the 1920s–1940s, in the period of the greatest ideological pressure, many brilliant thinkers managed to write and occasionally publish substantial portions of their work: Pavel Florensky, Aleksei Losev, Gustav Shpet, Mikhail Bakhtin and his circle, Lev Vygotsky, Vladimir Vernadsky, Konstantin Tsiolkovsky, Mikhail Prishvin, Viktor Shklovsky, Olga Freidenberg, Iakov Golosovker, and others. Along with professional philosophers, this list includes scientists, writers, and cultural and literary scholars, some of whom are celebrated in their respective fields. A coherent history of Russian *non-Marxist* and *non-émigré* thought of this epoch has yet to be written.

This deficiency becomes even more striking with regard to the latter half of the twentieth century. The cohort of Russian "philosophers in exile" virtually disintegrated with the deaths of the last survivors of the prerevolutionary Silver Age: Merezhkovsky (1865–1941), Berdiaev (1874–1948), Frank (1877–1950), and others. Consequently, almost all existing histories of Russian philosophy after the mid-twentieth century have been restricted to "Sovietology," exploring the official ideology and doctrine of dialectical and historical materialism and its various thematic divisions and internal debates.[12] Non-Marxist philosophy, with rare but notable exceptions,[13] has been mostly ignored or at best relegated to such narrow, tangential fields as aesthetics or poetics—areas in which Marxism had not established well-defined views. Not even the worldwide recognition of Mikhail Bakhtin, whose works represent a small but significant part of the Russian philosophical scene, has led to any concomitant attentiveness to the development of Soviet non-Marxist thought in general.

Even the most recent investigations of certain trends, such as cosmism, Eurasianism, or Orthodox thought, concentrate their historical narratives on preceding periods, especially the nineteenth and first half of the twentieth centuries. For example, George Young's focus in his study *The Russian Cosmists: The Esoteric Futurism of Nikolai Fedorov and His Followers* (Oxford University Press, 2012) is mainly Nikolai Fedorov (1828–1903) himself. In her book *Russian Eurasianism: An Ideology of Empire* (Johns Hopkins University Press, 2012), Marlène Laruelle concentrates on the first generation of Eurasianist thinkers of the 1920s. In *Modern Orthodox Thinkers: From the Philokalia to the Present* (InterVarsity Academic, 2015), the prominent scholar of Orthodox theology Andrew Louth only briefly surveys such late twentieth-century authors as Aleksandr Men' and Sergei Averintsev.

Only recently has late-Soviet philosophy begun to attract substantial scholarly attention in Russia. This new interest, however, has so far not produced any systematic research and is mostly limited to monographs and collections of articles on individual thinkers and problems.[14] The outstanding ROSSPEN Press series *The Philosophy of Russia in the Second Half of the Twentieth Century*, with Vladislav Lektorsky as its editor in chief, has published about twenty volumes dedicated to the work of prominent Russian philosophers of this period: Losev, Bakhtin, Lotman, Bibler, Mamardashvili, and other figures, many of whom the reader will encounter in my book.[15] However, only one volume in this monumental series focuses on general problems and discussions of the period in question, rather than on individuals, and these problems are mostly categorized not according to movements and schools, but by subject and discipline: philosophy of science, history of philosophy, the problem of human activity, the problems of dialogue and communication, and philosophical anthropology.[16]

In something of a temporal paradox, post-Soviet thought has already attracted more attention than late-Soviet. Thus, Alyssa DeBlasio's *The End of Russian Philosophy: Tradition and Transition at the Turn of the 21st Century* (Palgrave Macmillan, 2014) provides a persuasive analysis of Russian thought of the 1990s and the 2000s, focusing on the problem of its national self-awareness and claim to originality. Meanwhile, the preceding period of the 1950s to the 1980s remains mostly on the margins of contemporary research. This underscores the need to restore the meaning of this period as the crucial historical and intellectual link between Russian philosophy of the first half of the twentieth century (mostly idealist, existentialist, or Marxist) and its latest, post-Soviet development (mostly pluralistic-liberal or conservative-nationalist).

Major Trends of Russian Thought in the Post-Stalin Era

This book presents the history of ideas, not of institutions. Here for the first time, Russian philosophical thought of the latter half of the twentieth century will be covered in a single systematic investigation encompassing the most important trends and key figures both within the Soviet Union and in diaspora. Russian thought of this period, especially in the 1970s and the 1980s, cannot be mechanically divided into geographical zones. In many cases, thinkers within the Soviet Union and in emigration were the same people in different periods of their biographies, like Andrei Siniavsky and Aleksandr Solzhenitsyn, who were forced to emigrate in the middle of their careers (in 1973 and 1974, respectively). Even when thinkers remained geographically divided, they often belonged to the same intellectual trends and participated in the same discussions (e.g., Siniavsky in Paris and Grigorii Pomerants in Moscow represent the "pluralistic" outlook, while Solzhenitsyn in the US state of Vermont and Igor Shafarevich in Moscow are both proponents of "traditional" national values).

This book does not aim to cover every prominent thinker of this period (which would mean writing, instead, a dictionary or encyclopedia). Our task is to investigate the most characteristic and creative directions of Russian thought through their leading representatives.[17] Over the span of forty years, from Stalin's death to the death of the Soviet Union (1953–91), several philosophical movements emerged to challenge the ruling principles of Soviet Marxism, which itself had undergone considerable changes. Below, I will briefly outline eight major trends in Russian thought of the period under discussion.

1. Late-Soviet Marxism

One vector of transformation was the infusion of Marxism with nationalism, a process initiated by Stalin himself in his pamphlet *Marxism and Questions of Linguistics* (1950). Here Stalin abolished the class categories of traditional Marxism in favor of a notion of national unity, as exemplified in the integrity of the national language. This tendency resurfaced in the 1980s, with the increasing rapprochement of official Marxism and grassroots, nationalist ideology, which later grew into a political alliance of communists and neofascists. Another revisionist tendency, toward the humanization of Marxism, emerged in the mid-1950s with the publication in Russian translation of Marx's early *Economic and Philosophic Manuscripts of 1844*. This tendency suffered a severe political blow when the attempt to build "socialism with a human face" in Czechoslovakia was crushed by Soviet tanks in 1968, reinforcing the argument that humanism and Marxism were incompatible. The 1980s saw three new revisionist approaches to Marxism. The first was an attempt to revitalize and modify Marxism in the wake of the failure of the Soviet communist project. This version of *postcommunist Marxism* espoused the purification of Marxism from its Leninist and especially Stalinist contaminations and the incorporation of new realities, such as the persistent success of the market economy. The second approach suggested that Leninism and Stalinism had been consistent with the premises of Marxism, which must therefore be held responsible for all of communism's crimes against humanity. This version involved a radical critique of Marxism as a nonscientific and anti-humanistic theory, which, with its all-inclusive determinism, underestimated the sovereignty of consciousness, reducing personality to a function of the social system. The third approach, which can be called *post-Marxist communism* (as distinct from *postcommunist Marxism*), glorified the religious aspects of communism, abandoned by classical Marxism in favor of a quasi-scientific materialism. This position proclaimed the rebirth of communism as a moralistic and salvific doctrine, encompassing the insights of various Eastern and Western religions and challenging the soulless hedonism and consumerism of capitalist civilization. Thus Marxism was presented as the latest form of a "humanist religion" destined to save humanity from the pitfalls of bourgeois individualism through high spiritual ideals and collectivist aspirations.

2. Neo-Rationalism, Structuralism, and General Methodology

A number of new methodological approaches beginning in the early 1960s may be united under the title of *neo-rationalism*. Soviet structuralism came to the fore almost simultaneously with analogous movements in France and the United States. Structuralism revived interest in the forgotten and almost forbidden legacy of Russian formalism and at the same time brought it closer to the new disciplines and theories developed in the postwar period, such as cybernetics, semiotics, and general systems theory. Structuralism offered numerous methodological insights on the role of sign systems throughout history and culture. This project of rapprochement between the sciences and humanities was developed by the Tartu-Moscow semiotic school and by the Moscow Methodological Circle, which focused on the theory of systems and general methodology as related to the philosophical problems of social organization, artificial intelligence and cybernetics, and mathematical models and probabilistic approaches to language and the biosphere. Neo-rationalism pursued the systematic analysis of consciousness, the search for such properties of human activity and cultural models as are adequately cognized or organized by reason: logical and mathematical models, binary oppositions, methodological algorithms and reflective procedures, and so on. Neo-rationalism, and especially structuralism, achieved its greatest impact from the late 1960s to the early 1980s, when it boldly challenged the social mysticism of orthodox Soviet Marxism.

3. Personalism and Liberalism

Many thinkers of the period under discussion represent various trends of personalist and existentialist philosophy that posited freedom and individuality as their supreme values. Russian personalism, which is related to the heritage of Berdiaev and Shestov, is skeptical of rationalistic systems, and focuses rather on the formation and self-awareness of the personality, its moral and metaphysical choices and its attitudes toward nature and society. Personalism is inherently connected with pluralism. In its deeper background are neo-Leibnizean views on the individuality of multiple monads; more immediate sources include Dostoevsky, Rozanov, and European existentialism from Kierkegaard to Camus. The more politicized version of the same intellectual trend, liberalism, attracted influential supporters from fields of the natural sciences and the humanities. Emphases of this trend range from a foregrounding of the irrational and mysterious core of the personality, to valorization of human rights as the basis of social and scientific progress.

4. Culturology, or, the Philosophy of Culture

Culturology is the philosophy of cultural dialogue and the self-determination of cultural identity through "otherness." The cultural metaphysics of Oswald Spengler, Thomas Mann, Hermann Hesse, Florensky, and Bakhtin had a decisive impact on the formation of Russian culturology. Key concepts of this movement—"dialogue," "symbol," "otherness," "outsideness," "polyphony," "carnival"—emerged in opposition to both Marxism and structuralism, and characterized a specific methodology of the humanities as distinct from the natural and social sciences. Sharing a structuralist affinity for rational objectivity, culturology at the same time objected to the introduction of mathematical and cybernetic methods, attempting instead to develop special criteria of humanistic precision, and adopting certain methods from hermeneutics, phenomenology, and the spiritual-historical approach (W. Dilthey, H. Rickert). Culturology created its own methodological school of "dialogical logic" and "the dialogue of cultures," investigating the history of sciences and humanities from this standpoint. This intellectual wandering across the boundaries of cultures responded to a ripening public need to overcome loneliness and the self-isolation of Soviet society behind the "iron curtain" (both in space and in history).

5. The Philosophy of National Spirit

The grassroots ideology (*pochvennichestvo*) and neo-Slavophilism that (re)emerged in the late 1960s produced its own intellectual elite: writers, critics, and historians who attempted to create a philosophy of national spirit (which is typically but not invariably linked to rightist political views). Its major intellectual predecessors include the Russian Slavophiles of the nineteenth century and the Eurasianists of the 1920s. Twentieth-century German, French, and Italian sources, such as René Guénon and Giulio Evola, were also abundantly used. This intellectual trend focuses on the relationship between culture, nature, and nation and on questions of collective responsibility and guilt, and invokes such concepts as the biological energy, organic spirituality, and moral patterns of ethnic groups. In this approach, the rise and decline of ethnic formations are explained by biological rather than social factors, namely, by disproportionate infusions of cosmic energies into the biological mass of humankind. The philosophy of national spirit is fueled by many underground wellsprings of Russian culture, including extremely archaic, pagan beliefs. It produces both quasi-empirical doctrines about biological and geographical factors of ethnogenesis, and neofascist geopolitical utopias inspired by myths of the "Great Tradition."

6. Orthodox Christian Thought

Among the most influential trends of this period were varieties of religious thought, including Orthodox Christianity as well as synthetic, occult, or otherwise nontraditional teachings. Such major writers as Pasternak and Solzhenitsyn powerfully expressed Christian visions of history and contemporary society. Orthodox thought dates back to the heritage of the Eastern Fathers of the Church, while at the same time opens a dialogue with the traditions of other religions and with the world of contemporary European culture. In its most liberal version, Orthodox thought elaborates a philosophy of spiritual ascension that envisions humanity's development from paganism to the Christian revelation of Godmanhood. The younger generation of religious thinkers focused on such issues as Christianity's interaction with secular culture, science, feminism, communication networks, and contemporary philosophical and theological movements.

7. Cosmism and Universalism

Syncretistic or universalistic thought incorporates various gnostic, occult, Hindu, Buddhist, theosophical, and neo-pagan sources, often attempting to synthesize them with ideas of modern science (or science fiction) and technology. The legacy of Nikolai Fedorov, Konstantin Tsiolkovsky, Vladimir Vernadsky, Velimir Khlebnikov, and Nicholas Roerich is crucial for this trend. This religious universalism developed an original "meta-historical" and "trans-physical" vision that strived to absorb the religious wisdom of both West and East and pave the way for a future "inter-religion" and harmonious world order based on a universal theocracy. Various versions of Oriental mysticism and para-philosophical and esoteric teachings were intensely promoted and publicized by numerous intellectual groups. Another influential trend included the "philosophy of the common cause," originating in Nikolai Fedorov's ideas about the universal resurrection of the dead, physical immortality, and the technological transformation of the cosmos. Often identifying itself as "cosmism" or "anthropocosmism," this philosophy employs the broad categories of "universal reason," "noosphere," "immortality," "general resurrection," "the transformation and spiritualization of nature," "the conquest of the universe," and so on.

8. Conceptualism and Postmodernism

The latest trend corresponds to what was called postmodern and post-structuralist thought in the West; one of its original Russian varieties was conceptualism. This name usually refers to a well-known movement in Russian arts and literature of the 1970s and the 1980s, but it can also be aptly applied to a broad spectrum of critical and philosophical ideas that complement and illuminate this movement. Conceptualism assumes that certain conceptual schemes underlie the ideological construction of reality and determine its artificial, conventional character. Conceptualist thinking is imbued with irony, parody, and a sense of relativity, since "truth" and "reality" are regarded as dubious categories. Conceptualism's relationship to Marxism is somewhat reminiscent of the dispute between nominalists and realists in the epoch of the medieval scholastics: whereas Marxists assert the historical reality of such concepts as "collectivism," "equality," "progress," and "the people," for conceptualists these notions are purely mental or linguistic structures. Every cultural form is conceived as a combination of preestablished codes, such as the Soviet ideological language or the system of conventions in the Russian psychological novel. Conceptualism operates with mental universals and clichés in various genres of writing and artistic performance. It is essential to point out the proximity of conceptualism both to the postmodernist philosophy of pan-textuality (Jacques Derrida) and hyperreality (Jean Baudrillard), and to Buddhist or Taoist meditation.

Of course, the eight philosophical movements briefly outlined above do not exhaust the whole complexity of intellectual life in this period, nor do they even account for the "hybrid" work of certain particular authors. For example, Mikhail Bakhtin can be regarded both as a representative of personalist-pluralist thought and a founder of culturology. Andrei Siniavsky's work demonstrates smooth transitions between personalist and postmodernist paradigms. Georgii Gachev's thinking bridges such disparate trends as culturology, personalism, and the philosophy of national spirit.

Russian thought of this period is not just pluralistic but polyphonic: in the consciousness of the most creative thinkers, different positions and voices interact. Ideally, it would be productive to investigate the philosophy of this period at the intersection of two axes: (1) "Movement," encompassing the works of many authors, and (2) "Author," encompassing various aspects of several movements.

Of course, the life and work of a given author do not always match the boundaries of the period under consideration. Some thinkers, like Mikhail Prishvin and Iakov Druskin, belong to this period only through the final stage of their careers, while others, such as Vladimir Lefebvre and Boris Paramonov, through the early stage. In such cases, I concentrate on the works and problems characteristic of the authors in the given period, but at the same time I try not to lose sight of the overall horizon of their thinking.

This book investigates the first four major trends outlined above: Marxism, neo-rationalism, personalism, and culturology. The other four trends are examined in my book *Ideas against Ideocracy: Non-Marxist Thought in the Soviet Union (1953–1991)*, to be published by Bloomsbury Academic in 2020. These two books can be read separately, though their themes are interconnected within a single period and intellectual context.

The Structure of the Book

The order of the book's four parts is defined by the increasing influence of corresponding trends over a four-decade span: from the overwhelming hegemony of Marxism in the 1950s to the growth of structuralist, neo-rationalist, and personalist/liberal alternatives in the 1960s and the ascension of culturology in the 1970s. The 1980s, especially the period of glasnost and perestroika (1985–91), witnessed the renewed relevance of personalism and liberalism, increasingly open and critical debate around Marxism, and the emergence of postmodern literary and intellectual movements (the latter trend is discussed in *Ideas against Ideocracy*).

Each part begins with an overview of the major trend in question and a history of its formation. The subsequent chapters are devoted to individual authors who represent the most characteristic approaches and subspecies of the general trend, considered mainly chronologically.

The book's full structure may be seen in the following more detailed version of the table of contents.

Part I. Vicissitudes of Soviet Marxism

1. From Lenin to Stalin
2. Stalin's Later Thinking. From Class to Nationality
3. The Renaissance of Early Marx. From Class to Humankind
4. The Renewal of Dialectics. Evald Ilyenkov
5. The Philosophy of Human Activity. Genrikh Batishchev
6. The Renewal of Ethics. Iakov Milner-Irinin
7. Discussions around Aesthetics. Mikhail Lifshits and Aleksandr Burov
8. The Philosophy of Science. Technology and Nature
9. The Marxist Critique of Bourgeois Philosophy
10. The New Moralistic and Grassroots Turn in Marxism. Arsenii Gulyga and Iurii Davydov
11. Revisions of Orthodox Marxism in the Era of Glasnost. S. Platonov
12. The Self-Destruction of Soviet Marxism. Aleksandr Iakovlev
13. Back from Science to Utopia. Mystical Neo-Communism

Part II. Neo-Rationalism, Structuralism, and General Methodology

1. From Formalism to Structuralism. The Fate of the Formal School
2. General Premises and Particular Features of Russian Sructuralism
3. The Philosophy of the Semiosphere. Iurii Lotman

4. General Methodology and the System of Thought-Activity. Georgii Shchedrovitsky
5. Reflective Analysis. Vladimir Lefebvre
6. Probabilistic Philosophy of Nature and Language. Vasilii Nalimov
7. Phenomenology and the Theory of Consciousness. Merab Mamardashvili

Part III. The Philosophy of Personality and of Freedom

A. Personalism

1. Personalist and Existentialist Trends in Russian Thought
2. Nature and Personality. The Writer Mikhail Prishvin as Thinker
3. The Religious Existentialism of Iakov Druskin
4. Between Historicism and Personalism. Lidiia Ginzburg
5. Personalism, Pluralism, and Spiritual Universalism. Grigorii Pomerants
6. Russian-Jewish Personalism. Boris Khazanov
7. Personal Freedom and Planetary Consciousness. Mihajlo Mihajlov
8. The Paradoxalist Boris Paramonov. Sexual Liberation against Nationalism
9. Joseph Brodsky as Thinker. Privacy as the Ultimate Value

B. Liberalism and Westernism

1. Liberalism, Conservatism, and Religiosity
2. Freedom and Solidarity in Émigre Thought
3. Skepticism and Pluralism. Aleksandr Esenin-Volpin
4. Liberal Dissident Scholars. Arkadii Belinkov and Andrei Amalrik
5. Liberalism and Science in Political Thought. Andrei Sakharov
6. Liberal Historians. Natan Eidelman and Aleksandr Ianov
7. The Paradoxes of Late-Soviet Westernism

Part IV. Culturology, or, the Philosophy of Culture

1. The Concept of Culture in Culturology
2. Dialogism and the Methodology of the Humanities. Mikhail Bakhtin
3. Dialectical Idealism and the Phenomenology of Culture. Aleksei Losev
4. Culture, Myth, and Imagination. Olga Freidenberg and Iakov Golosovker
5. Philosophy and Philology. East and West. Dmitrii Likhachev and Nikolai Konrad
6. Dialogical Logic in the Interaction of Philosophies and Cultures. Vladimir Bibler

7. The Philosophy of Culture and Christianity. Problems of Hermeneutics. Sergei Averintsev
8. Living-Thinking through the Diversity of Cultures. Georgii Gachev

Several of the chapters listed above are further divided into sections describing various aspects of thought of certain of the most complicated thinkers (such as Iurii Lotman or Sergei Averintsev).

Part I

Vicissitudes of Soviet Marxism

1.	From Lenin to Stalin	17
2.	Stalin's Later Thinking. From Class to Nationality	19
3.	The Renaissance of Early Marx. From Class to Humankind	23
4.	The Renewal of Dialectics. Evald Ilyenkov	27
5.	The Philosophy of Human Activity. Genrikh Batishchev	35
6.	The Renewal of Ethics. Iakov Milner-Irinin	40
7.	Discussions around Aesthetics. Mikhail Lifshits and Aleksandr Burov	43
8.	The Philosophy of Science. Technology and Nature	48
9.	The Marxist Critique of Bourgeois Philosophy	51
10.	The New Moralistic and Grassroots Turn in Marxism. Arsenii Gulyga and Iurii Davydov	54
11.	Revisions of Orthodox Marxism in the Era of Glasnost. S. Platonov	60
12.	The Self-Destruction of Soviet Marxism. Aleksandr Iakovlev	65
13.	Back from Science to Utopia. Mystical Neo-Communism	69

1. From Lenin to Stalin

With the exile of the most prominent non-Marxist thinkers—Nikolai Lossky, Nikolai Berdiaev, Semyon Frank, Ivan Ilyin, and others—and the suppression of all non-Marxist philosophical associations and periodicals, Marxism was firmly entrenched in 1922 as the official Soviet ideology. The program for the integration of Marxist philosophy with state politics was outlined in Vladimir Lenin's article "On the Significance of Militant Materialism" (March 1922), published in one of the first issues of the new journal *Pod znamenem Marksizma* (Under the Banner of Marxism). Lenin's program called for an alliance of Marxist philosophy with the natural sciences and insisted on their collaborative critique of bourgeois idealism and religion. Lenin's death in 1924 prompted a reassessment of Marxism on the basis of his creative development of it;

Leninism would now be understood as the next and highest stage of Marxism, as the Marxism of the epoch of proletarian revolution and the construction of communism.

Lenin's main contribution to philosophy consisted of two works: the book *Materialism and Empirio-Criticism* (1908–9), and the so-called *Philosophical Notebooks*, a collection of marginalia (written in 1914–15, and published posthumously in 1929–30) to Hegel's treatises *The Science of Logic* and *The History of Philosophy*, including a short draft entitled "Toward the Question of Dialectics" (1915). Insofar as the philosophy of Marx and Engels is formulated in Marxist tradition as "dialectical materialism,"[1] Lenin was concerned with elaborating both interconnected parts of this conception. In the book, Lenin defends materialism against physical idealism and neo-Kantian revisions of Marxist doctrine popular among Bolsheviks in the early twentieth century. In his marginalia, Lenin pays tribute to dialectics as the component of Marxism adopted from Hegel. The relationship between the two constituents of dialectical materialism became the most dramatic theoretical topic of the 1920s, when relatively free discussion of philosophical issues was still permitted. Soviet Marxists divided themselves into two camps: the "mechanists," headed by Nikolai Bukharin, prioritized the materialistic component of Marxism and subordinated philosophy as a discipline to the methodology of the natural sciences, while the "dialecticians," headed by Abram Deborin, emphasized Marx's Hegelian legacy and the active role of philosophy in guiding the development of science. By the end of the decade, the "dialecticians" seemed to have gained the upper hand, especially after the publication of Engels's unfinished treatise *The Dialectics of Nature* (1925) and Lenin's *Philosophical Notebooks*, which provided authoritative arguments for a critique of "mechanist" materialism. However, in 1930–1, the ideological organs of the Communist Party, under the leadership of Iosif Stalin, intervened in the debate and condemned the "dialecticians" as "Menshevist idealists."[2]

This strategy was characteristic for Stalin (1879–1953): he would take a stand between two opposing camps, and denounce both for perverting authentic Marxism. In politics, Stalin fostered the establishment of a central dogma (the "general party line") via the tactic of "divide and conquer," which enabled him to amputate extreme views on the left and right, which he deemed "Trotskyite and Bukharinite counterrevolutionary deviations." This strategy of totalitarian "removal of opposites" was applied also to the field of philosophy, where the extremes of "bourgeois mechanicism" and "Menshevist idealism" were rejected for the sake of a unified doctrine that precluded any further debate. The most authoritative exemplar of such synthesis was contributed anonymously by Stalin himself, in the form of a chapter in *A Short Course in the History of the All-Union Communist Party (Bolsheviks)* (1938)—the book that became the ideological catechism of Stalin's epoch—titled "On Dialectical and Historical Materialism."[3]

Stalin begins his presentation of dialectical materialism with dialectics, opposing it to bourgeois metaphysics; and concludes with materialism, opposing it to bourgeois idealism. He is careful to maintain the balance between the two components. Dialectics is presented first, which to the Soviet mind suggests this category's priority, but symmetry is restored as greater emphasis is laid on materialism in the subsequent exposition, since the second part of the chapter is devoted exclusively to historical materialism, which by its name and nature is more materialistic than dialectical. The core concept of historical materialism is that all historical phenomena can be categorized as primary or secondary, constituting, respectively, the economic basis or the political and ideological superstructure. Though the relationship between base and superstructure presupposes dialectical interaction, the principal determination comes from the base, giving priority to a materialist interpretation of history.

Thus, if in 1922 all the movements competing *with* Marxist philosophy were banished from the USSR, then after 1930 the same fate befell all the movements competing *within* Marxist philosophy. For at least twenty years, in the 1930s and the 1940s, dialectical materialism functioned as an absolutely consistent and incontestable doctrine; the enforced unanimity of its recognition precluded any debate or creative interpretation among philosophers. During and after the Second World War, there were some attempts to deemphasize Marx and Engels's reliance on the legacy of classical German philosophy, and to underscore both their theoretical novelty and their affinities with the legacy of Russian revolutionary democrats. However, these political maneuvers did not touch the essence of the dialectical-materialist synthesis, which Stalin's mighty hand seemed to have set in stone. Ironically, the first to question this unshakable system was Stalin himself: in order to remain totalitarian, ideology must leave room for self-revision, which is usually presented as yet another grand achievement and confirmation of that same ideology.

2. Stalin's Later Thinking. From Class to Nationality

The year 1950 may serve as a signpost dividing the history of Soviet Marxism into two periods: (1) the rise and strengthening of dogmatic Marxism (primarily via Stalin), and (2) its gradual loosening and disintegration. It was Stalin himself who initiated the transition; the publication of his pamphlet *Marxism and Questions of Linguistics* (1950)[4] became a strong impetus for the subsequent demolition of Marxism, at least in its Soviet version.

The Marxist doctrine of historical materialism rests on two assumptions: the determination of an ideological superstructure from an economic base, and class struggle as the motive force of history. Stalin's focus in the pamphlet is the phenomenon of language, a topic which could have virtually no grounding in the works of Marx and Engels themselves other than a few isolated remarks. However, like all the arts and sciences of Stalin's time, linguistics was obliged to rely on the principles of dialectical materialism; thus the "new doctrine of language" espoused by the academician Naum Marr (1867–1934), the father of Soviet linguistics, was considered infallibly Marxist. Marr theorized the relationship between language and class, claiming that language was yet another determinant in class struggle, insofar as it was a tool for power. In Marr's view, the language of the Armenian poor had more in common with the language of the Georgian poor than with that of the Armenian aristocracy. Thus, the integrity of a national language is belied by class divisions that conform to Lenin's doctrine concerning the existence of two class cultures within every national culture: the progressive and the reactionary, *tertium non datur*. Marr's ideas dominated Soviet linguistics until long after his death, even to the extent that his opponents were politically persecuted and removed from their academic positions.

Unexpectedly, Stalin attacked Marr and his followers, distinguishing them from "true Leninists" with a surprisingly un-Marxist counterargument. In his pamphlet on linguistics, Stalin writes that "culture and language are two different things. Culture can be either bourgeois or socialist, but language, as a means of communication, is always an all-national language, and it can serve both bourgeois and socialist culture."[5] "Language as a means of social communication between people equally serves all classes of a society and displays in this respect a kind of indifference toward classes."[6] From some other source, such judgments could easily be ascribed to simple common sense, but from the perspective of orthodox Marxism, a view Stalin himself had forcefully expounded in "Dialectical and Historical Materialism," this interpretation of language borders on heresy. By Stalin's argumentation, language is a non-class phenomenon; moreover, it belongs neither to the "base" nor the "superstructure"—the categories that together constitute the conceptual matrix of historical materialism.

In a letter to Stalin, one of his readers asked for clarification, wondering "if it would be right to consider language a phenomenon peculiar both to the base and the superstructure; or would it be more accurate to consider language an intermediate phenomenon?"[7] Stalin rejected both these interpretations, arguing that language is used in all social, economic, and cultural spheres. "In short: language can be placed neither within the category of bases, nor within the category of superstructures.... Nor can it be placed within a category of intermediate phenomena between base and superstructure, because such 'intermediate' phenomena do not exist."[8]

Stalin mentions yet another possible interpretation—could language, perhaps, be numbered among the forces of production, maybe even as a tool?—but immediately dismisses this last potential reconciliation with orthodox historical materialism (or *histmat* as it was abbreviated in the Soviet Union). Tools, he would counter, produce material goods, while "language produces nothing or 'produces' only words." Language is thus no means of production; "if it were, chatterers would be the richest people in the world."[9]

For his contemporaries, Stalin's thesis suggested the ghastly impression of a philosophical black hole into which language drops and vanishes. Ultimately, Stalin never explains how language fits in the system of positive Marxist concepts, but instead "deconstructs" the Marxist notion of it, and demonstrates language's elusive and irreducible character. Like a theologian expounding on the nature of God based on his *non*-attributes, Stalin gives only a series of negative definitions, shrouding language in a mystical miasma beyond the grasp of rationale: language is neither this nor that; neither base nor superstructure; neither both, nor some mediation between them. Stalin's non-definition of language represented a bizarre void in the rigid network of Marxist categories. Indeed, if we recall that young Stalin studied for several years in a Georgian Orthodox seminary, and that the founder of negative (apophatic) theology, Pseudo-Dionysius the Areopagite, was, according to certain findings, a Georgian, the comparison of the negative theological approach to Logos and Stalin's negative philosophy of language seems less arbitrary. Importantly, Soviet philosophy after Stalin would see the emergence of such other irreducible phenomena as "personality" or "spirituality," which further widened the black hole in the Marxist galaxy. The loosening of the net in one cell inevitably led to its overall slackening.

It is ironic that the Marxist network of categories should have been loosened thus by the same man who had done more than anyone to forge it into an unbending iron cage. One possible explanation is that Stalin moved away from Marxist doctrine after the war in order to advance a nationalist mindset that he may well have borrowed from the defeated fascist regimes. Russian history has often seen its victorious leaders adopt the tactics of their vanquished enemies: thus did Muscovite Rus appropriate a Tatar administrative system in the fifteenth century; thus did the French revolutionary and republican ideals infecting young Russian officers after the seizure of Paris in 1813 lead directly to the Decembrist revolt of 1825. It is no coincidence that after the victory over Nazi Germany in 1945, Stalin launched a domestic campaign against "cosmopolitans"—who were mainly Jews—and proclaimed the "leadership" role of the Russian people as "the first among equals." Stalin's postwar ideological program demanded a revision of the entire Marxist conception of class as the determinant force of the historical process, in order to promote the category of nation. He may have been groping for an ideological revision of the classical Marxist postulate concerning the "dictatorship of the proletariat" so as to broaden and consolidate the social basis for a communist utopia. In fact, Nikita Khrushchev would officially ratify this revision eleven years later in the Third Program of the Communist Party of the Soviet Union (1961), whereby the country was said to have attained the status of an "all-national state"—a necessary stage of social integration on the road to a communist society where classes would be completely abolished. Clearly, moreover, Stalin initiated the rapprochement between official Marxism and Russian nationalism that would dominate the ideological agenda in the late Brezhnev and post-Brezhnev era.

Of course, rearranging the Marxist conceptual framework such that nationalist ideals would supplant class ideology was a tricky business. Such a project contradicted the entire Marxist tradition that had been imprinted upon every Soviet citizen even in elementary school. This is why Stalin left himself a loophole in the narrow field of the philosophy of language, wherein the notion of national integrity is clearly pertinent, while the application of class theory, though irreproachable from a Marxist ideological standpoint, is easily made to appear absurd. Stalin removes the categories of base and superstructure relevant to economic determinism so as to clear a space for the "organic" categories of national life—first and foremost, language. "History shows that national languages are not class languages; rather they are common to a whole people [*obshchenarodnye*], shared by all the members of a nation, uniform for a nation [*edinye dlia natsii*]."[10] From all the negative definitions of language, Stalin produces one positive conclusion: language implements the unity of national life and allows this unity to prevail over class divisions and conflicts. Thus, Stalin succeeded in introducing a nationalist twist in postwar Soviet ideology in the modest form of linguistic theory.

It is unlikely that any other philosophy of language has ever influenced a society as profoundly as Stalin's forty-odd-page pamphlet did the USSR. Not only was "Marxist linguistics" utterly turned on its head, but the entirety of the humanities now adopted a position against "vulgar sociologism"—which in effect meant orthodox Marxism. The class approach was still favored in analysis of the international scene, where the struggle against the "world bourgeoisie" remained in full swing, but domestically, it was to be eliminated, so that an "all-national" ideology could succeed it.

Another "magnum opus" by Stalin, *The Economic Problems of Socialism in the USSR* (1952), was twice as long as the work just discussed, but proved less influential. Published only five months before Stalin's death,[11] it did not have a chance to produce as radical and lasting an effect as his linguistic theory, though, had its ideas taken root, the consequences may have been even greater. This work concerns the primary aspects of Marxist social and economic teachings, including the fundamentals of historical materialism. Its topics encompass commodity production and the law of value under socialism; the elimination of the opposition between the urban and the rural, and between mental and physical labor; and the disintegration of a world market and the deepening crisis in the global capitalist system. Most of Stalin's insights remained intact in subsequent Soviet textbooks of Marxist philosophy and political economy, and would influence the composition of the Third Program of the Communist Party of the Soviet Union, albeit with Stalin's name nowhere to be seen.

Philosophically, this treatise's most significant part is its first chapter, which concerns the character of economic laws under socialism. Its main thrust is to condemn as subjective and voluntarist the idea that the Soviet authorities could abolish or modify the objective laws of society. The Soviet theoreticians who had advanced such notions made reference to Engels, who predicted in *Anti-Dühring* (1877) that alienated social laws, though dominant for centuries, would in the future be applied reasonably and come under the governance of the people. In Stalin's view, Engels had in mind the mastering of objective laws through their cognition and skillful application, not the creation of new laws and abolition of old ones. "Marxism understands the laws of science—whether natural science or political economy—as a reflection of objective processes, which occur independently of people's will. People may discover these laws, come to know them, study them, take them into account in their actions, use them for society's benefit, but they cannot change or negate them. Still less can they form or create new laws of science."[12]

A curious philosophical consequence of this idea would be that the laws of socialism would have had to exist before socialism itself; the construction of socialism would have followed economic laws independently of the will of its creators. For example, if we follow Stalin's logic, the "planned and balanced development of the national economy," considered to be the main economic law of socialism, could not have been invented by the devisers of the Five Year Plans, insofar as these persons were attempting to subject the entire economy to the "political will of the party." Centralized state planning and administrative decision-making, it turned out, was fulfilled by historical laws, not by government authorities (nor even Stalin himself). Like the laws of nature, economic development should be taken as a self-contained and objective entity that the Bolsheviks merely recognized and implemented. Stalin's emphasis on the objectivity of social laws is reminiscent of Plato's objective idealism, according to which the laws of the Republic preexist within a supernatural mind and are enacted by loyal citizens. Perhaps all practical utopianists, whether they proceed from idealist or materialist assumptions, feel the need to ground "prescriptive" laws, as enforced via political power, in the "descriptive" laws of nature itself.

On the whole, Stalin's later writings stand as one of the two most important contributions to the evolution of Soviet Marxism after 1950. Many of the socioeconomic ideas later appropriated by ideologists under Nikita Khrushchev and Leonid Brezhnev, including the significance of the law of value, the self-sufficient mechanism of economy, and the principle of profitability (*khozraschet, rentabel'nost'*), derive from Stalin; as do subsequent attempts at reconciling Marxism with nationalist ideology.

The other crucial contribution to the evolution of Soviet Marxism came from Marx himself, with the publication of his early writings.

3. The Renaissance of Early Marx. From Class to Humankind

Stalin's death in 1953 encouraged the new mood of openness and gradual relaxation of the regime that came to be known as the Thaw (*ottepel'*). The future of communism, cleansed of the deceased leader's dogmatic distortions, was now conceptualized as a revival of the political and philosophical ideals of the doctrine's founders. In 1956, the same year Khrushchev denounced the atrocities of Stalin's regime at the Twentieth Congress of the Communist Party of the Soviet Union and promulgated a critique of Stalin grounded in Lenin's last will and testament, the party publishing house released a volume of Karl Marx's early writings previously unpublished in Russian. The appearance of Marx's *Economic and Philosophic Manuscripts of 1844*[13] was an enormous event for Soviet and Eastern European intellectuals; their reception of it laid the foundation for a new, "humanized" version of Marxism that was to establish a "socialism with a human face," and whose political impact would be felt until the Prague Spring of 1968.

What, in the eyes of Soviet philosophers, made the rough drafts of a twenty-six-year-old "Young Hegelian" so compelling? The previous version of Marxism, canonized by Russian Bolshevism under the leadership of Lenin and Stalin, stressed the necessity of class struggle, socialist revolution, and the dictatorship of proletariat. Political and economic issues occupied the foreground, while the ultimate goals and human justifications for such a program were considered self-evident: the proletariat and its communist party were regarded as the bearers of the true, class-based humanism, which could only be achieved through the revolutionary activity of the toiling masses and their avant-garde party. Humanism, as a universal moral value blind to class demarcations, was seen as a bourgeois abstraction, meant to mask the truth of class motivation. This suspicion originated with Marx and Engels's *Communist Manifesto* (1848), which emphasizes the struggle between the bourgeoisie and the proletariat as the motive force of contemporary history; all their subsequent works, moreover, including *Capital* (first published 1867), were devoted to specific socioeconomic issues, rather than to the ultimate ideals and humanistic goals of the communist movement.

But in his earlier manuscripts, Marx had formulated the meaning of communism as a solution to some of the profoundest problems of human existence, most significantly the issue of estrangement and alienation. Borrowing these terms (*Entäusserung* and *Entfremdung*) from Hegel, Marx interprets them not (like his predecessor) as a productive self-estrangement of spirit (*Geist*) in nature and history, but as the ruinous self-estrangement of social man from his species-being (*Gattungswesen*) through the institution of private ownership. At this early stage of his thought, the crucial phenomenon for Marx is not Hegel's absolute spirit, nor yet is it class struggle; instead, it is "man's essential nature" (*menschliches Wesen*), as manifest and amplified in labor relations and articulated in all the richness of human sensuousness. Marx develops an anthropological theory, much in accordance with Feuerbach's views, but oriented socially and economically rather than psychologically and ethically. The central object of this theory is the reappropriation of the human essence via the overcoming of private property, identified as the cause of the alienation of workers from their products. The entire communist project, then, is designed to reclaim the investments of human nature from the estranged world of private property, and return them to species-being, conceived as a harmonious mode of social collaboration conducive to the fulfillment of all substantive human capacities.

Marx's anthropological principle presumes that this essential humanness is degraded in the existing antagonistic society; revolutionary transformation will thus be required if the products of human activity, currently perverted by private property, are to be repossessed by humanity as a whole. What is more, this "humanity" potentially encompasses not only people, but the entirety of external nature as a part of man's "inorganic body," which is increasingly humanized through industry and the arts and sciences. The alienation of man as both a private owner and an exploited worker must be resolved through the mastery of the estranged forces of society and the raw potential of nature.

> *Communism* as the *positive* transcendence of *private property*, or *human self-estrangement*, and therefore as the real *appropriation of the human* essence by and for man; communism therefore as the complete return of man to himself as a *social* (i.e. human) being.... This communism, as fully developed naturalism, equals humanism, and as fully developed humanism, equals naturalism; it is the genuine resolution of the conflict between man and nature and between man and man—the true resolution of the strife between existence and essence, between objectification and self-confirmation, between freedom and necessity, between the individual and the species. Communism is the riddle of history solved, and it knows itself to be this solution.[14]

These principles of early Marxist social anthropology (or anthropological communism) reinvigorated the post-Stalinist development of Soviet thought and shaped a new generation of philosophers and humanistic scholars who began their careers in the mid-1950s. Of course, subsequent changes can hardly be ascribed solely to the impact of the early Marx; rather, the unprecedented enthusiasm for his manuscripts was a sign of an urgent demand for social and intellectual renewal.

One important change in post-Stalinist Marxism was the philosophical shift from an emphasis on class determinants to concerns common to all humankind. It became possible to speak about "man as such," or "human essence," whereas previously such concepts would have been condemned out of hand as bourgeois humanism or reactionary abstractions, the products of a non-class approach (as distinguished from *classless*, which was considered to be the highest goal of human progress). By no means was this new tendency meant as a compromise with bourgeois ideology; the point was that the bourgeoisie had previously cloaked its class selfishness in *pseudo-universal* values. It was now up to socialism to rehabilitate the concept of humanism as transcending the narrow class horizon of the bourgeoisie.

Consequently, from 1956 on, we see a growing epistemological interest in theorizing such notions as the universal, the general, and the generic, or that of the abstract versus the concrete—a shift corresponding to the new emphasis placed on universal goals and the spiritual unity of humanity. These perennial issues of Western philosophy become vital for the most active representatives of the neo-Marxist intellectual generation, among them, Evald Ilyenkov and Genrikh Batishchev.

Within the orthodox, two-part conception of dialectical materialism, a greater emphasis was now put on dialectics, since it promised to overcome the one-sidedness of materialistic determinism and to demonstrate the inverse influence of consciousness on the external world. Some of the arguments that in the 1920s had been directed against the mechanist faction by the dialecticians were now revived, though without explicit reference to their origin, discussion of which remained taboo. At times, however, this new dialectical reasoning went even further than its early Soviet precedents, inasmuch as it stressed the human, "spiritual" (*dukhovnyi*) source of dialectics as opposed to its derivation from objective nature. The entire focus of neo-Marxist philosophy in the Thaw period shifts to a concern with "activity" or "life activity" (*deiatel'nost'* or *zhiznedeiatel'nost'*)—quite a departure from orthodox Marxist determinism, according to which social being determines social consciousness. In part, this shift may be attributed to the influence of French existentialism and Sartre's interpretation of dialectics as the inner property of the subject rather than an objective process of the external world. It is, however, significant that the Russian word for "reality" (*deistvitel'nost'*) implicitly contains the idea of "action" (*deistvie*). With this shift, the entire social order, the world of circumstances, is reinterpreted as an objective product of human activity that becomes alienated from the creative subject, subsequently opposing it as a determining force. Thus the concept of determinism, once prescribed as a Marxist antidote to nonscientific, utopian, or populist views, comes to be associated with the alienation of the subject from its own creative potential.

With this new generation of Marxist philosophers, communism once again becomes a philosophical, even metaphysical concept (as opposed to a merely social or political phenomenon). All the antinomies that had tormented the European mind since Kant, Fichte, and Hegel—the subject/object dualism, the paradox of self-alienation, and so on—appear to find their solution in communism, insofar as it reappropriates the external world to the collective subjectivity of humankind. Marx's famous definition of communism as "the true resolution of the strife between existence and essence, between objectification and self-confirmation,"[15] readily lends itself to any humanistic or religious adaptation, containing as it does a chiliastic vision of post-history, of paradise on earth. No wonder Soviet philosophers in the late 1950s and early the 1960s willingly indulged in discussions about a communist future and communist ideals, especially as the realization thereof was announced as an urgent and feasible goal by the Third Program of the Communist Party. "The Party solemnly proclaims: the present generation of Soviet people will live under communism"; this was not just a political slogan for the later Khrushchev period, but also a benediction for the philosophers who would boldly conceive the next historical epoch as reconciling all the contradictions from which previous, antagonistic social formations had suffered and groaned. Before the Thaw, Soviet philosophers had been obliged to adjust their views to the slightest changes in party politics; now this same politics demanded that they elaborate a strategy for building humanity's ideal future.

The drift described here, from class to universal human values, was inversely congruent with Stalin's attempt to deemphasize class doctrine in favor of all-national unity. Hereafter, with this revision of the class category as their fount, two intellectual mainstreams began increasingly to diverge. Both headed away from class concerns, one toward nationalism and nativist ideology, the other pursuing liberal and universalist tendencies. Ironically, the point linking these two vectors—that is, Marxism itself—lost its clout, and within a decade or so, one would be hard pressed to identify any common ground between nationalism and liberalism except for their growing contempt for Marxism. Thus, the Soviet experience suggests that as soon as Marxism pushes past class doctrine in search of a broader social foundation, whether nation or humanity, it loses its footing and gradually surrenders to alternative doctrines.

The peculiarity of the renovated Soviet Marxism of the 1950s and the 1960s is its sincere attempt to embrace universal values without abandoning its class character. The feeling that they were standing on the doorstep of a classless society of pure communism made the new generation of Soviet Marxists far more broadminded than their predecessors who had come of age amid the conformity and dogmatism of the Stalin era. This new generation included such thinkers as Merab Mamardashvili, Georgii Shchedrovitsky, and Georgii Gachev, who overcame Marxist inertia and succeeded in producing their own schools or methods of thought, which will be discussed in the chapters that follow as non-Marxist movements. In the sections below, we will examine the works of Evald Ilyenkov and Genrikh Batishchev—Soviet philosophers who remained principally faithful to Marxism and strived to revitalize its original spirit, even at the price of occasional conflict with ossified and institutionalized Soviet representations of the doctrine.

Figure 1.1 Evald Ilyenkov.

4. The Renewal of Dialectics. Evald Ilyenkov

Evald Ilyenkov (1924–1979) is probably the most prominent example of a late-Soviet "pure" Marxist who never deviated, at least consciously, from dialectical materialism. He would marshal all the vigor and elegance of his reasoning to defend ideas that, by the 1970s, had come to seem outdated to many of his peers, even those who had been enthusiastic about them in the 1950s.[16] From 1953 until his untimely death, Ilyenkov worked at the Institute of Philosophy at the Academy of Sciences in Moscow. His productivity was perennially constrained by institute higher-ups, who made every effort to keep his publications and travel abroad to a minimum.

Ilyenkov's philosophical background was, for a Marxist, typical. Favorite thinkers to whom he devoted several essays included Spinoza and Hegel; and Plato, Descartes, Kant, Fichte, and Feuerbach stood in the second row of his pantheon. As for Schopenhauer, Nietzsche, Husserl, Heidegger, and Sartre, not to mention other post- and non-Marxist philosophers—from Ilyenkov these came in for little more than dismissive mention. Though well-educated and erudite, Ilyenkov may in no way be considered a "liberal"; he was intolerant of even the slightest deviations from what he believed to be genuine or classical Marxism, and a considerable part of his writings consists of vociferous attacks on bourgeois and revisionist theories. He strongly objected, for instance, to the Polish philosopher Adam Shaff's attempt (relying heavily on the early Marx) at a reinterpretation of communism, partly in Kantian terms, as an endless humanistic approachment of a communist ideal that can never be finally attained, since alienation is ingrained in the depths of a human nature invariably constrained and distorted by social bonds. For Ilyenkov, Marx's principal thought is that the human essence is the totality of social relationships, not something "abstract" contained in a particular individual. Alienation between man and society cannot be infinite, since man himself is an inherently social being. It is the privatization of property that alienates man from society; the abolition of private property, then, puts a definite end to alienation and restores to a "particular" individual—reappropriates for them—their genuine social essence. A person comprehends and enjoys their own "species (panhuman) nature" in everything that is created by humanity as a whole and that belongs to him or her as a social being.

Ilyenkov's major contribution to Marxism is his epistemological work on the method of materialist dialectics, especially his first (and unsurpassed) monograph *The Dialectics of the Abstract and Concrete in Marx's "Capital"* (written 1956, published 1960). This was a cogent reassertion of "Hegelian" elements in Marx's legacy, and a refutation of positivist and empiricist approaches, which are so easily mistaken for materialism. The problem harks back to an enduring issue in Western thought: the status of universals. Materialism is sometimes alleged to deny the objective existence of general entities and to reduce them to signs or concepts, assigning real existence only to singular objects and individuals, but according to Ilyenkov, authentic Marxism has nothing to do with this nominalistic position adopted by empiricism and later by logical positivism. In his view, it is individuals as such, not universals, that constitute abstractions divorced from the wholeness of reality, which is at the same time general and absolutely concrete. In Ilyenkov's favorite example, such a concrete totality obtains in a society, which encompasses all relationships between individuals; whereas a separate individual, as a psycho-physiological unit, is nothing but an abstraction, a misconstrual of the human essence, insofar as this essence is realized only in society as a whole. Empiricists and logical positivists identify the concrete with a singular thing or "atomic fact" (Wittgenstein), but, for Ilyenkov, this singularity is the utmost abstraction, achieved as it is, literally, by *abstracting*, that is—to recall this word's etymology—*pulling* this thing *away* from its relationships to other things with which it constitutes one concrete whole: this society, or this forest, of which a single tree is only an abstraction.

Ilyenkov's interpretation definitely draws Marx closer to holism and leaves obscure the distinction between "concrete" and "whole," on the one hand, and "abstract" and "partial" on the other. Ilyenkov does not conceal that

> abstractness appears here as a synonym of individuality, that is, of particularity and even singularity.... A concrete object ... is a historically formed, integral object, similar not to a separate, isolated atom, but rather to a living organism, a socioeconomic formation.... This is why Marx so frequently uses the concept of the organic whole, an organism (or totality) as a synonym of the concrete.[17]

Hence Ilyenkov's vociferous polemics against both nominalism and realism, or in modern terms, against empiricism and idealism—which, in his view, presuppose and beget one another, since the abstraction of the singular from the general implies, by the same token, the abstraction of the general from the singular. "Consistently nominalistic empiricism invariably returns to the ideas of realism—to the picture of something general (abstract), which has the status of an object existing in some impersonal thinking."[18] Only materialist dialectics, proceeding from the whole as determinative to its parts, can avoid this double mistake of empiricism/idealism, which proceeds from separate individuals to their abstract general qualities.

The rationale for this epistemological error is the historical alienation from society whereby an individual imagines their own singularity as a concrete reality and perceives the social order as a mysterious abstraction, which, like the law of value, governs him or her from the outside. In reality, the abstractness of laws in a bourgeois society replicates the abstractness of an individual him- or herself who, alienated from his or her integral human capacities, is reduced to the "abstract function" of a profession—a tailor or locksmith, and so on. Marx not only anticipated the abolition of private *property*, but also elaborated the dialectical method of abolishing the epistemological illusions concomitant with the fetishizing of particular things and individuals. This is the method of ascension from the abstract to the concrete, by which all separate, analytical, abstract definitions of an object come together to convey its concrete complex unity as an ensemble of diverse and indivisible qualities. Ilyenkov's point is that generalization is at the same time a process of concretization, since abstract particulars grow together in the human mind to comprise an authentic vision of a concrete object. The highest goal of cognition is the concrete, inasmuch as it integrates a variety of abstract definitions. The ascension from the abstract to the concrete is the epistemological equivalent of the social process by which an abstracted individual reappropriates the richness of social potentialities into an integral human being, who thus stands as a "personality."

For Ilyenkov, dialectics is the highest mode of thinking, one that coincides with the essence of thinking as such. Following Hegel, he distinguishes three stages of thinking, or three types of mind. The first is the dogmatic, which takes up one abstract side of the truth and stubbornly rejects the other. The second is the skeptic, usually a further-along or disappointed dogmatic; this type grasps both sides of the truth, but they remain equally abstract, hence relative. The third, the dialectical mind, comprehends how these two sides collide with and contradict one another, and how they resolve their contradiction in the wholeness of a concrete object.[19] In other words, dogmatism and skepticism halt on the abstract definitions of an object (an absolute *one*, or relativist *many*), while dialectics goes further, to the concrete contradiction embodied in a real object.

In his works on dialectical logic, Ilyenkov insists that the principle of contradiction reflects the living processes of reality, while the principle of non-contradiction, peculiar to formal logic, deals only with signs and symbols. He rejects the conventional opinion, shared by analytical philosophy and logical positivism, as well as by some Marxists, that thinking is inseparable from language and can be accomplished only in language. "Do not people, in their acts of forming things, show themselves to be thinking beings? … This is why logic is a science of those forms through which thinking is implemented not only in language, in the acts of speech or its graphical representation, but in the purposeful ('smart') actions of a person. Of a social person, not an individual."[20] While formal logic demands that contradictions be eliminated, dialectical logic aims to disclose them and to explain, by them, all existing phenomena, since mental activity, social practice, and every other form of the universal movement of matter derive their energy from the collision of contradictions.

The core of Ilyenkov's thought is a Marxist reinterpretation of philosophical categories traditionally considered extraneous and foreign to Marxism, for instance, the "ideal," the "general," the "fantastic," and the "personality." Playing upon the Hegelian, "idealistic" origin of Marx's dialectics, Ilyenkov adduces incontrovertible arguments against empiricism, or "vulgar materialism," regarding the problem of the ideal. The ideal, for Marx, is nothing but "the material, transplanted into man's head and transformed in it."[21] Proceeding from this formulation, Soviet Marxists had typically considered the ideal to be a reflection of the material in the human mind, or as Lenin put it, "a subjective image of the objective world"; the ideal resides, therefore, only in the subject of knowing, that is, in the neurodynamic processes of the subject's brain. Reversing this influential interpretation, Ilyenkov argues that the ideal indeed does exist in the objective world, insofar as the world is already transformed by human "idealizing" activity. An example of such an objective ideality would be the form of value (in political economy), which is independent of the material qualities of the commodities whereby it is represented. Ilyenkov compares this with traditional theology's concept of the soul: value is universal, incorporeal, imperceptible to any physical or chemical analysis, but nevertheless exists and determines real processes in the economy, trade exchanges, and people's material welfare.

Marx called the form of value "ideal"—despite its not being confined to a person's head—because society has its own sphere of idealities, which cannot be reduced to an individual's brain processes. Moral norms, legal institutions, religious rituals, professional regulations, language structures—all these forms of social consciousness are undoubtedly ideal, notwithstanding their status as extrinsic to individual consciousness, their objective determination of it from the outside. Such reasoning is reminiscent of objective idealism, and Ilyenkov refers sympathetically to Plato and Hegel, repeating Lenin's thought that an intelligent idealism is far more relevant than a stupid materialism. Naturally, as a Marxist, Ilyenkov takes care to distance himself from idealism: all these objective idealities, he emphasizes, are not supernatural entities, but the products of human social activity transcending the boundaries of separate individuals and the capacities of their brains. The economic form of value is ideal inasmuch as it is an objectified form of human vital activity, placed outside this activity, as a form of commodity itself.[22] For objective idealism, things by themselves contain the ideal model preceding and pre-forming their material existence, while dialectical materialism derives their ideality from the formative activity of the human as a social being. For Ilyenkov, ideal objects exist only in a cultural realm, not—as idealists would have us believe—in nature. There is nothing ideal, that is, except the person, understood not as a separate individual, but as a sum total of relationships between people, their cooperative labor bringing ideal forms forth into society.[23]

It is characteristic of humans to misconceive the exteriorized products of their own accomplishment, taking them for the natural, inherent, self-contained forms of the surrounding world. Hence the task of dialectical materialism to clearly demarcate not only the subjectively ideal in the human mind from the objectively ideal in human society, but also the objectively ideal in society from what is objectively material in nature. Ilyenkov explains the errors of "vulgar" materialism and of objective idealism by the illusion of fetishism, which reduces ideal qualities to matter (e.g., cerebral cells or neurodynamic functions) and, by the same token, reduces material objects to ideal entities (e.g., ideas, pure spirit, or archetypes). The interdependency of these two philosophical illusions was uncovered by Marx: "The crude materialism of the economists who regard as the *natural properties* of things what are social relations of production among people, and qualities which things obtain because they are subsumed under these relations, is at the same time just as crude an idealism, even fetishism, since it imputes social relations to things as inherent characteristics, and thus mystifies them."[24] Thus, for Ilyenkov, vulgar materialism, which sees the ideal as a quality of an individual brain, and objective idealism, which sees matter as the embodiment of a universal spirit, both derive their illusions from fetishism, in the sense of an inability to distinguish between the material and the ideal. It is only dialectical materialism that allows us to establish the objectivity of the ideal as a social and cultural phenomenon, without confusing it with the objectivity of matter (as given in nature) or the subjectivity of the ideal (as given in psychology).

In his later work, Ilyenkov paid greater attention to ethical and psychological issues, as set forth especially in his popular book *Of Idols and Ideals* (1968) and in a series of works devoted to personality formation and the education of blind and deaf children. In his discussion of personality, Ilyenkov seeks to counter the existentialists' valorization of the unique over and against the general, and their perceived foregrounding of the solitary and asocial individual to an impersonal society. For Ilyenkov, the general is not some "abstract category," a stultifying identicalness or "equality" extracted from all separate individuals or imposed on them; the general, he maintains, is rather the comprehensive social network and interplay between people. Ilyenkov never tired of repeating his favorite formulation by the early Marx: "[T]he human essence is no abstraction inherent in each single individual. In its reality it is the ensemble of the social relations."[25] It is only by partaking in this generality through interactions with other people that one embraces the essence of humanity and actively transforms one's own innate physiological qualities into the self-conscious unity of a real personality. "The personality is the totality of a man's relationships to himself as to 'the other'.... Thus 'the body' of a personality is not a separate body of a specimen of the *homo sapiens* species, but at least two such bodies—'I' and 'You,' united as if into one body by social-human bonds, relationships, mutual ties."[26] In other words, an individual develops into a personality inasmuch as he or she appropriates relationships with other individuals as with his or her own self. A personality is an interrelationship, a reciprocality, not an isolated physiological or psychological unit. A personality lives not in the animal, but in the human body, which includes all such artificial "organs," created by humanity, as tools, machines, words, books, TV networks, and so on. To appropriate this collective body of humanity, to socialize one's animal body, means to become a personality. Loneliness, it follows, is a setback of personalization, which may truly be achieved only through the internal assimilation of as many social ties and cultural values as an individual can muster. Thus it would be incorrect to make reference (as Marxists frequently did) to the "socialization of the personality," since personality in itself is a social phenomenon; rather, one should speak of the socialization of an individual, of the natural body of (in particular) a newborn.[27]

Ilyenkov criticizes traditional psychology (including the Soviet variant) for its focus on individual, physiologically determined properties, recommending instead the early Marx's vision of psychology as a science of the human essence not isolated in a biological specimen, but deployed in the integrity of social and cultural resources.

> Only through the objectively unfolded richness of man's essential being is the richness of subjective human sensibility … either cultivated or brought into being.… It will be seen how the history of *industry* and the established *objective* existence of industry are the *open* book of *man's essential powers*, the exposure to the senses of human *psychology*. Hitherto this was not conceived in its inseparable connection with man's *essential being*, but only in an external relation of utility.[28]

This does not mean that the history of industry may be substituted with psychology but implies, rather, that psychology should study human personality in all the complexity of its social nature, externalized in the diversity of sensuous objects. Again—just as in all other methodological applications of dialectical materialism—according to Marxist psychology, a person must reappropriate what was alienated from them in the commodified setting, and reinterpret all the material wealth of society as the fulfillment and expression of human capacities, subject to psychological research.

These philosophical considerations were tested in the pedagogic experiments to which in his later years Ilyenkov devoted much attention, in cooperation with Aleksandr Meshcheriakov, a well-known educator of deaf-blind children.[29] If a newborn is devoid of the most vital sensuous channels to perceive the outward world, is his or her subsequent growth into an intelligent, mentally developed person a smashing argument in favor of idealism? In the United States, the story of Helen Keller has frequently served to confirm that innate mind, or soul, is more or less independent of extraneous factors and stimuli. On the other hand, Soviet scholars of the new post-Stalinist formation, such as D. I. Dubrovsky and A. A. Malinovsky, also tended to take an "innatist" position, albeit from the purely materialistic standpoint of genetic laws and inborn neurophysiological microstructures. In these polemics, Ilyenkov took a firmly anti-innatist and anti-reductionist stance, one he deemed most befitting the classical Marxist view. At stake in the debate was the conception of the social origin of mind. The upbringing of a deaf-blind child bereft of vital physical functions is conducive to quite purely experimental conditions; for Ilyenkov, these attest to the social, not physical, origin of human intellect, will, and self-consciousness.

Ilyenkov attempted to counter the arguments of both idealists and physiological materialists, whom he categorized under the joint rubric of "physiological idealists."

The successful training of deaf-blind children proves that it is not the inborn abilities of seeing and hearing that determine the development of their mind, but social interaction with their educators, who provide them with the collective mind of humanity. An adult takes a child holding a spoon by the hand and produces the intelligent movements of eating and drinking, until the child's hand, at first passive or even resisting, begins to help the adult, and then independently carries on the logic of the same movements: this is how social interaction works through the palpable forms of material culture. "Adjusting himself to the world of things, that is appropriating them actively, a child appropriates the social human intellect and its logic, objectified in these things, that is turns into an intelligent being, a plenipotentiary representative of the human kind."[30]

Ilyenkov recalls with satisfaction an episode at a conference when one of his pupils, at the time studying at Moscow State University, was asked: "Does not this experiment refute the old truth of materialism that there is nothing in the mind that would not have been in feelings? These people do not see and hear, but understand better than we do?" The deaf-blind student answered on his own behalf: "Who told you we do not see and hear? We see and hear through the eyes and ears of all our friends, of all people, of all humankind."[31] This, Ilyenkov adds, was the proper reply of a Marxist psychologist, for whom even the physical abilities of a human being are not purely physical or animal properties, but are shaped in the course of social interaction. Each person is a society in miniature, which is why a disabled person can compensate for particular deficiencies by using the resources and abilities of the whole society.

Ilyenkov's arguments, like the entire Marxist position on this question, are open to criticism because the very status of seeing and hearing is ambivalent: on the one hand, these are innate abilities, but, on the other, they serve the perception of the outside world, and a child's intellectual growth in the absence of these abilities may serve as evidence both for and against innatism.

Ilyenkov's ethical orientation is decisively atheistic. In his youth, as an officer in the Second World War, under the impression of unbelievable sufferings and hardship, he wrote in his diary: "A feeling grows stronger in me, that we need God very, very much … Exactly the sort of God that Lev Tolstoy had."[32] However, later, as a mature philosopher, he fiercely rejected any compromise with religion. His favorite saying was "Where there's divinity, there's poverty" (in Russian, a play on the shared etymology of the words: *gde bozhestvo, tam i ubozhestvo*)—a reference to the famous Feuerbachian (and Marxist) postulate that faith in God devastates and impoverishes the essential powers of the human.

However, Ilyenkov, unlike the majority of his fellow Marxists, did pose himself the question of the ultimate goal of humankind. No metaphysical speculation would be appropriate for a convinced materialist, and so he situated his "Marxist eschatology" in the cosmic dimension. One of his earliest pieces, "The Cosmology of Spirit. A Philosophical and Poetical Phantasmagoria Relying on the Principles of Dialectical Materialism"—written in the 1950s, but published only in 1991—demonstrates, in Ilyenkov's thought, an astonishing originality and imaginative force that in time would be partially surrendered as he gradually adjusted to the needs of arid, official

Marxism. Here Ilyenkov proceeds from Engels's postulate in *The Dialectics of Nature* that matter in all its transformations never loses a single attribute; therefore, "with the same iron necessity that [matter] will exterminate on the earth its highest creation, the thinking mind, it must somewhere else and at another time again produce it."[33] Ilyenkov agrees with Engels that the second law of thermodynamics, establishing the progressive dispersion of energy and the growth of entropy in the universe, inevitably draws humankind to thermal death: the sun will go out, like other stars, and life will be doomed to extinction. But since the human mind accumulates solar energy in higher proportions than other matter, and since the human mind can transform matter according to its own laws, Ilyenkov foresees the crucial role of the mind in future cosmic evolution.

Here we might expect from Ilyenkov some variant of Teilhard de Chardin's vision of the universe completely intellectualized and transformed into noosphere—the kingdom of the mind. But for Ilyenkov, this would likely have been too idealistic a move, since it is the mind that should remain an attribute of matter, not vice versa. Hence a unique suggestion: in the final stage of the freezing universe, humankind should blow it up, in order to begin a new cycle of cosmic evolution. In this cataclysm, a thermonuclear explosion on the scale of the whole extant universe, mind itself would surely perish—but in self-sacrifice for the sake of its "mother," the universal matter that, beginning with this explosion, would engage in a new cycle of evolution that would inevitably bring forth a new generation of thinking beings.

> The death of the thinking mind becomes a truly creative act—an act that transforms the freezing wastes of interplanetary space, absorbed into darkness, into revolving masses of burning, bright, warm, sunny worlds— systems that become the cradles of new life, a new blooming of the thinking mind, immortal as matter itself.... In so doing, the thinking mind sacrifices itself; in this process, it cannot survive. But its self-sacrifice is performed for the sake of its duty toward Mother Nature. The human being, the thinking mind, returns to her its old debt. At one time, during her youth, nature gave birth to the thinking mind. Now, the other way round, the thinking mind, at the cost of its own existence, gives back to Mother Nature, dies in her "thermal death," a fiery new youth—a state in which she is capable of beginning anew the grandiose cycles of her development that someday, in another point of time and space, will lead again to the birth, from her cooling depths, of a new thinking brain, a new thinking mind.[34]

This inspired, myth-like conception is reminiscent of great philosophical visions of the past: for instance, that of Empedocles, who, according to legend, threw himself into the mouth of a volcano to merge his spirit with the fiery, ecstatic life of nature; or Nietzsche's myth of the rotation of time and the eternal return. But if we compare Ilyenkov's cosmological hypothesis with its immediate philosophical ground, Marxism—which is marked by a glaring historical optimism—this vision strikes us as deeply pessimistic. What is the use of social struggles and revolutions, the building of a classless communist society, and the subjugation of wild, spontaneous forces of nature if, in the final analysis, the only destiny humanity can strive for, the best it may eventually attain, is the noble suicide? The heroic self-sacrifice is intended for the benefit of cosmic evolution, and ultimately for the emergence on its future basis of new forms of mind: this action is all that elevates the thinking mind over the level of matter itself, and constitutes the only alternative to its resignation to an ineluctable natural end. This suicide, strange as it may seem, remains the last word of Marxist teaching on the ultimate meaning of human existence. This had a tragic repercussion in the fate of Ilyenkov himself, who, at the height of his career, overcome by professional and personal crises, took his own life.

Ilyenkov was probably the last significant Soviet philosopher to be unconditionally devoted to Marxism. He was talented, erudite, and refined enough to make Marxism his deliberate intellectual choice and to conduct sophisticated polemics with the doctrine's opponents and revisionists. This sophistication made Ilyenkov suspicious of straightforward Soviet dogmatics, even as, given his lifelong attachment to the philosophy of Marx and Lenin, to him the new generation of independent and dissident intellectuals seemed ridiculous. The loneliness of his position reached its peak in the late 1970s during work on what would be his final book, about Lenin's vehement attacks on Mach, Bogdanov, and other "empirio-criticists"—at a time when Moscow's most advanced intellectuals had moved far, far on: to Russian religious philosophy and Western structuralism, Nikolai Berdiaev and Roland Barthes, Oswald Spengler and Herman Hesse, and to the latest cultural and anthropological studies. During this period Ilyenkov was perceived as a whimsical holdover of Khrushchev's Thaw, an avatar of the old-timey infatuation with Marxism it was hard to believe still survived.

But none of this should diminish the importance of Ilyenkov's most creative endeavors of the mid-1950s and the 1960s. He was an exceptional Soviet Marxist, possessed of a zest for thinking and the urge to inspire his colleagues by the power of the dialectical method. He was the first to reinstill Soviet Marxism with elements of Hegelian dialectics (and, to a degree, of Hegelian idealism) since the time of Soviet Hegelians' ("Deborinites'") defeat by Stalin's ideologues in 1930. Ilyenkov was second to none in validating the objective status of the ideal and the universal as elements of social practice and as categories of Marxist materialism. Finally, Ilyenkov had an impact on numerous philosophers of his generation, including Genrikh Batishchev, Feliks Mikhailov, Iurii Borodai, Iurii Davydov, Georgii Shchedrovitsky, Merab Mamardashvili, and Georgii Gachev, who at the outset of their professional careers were strongly influenced by Ilyenkov's methodological quest and dialectical reasoning, however far their ways would part in the decades that followed.[35]

5. The Philosophy of Human Activity. Genrikh Batishchev

If Evald Ilyenkov foregrounded the problem of the ideal so as to incorporate it into the world of concrete social phenomena, his disciple and eventual opponent Genrikh Batishchev (1932–1990), who from 1962 to the end of his life worked as a senior researcher at the Moscow Institute of Philosophy, elaborated a related problem not sufficiently treated in classical Marxist thought: that of human activity. In his *Theses on Feuerbach*, Marx himself connected these two problems, remarking that the chief shortcoming of all previous materialism was its passive and contemplative approach to the material world as a totality of objects. "Hence it happened that the *active* side, in contradistinction to materialism, was developed by idealism—but only abstractly, since, of course, idealism does not know real, sensuous activity as such."[36] Ilyenkov sought to overcome this defect of pre-Marxist materialism by divorcing abstraction from the ideal. For his part, Batishchev would undertake the complementary task of demonstrating that human activity may be divorced from the ideal and rooted in the sensuous, material foundation of human existence. The relationship between these two approaches could be schematized thus: Ilyenkov's thought makes a downward movement, from the heights of ideality to the material world, while Batishchev moves in the opposite direction, from the given organic status of humans to the horizon of their creative activity.

First of all, Batishchev critiques two directions in contemporary philosophy concerning the place of the human in the world. One is objectivism, or ontologism, which claims to explore the existing world as such, beyond the limits of human subjectivity. Positivism, empiricism, psychoanalysis, and structuralism all fall under this general category, since they proceed from an assumption of nonhuman, objective causality. The human thus stands as a tool at the disposal of impersonal and anonymous mechanisms variously defined as forces of production, or the nature of the human species, or subconscious drives, or language structures. The other extreme, which can be called subjectivism (or activism), grounds human activity in consciousness or will, and opposes it to the dead materiality of the external world. According to this view, one is a free, self-determining entity whose activity is owed to no external influences in the objective world; one willfully creates one's own destiny. Objectivity can affect this activity only by hindering it, as an obstacle or mechanism of alienation. Fichte, Schopenhauer, Nietzsche, and philosophers of existentialism and personalism are representative of this subjectivist tendency.

These two extremes, argues Batishchev, may be combined into a single theory, one that is deterministic and activist at the same time. Though his philosophical critique is directed at bourgeois philosophy, his implicit target is orthodox Soviet Marxism, which on the one hand proclaims its allegiance to scientific objectivity and historical determinism, but on the other, condones the most arbitrary and violent activism of communist leaders. Batishchev demonstrates that the conceptions of social determinism and ideological voluntarism are, despite their seeming incompatibility, internally connected and mutually dependent, which makes possible the very phenomenon of Soviet Marxism with its oxymoronic scientific utopianism. To the same degree that reality is alienated from human activity and reduced to laws of material causality, activity is alienated from objectivity and reduced to pointless arbitrariness and militant invasions into the organic life of nature and society. In other words, activity and objectivity are alienated one from the other, as epitomized by the Stalinist model of socialism, with its theoretical insistence on the material determination of social life and—at the same time—its practical obsession with ideological intervention into material conditions.

Challenging the alienating dichotomy between human activity and objective reality, Batishchev theorizes objectivity as an indispensable and primordial quality of activity itself. The truth, for Batishchev, consists "not in the choice between the insignificance of the substance of the objective world (activism) and the insignificance of man (objectivism), but in understanding the substantial character of human activity."[37] This means that activity is not opposed to external objects, but is objective and substantial in its very essence. "Human activity is objective [*predmetna*].... Objectness [*predmetnost'*] fills up activity and constitutes its own primary definition."[38] From this standpoint, the opposition between human activity and the world of objects is chimerical. In Russian, the etymological correspondence between reality (*deistvitel'nost'*) and action (*deistvie*) supports Batishchev's argument that activity does not come to reality from somewhere outside, but is the inherent propensity of people who dwell and act within the real.

This raises the question: how does the human differ from all other organisms, which also constitute a part of objective reality? According to Batishchev, the human is distinct in behaving vis-à-vis the world not like an organism, using it to satisfy limited biological needs, but perceives the value and meaning of objects outside the self. Human activity transcends its own organic boundaries and addresses objects in their internal structure and essence. One is object-oriented to the degree one can overcome one's own specificity as an object, and thus become a subject in the true sense of the word. One's subjectivity is not opposed to, but conditioned by, one's relationships with the world of objects, one's capacity to perceive these objects as they are, and not only through the distorting prism of one's utilitarian needs. "[M]an finds *himself in the world of objects* and only in it, but *by no means* as one of its objects or its totality. He conditions himself by this *objectness* and by nothing else, but at the same time it is *he* who conditions *himself* by it."[39] Objectness does not determine an individual person from the outside but becomes a component of his or her self-definition and self-determination as a subject. One positions oneself through an activity that is selfless (in the literal rather than moral sense), that is, through actions that reflect the laws of objects instead of imposing on them the laws of a particular human organism. In this sense, the human may be regarded not as the "highest" animal—which is still a part of nature—but a sort of representational descendant of nature as a whole, a universal being free from any organic limitations.

The human is therefore a transcendent being that, albeit unable to escape the objective world, may yet enter into and understand it, and apply to objects their own measure. According to Batishchev, objectification and transcendence are the very same process, in which an individual realizes him- or herself as an objective reality, and comprehends reality as a constituent of the self. The entire world of objects is an actual or potential manifestation of diverse human abilities that discover the internal measure of things and transform them according to this measure—much as a violin embodies the artistic and musical potential of wood. Instead of looking at the world as a totality of physical bodies, we should see in it the embodiments of human capacities; by the same token, the principle of activity enables us to disembody the objectified world and discover its constructive, human dimension. "Activity is precisely the concrete identity of disembodiment and embodiment."[40] Through activity, since it is essentially objective, human potential is embodied; at the same time, the bodies created by this activity demonstrate the disembodiment of the natural world. The disruption between these two aspects of activity gives rise to alienation: activity produces objects that fail to be disembodied, owing to the social fetishism of the commodity. This is how things come to dominate people, to claim their own reality independent of the activity that engendered them.

Following Marx's early analysis of alienation, Batishchev's critique of capitalism and bureaucratism espouses in their stead what he calls "humanistic revolution," which must be permanent and not limited to the period of transition from capitalism to socialism. Revolution should not only transfer the domain of objects from one proprietor to another, from the bourgeoisie to the working class, but ought to prevent the rise of further alienation in the society of bureaucratic socialism. This means that objects themselves should be disembodied and foregrounded as extensions of free human activity. According to Batishchev, freedom *from* or freedom *for* are a matter of misinterpretation. The former is self-contradictory, because activity itself is only free insofar as it implements itself through the limited substance of specific objects. One cannot be free from freedom itself, that is, from the substantiality and objectivity that make free activity meaningful. Neither can one speak of freedom *for*, since freedom has no goal outside itself, but comprises its own goal. Batishchev refers to Marx's view that man enters the "true kingdom of freedom" insofar as "the development of human powers becomes an end in itself."[41] Thus Batishchev attempts to restore the entire spectrum of Marx's initial project of human self-transcendence. Such a project assumes that human activity imposes objective self-limitations, alienates itself through reification, and then overcomes this reified condition and restores its freedom, which is a goal in itself.

Proceeding from the category of contradiction central to Marxist dialectics, Batishchev asserts that human activity is deeply contradictory; first, because it unites the opposites of embodiment and disembodiment, and secondly, because it engenders its own opposite, alienation, which is overcome by means of activity itself. The first law of Marxist dialectics advances the unity and struggle of opposites; thus, it not only describes the relationship of opposites, but is contradictory itself; that is, it includes the contradiction between unity and struggle in its own formulation. Each phenomenon must be interpreted in terms of its inner contradiction; however, this contradiction is not a static polarity, but rather a dynamic interaction, with the potential for unification.

According to Batishchev, this basic law of dialectics can be distorted in two ways: by neglecting either the struggle or the unity. Batishchev identifies and criticizes these philosophical "perversions," calling them "distinctivism" and "antinomism," which evidently correspond to his dichotomy of objectivism/activism.[42] Distinctivism, which is typical of empirical and positivist schools, as well as of structuralism, reduces contradiction to distinction, or difference, which downplays the energy of internal opposition. From a distinctivist standpoint, different aspects of phenomena coexist without inner tension or antagonism, even remaining completely indifferent to one another. This presupposes a purely rationalist description of the world as it is—in the variety of its differences, but without insight into the nature of contradiction as the source of its internal dynamics. Another bias of contemporary thought is the reduction of contradiction to antinomies that can never be resolved, since both extremes are presumed to be equally valid, hence irreconcilable. This promotes dualistic views of an irrationalist and even tragic bent—those expounded by existentialism and, to a certain degree, by the Frankfurt School, with its negative dialectics. Since contradiction cannot be resolved, the world is condemned to eternal, agonizing struggle and self-destructive antagonism; human reason and purposeful activity are ultimately helpless before alienation and absurdity. Batishchev advances full-fledged contradiction as the quintessential Marxist concept: it is the source of all dialectical conflicts, but does not deny the ultimate goal of conflict as the perspective of its own resolution. Human activity, then, develops through the opposition of embodiment and disembodiment. The antinomistic element of this relationship is manifested in alienation, which opposes the world of self-sufficient objects to human activity, but the antinomy of this self-inflicted dehumanization of humanity is overcome by a proliferation of new activity, which becomes historically self-conscious and, through revolution, reappropriates the alienated world as a sphere of human self-realization.

Batishchev's works published in the 1960s stand as perhaps the last expression of a "sincere" Marxism, one that is equally hostile to non-Marxist views and to dogmatic perversions within Marxism itself. Batishchev still believes that all contradictions and polarities—between essence and existence, personality and structure, immanence and transcendence—can be resolved with Marxism, as a project of universal dialectical synthesis through active human self-transcendence and self-realization. To some degree, his work may be compared with that of Georg Lukács, who also attempted to reconcile the implicit contradictions between determinism and activism as the two cornerstones of Marxist theory. Unlike Lukács, though, Batishchev makes no use of Lenin's theory of reflection, emphasizing instead the opposite pole of Marxism: the active transformation of the world. However, his interpretation of human activity as the voluntary submission of the subject to the intrinsic nature of objects still smuggles in the theory of reflection, which presupposes a materialistic and deterministic definition of consciousness as the undistorted mirror of the real. The substitution of activity for reflection seems inevitable, given Batishchev's keenness to remain within the boundaries of human immanence without recognizing potential sources of human activity other than the material world. If activity proceeds according to the laws of objects, it inevitably slips into *re*activity, the practical reflection of the world as it is.

Paradoxically, the interaction of the individual and the world as postulated by Batishchev would reduce the individual's active role solely to the ability to act according to the demands and tendencies of objects themselves. Perhaps the fundamental deficiency of Batishchev's project is rooted in the very concept of "sensuous human activity" as proposed by Marx. By eliminating the idealistic element of activity and limiting it to sensuousness, the very foundation of activity is undermined, since sensuousness is first and foremost the ability to perceive the surrounding world. Marx himself, in his discussion of sensuous practice, emphasizes the capacities of seeing, hearing, touching, and so on, as genuinely human capacities, the development of which is a goal in itself. But if the mere perception of the external world in all its subtlety is the crux of human activity, then activity itself is understood as the progressive development of perception—a passive cognitive capacity. Sensuous activity is the activity of perception, not creation; not surprisingly, Batishchev, following Marx, avoids using the terms "(self-)expression" or "imagination" in his discussion of the ultimate goals of humanity. Creation and expression, as distinct from sensuousness, presuppose sources of activity other than the external world; they originate in human transcendence thereof. This transcendent aspect of creativity is indeed "the active side ... developed by idealism," and cannot be convincingly explained by the materialist model. "Sensuousness" as distinct from ideal creativity is either oriented to passive perception of objects or identified with an organic activity of the sort shared by humans and animals. Sensuous activity as such appears to be a contradiction in terms, since activity exceeds the boundaries of perception. Batishchev's work turns out to be most valuable in its lucid demonstration of the theoretical tragedy of materialism—the impossibility of building a theory of human activity on the basis of a purely monistic and immanentist worldview.[43]

This would explain why, in his later evolution, Batishchev turned to religious seeking, first inspired by the Oriental mysticism of the painter and theosophist Nicholas Roerich (1874–1947), and then converting to Orthodox Christianity. The main theme of his later work (1980s) is the philosophy of creativity that develops the dialectic of embodiment and disembodiment, the objectification and transcendence he had initially elaborated on Marxist grounds.[44] At this later date, however, his work, sustained in the framework of Hegelian and Marxist discourse, loses its prominence amid more articulated phenomenological, hermeneutic, and post-structuralist approaches to the same circle of problems.

6. The Renewal of Ethics. Iakov Milner-Irinin

A line of thinking that similarly harked back to "authentic" Marxism may be seen in the development of ethics after Stalin. Overall, ethics was one of the most conservative branches of Soviet Marxism, and one that in seventy years produced almost nothing original or innovative. From the standpoint of classical Marxism, ethics is a subordinate discipline, because all standards and norms of personal behavior are determined economically and socially. Ethics is thus at best a kind of applied sociology, and at worst—in its capacity as an "independent science of universal values"—the distorted ideological reflection of the norms by which the dominant class perpetuates its dominance and oppresses other classes. All claims concerning absolute and eternal ethical norms, applicable to people of every class and epoch, are the insidious illusions unmasked by historical materialism.[45]

According to Soviet Marxism, the success of the socialist revolution meant that the regulative norms of behavior, such as collectivism, internationalism, and the dignity of labor, are dictated by proletarian morality. Lenin identified genuine morality as whatever promotes the ultimate triumph of communism: "Morality is what serves to destroy the old exploiting society and to unite all toiling people around the proletariat, which is building a new society of communists."[46] Soviet leaders found this formulation ideally convenient, since it could rationalize or righteous-ize any crime committed for the sake of the communist cause, including denunciations of close friends or even one's parents—as in the case of the pioneer Pavlik Morozov, whose "heroic" denunciation of his own father as a kulak accomplice was made a moral exemplar for all Soviet schoolchildren—and the mass repression of the "enemies of the people." The same formulation, however, signified the abolition of ethics as such, which was replaced by purely political considerations. The highest ethical standard coincided with conformity to the general line of the party, which, according to Lenin, was "the mind, honor, and conscience of our epoch."

Nevertheless, philosophers in the post-Stalin period did try to elaborate some fundamentals of Marxist ethics separate from mere political conformism. Under Stalin, the most frequently cited ethical formulation from Marx was his likening of morality to an inner policeman, implying that conscience is imposed by the external social order. After Stalin, the emphasis shifted to another citation from Marx, which asserted that communism presupposes the observation of the "basic standards of human morality." Some of the more advanced Soviet Marxists went so far as to include certain biblical commandments among these fundamental rules, such as "Honor thy mother and father" and "Thou shalt not kill," at the same time, of course, denying their religious origin and presenting them as manifestations of the people's wisdom. The most ambitious task for Soviet Marxist ethics was to find the dialectical connection between universal ("panhuman," *vsechelovecheskii*) and class values. The theory shared by the majority of Soviet ethicists was that the morality of the exploiting classes is antithetical to panhuman morality. It is only under a socialist or communist system that panhuman values, or "truly human morality," can find adequate expression in the social behavior of people. This formula of the dialectical unity of panhuman and communist morality was eminently suitable for both the justification of existing political regimes and the criticism of their "isolated" shortcomings. On the one hand, communist values, by definition, must contain a panhuman appeal, which sanctifies the construction of communism in the USSR. On the other hand, panhuman values will be fully integrated only in a mature communist society—a viewpoint permitting the critique of conditions past (the cult of personality, mass repressions of innocent people) and present (bureaucratism, etc.) as the exposition of blatant deviations from panhuman morality.

Perhaps the most original contribution to Marxist ethics in the Soviet period came from Iakov Abramovich Milner-Irinin (1911–1989), who tried to reconcile Marxist-Leninist views with the Kantian approach to ethics as a purely normative science. In 1963, the Soviet Academy of Sciences refused to publish Milner-Irinin's book on ethics, claiming that it deviated from Marxist teachings, and when he succeeded in publishing an article on ethics in a Georgian journal, it was severely attacked by official Soviet philosophers.[47] Milner-Irinin treats ethics as a normative science, distinguishing it from all other sciences, which are descriptive and relate to what exists. This postulate was in and of itself considered anti-Marxist, since, from the standpoint of historical materialism, all ethical norms reflect objectively existent social conditions. Milner-Irinin also emphasizes, to the indignation of orthodox Marxists, the abstract character of ethics, whose norms can be applied to any and all historical contexts:

> With regard to abstractness, ethics is akin to logic; I would describe it as the logic of human happiness.... The principles of true humanity are necessarily abstract since they can and must be applied, as the moral law, to each and every case of life without exception.... The concreteness of truth in the science of ethics consists precisely in its abstractness.[48]

Milner-Irinin argues that there can be only one science concerning what should be, namely ethics, an assertion that also contradicts the Marxist definition of "scientific communism" as the discipline that elaborates prescriptions for the future and guidelines for revolutionary transformation.

Milner-Irinin, however, had no intention of challenging Marxism; on the contrary, he saw his task as that of laying the foundation for a truly Marxist ethics. He discovers in Marx, not only in the early manuscripts but also in *Capital*, clear statements about a "universal human nature" and the "innate rights of man." Ethics thus acquires its own grounding, its specific subject matter, irreducible to any social or historical dimension. An echo of the early Marx, moreover, may be heard in the later one, who wrote: "We must know what human nature in general is, and how it undergoes modifications in each historically given epoch."[49] Ethics concentrates on this "human nature in general," on the "development of the richness of human nature as an end in itself" and "a constant premise of human history."[50]

Milner-Irinin distinguishes between two Marxist definitions of human essence: first, the human as a social, tool-making animal, and secondly, the human as a creatively transforming and revolutionary being. The first definition is materialistic, the second idealistic, though not in a way that contradicts scientific materialism. Materialism is scientific in its description of the human essence as it is, whereas ethics is scientific in its attempt to prescribe the ideal goals of human existence. Ethics, therefore, can be constructed on a properly materialist basis, since this demonstrates the path by which *what really is* is transformed into *what ideally should be*. In the primitive stages of history, the spiritual aspect of human life is subordinated to material needs and limitations, but in the course of history, the material aspect becomes increasingly dependent on the ideal contents of life: "[I]n the world of communism the material aspect of life is only the shell of its high ideal (spiritual) content."[51]

From this point of view, communism is "what should be," a Kantian world of absolute norms and "ends in themselves"; Milner-Irinin thus inadvertently highlights the Kantian subtexts of Marxist theory. These elements of transcendental, anthropological idealism are the byproduct of Marx's attempt to abandon the objective idealism of Hegel. Indeed, if the absolute idea is eliminated as the cause of the historical process, then ideals are relegated to the teleological dimension of history—the future kingdom of communism and a realm of absolute ethical norms and prescriptions. To a certain degree, by turning the Hegelian system "right side up," with matter instead of idea as its foundational principle, Marx reinstates the Kantian dimension of the ideal, which is expelled from the objective world in order to constitute the world of human goals and collective subjectivity. This would explain why nearly every attempt to reinstate the meaning of spirituality on the basis of Marxist historical materialism invariably leads to Kantian revisions of Marxism, as can be seen, for example, in early twentieth-century Russian Machism and empiriomonism (as represented by Aleksandr Bogdanov and Anatolii Lunacharsky), which defended the value of collectivist subjectivity and its voluntarist formation of the future, even to the extent of "God-building," an anthropological religion condemned by Lenin. Lenin's assertions notwithstanding, Kantian revisions of Marxism do not necessarily deny materialism as the foundation of human knowledge and spirituality, but add to it a new dimension of moral norms and goals. Milner-Irinin employs this teleological potential hidden in Marxist theory by arguing that materialist ethics proceeds from the fact of human materiality (the human as a tool-making animal) and ascends to the level of ultimate goals where the human being transforms itself into a self-conscious and "ideal" entity. Milner-Irinin's precedent shows that ethics as a normative science can easily be identified as a Kantian ingredient in Marxism, and that no Marxist ethics is possible without some Kantian extension and revision.

If Ilyenkov reinterprets Marx from a Hegelian point of view, claiming the objective social existence of such ideal forms as the economic category of value, then Batishchev and Milner-Irinin reappropriate Kantian components of Marxism, the categories of creative activity and ethical norms. In both cases, however, the revitalization of Marxism accentuates precisely those elements that were most suspect in the eyes of orthodox Soviet Marxism, but that had been imparted to Marx's thought from his great predecessors in German idealism. Marxism proved to be a vehicle for the transmission of ideas that were scarcely Marxist in the strictest sense of the term. The later development of Russian philosophy shows a gradual differentiation of these non-Marxist trends within Marxism; and their increasing alienation from, and opposition to, Marxism, which is seen most clearly in the works of Mamardashvili, who moved from a Kantian-Hegelian reinterpretation of Marxism to a critique of Marxism as such.

7. Discussions around Aesthetics. Mikhail Lifshits and Aleksandr Burov

Aesthetics proved to be one of the most developed fields of Soviet Marxism. Undoubtedly, this was an outcome of Russian cultural tradition, which places high value on literature, art, and various modes of criticism. Even in the nineteenth century, many principal philosophical issues were discussed within the framework of literary theory, where Vissarion Belinsky and Nikolai Chernyshevsky laid the foundation for the so-called revolutionary-democratic ideology, which was considered to be the most progressive form of pre-Marxist thought. In the 1920s and the 1930s, aesthetics was probably the only field where ardent philosophical discussions could still take place under conditions of increasing ideological pressure.

One of the most active participants of those debates, Mikhail Lifshits (1905–1983), a collaborator with Lukács, and one of the editors of the important volume *Marx and Engels on Art*[52] (1933), survived Stalin's repressions to become a prominent figure in the post-Stalin period. He is an exemplary representative of the traditional Marxist approach: rather feeble in the area of postulating new ideas, but evincing considerable vigor and wit in critiquing bourgeois art. The majority of Lifshits's books are critical interpretations of the avant-garde and modernism, which he considered symptomatic of the degradation of bourgeois culture. As distinct from Lukács, who had elaborated his own comprehensive system of Marxist aesthetics, Lifshits confined himself mostly to feuilleton-like articles describing what he perceived to be the absurdity of the latest Western trends, for example, abstractionism and pop art. The title of his most popular article, "Why I Am Not a Modernist," was a deliberate allusion to Bertrand Russell's pamphlet *Why I Am Not a Christian*. Lifshits's main argument against modernism is that its distortions of reality are based in the bourgeois fear of, and desire to escape from, history. He claims that contemporary art, having lost touch with the real world, has become the projection of solipsistic and subjective moods, and may be seen as the nightmare of the agonizing bourgeois consciousness. These modern art forms, he maintains, have lost the historical perspectives that had been very much present in the nineteenth-century art of critical realism.

Lifshits, like Lukács, was not particularly enthusiastic about the Soviet art of socialist realism, but he cautiously avoided this dangerous issue, concentrating instead on the opposition between "good" critical realism and "bad" decadence and modernism. He took special pains to harp on affinities between artistic modernism and fascist ideology, on the grounds that each constituted an extreme extension of irrationalism. Even granting that such leaders of the avant-garde as Picasso could be anti-fascist in their general views and in the intentions of their artistic work, as in Picasso's *Guernica*, he insisted that the artistic methods of modernism were an expression of the same mythological and magical mentality as the fascist aggression against reason and personality. In the 1960s and the 1970s, Lifshits was probably the only remaining philosopher in the Soviet Union to still be loyal to an orthodox Marxism as a rational and scientific doctrine, and to oppose this to the irrationalism of the latest "rotten" bourgeois ideology, with fascism ever lurking as its inevitable heir. For Lifshits, Marxism was the best fruit of the European Enlightenment, while the bourgeoisie of the twentieth century betrayed its own legacy of classical rationalism and fell back into the darkness of paganistic animism and mythology. In spite of his elegant, aphoristic style and clear system of argumentation, the younger generation of Soviet philosophers looked upon Lifshits as a Marxist relic, bright and ambitious, but irrelevant. He had no tolerance for the existentialism, psychoanalysis, or structuralism his younger colleagues sought to incorporate into their rejuvenated versions of Marxism.

Lifshits was probably one of the last Soviet thinkers to sincerely and ardently oppose the idea that diverse opinions may lead to objective truth. To a certain degree, he anticipated the attack on pluralism that would come from Solzhenitsyn, albeit from a quite different—religious conservative—point of view. For Lifshits, just as later for Solzhenitsyn, pluralism shows generosity and openness to a multiplicity of viewpoints only such that each perspective, in relation to the multitude of others, becomes insignificant and can be ignored. Lifshits finds this "repressive tolerance" scarcely better than repressive intolerance, the totalitarian exclusion of dissenting points of view. To some extent, he even finds intolerance preferable, insofar as it adheres to rigorous standards of truth. Intolerance presupposes that there exists a single truth, in relation to which any viewpoint may be of significance, either as its confirmation or denial. "[T]ruth is not a matter of intellectual comfort; it is not a private concern and is not divisible into points of view. In this sense, it is, if you will, exclusive.... Total unanimity among humankind is the ideal, like absolute truth."[53] Among Soviet thinkers Lifshits represented the starkest evidence that Marxism in the Soviet Union had morphed into a kind of Thomism, which was perfectly aware of, and yet could not help extolling, its own scholastic nature. Orthodox Marxism, according to Lifshits, "puts a limitation on thinking, but in the same way as rhyme or rhythm puts a limitation on the poet. Limitations of this kind lead to perfection; they constitute the foundation of all human culture, which expresses the infinity of contents in relatively finite forms. Where there is no intelligent, voluntary self-limitation, there is the kingdom of all-permissiveness and stupidity."[54] This passage is reminiscent of the arguments of many Church thinkers, both Catholic and Orthodox, who were criticized for their strict adherence to Church dogma, which seemed to undermine the creativity of their conceptions. The great Russian Orthodox thinker Pavel Florensky, for instance, maintained that any creative activity is based on some inner form or canon, and if one's thought abandons the Great Canon established by the thousand-year dogmatic tradition of the Church, then one falls prey to a variety of minor canons or transitory fashions, which decreases the potential of creativity and reduces it to eclecticism. Lifshits championed Soviet Marxism, not as an official ideology susceptible to the vagaries of ideological fashion and the zigzags of party politics, but as a powerful intellectual canon from which perennial values of culture and philosophy may emerge, similar to those created in the West on the basis of Christian dogmatics.

In the late 1950s, especially upon publication of Aleksandr Burov's *The Aesthetic Essence of Art* (1956), aesthetics became a pressing philosophical issue. This book came as a revelation, since the very word "aesthetic" had been virtually forgotten by this time, pushed aside by such typical Soviet categories as the "ideological" or "social" essence of art. For Burov (1900–1957), an architect by profession, "aesthetic" meant something quite specific: it referred to the sphere of human ideals, realizable only by social means, but ultimately directed toward the creation of a "beautiful, full-valued, harmonious human being, and truly human relationships."[55] This was an unusual approach to beauty: previously, Soviet aesthetics had been relentless in its insistence that beauty and art were only tools for class struggle and the expression of class-oriented ideological views. With Burov, aesthetics shifted from the instrumental realm of social development to be placed, instead, among the highest goals of human self-accomplishment in the distant future. Burov supported Marx's earlier view, expressed in his *Economic and Philosophic Manuscripts*, that, upon being liberated from urgent physical need, the human begins to create also according the laws of beauty. "In any practical human activity, an object becomes beautiful only insofar as man recognizes in it his own self, his creative possibilities, the richness of his human essence."[56] Here we can easily recognize the influence of older, Kantian and Schillerian, definitions of beauty as "purposefulness without purpose," by which one may attain the self-realization of one's capacities, distorted as these have otherwise been by the division of labor and by the subordination of the human to the violent laws of nature and history. The aesthetic dimension of existence, therefore, is superior to social and historical existence. This is implied in Burov's assertion that "the entire essence of art, not only its form, must be defined as aesthetic."[57] What is specific to art, and sets it apart from other spheres of human activity, is that its object is the human in the entirety of its every quality and capacity; the human as a "generic being," not reduced to any partial social, historical, psychological, or physiological functions. "Man as the personification of the highest and most perfect life is an absolute aesthetic object .... From the standpoint of this ideal, man judges aesthetically regarding all other phenomena of reality, which accounts for the 'humanization' of these phenomena so characteristic of art."[58]

At this stage of Soviet philosophical development, the *aesthetic* becomes the supreme teleological, almost theological category, indicating the final goal of all economic and political transformations: one's self-enjoyment in the products of one's free creativity. In no other period in Russian intellectual history was the "aesthetic" elevated to a loftier ontological status than in the late 1950s and early the 1960s—higher than the "social," "scientific," "ethical," and certainly "religious." General philosophical textbooks routinely treated aesthetics in the last chapter, after dialectics, logic, history, science, and ethics, because the field of beauty seemed to be the "last" in the order of actual tasks of communist construction, but simultaneously the "most advanced" in terms of its final goals and the comprehensive prospects of the communist future. Politics, ethics, and science remained important, but aesthetics would ultimately prevail. When communism is implemented, politics and science will come under the aegis of aesthetics. If the system of communism was akin to a religious faith, aesthetics was a kind of final revelation, a harbinger of things to come in the most distant future. All human capacities would develop to the utmost, and the human being would perform every action according to the laws of beauty itself. The idea that aesthetics is a mode of cognition that embodies the wholeness of human capacities is probably one of the last remnants of utopian thinking. That a human being can be approached as a whole is questionable; and that every human being should someday acquire the all-encompassing abilities of a Renaissance-like titan sounds like some totalitarian fantasy.

It was thanks to Burov and like-minded aestheticians that the goal of communism was presented as liberation of the human from the fetters of social and economic necessity; the attainment, for everyone, of pure human existence, which is nothing but the creation and enjoyment of beauty, being an end in itself. It is no surprise that, at this later stage, as formerly ardent communist *political* aspirations waned, the intellectual priorities of Soviet society shifted to art, science, ethics, and religion.

Burov's book sparked a heated dispute on the essence of the aesthetic, which continued for about fifteen years, until the early 1970s. Scholars divided into two parties depending on their acceptance or rejection of this new aesthetic vision. "Traditionalists" defended the "cognitive" specifics of art as a method of knowledge, a way to reflect objective reality. The peculiarity of art, then, is its imaginative (*obraznaia*) form, distinct from the conceptual (*poniatiinaia*) form of scientific knowledge. Art operates with concrete, sensuous, and individual images, while science presents general ideas in the form of abstract notions and formulas but they have, essentially, the same object and goal. This view, originating in Hegel's aesthetics, was traditional in Russian literary criticism of the nineteenth century, and was preserved in Soviet philosophy as the "truly Marxist" approach.

The "innovators," also proceeding from Marx, argued that art is a sociohistorical activity, which creates its own object, not merely reflecting or reproducing the existing world. The criteria of what is beautiful cannot be found in nature itself, but only in the process of social practice, by which the individual transcends nature and asserts his or her generic qualities as a social being. Accordingly, the first group of aestheticians, comprising Gennadii Pospelov, G. A. Nedoshivin, and Mikhail Ovsiannikov, was called the *prirodniki*, or the "naturists," while their opponents, Leonid Stolovich, Iurii Borev, and Semyon Goldentrikht, adopted the name of *obshchestvenniki*, or the "societalists." For the latter, social reality cannot be divorced from human subjectivity, which becomes an objective factor in the formation of aesthetic tastes. For example, the color red, physically identical in a rose, blood, and a banner, bears the various symbolic and aesthetic meanings of love, suffering, struggle, and so on. The goal of art is not merely to reflect, but to "appropriate and transform" (*osvaivat' i preobrazhat'*) external reality and create a new, aesthetic reality grounded in human imagination and aspiration to the ideal. Some parallels can be found between Ilyenkov's view on collective human subjectivity as a form of objective reality and the aesthetic views of the societalists.

In these debates, the societalists were supported by a group of still more radical aestheticians, including Boris Shragin, Leonid Pazhitnov, Karl Kantor, and Iurii Davydov, who espoused the so-called "practical-productive" conception of art. Taking their cue from the early Marx, they stressed sensuous practice as the common denominator of labor and artistic creativity. This viewpoint had little to do with the "objective cognition" of the naturists, and advanced the societalists' tendency of the "active intervention" of consciousness into life. Whereas the societalists were more preoccupied with the problems of aesthetic consciousness and its active role vis-à-vis reality, the "productivists" stressed the sensuous aspects of art by which new real things are brought into the world. For them, beauty is the outcome of the labor process, by which the richness of human capacities and essential powers are realized in specific things. It is not consciousness but human sensuousness that creates aesthetic objects. This is why architecture and ornament belong to the sphere of art, despite not being designed to reflect some external reality, and thus escaping the principle of "socialist realism."

8. The Philosophy of Science. Technology and Nature

From the outset, Marxism insisted upon the rapprochement of philosophy with the natural and social sciences, going so far as to claim the death of philosophy as an isolated discipline. In the place of metaphysics—disparaged as a remnant of the religious impulse—Marxism proclaimed dialectical materialism as the general methodological basis for scientific inquiry. Friedrich Engels's *The Dialectics of Nature* was first published in the Soviet Union in 1929, but became most influential in the 1960s and the 1970s when Soviet Marxism turned its attention to issues of the natural sciences and technological advancement. Previously, dialectical materialism had confined itself to the interrogation of such nineteenth-century scientific advances as Darwinism or the laws of thermodynamics. Subsequent theories were looked askance at, as potential threats to the materialist model of reality. This suspiciousness was manifest most famously in Lenin's denunciation of Mach's and Oswald's interpretation of nature as the play of energies rather than the interaction of material bodies. Lenin's objection was not directed at the empirical discoveries themselves, but at the idealistic interpretations that could be inferred from them. Later, however, Soviet Marxism sought to test the validity of such new discoveries as the theory of relativity, quantum mechanics, genetics, and cybernetics, formerly rejected as extensions of the bourgeois worldview and contrary to the principles of materialist determinism. For example, genetics had been condemned as incompatible with the Darwinist principles of evolution by natural selection, because it deemphasized the influence of the material environment on the progress of a species. In the post-Stalin period, in response to great scientific and technological advances in the West, Soviet progress in these areas was thought to depend upon the organic reconciliation of modern discoveries with the basic postulates of dialectical materialism. Thus we see a sharp change in the philosophical evaluations of cybernetics taking place in the mid-1950s. *The Concise Philosophical Dictionary*, published in 1954, defines cybernetics as "a reactionary pseudoscience that emerged in the United States after the Second World War, and was disseminated extensively throughout other capitalist countries: a form of contemporary mechanicism.... [C]ybernetics is not only an ideological weapon of imperialist reaction, but also a means for the implementation of its aggressive plans."[59] However, already in the 1955 edition of the same dictionary, the term "cybernetics" is absent, whereas in the 1963 edition this field is lauded as "a splendid example of the new type of interaction among sciences," since it "provides extensive material for the philosophical doctrine regarding the forms of the motion of matter and for the classification of sciences."[60] Many examples could be cited of this sort of philosophical appropriation of scientific and technological developments—a hermeneutic change effected with astonishing speed in the Khrushchev period.

As the Communist Party's projection (1961[61]) of the attainment of communism within twenty years grew increasingly untenable, Soviet thinkers turned to such aspects of Marxist philosophy as might streamline the game of catchup the country would need to play if it was to remain economically and technologically competitive with the West. Social aspects of Marxist doctrine were deemphasized, and for the first time Soviet philosophy concentrated on concepts catering to the new program of accelerated scientific progress. Beginning in the early 1970s, this shift manifested itself in the leading Soviet philosophical journal, *Voprosy filosofii* (Questions of Philosophy), as discussion of Marxist ontology, epistemology, ethics, aesthetics, and so on was pushed aside in favor of articles on philosophical aspects of the history and contemporary status of science. This tendency remained until the coming of perestroika, when the journal once again foregrounded problems of ontology and ethics and even metaphysics—albeit now from a non-Marxist perspective.

Already in the early 1950s, the theory of relativity had undergone a vigorous rehabilitation in accordance with Marxist principles. It was reinterpreted as a confirmation of the dialectical interdependence of the categories of time and space, matter and energy, and of the principle of the unity of opposites. Quantum mechanics was seen as a development of the traditional connection between cause and effect, but this was compensated for by the observation of statistical regularities among fields of particles, which reconfirmed the validity of determinism from a more general perspective. Cybernetics and information theory were especially difficult to digest, privileging as they did the mental process over material reality, which now seemed relegated to the status of a symbolic structure. Making up for this feature, however, was the interpretation of information as a new form of matter, which thus conformed to the principle of material self-organization, albeit at the highest level of mental activity.

The contortions required for these ad hoc explanations gradually hollowed out the concept of dialectical materialism, insofar as matter seemed to have become something amorphous and nominal. If mathematical abstractions, cybernetic algorithms, and quantum deviations could all be interpreted as "matter," then matter itself lost all its identity.

Cosmology occupied a crucial position in this scientific renaissance, because of the demonstrated superiority of Soviet technology in this area, as attested by the launching of the first human into space. In philosophical circles, this event was regarded as an argument for atheism: the celestial spheres traditionally associated with the divine were found to be the domain of a cold and empty materiality. One area of theoretical difficulty concerned the so-called Big Bang theory, which seemed to contradict the principle of the eternal nature of matter, that is, the accepted Marxist presumption that matter was neither created nor capable of being destroyed. This problem was sidestepped by suggesting that the temporal perspective occupied by human science could only relate to our observable metagalaxy, while the universe on the whole inevitably defied interpretation; thus, the viability of the materialist postulate was preserved.

One outcome of the renewed interest in scientific advancement was the relatively liberal intellectual climate created for scientists themselves. Debates and disputations were routinely permitted, and methodological discourse was not stringently policed to enforce adherence to orthodox Marxism. For example, a leading Soviet astronomer, Igor Shklovsky (1916–1985), published a sensational (and popular) book arguing that the existence of intelligent extraterrestrial life was highly probable and proposing the formation of a program dedicated to establishing contact with alien civilizations, without any explicit consideration of their class structure. A few years later, he revised his position on the basis of statistical claims that seemed to greatly diminish the probability of biogenic conditions occurring elsewhere in the universe. Significantly, neither of his positions came under the critical scrutiny of the official philosophical apparatus, which bracketed ideological concerns in favor of freedom of scientific speculation.

The growing discrepancy between official Marxism and the philosophical interpretation of science may be seen not only in the opposition between ideologies and scientists, but even within the work of a single thinker. Consider, for example, the eminent physicist Moisei Markov (1908–1994), who in the book *On the Nature of Matter* developed a new model of the universe. Here Markov advances the quantum-theory concept of the "mass defect," which interprets elementary particles as alternative universes, the implication being that our universe might be an atom in a meta-universe. Since he proceeds from quantum theory, he is anxious to distance himself from its idealistic interpretations, which logically follow from the decisive role of the observer in the physical investigation of the microworld. As he sees it, the mistake of idealism lies in its denial of the objective status of elementary particles, but what is characteristic of this renewed Marxist methodology is that metaphysical, or mechanistic, materialism is likewise mistaken in attempting to banish subjective moments from human knowledge. The only reliable position, then, is dialectical materialism, which provides for a balanced approach to the interaction between subject and object in the process of cognition: though the observer's position determines, to some degree, the result of the experiment, it is not purely subjective, but presents a part of the objective world. Overall, in opposing dialectical materialism to metaphysical materialism rather than to idealism, Markov puts more emphasis on dialectics than on materialism. However, all these philosophical concepts are put aside when Markov addresses the strictly physical problem of the *fridmon* class of elementary particles (named in honor of the Russian physicist Aleksandr Fridman, or Friedmann, 1888–1925) that potentially constitute "partially enclosed" universes. In Markov's view, the mass of the universe can decrease in proportion to the energy of interactions between various parts of the universe; thus, the universe as a whole may appear to an outside observer as a microscopic object, however great the multitude of galaxies it contains. "We see that contemporary physics makes possible a completely new interpretation of the notion of 'consists of.'.... The universe as a whole may prove to be a microscopic particle. A microscopic particle may contain in itself an entire universe."[62] The opposition of such concepts as "large" and "small," "elementary" and "complex," becomes irrelevant in a world where a quantum particle is not only a component of a universe, but encompasses a universe of its own. This picture of particles comprising/containing universes would seem to be quite amenable to dialectical explanation, but Markov avoids exploiting this ideological advantage. Although he shows himself, elsewhere, capable of gestures of philosophical conformism, when it comes to his own theoretical interests he is careful not to pollute science with ideological lip service. This tendency is characteristic for many outstanding scientists of this period; while showing some signs of loyalty to the party line, they strove to keep these separate from their scientific investigations.

There was, perhaps, only one major Soviet scientist in this period courageous enough to speak openly against dialectical materialism as the methodological foundation of the natural sciences and culture in general. Aleksandr Liubishchev (1890–1972) was a provincial professor of biology who, in addition to his contribution to the particular fields of genetics and taxonomy, displayed a unique breadth of cultural and philosophical interests. Some of his philosophically mostly significant works were published posthumously, including *Science and Religion* (2000) and *The Lines of Plato and Democritus in the History of Culture* (2000). He also authored numerous detailed diaries and letters, many of which he sent not only to friends and colleagues, but also to scientific and literary journals, and which sometimes grew into lengthy articles or essays. It will be up to future researchers to systematize Liubishchev's views after all his works are published, but one achievement of his is beyond any doubt: a coherent challenge to official Soviet materialism, which dogmatically asserted the primacy of matter and the secondariness of consciousness. Referring to Lenin's famous equation of matter with objective reality, Liubishchev wrote in one of his philosophical letters:

> Is not consciousness a special sort of being? Everything that is external to my consciousness and independent of my consciousness is real, but, for example, your consciousness is independent of my consciousness, therefore, for me, it is matter, and my consciousness is matter for you; therefore, consciousness also is matter. In this area, dialectical materialists have offered nothing but stupidity and impudence.[63]

The materialist definition of matter in its opposition to consciousness is exposed here in all its absurdity. Liubishchev dared to identify himself as a "militant idealist." In the field of biology, he defined himself as a vitalist, and insisted on the principle of the irreducibility of life to the laws of physics and chemistry. Throughout his career, he resisted dogmatic tendencies in science, whether the anti-genetic bias of Lysenko's "materialist biology," or the so-called "synthetic theory of evolution," which attempted to unite classical Darwinism with genetics. Liubishchev's was likely a more critical than creative mind, but his brand of dissidence was no less vital for scientific developments in the Soviet Union than his positive achievements in any particular discipline.[64]

9. The Marxist Critique of Bourgeois Philosophy

As the creative momentum of Soviet Marxism began to wane, it came to focus ever more on critiquing "bourgeois" Western philosophy. For many philosophers, this area represented a comfortable opportunity to explore intriguing strains of contemporary thought, even if ultimately these latter had to be condemned. There were scarcely any recent Russian translations of the texts they would consider. For example, scholars interested in Kierkegaard or Husserl had to rely on the two or three translations published before the October Revolution. As for later thinkers, such as Heidegger, Sartre, Jaspers, or Derrida, the first translations of their major works began to appear only in the early 1990s. Thus, the task of the Marxist scholar involved both exposition and criticism, which were conflated in such a way as to render the primary texts susceptible to easy refutation. The dialectical method employed by Marxist critics tended to isolate decontextualized fragments in order to claim that the thinker in question painted an incomplete or distorted picture. The essence of the bourgeois worldview was, from a Marxist standpoint, defined by a progressive alienation from the reality of history. Blind to social context, then, the bourgeois philosopher was condemned to elaborate only a fragmented perspective.

For example, existentialism (as represented by Kierkegaard, Heidegger, Sartre, and Camus) was criticized for overemphasizing subjectivity while ignoring the impact of sociohistorical factors on the life of the personality. The existentialist preoccupation with such concepts as nothingness, nausea, absurdity, and alienation was deemed emblematic of a dead-end bourgeois individualism whose last resort was a frustrated and anarchistic rebellion against objective circumstance. "The existentialist categories of 'fear' and 'anxiety,' 'communication' and 'freedom,' express the tragic situation of the contemporary individual in capitalist society, splintered by alienation."[65] Structuralism, in its turn, was interpreted as a justified reaction against existentialist extremism, but, at the same time, was accused of going too far in the opposite direction, relying on the overly analytic procedures of the natural sciences and cybernetics at the expense of historical-diachronic dimensions of cultural studies. The very concept of structure was thought to operate in a purely mathematical way, without any organic connection to social processes. Pragmatism and behaviorism were criticized as expressions of bourgeois utilitarianism, as they jettisoned objective truth as a category of value in favor of instrumental interpretation of observable phenomena. Neopositivism, though relatively acceptable from the Soviet standpoint compared with other trends, was nevertheless condemned as an "anti-philosophy," an attempt to eliminate philosophical problems by reducing them to questions of language, which again betrays the fear of reality characteristic of all bourgeois thought. The fault of phenomenology, meanwhile, was the alleged internal contradiction of its earlier scientific claims and later turn to the justification of the lifeworld as given spontaneously to human intuition and unreflective faith. "Husserlianism simultaneously claims the role of a rigorously elaborated philosophical system, supposedly championing reason and asserting new logic, but in the final analysis it is a subjective-idealistic philosophy devoid of scientific foundation, and contributing to the war on reason and science."[66] The grammatical inconsistency of this sentence itself highlights the tendency of Marxist critics to conflate their own evaluative perspective with seemingly objective expositions of philosophical ideas. The word "simultaneously" presupposes that Husserl contradicts himself, but the critic's descriptive gesture remains incomplete as the sentence drifts into her own opinion, expressed by a new grammatical construction ("but in the final analysis") that leaves that "simultaneity" dangling. Finally, all varieties of religious philosophy—including neo-Thomism—made easy targets for an atheist Marxist critique; these were, invariably, false narratives of appeasement masking the truer historical source of alienation by positing a transcendental realm, which vitiates real-world human self-determination and social engagement.

By the same token, any claim of Western innovation was derided for its metaphysical pretensions, as it ignored the dialectical interdependence of reality's various aspects. Ironically (although perhaps understandably in terms of "sibling rivalry"), Western thinkers who employed a dialectical approach, such as Adorno or Marcuse, were condemned even more fervently for their mystification and revision of the Marxist legacy. The Frankfurt School's revolutionary project was criticized for relying almost exclusively on support from non-proletarian factions, such as student and racial-minority activists, and its critical sociology was rejected as a negativistic distortion of Hegelian and Marxist dialectical thought, insofar as it abandoned the synthetic and constructive stage of the dialectical triad, and overstated the antithetical moment of negation.

If we ignore its vituperativeness, the Soviet Marxist critique of bourgeois philosophy seems to follow a largely Hegelian blueprint in insisting on the assimilation of successive stages of philosophical thought into a dialectical totality. Unlike Hegel, however, Marxist critics focused exclusively on the negative aspects of the philosophical systems they considered—especially those of the post-Marx period. The few positive phenomena of pre-Marxist thought were held to be Democritus and Heraclitus—the founders of materialism and dialectics; the representatives of the French Enlightenment Voltaire and Diderot; and Hegel and Feuerbach, the pinnacles of these dialectical and materialist traditions. From this point of view, the decadence of Western thought began with Schopenhauer and Nietzsche, and no major original or progressive philosopher came into existence after Marx, Engels, and Lenin. "In the period of the 1840-60s, in the bourgeois philosophy of the main countries of Western Europe, there occurred a decomposition of classical forms of idealism,"[67] and this degradation of non-Marxist philosophy continues to the present day. Whereas for Hegel the history of philosophy represents the progressive self-revelation of absolute spirit, with each successive thinker offering a fuller account of the dialectical truth, for Soviet Marxists, the post-Marx philosophical climate is characterized by increasing degeneracy. In this light, Heidegger was considered more dangerously subjective than, for instance, Kierkegaard; and Dewey assessed as less insightful than Peirce.

Another source of Soviet hostility to Western thought—albeit one that would never be acknowledged—was the Slavophilic influence, as represented, in particular, by Vladimir Solovyov's early treatise *Critique of Abstract Principles* (1880). Like Russian thinkers of the nineteenth century, Soviet Marxism tended to criticize Western philosophy as a fragmented array of partial insights, each abstracted from what, for their part, the Slavophiles declared the "living truth" of a holistic intuition. Thus, during this period, the Soviet approach to Western philosophy can be viewed as a mixture of Hegelian dialectics and Slavophilic "totalism" (*tselostnost'*), both elements serving as a vehicle for the assertion of Marxist ideological superiority.

The Soviet classifications of the principal directions of contemporary Western thought were not coherent, often becoming muddled even within a single edition. For example, the monumental and authoritative reference text *Contemporary Bourgeois*

Philosophy, published by Moscow State University in 1972 and including contributions by the top experts in the field, asserts on page eight that in the middle third of the twentieth century, various petty schools of idealism were consolidated into five main directions: phenomenology, Catholic-Protestant religious philosophy, existentialism, pragmatism, and neopositivism. On page ten, however, it is claimed that the *three* primary movements of bourgeois philosophy of the mid-twentieth century—neopositivism, existentialism, and neo-Thomism—are currently coalescing into *two* tendencies, the positivist-"realistic" and the irrationalist-religious, which, by the early 1970s, manifest themselves as the opposition between the structuralism of Levi-Strauss and Foucault and the anthropologism of Marcuse and Fromm. It remains unclear how many "primary movements" really existed in the mid-twentieth century, three or five. Generally, the unification of bourgeois philosophical movements was interpreted as imperialism closing ranks in the struggle against communist ideology; whereas these movements' diversification was supposed to signify the exhaustion of their underlying purpose, a crisis of ideas. One subtle distinction within Soviet philosophical criticism concerned the question of whether contemporary bourgeois philosophy reflected any actual issues. Soviet conservatives denied even this possibility, while more liberal scholars recognized that "bourgeois philosophers sometimes pose real problems (e.g., various aspects of freedom, the logical structure of sciences, the relationship between causality and predictability, etc.), which is explained by the fact that their class is still interested in the development of productive forces."[68] The solution to these problems was, of course, invariably presented as false, while it was noted that these very "mistakes and deviations are instructive in their own way, on the condition that they are unmasked in time and challenged by a truly dialectical-materialist solution."[69]

10. The New Moralistic and Grassroots Turn in Marxism. Arsenii Gulyga and Iurii Davydov

In the 1970s, a grassroots ideological revival among the intelligentsia began to influence the doctrines of official Marxism. Notably, in this period bourgeois philosophy is increasingly and negatively associated with the West, while Marxist philosophy is identified with the national tradition of Russian thought. A similar shift had occurred in Stalin's later years, during the "war on cosmopolitanism," but that had been a merely official political doctrine, unconvincing to the intellectual elite. Now the newly awakened nationalism often felt unobliged to accommodate existing Marxism; it was more a matter of Marxism being inclined to take nationalism into account.

A curious example of this symbiotic relationship can be seen in the work of Arsenii Gulyga (1921–1996) and Iurii Davydov (1929–2007). Both philosophers initially gained prominence as staunchly Marxist critics of "reactionary bourgeois philosophy," but their positions gradually moved in the direction of what could be called "ethical absolutism." Gulyga became preoccupied with classical German idealism, devoting several books to the lives and philosophies of Kant, Hegel, and Schelling, whom he regarded not only as predecessors of Marx but also as exponents of vital and universal spiritual values. Later, he turned to the legacy of Russian thought, especially the teachings of Vladimir Solovyov and Nikolai Fedorov, whom he considered to be the best exemplars to guide the social and moral regeneration called for by the contemporary crisis of technological and individualistic mentality. At the same time, he never abandoned his Marxist motivations, even with the advent of glasnost, when renunciatory self-reappraisal became commonplace. He was able to reconcile his Marxist views with the new spirit of idealism and national pride by making recourse to collectivism, a feature common to both bodies of thought. In this context, the spirit of conciliatory and all-encompassing unity (*vseedinstvo*) that collectivism grounds itself in derives from the religious doctrines of Russian Orthodoxy. For many decades, Soviet Marxism had denounced religious systems and persecuted all thinkers who incorporated religion in their works. The landmark of such persecution was Lenin's 1922 exile of about 160 of the most prominent Russian thinkers—whose legacy, enriched by their subsequent activity outside Russia, returned to the Russian intellectual scene in the late Soviet period, as attempts were made to integrate their work with the Marxist tradition.

Davydov devoted the better part of his career to critiquing Western sociological theories, beginning with Plato and Aristotle and concentrating later on the philosophy and aesthetics of the New Left. The primary targets of his criticism are the allegedly elitist theories of art espoused by Schopenhauer and Nietzsche, as well as the sociology of the Frankfurt School, which Davydov condemns as a nihilistic denial of the bonds of civilization. In his view, nihilism—as incarnate in the works of such existentialist radicals as Sartre and Camus, and such "pseudo-Marxist" radicals as Marcuse—constitutes the greatest of all the dangers represented by contemporary Western thought. These thinkers exemplify a dangerous hedonistic worldview (characterized by such New Left slogans as "paradise now" and "all power to the imagination"), which undermines the true moral obligation of the individual toward his or her fellow citizens. In his most important book, *The Ethics of Love and the Metaphysics of Self-Will*, Davydov contrasts the teachings of Tolstoy and Dostoevsky with those of Sartre and Camus. He equates existentialism with an absolute metaphysical egoism and posits the alternative of self-sacrifice as the true foundation of human morality, originally established by the great Russian prophets, Tolstoy and Dostoevsky.

Both Gulyga and Davydov bracket the religious aspects of morality, as they desire to found their ethical views without explicit recourse to transcendental systems. For both thinkers, moral categories like responsibility and self-restraint are self-justifying. Thus, by subtracting the religious impetus from the moral imperatives of Tolstoy and Dostoevsky, and deemphasizing the revolutionary and atheistic strains in Marx and Engels, they are left with an equation of purely ethical prescriptions. In this way, moral responsibility, which for them is characterized by the supremacy of the social bond and shared human destiny over and against the vagaries of individual will, can be derived and validated equally by way of Marxist humanistic doctrine or Russian religious traditions.

Both philosophers valorize the Russian peasant commune as the exemplary moral institution, since villages are administered by the collective will and the recognition of mutual obligation. Gulyga and Davydov identify the advent of the modern age, and the growth of the city, with an erosion of traditional morality, as explicitly demonstrated in Western historical developments. They therefore champion a traditional, patriarchal set of values as a noble challenge to the progressive disintegration of Western society. Intentionally or not, they support a social model that combines elements of socialist and feudal moral orders, insofar as it opposes the primacy of the individual. This way, they are able to celebrate the Marxist model of social unity as a distinctly Russian mode of resistance to morally corrupt Western individualism.

A prolific writer, Davydov in the 1960s–1980s published nearly a dozen books, mostly devoted to critiquing various trends of contemporary "bourgeois" thought. Identifying him as a Marxist theoretician requires some qualification, since he did not elaborate any traditionally positive aspects of Marxist doctrine, such as the categories of dialectical and historical materialism. With Davydov, Soviet Marxism moves away from its previous association with systematically elaborated philosophy, becoming instead a method of critiquing various ideologies through the disclosure of their social origins. Soviet Marxism, of course, often had the whiff of utopianism, but Davydov harks back precisely to Marx's *anti*-utopianism, his focus on the exposition of ideology. This transition from a constructive to deconstructive use of Marxist theory was typical for the evolution of Soviet Marxism from the 1950s to the early 1980s. For Ilyenkov and Batishchev, Marxism was still a method of systematic thinking aimed at certain positive philosophical innovations and generalizations, such as the ascension from the abstract to the concrete, or the overcoming of alienation through human activity. Later, however, these intellectual claims were progressively eroded in proportion to the growing stagnation of Soviet society, which seemed to render absurd any attempt to take the scientific pretensions or practical implementation of Marxism seriously. Textbooks and monographs on dialectical materialism and scientific communism remained ubiquitous, but more creative minds tended to avoid this approach altogether. Those not creative enough to challenge official philosophy with alternative conceptual schemes, and inclined to stay within the bounds of Marxism, attempted to revitalize the doctrine via confrontation with non-Marxist theories. The favored philosophical genre of this period was collections of polemical articles with titles like *Marxism and Existentialism* or *Analysis and Critique of Contemporary Bourgeois Philosophical Anthropology*. The erudition of these authors led them far beyond Marxist scholasticism, but their methodology necessarily kept them within a predominantly Marxist paradigm.

Davydov was a representative of this critical and "humble" Marxism, which succeeded the ecstatic stage of the 1920s, the dogmatic one of the 1930s, and the renewed enthusiasm of the 1950s. This later version of Soviet Marxism sought to defend "eternal values" from the corrupt West, rather than challenge the stagnant West with revolution. No longer, in this period, does Marxism stand as the bold vanguard of a new society but, rather, as protector of the traditional humanistic values threatened by all manner of post-Marxist radicalism, from both right and (especially) left. This exaltation of moral values is peculiar to Davydov's version of Marxism, and runs counter to the well-known hatred of Marx himself for traditional morality as a sham, an amalgam of ideological and religious illusions. For Marx, moral rules conceal the real economic and social motives of human behavior. For Lenin, as mentioned above, the only *true* morality is whatever serves the final victory of communism. Certainly this is an unconventional definition of morality, since it justifies in principle any crime or repression so long as the cause is served. However, by the 1960s and especially the 1970s, Soviet society had so deteriorated in socioeconomic terms that, ironically, the only sphere in which materialist ideology could claim to still compete with the "decadent" and "corrupt" West was morality. The silent (albeit increasingly hinted-at) presupposition of *Marxist moralism* in this period was that capitalism had proved to be more efficient vis-à-vis economic and technological progress, but that Soviet society remained superior in its moral dimension, since human exploitation had been eliminated, and for each individual the interests of society superseded self-interest. Thus, Soviet Marxists' increasing emphasis on morality may itself be Marxistically interpreted as a reflection of the economic shambles Soviet society found itself in.

Davydov's first two books, *Art and the Elite* and *Art as a Sociological Phenomenon: Toward a Characterization of Aesthetic-Political Views in Plato and Aristotle*, deal with the social role of art. He is careful to dissociate himself from the vulgar sociologism that had been popular in the Soviet Russia of the 1920s and had claimed to reduce all aesthetic phenomena to their social origin, such that any writer or artist was interpreted as a representative and exponent of a particular class position. For Davydov, the sociology of art is called not to reduce art to social phenomena, but to deduce the possible social ramifications of a given work of art, regardless of its origin. This "deductionism," as opposed to "reductionism," presupposes that "the sociology of art is interested in artistic culture not so much as a consequence of certain historical conditions, but as the cause of subsequent human actions."[70] In other words, art itself produces a certain social situation, a specific type of communication between creator and perceiver, which may serve as a starting point for the transformation of society as a whole. Art is not only the highest aspiration of a free society but also a vehicle for the construction of such a society. Here Davydov echoes the early proclamations of Marx regarding the importance of free time and artistic creativity as a measure of social progress. These ideas were certainly foregrounded in Kantian and Schillerian aesthetics and later developed by Wagner in his theory of art as a mode of social revolution. However, Davydov argues that, instead of leading to a transformation of society, such an exaltation of art leads to the formation of an elite faction within society. He thus critiques all aesthetic theories that limit the communicative potential of art as receivable by only a small circle of cognoscenti.

Davydov finds the first manifestation of such aesthetic elitism already in the theories of Plato and Aristotle, who exaggerated, in his view, the ideal and contemplative aspect of art (as located in the audience) at the expense of its productive and laborious (in the neutral sense) nature (as embodied in its creator, typically an artisan who would not have belonged to the audience's class). This disjunction, drawn by the ancient Greeks, between creator and audience gave rise to an elitist aesthetics, which utilized the artist's creative labor to enhance the leisure of the ruling classes. What resulted was the "alienation of knowledge from the object,"[71] with the bearers of aesthetic knowledge socially alienated from art's producers. Davydov further traces this bifurcatory tendency in the aesthetics of Wagner, Schopenhauer, Nietzsche, and Spengler, following it into the contemporary work of Ortega y Gasset and Adorno, who treat with disdain the increasing popularizing tendency of twentieth-century art, and valorize elitism as an aesthetic "negation" of dominant social structures. For Davydov, elitism is an amplified form of individualism—whose challenge to existing society is of necessity illusory. In his view, the alternative to false social relationships would be not antisocial escapism, but the "creation of such forms of collectivity as would not oppose human individuality as its abstraction and *alienation*."[72]

The main focus of Davydov's later works shifts to the philosophy of the New Left movement and its theoreticians, such as Marcuse, Adorno, and the Frankfurt School in general.[73] The counterculture of the younger generation, which appeared to present the most radical challenge to the Western capitalist establishment, is interpreted by Davydov as an extension of the capitalist mentality. For example, Marcuse's proclamation of the "end of utopia" as the real possibility of the unlimited realization of human desires strikes Davydov as a case of hyper-consumerism. No longer, that is, is the consumer mentality limited to the desire for reified goods; now it demands the immediate gratification of all impulses through the use of drugs, sexual license, freedom from work, and so on. While Marcuse, after Freud, espouses a revolutionary "pleasure principle" to replace the repressive principle of reality, Davydov champions the primacy of reality, with its deliberate limitation of desire in favor of labor and morality (the "morality of labor," in Davydov's terms). Davydov's argument is that contemporary capitalism has betrayed what was progressive in its past by shifting its focus from productivity to consumerism. Thus, the counterculture does not so much challenge capitalism as embody capitalism's disintegration into mystical hedonism, raising the most mundane aspects of bourgeois consumerism to the status of a religious cult. The commodity most in demand with the New Left is paradise itself, the blissful vocation of leisure and sensual satisfaction. For Davydov, the counterculture is synonymous with such pejorative categories as avant-gardism and nihilism, since it denies traditional moral values grounded in a continence the counterculture would dismiss as repression.

Other features of this mentality include a "voluntarism asserted in contrast to the traditional European idea, which traces its origin to Plato and Aristotle, of the primacy of reason over will"; and "aestheticism—the aspiration to 'liberate oneself' from any and all limitations imposed on man not only by specific social conditions but by 'sociality' in general."[74] Here, again, we observe that for Davydov, sociality means conservation of existing social models rather than the radical rupture envisioned by proponents of the New Left. Ultimately, Davydov concludes that capitalism is experiencing a crisis of socialization, whereby young people increasingly refuse to take their place in the world of adults, preferring to remain children forever. Hence, the transference of values and ethical norms from one generation to the next has collapsed.[75] For Davydov, this "infantilism" as he calls it is the dead-end of capitalist civilization, which has become loath to produce anything, desiring only to consume.

Thus did the Soviet variety of Marxism, unlike its radical leftist modifications typical of the West in the 1960s, insist on the validity of social constraints as something indispensable for maintaining cultural productivity. A question arises, though: Why did Marxism in the Soviet Union stray so far from the theory of revolution, coming to be a doctrine of moral restraint and self-sacrifice? One possible explanation is that, since Marxism had become an official ideology, it was accordingly preoccupied with morally justifying the existing society's repressive structures. Davydov's views underwent a remarkable evolution in this regard. In 1966, he sympathizes with Wagner, for whom "art stands as the criterion of the authenticity of revolutionary changes and the measure of their expediency at each stage of revolution."[76] But in 1978, Davydov criticizes Adorno for an almost identical statement: "The measure of the social authenticity of music today is how much … it stands in opposition to the society in which it arises and exists, how … 'critical' it is."[77] There are at least two reasons for this shift in Davydov's evaluation: first, the further in the past, the more acceptable are non-Marxist ideas for a Soviet Marxist (the long-dead Wagner is preferable to the virtual contemporary Adorno); and second, the further in the future, the more stabilized and reluctant to radical change is Soviet society itself, thus making any association between art and political opposition sound like heresy.

There is, however, also a third, and most important, reason, explicitly stated by Davydov himself: the increasing rapprochement between Soviet Marxism and Russian conservative moral(istic) thought. For Davydov, Soviet Marxism proves to be the continuation of the illustrious traditions of Russian religious moralism, associated especially with the legacy of Tolstoy and Dostoevsky. In his book *The Ethics of Love and the Metaphysics of Self-Will*, Davydov all but abandons his Marxist allegiance and finds a more authentic source for his moralistic stance in a grassroots ideology of ethical fundamentalism. He argues that morality must have an absolute foundation, and thus stands opposed to any kind of individualism (and also, we might emphasize, to class determinism). Davydov analyzes parallels between the philosophy of Camus and Sartre, which proclaims an absolute existential freedom, and such characters in Dostoevsky's novels as Raskol'nikov, Svidrigailov, Stavrogin, and Ivan Karamazov, who, through experiments with their own lives, attest to the destructive and self-destructive effects of this freedom. The exaltation of individual freedom undermines the basis of individuality and threatens to lead to suicide, since the meaning of life can be found only in life for other people; hence, the morality of self-sacrifice professed by Russian thinkers.

> From the standpoint of Russian moral philosophy, the cause of the moral dead-end in which the West finds itself, but which once also threatened Russia, is the collapse of a moral absolute, and of the belief that the distinction between good and evil, virtue and vice, nobility and baseness, is utterly irrevocable. There is thus only one prospect for escape from this dead-end: relying on the people's moral essence, which has not yet disintegrated, … to revive the faith in the absolutism of moral absolutes, the validity of moral truth, also among those educated and cultured strata of Russian society already engaged in the "civilized" processes that are the source of *ethical skepticism*.[78]

This negatively charged identification of civilization with skepticism is characteristic of Davydov's later sympathies with patriarchal society, with its enduring system of absolute values. Davydov never specifies the source of his desired absolutism. His morality is not explicitly rooted in any religious faith, and in some writings, he argues that humanism is incommensurate with Christianity.[79] Thus, humanism in search of an absolute foundation comes to coincide with the immanent moral integrity of the nation. Though Davydov is careful to distinguish his views from outright nationalism, he claims that out of all existing nations, Russia is the only one to assume the burdensome responsibility for the fate of the world, while Western nations have all succumbed to the pursuit of material and economic *self*-interest. "In its practical-historical realization, the idea of self-abnegation and self-sacrifice asserted solely by the Russian people, appears in this exposition first of all as 'being for the other' ('for others,' ultimately for everyone). By sacrificing itself for everyone, the nation saves itself."[80] Actually, Davydov identifies his own philosophy with the position of another of Dostoevsky's characters, Shatov, who proclaimed that the Russian nation is the bearer of God.

Ultimately, what remains from Marxism in Davydov's interpretation is only "the simple rules of morality"—a citation from the later Marx[81] that became the sole theoretical support for those newly arisen grassroots philosophers who nevertheless claimed allegiance to "genuine" Marxism; even as, in reality, Marx was thus reduced to a platitude that could as easily have been uttered by any Soviet schoolteacher or administrator. Despite the obvious incongruence of Davydov's philosophy with Marx's theories, one aspect of this transformation of Marxism should be taken seriously. The "primacy of social being" espoused by Marxism proved to be a useful justification for a moralism that negates the freedom of individuality and condemns, rather than supports, revolutionary initiative. Is not the moralism of later Soviet Marxists somehow embedded already in the initial project of Marx's communism, which appeals to collective values shared by all members of society? If communism, according to Marx's predictions, reproduces, at the highest industrial level, the spirit of communality peculiar to primitive, "non-antagonistic" society, then the further communism recedes into the distant and unattainable future (as was the case with Russia in the 1970s to the 1980s), the more persistent and appealing become the values of traditional society in its pre-civilized and pre-relativized state. The transformation of Marxism into a rationale for moralism and traditionalism may thus be viewed as an organic component of the original mythological roots of communist eschatology, oriented toward a golden age in the future, but taking as its model the nostalgic past.

11. Revisions of Orthodox Marxism in the Era of Glasnost. S. Platonov

With the advent of perestroika, Russian philosophers were permitted for the first time to criticize Marxism openly. Paradoxically, Marxists themselves were most eager to exploit this potential and to settle accounts with their orthodox past, while for non-Marxists the downfall of the official *diamat* (dialectical materialism) meant an opportunity to express their views publicly. Thus, the most active critics of Marxism came from the higher ranks of party officials, such as Aleksandr Iakovlev, a member of the Politburo and second in command to Mikhail Gorbachev, or Aleksandr Tsipko, a consultant in the Central Committee's international department.

This new sense of openness was fostered by Gorbachev himself, who as early as 1986 began to contradict Marxist prescriptions; for example, he publicly attributed to Lenin an unspecified passage to the effect that "there are situations in which ... panhuman values" are more important than "class or proletarian values."[82] Furthermore, Iakovlev, as his closest ally and head of the party ideological apparatus, consistently condemned all forms of Marxist scholasticism and called for a rejuvenation of the Soviet humanities and social sciences on the basis of contemporary Western methodologies.

Several lines of argumentation developed regarding the cause of communism's failure. Critics debated whether to attribute it to the distortions of those who attempted to implement Marx's vision, or to find implicit fault with Marxism itself. The first position, represented by Aleskandr Butenko, Otto Latsis, and Gennadii Lisichkin, among others, presupposes that it was Lenin and/or Stalin who were to blame for Marxism's totalitarian drift toward traditional patterns of allegedly "Asiatic" despotism. In other words, a more faithful application of Marxism would have produced a different outcome. For instance, if the New Economic Policy (NEP), launched by Lenin, had been continued by Stalin, or if Bukharin had come to power instead of Stalin, then Marxist theory would have come to its fruition.

The exact historical moment this distortion is supposed to have happened varies: some point to the inadequacy of the Russian assimilation of Marxism in the 1880s; others to the Bolshevik deviation from the broader social-democratic movement after 1903; and still others blame an untimely and undemocratic October Revolution of 1917, which gave rise to a too-militant communism. Mikhail Kapustin, for example, advanced the idea that the socialism constructed in the USSR was nothing but the crude, egalitarian, "barracks-like" communism Marx himself warned against in his *Economic and Philosophic Manuscripts of 1844*. From this point of view, neither Stalin nor Lenin could be called authentic Marxists.

Another line of argument, likewise based in a reverence for Marxist thought, was oriented toward the construction of a revised communist future, rather than toward the conventional criticism of Stalin's perversions of communism. This approach is reminiscent of the spirit of Marxist revival in the 1950s. The early stage of Gorbachev's perestroika seemed to regenerate the mentality and aspirations of Khrushchev's Thaw, not only in its anti-Stalinism, but also in its romantic and humanistic appeals to the legacy of the early Marx, and its determination to build a "communism with a human face." The period between Brezhnev's death (1982) and Gorbachev's deconstruction of communism, which became explicit only in 1987–8, was dominated by a revisionist impetus reminiscent of the early years of Khrushchev's leadership. Brezhnev's neo-Stalinism seemed to be a thing of the past, whereas the future offered the promise of "genuine" communism, which, since it was opposed to the militant model of communism traditionally ascribed to Soviet Marxism, could even be identified as a doctrine of postcommunism, one that might realize the most fundamental Marxist ideals.

The postcommunist vision was presented most persuasively by S. Platonov, a pseudonym for a group of three writers, social commentators, and political journalists: Viktor Aksenov, Viktor Krivorukov, and Sergei Chernyshev. "S. Platonov" ("1949–86") had supposedly worked in a defense-oriented research institute, and sought to enter into dialogue with Soviet leaders in order to suggest a new theoretical view of Marxism, one that might help overcome the dead-end of the Brezhnev stagnation. In 1983, Iurii Andropov, general secretary of the Communist Party of the Soviet Union, publicly proclaimed that the Soviet people had yet to define their historical and social identity, asking: "Who are we and where are we going?" This question provided the impetus for a quest for theory, with Platonov among the brightest of those who offered answers. His (in reality, their) writings primarily took the form of letters to party leaders, whose responses were so favorable as to suggest that Platonov's views may have influenced Gorbachev's early policies, especially those concerning the "new thinking" (*novoe myshlenie*) and his attitude toward the West.

S. Platonov's only publication, *After Communism* (1989), is a book-length collection of his letters and unfinished fragments. A fervent believer in the Marxist cause, Platonov argues from the point of view of a person dissatisfied with the Soviet modification of Marxism. However, rather than accuse it of being a perversion of the Marxist ideal, he theorizes it as a necessary stage in the realization of Marx's vision. The basic project of Marx was the overcoming of alienation, which also implied human liberation from the laws of economic and historical determinism. Thus, Marxist historical materialism, proclaiming the priority of matter over consciousness and of economic conditions over ideological superstructures, is not a universal method, but pertains only to the prehistory of humanity, to those antagonistic formations where people function as tools of the social forces that dominate them. Marx was correct in his descriptions of the laws of capitalist political economy, but the Soviet Marxists who attempt to formulate laws of socialist economics are wrong. Platonov notes sardonically that the "political economy of socialism"—an illustrious official discipline taught in every Soviet university—does not really exist, not because Marxists have failed to elaborate it correctly, but because it is impossible in principle. The very essence of socialism presupposes the undermining of the laws of economics as the determining basis of social relationships; in their stead, ideology and the activity of human consciousness take priority. Hence the October Revolution resulted not only in the reversal of oppressed and oppressing classes but, more importantly, in the reversal of the relationship between the base and the superstructure. "By the same token, the very relation between social being and social consciousness is reversed," asserts Platonov, referring to Engels's famous statement: "People who at last become the masters of their social being become, as a result of it, the masters of themselves—free people."[83] It was ideology, then, that came to be the basis of historical development under socialism; people had liberated themselves from the oppression of economic laws. According to Platonov, Marxism should now renounce its allegiance to the method of historical materialism and elaborate a new worldview that prioritizes the role of the subject in the conscious transformation of history. As he puts it: just as the anatomy of a horse is useless in modeling the construction of an automobile, knowledge of historical laws cannot form the basis of the construction of communism.

In full accordance with the Marxist principle of collectivism, Platonov argues that the role of the subject belongs not to a separate individual, but to the collective subject manifested by the ruling party. "Thus, the crux of the crux, the engine of engines, of the mechanism of social development in the communist epoch is the conscious activity of a subject—the ruling party."[84] Platonov calls for the ruling party to throw aside all objectivist prejudices of classical determinism and proclaim the absolute autonomy of the subject as the only determinant of future human history. He claims that this aspiration is the soul of Marxism, economic and historical determinism being only a necessary tool for the explanation of pre-communist formations.

Platonov likewise critiques the traditional Soviet assumption of communism as the *telos* of the Marxist project. In Marx's early manuscripts, communism appears only as the negation of capitalism and the first stage in the creation of a truly humanistic society. Public property is merely the negation of private property, not the liberation of people from property relations as such. In Platonov's view, the genuine goal of Marxism should be not the glorification of labor and production, but their eventual annihilation, since they still objectify and reify interpersonal relations. "Labor is a category signifying a kind of activity under which people are connected by alienated relations, i.e., relations of production."[85] Thus, there are three grand epochs of human development, in which reign the kingdom of natural necessity (prehistory); the kingdom of conscious necessity (the epoch of communism); and the kingdom of freedom (the epoch of humanism). Communism, as such, has no vital attraction for people, which explains why the enthusiasm for communist perspectives has been eroded in Soviet society. The point is that communism is not an end in itself; it is merely a transitional phase, a conscious self-subjection that overcomes natural law, but is not the goal for "any competent Marxist, who knows the law of the negation of the negation, and understands that history cannot stop on communism."[86] Communism, as the negation of capitalism, will, in its own turn, be negated by humanism, putting an end to the dominance of public property as the last stage in the process of liberation from property relations. Platonov predicts that humanism will embrace all types of ownership and create a pluralistic economy, incorporating the property of associations, territories, organizations, and humanity as a whole.

Out of this pluralism comes Platonov's recommendation of a more friendly and flexible relationship with the West. He does not doubt the validity of Marx's and Lenin's predictions of the inevitable collapse of capitalism, but argues that these predictions were already fulfilled in the wake of the Great Depression, after which Western society ceased being capitalist. Platonov calls the purportedly postcapitalist economic system "elitist," arguing that its basis is no longer private property as such, but property concentrated in the hands of conglomerates, such as corporations. Thus, it is socialized property, though not to such a degree as under socialism. This means, first, that "elitism, as distinct from capitalism, does not contain in itself any principally insoluble economic contradiction that would fatally condemn it to death."[87] Secondly, this notion suggests that there is no antagonism between elitism and socialism, since they represent two varieties of social property. Thus, cooperation between the Soviet system and the West is hardly to be frowned on; to the contrary, from the Marxist point of view it is a natural step in the development of humanism.

Not only does Platonov recommend cooperation between East and West, he also foresees the eventual synthesis of their socioeconomic systems in a future humanist society. Indeed, the increasing divergence between the two basic values of humanism, equality and freedom, may, he notes, be traced back to ancient Greece. In this light, Hegel comes in for criticism, for deeming inequality between individuals a necessary condition for the growth of freedom; and Marx is lauded as the first to recognize the interdependency of freedom and equality. In Marx's famous formula, the ideal of humanism is a comprehensive, harmonious development of personality, realized through a social association in which "the free development of each is the condition of the free development of all."[88] If the value of individual freedom was fostered best in the capitalist West, it is the communist East that best embodies the ideal of equality. Under humanism, this opposition of two values is dialectically preserved and, at the same time, superseded. This contradiction "becomes the source of development for each personality and society as a whole; the identity of equality and freedom is repeatedly violated and restored on a higher level."[89]

Marxism, in Platonov's interpretation, becomes an argument for a very cautious and moderate theory of convergence between communism and capitalism. Though Platonov's conceptual scheme and terminology are characteristically Marxist, his arguments, in essence, are social-democratic; as a result, his theory approaches that of the "third position," advocated by solidarists in the West as an alternative to both capitalism and communism. However, the revisionist and evolutionary components of Platonov's Marxism are paradoxically balanced with a voluntarist faith in the crucial role of the collective subject, or "hegemony," embodied by the Communist Party, which subordinates people to its absolute will in order to liberate them from the laws of economic determinism. This theory may be regarded as a product of intellectual despair, since it offers two boldly antagonistic platforms of reform: to recognize the reality of the capitalist West and to promote the dominant role of the party. It is rare to encounter contradiction in such a pure and blatant form; in the case of Platonov, it demonstrates the incongruence between this "updated" Marxism's revisionist (or moderate) and voluntarist (or radical) components, however much they pretend to form a coherent ideological unity.

Platonov represents one version of late-Soviet disillusionment with communism. Another revisionist project focused on the disclosure of the internal contradictions within Marxism itself, attempting to distinguish its outmoded aspects from those that remained valid for the future. According to such authors as Igor Pantin, Evgenii Plimak, Vadim Pechenev, and Georgii Bagaturiia, the method of dialectical materialism still had merit, especially as applied to the analysis of history. However, Marx's social and political views, including his affirmation of revolution and communism, had not withstood the test of time. These authors tended to regard the inconsistency of

Marx's theories as not so much a weakness as part of their inner dynamics, and a potential source of creative innovation. For example, historical materialism allows us to explain why the ideal of communism could not be realized in such an economically underdeveloped country as Russia. Moreover, it accounts for the utopianism of the entire communist project, since the laws of historical determinism are not conducive to the intended leap from the kingdom of necessity to the kingdom of freedom. Thus, this line of revisionism proposes a critique of Marxism on behalf of Marxism itself, leading to rather ambivalent results, since the righter Marx was as a materialist, the wronger he was as a communist.

Common to all three of these revisionist lines of argumentation is their attempt to retain the vitality of Marxism as a relevant, if not absolutely efficient, cure for the diseases of the Soviet social system. In the first case, Marxism is rescued from the perversions of its successors and restored to its infallible purity. In the second, Marxism's historical insights are ratified, although history has moved beyond the horizon of its fulfilled predictions, rendering some of its methodologies, such as historical materialism, applicable only to the past; however, Marx's humanist aspirations are now more relevant than ever. In the third case, Marx's legacy is evaluated in a piecemeal fashion, with various elements either confirmed or rejected in their own right. Thus, these three lines form a spectrum of approval, ranging from total acceptance, to historically relative justification, to a discernment between correct and incorrect aspects of Marx's teachings.

Revisionist lines of this sort prevailed in the early stages of perestroika, but the critique that eventually won out over all others proved the most radical in its merciless rejection of Marxism's entire premise. Marxism came increasingly to be seen as the culprit in all the crimes of the twentieth century, especially communism and fascism (the latter being interpreted as an extremist reaction to communism's extremes). Such a reversal of values is typical of the Russian ideological imagination, which often makes recourse to a binary evaluative model.[90] No middle ground is possible; if, in the past, Marxism was lauded as the way to the promised land, now it must appear as a satanic ruse.

12. The Self-Destruction of Soviet Marxism. Aleksandr Iakovlev

This radical line of critique was prepared, initially, by criticisms leveled at the Stalinist perversion of Marxism, but with time, critics became increasingly preoccupied with the earlier, Leninist, stages of the Russian Revolution, until, in the final analysis, critical attention was turned to Marxism itself. In this last stage, the very core of Marxist philosophy was decried as the cause of the subsequent inadequacies and self-destructive tendencies of the Soviet socioeconomic and political systems. According to this radical view, Russia is not to be blamed for distorting Marxism, but Marxism itself must be seen as culpable for Russia's misfortunes, as well as for the sufferings of many other nations in the twentieth century. This radical anti-Marxism, which arose in perestroika's latter period, considered Stalin and Lenin not apostates from Marx's teachings, but genuine Marxists, who therefore had no choice but to institute communism through violence and dictatorship. Paradoxically, this point of view is quite close to the official party propaganda that had always cast the Soviet regime's origins as truly Marxist (hence the term "Marxist-Leninist"). However, this radical critique came to the opposite conclusion about Marxism itself, condemning the ideology for the subsequent crimes and atrocities committed by the state.

The best-known proponents of this line of argumentation came from the most powerful circles in the party hierarchy, including Aleksandr Iakovlev (1923–2005), who had headed the propaganda department of the Communist Party's Central Committee under Brezhnev and who, as a member of the Politburo under Gorbachev, was instrumental in setting the ideological policy of perestroika and glasnost. In 1992, after his retirement, he published a book discussing the anti-Marxist views that had gradually led, under the author's political leadership, to the dismantling of Soviet communism. To a certain degree, his critique makes use of the numerous arguments Western anti-Marxists had been elaborating for over a century. Though Iakovlev's ideas are not very original in themselves, they are important inasmuch as they led to the practical deconstruction of Marxism as the ruling ideology of a world superpower.

Rejecting Marxism's scientific claims, Iakovlev argues that, from the very start, its tragedy was its aversion to any dialogue, its principles being grounded in unshakable, monological "truths." Furthermore, although its postulates are ostensibly based on dialectics, it gives a simplistic interpretation of the category of contradiction, underestimating the unity of opposites.

According to Marx, any class exists only through its antagonism with another class. A class can be only either exploited or exploiting: interclass relations are defined by conflict of interest. Iakovlev deems this thesis fundamentally incorrect: the opposition between classes does not necessarily mean conflict or contradiction. There exists a harmony of opposites, a collaboration and solidarity among classes. And only because of this, society lives and develops. Every organization is a harmonic collaboration; each division of labor, a mutual complement of different and opposing functions.[91]

Along with dialectics, Iakovlev critiques the other pillar of Marxist philosophy, materialism, specifically with reference to information theory. "Both materialists and idealists are equally right and wrong because matter and spirit are secondary, while information is primary."[92] For Iakovlev, matter is the energetic resource of the informational process, while spirit is information in its most complexly organized form. All levels of what Marx considered to be materiality, from the elementary particle to human society, are interpreted by Iakovlev as informational systems. History, therefore, is a process of the evolution and accumulation of information, not the succession of material modes of production.

Another concept used by Iakovlev is "feedback," which presupposes the interaction and interdependency of all elements within a system. The Marxist distinction between the base and the superstructure, the former determining the latter, fails to recognize the importance of feedback. In a complex informational system like a society, the privileging of any single component as foundational is a dubious philosophical move. Marx derived human progress solely from the growth of the material means of production, but all of these, from the hammer to the computer, are products of the human imagination, which cannot be discounted as a decisive factor in history. Historical materialism cannot, in Iakovlev's view, provide an explanation for such different cultural monuments as the Egyptian Sphinx or the Greek Parthenon merely on the grounds of their having been built by slaves, which is the traditional Marxist conception.

Iakovlev's critique does not limit itself to the legacy of the later Marx, with its primarily economic preoccupation, but also opposes the humanist Marx of the 1844 *Manuscripts*, which, as described above, had been used in the 1950s to revitalize the spirit of communism. His main target here is the Marxist idea of a human species-being, which is opposed to the contingent or empirical human being—the individual. Marx argues that species-being is not an abstract quintessence of humanness, present in each separate person, but rather the sum of all social relationships. Iakovlev sees this species-being, nonetheless, as a generic "essence" of the human; and Marxism's emphasis on its eventual realization in the ideal society, as reducing the discrete individual to an auxiliary tool for the implementation of social utopia. The theory of species-being is more readily applicable to "collectivist" insects than to human beings, whose center of self-determination is individual as opposed to generic.[93] For Iakovlev, all the social forms that Marx identifies as distorted modes of human self-alienation, such as private property, the monogamic family, and religious belief, are the necessary manifestations of human individuality, which requires economic, biological, and spiritual forms of intimacy and privacy that cannot be reduced to a collectivist mode of production. Hence, the Marxist categories of alienated behavior, conceived as historical perversions of the human essence, pertain only when that essence is postulated as a collectivist totality of social relationships. From a liberal perspective (such as that of Iakovlev here), these same categories constitute necessary expressions of human nature, making socialist collectivism the most devastating form of alienation known to history.

In Iakovlev's view, Marx's theoretical errors all derive from his faulty essentialism, with essence and phenomenon contraposed. Marx's "initial conviction that appearance is not very essential, that one should not trust what one sees and what is near, contains the premise for the reduction of reality, of life as it is."[94] Marx's essentialism has two aspects, theoretical and practical. From a theoretical standpoint, Marx postulates an essential human nature behind the empirical life of society. This hermeneutics of suspicion leads him to proclaim that the historically given social order is a perversion of humanity's true *telos*, and so must be overthrown. Hence, Marx's practical essentialism calls for a world revolution that will destroy false phenomena and give full expression to the previously alienated essence of humanity. One could conclude that capitalist society does not alienate humans from their generic essence, but it is, rather, Marx's theory itself that abstracts and alienates human essence from existing society, postulating its realization only in a distant, utopian future. Marx's fundamental mistake, according to Iakovlev, is that, encountering Hegel's theory of the essential self-alienation of absolute spirit and its progressive historical self-realization, he has taken this conception as a given. Having inherited Hegelian essentialism, albeit reinterpreted in economic terms, Marx, then, was attempting to accelerate history's self-realization by force, but ended up not alleviating alienation, but only intensifying it.

Iakovlev's radical critique of Marxism found several supporters among such former dedicated communist ideologists as Aleksandr Tsipko (born 1941), who was the first "official" Marxist to publish attacks on Marxism as the theoretical foundation of Soviet totalitarianism.[95] Tsipko emphasizes that Marxism is self-contradictory, for it proclaims the objectively ineluctable laws of history and simultaneously prescribes a means of altering the historical process.

> On the one hand, Marx can be regarded as a materialist in his understanding of history, as an enemy of voluntarism, of the external, volitional intrusion into the natural course of events.... But on the other hand, there is a very strong presence of German transcendental idealism in the Marxist understanding of life and history, including the conviction that a self-conscious "I" creates the world. Already in their *German Ideology*, Marx and Engels attended to this primordial, organic link between the Fichtean doctrine of "I," of "impetus," and the communist teaching.... The communist Marx and Engels converted this Fichtean impetus, the doctrine of the creative self-consciousness, into the idea of revolution, of a constructive violence that creates the world.... Every aspect of Marx's teachings, without exception, is permeated by this contradiction between materialist and idealist, transcendental components.[96]

Tsipko argues that Marxism is not a move from utopian to scientific socialism, as Engels claimed, but an explosive mixture of science and utopia, by which abstract ideals are disguised in scientific concepts so that they can be practically enforced.

The following aspects of Marxism were subjected to interrogation during the glasnost period: first of all, Marx was accused of misunderstanding human nature, especially insofar as private property was concerned. According to this line of argumentation, private property is a necessary institution that provides individuals with a sense of security and freedom, protecting them from the oppression of an authoritarian state. Of course, this critique was new only for Soviet citizens: as early as the 1850s, French socialist Pierre Proudhon had warned Marx that the abolition of economic competition would inevitably lead to the seizure of absolute power by the central organs of the commune. Secondly, Marx was criticized for underestimating the vitality of the capitalist system, treating it merely as a stage to be superseded by communism, and failing to account for its dynamism and mutability. Marx derived his understanding of capitalism from a model constructed during the first decades of the nineteenth century, based on a purely anarchic conception of free enterprise. As a result, he remained blind to the possibility of the marriage of a market economy with governmental regulatory mechanisms, and continued to oppose all forms of private economic initiative as antagonistic to his vision of an absolutely rational communist society. Marx's faith in his original plan for a proletarian war on the bourgeois order never wavered, even in the face of later historical developments in his lifetime that suggested that elements of a planned and rational socialist system might be beneficially integrated into a capitalist mode of production without resorting to revolutionary upheaval. Thirdly, critics argued that Marx's internationalism kept him from foreseeing the rise of nationalism that would characterize twentieth-century world politics, eventually leading, within the Soviet Union, to the integrated communal state's atomization into distinct, sovereign national entities. In a similar vein, Marx was seen as having exaggerated the crucial role of class consciousness, while underestimating other modes of identity, such as the racial, familial, regional, professional, sexual, and so on. A fourth line of criticism focused upon the Marxist neglect of the moral and spiritual aspects of human life in favor of a purely materialist model, which resulted in *Homo Sovieticus*'s development into an increasingly apathetic and parasitical being.

The upshot of these various polemics was that Marxism could offer only condemnations of capitalist shortcomings, and abstract visions of a paradise deferred. Despite its scientific claims, Marxism turned out to be a utopian project that failed to address the practical aspects of orchestrating a national economy and building a healthy, productive society.

13. Back from Science to Utopia. Mystical Neo-Communism

Despite the comprehensive critique offered in the wake of perestroika, Marxism still had fervent supporters in Russia, who now proposed a revisionary reading of Marxist philosophy that foregrounded its spiritual profundity and eschatological promises. For this new generation of intellectuals, Marx was a prophet of human self-salvation. They read Marxist philosophy as a religion of immanence, one that assimilated the best features of previous religious systems: in particular, the formulation of the highest goals of humanity, and the mobilization of spiritual power toward the attainment of these goals.

One prominent member of this movement, Sergei Kurginian (born 1949), received considerable attention for his close affiliation with conservative, pro-communist forces in Gorbachev's later years, and coauthored a book called *Postperestroika* that develops the notion of communism as the religion of the future. To quote the popular Russian magazine *Sobesednik* (Interlocutor) in 1991:

> Sergei Kurginian is a mysterious individual. [He is] the director of the *Na Doskakh* [On the Boards] Theater, an associate of the *Pamiat'* [Memory] and *Interfront* [Interfront] movements, the last mystical hope of neo-Bolsheviks, the savior of the Communist Party of the Soviet Union, the theoretician of communism as a new religion, and the head of the enigmatic corporation The Experimental Creative Center.[97]

Postperestroika served as a manifesto for conservative elements dissatisfied with Gorbachev's westernizing and liberal tendencies, and hopeful for the restoration of the country's communist orientation. However, given the blatant exhaustion of the Soviet model's economic and ideological resources, the communist project needed a radical revision that would revitalize its spiritual appeal. The religious origins and eschatological claims of communism,[98] seemingly forever superseded by its Marxist scientific and atheistic interpretation, now move to the forefront, making it once again a doctrine of salvation:

> We regard communism not only as a theory, but also as a new metaphysics that leads to the creation of a new, global religious teaching.... It contains many fundamental features vitally important for civilization, features of a new world religion with its own saints and martyrs, apostles and creed.... Among the indisputable predecessors of communism we identify Isaiah and Jesus, Buddha and Lao Tse, Confucius and Socrates.... Today there is no alternative to the communist meta-religion that would be spiritually commensurate with the power of communist ideas.[99]

From this standpoint, the abandonment of communism in the USSR is a global catastrophe, on the same order as the crucifixion of Christ. All the loftiest values that make life meaningful—brotherhood, freedom, justice, and so on—and that the Christian Church and then the French Revolution had failed to implement, were later inherited by Russian communism. With the extinction of this last heroic impulse in history, nothing is left to humanity in the twenty-first century but purely animal existence, which will take the form of either dull bourgeois consumerism or the fascist exaltation of the man-beast.

> The whole brilliance and appeal of the red ideal was in its spiritual power, its ability to oppose and challenge death, to give a tragic fullness to life and a tragic significance to the fact that life's end does not cut short the thread of the common cause, but is just another step on the way to the temple encompassing all humanity.[100]

Kurginian's ideal is a "red monastery," where people accomplish technological and simultaneously spiritual breakthroughs, selflessly devoting themselves to exhausting labor for the sake of society.

In his later works, Kurginian states more precisely the reason for his dissatisfaction with classical Marxism: it was too bound up, he argues, with the positivistic and bourgeois-materialist trends of the nineteenth century. Just as the theory of relativity does not abrogate Newton's laws, but rather incorporates them into a larger scientific framework, classical Marxism needs its own Einstein to reestablish communist theory on a firmer ground than materialism. Marxist theory's main drawback is its reduction of the spiritual essence of communism to economic determinants. Marx was correct in his relentless unmasking of the illusoriness of traditional, liberal humanism, but his theories failed to provide a supra-humanistic project that might give religious impetus to communist struggles and strivings.

The history of the Russian Communist Party, as founded by Lenin and shaped by Stalin, reveals this inherent deficiency of the Marxist project: built like a monastic order, it nevertheless lacked any religious goals that would justify its holy aura and hierarchical structure. "The contradiction between the theocratic structure of power and the defectiveness of the spiritual political center" led to the victory of a "party clan, the clan of an intellectually castrated and spiritually destitute pseudo-priesthood."[101] This critique of Soviet communism as a false theocracy goes hand in hand with Kurginian's enthusiasm for a "true" theocracy, based on communism as a global religion. In his view, the shortsightedness of Soviet rulers distorted the prospects for a worldwide theocracy, despite its organizational structures being already in place. The bonds of comradeship, the imperative of self-sacrifice, the absolute devotion to a common cause, the subordination of personality to the party—all these formal attributes of a religious order lacked any organic connection to the party's Marxist program, which instead pursued material productivity and prosperity. In Kurginian's view, this is how the party degenerated in Brezhnev's and especially Gorbachev's time, when it finally surrendered to the ideology of consumption. Kurginian attributes the failure of the communist idea in its Marxist conception not merely to the subjective betrayal of late-Soviet leaders, but to the basic deficiencies of its original materialist doctrine. If the ultimate goal of humanity is prosperity, then communism as an *economic* epitome must logically be abandoned as soon as it reveals its inferiority to the capitalist mode of production; this is what happened in the wake of perestroika, leading to the disintegration of the communist superpower.

Communism, however, as Kurginian conceives it, stands opposed to materialism. In his redefinition of the communist project, capitalism and communism are not two successive stages in the linear progress of humanity, but two independent and concurrent systems having developed from ancient times, the latter prevailing in the East, the former in the West. The progressive dimension of history involves the transition from primitive hunter-gatherer to agrarian societies and beyond, to industrial and postindustrial models; within each stage, however, one finds the coexistence of communist and capitalist property types.[102] Capitalism was based on the right to private ownership, whereas communism promoted state and social forms of property; the economic effectiveness of both models is confirmed by the history of civilization. Furthermore, the current tendencies of postindustrial development underscore the value of planned organization and state regulation of economic life, which, in Kurginian's view, allows Eastern countries to compete successfully with the West in super-technological markets. Even more importantly, communism is superior to capitalism in its moral and spiritual potential, since it replaces the selfish profit motive with the well-being of society. According to one of Kurginian's prophecies, "in the near future, the communitarian, nontraditional [i.e., non-capitalist, postindustrial—ME] principle will predominate in the sphere of production. This means that communism will begin to triumph on a worldwide scale. The market will shrivel up, giving way to a programmatic-projective organization of production."[103] Curiously, this prediction was made one week before the attempted coup in August 1991, which led to the ultimate demise of Soviet communism. However, the downfall of "red" communism—that is, the communism based on Marxist theory—signifies for Kurginian only the failure of its classical model, and the beginning of its transformation into "white" communism, poised to unite all mystical forces of light in their struggle against the forces of darkness.

One period in the history of Russian communism stands, for Kurginian, as a missed opportunity for religious revival: the "God-builders" movement in the Bolshevik faction of the Social-Democratic Party (1906–13). God-builders such as Lunacharsky, Bazarov, and Maksim Gorky interpreted Marxism as a new world religion and a means to a superior organization of humanity's collective will. They insisted that, unlike previous religions that worshipped transcendental deities discovered through supernatural revelation and preserved by a church, the communist "religion" would create or "build" its own deity. The God-builders criticized orthodox Marxist materialism, defended by the Menshevik leader Georgii Plekhanov, and attempted to derive a communist theology and teleology from the notion of "collectivist subjectivity," as opposed to the materialist emphasis on objective reality. In this philosophical dispute, Lenin turned aggressively against his political allies and supported Plekhanov; his vituperative stance would be codified in a consistent condemnation of "God-building," or any religio-communist mixing, in official Soviet ideology. It is to this pre-October, aborted program of the reunification of communism and religion that Kurginian professes his allegiance. He contrasts communism as a mystical doctrine to the profane humanism of socialism, which merely attempts to extend capitalist comfort to a broader population. For Kurginian, communism is far closer to the eschatological visions found in Richard Wagner and the anthroposophy of Rudolf Steiner; and to the "mystical pragmatism" of Andrei Belyi and Andrei Platonov, who believed the universe must be transformed by a technology endowed with spiritual power. According to this view, a human being is only one of the participants in an all-encompassing cosmic drama, where gods and people (living *and* dead) fight together against the forces of evil. However, Kurginian identifies two versions of this mystical dualism: one where the final triumph of light is predetermined by providence or a supreme being; the other, where only the activity of people can determine the fate of the universe. Communism is founded on the second viewpoint, which is why it requires an extreme concentration of all human spiritual resources in their unification against the forces of darkness.

How these forces of light and darkness are distributed in the contemporary world, Kurginian leaves generally unexplicated, except to specify that evil is concentrated in the hedonism of Western civilization, while good is associated with the moral values of communism and the Eurasian mentality. By Eurasia, Kurginian understands the unique synthesis of Orthodox Christian and Islamic polities, which geographically coincides with the territory of the Soviet Union and its European and Asian satellites, and which is spiritually led by Russia. Russia is destined to inspire and organize all the creative and cultural forces in humanity, resisting the expanding chaos and destruction represented by the atomistic individualism of consumer society. "[T]he ongoing war is an ontological war, the war of a cultural hero with a Serpent, cosmos against chaos, the state against the horde."¹⁰⁴ Kurginian is skeptical about the reformist platform of Russian democrats calling for the formation of a market economy and the emergence of a middle class of businesspeople, managers, and entrepreneurs; in his view, Russia will never be a land of capitalists. But neither is it destined to be the land of the proletariat, as Lenin predicted, or the land of peasants envisioned by Slavophiles. Essentially, Russia is a country of warriors, and since the contemporary world gives rise, on an unprecedented scale, to commercial, technological, financial, and informational warfare, Russian warriors can become managers, scientists, or businesspeople without losing their militancy. This is not simply a matter of militarism or an aggressive foreign policy, but a "theology of struggle," a struggle waged by the providential forces of light against darkness. Marxists, Slavophiles, and westernized democrats misunderstand the Russian spiritual identity, interpreting it in economic terms. However, Russia from the very beginning

> experienced a need for an idea with global-messianic potential, capable of unifying Eurasia. She found this in communism. The categories of Russian quality of life can be "competition, victory, and feast [*prazdnik*]," perhaps even "prestige," but never prosperity and tranquility ... Russia has always lived and will live in accordance with a project of mobilization .... Russia will always profess, in any form and on any occasion, its religion of intense struggle between Light and Dark; this is the theology of struggle. It will always stand opposed to hedonism, the cult of luxury. ... The primary category for Russia will be sanctity, not satiety. If she is tempted by satiety, Russia loses everything, including her daily bread.... However paradoxical it may sound, today to be a realist means to be a mystic and metaphysician. ... The red field, communist eschatology, and communist mysticism have existed, exist, and will exist in Russia and, most probably, these ideas ... will find their place within the Eurasian expanses, merging with Orthodox, Sufic, Buddhist, and possibly Catholic mysticism.... Communism has nothing in common with socialism, though [people] connect them. Communism is mystical and theist, whereas socialism is profane and hedonistic, and bears a tediously secular character.¹⁰⁵

Kurginian's mystical communism has much in common with the well-known Eurasian theory elaborated by Russian political emigrants such as Nikolai Trubetskoi and Lev Karsavin in the wake of the October Revolution. Nearly all the basic elements of their conception are adopted by Kurginian: the spiritual superiority of Eurasia over the West; the historical and geographical unity of the Russian and Turkic peoples as constitutive of Eurasian identity; the subordination of the individual to the symphonic personality of the nation; the coexistence and integration of Orthodox Christianity and communism; and the determining role of an ideocratic state in organizing all aspects of public life and dominating both the spiritual and ideological spheres. However, Kurginian preferred not to associate himself with the Eurasianists, thereby distinguishing himself from the extremes of the Russian right, also inspired by the

Eurasianist legacy. For Eurasianists, communism was only a transitory ideological and social phenomenon—to be incorporated, ultimately, by the longstanding spiritual traditions of Eurasia; whereas for Kurginian, communism appears to be an eschatological perspective for all humanity, supported by the cultural and religious legacies of Eurasia, above all, the traditions of communal property and collectivist morality. He does not subordinate communism to Eurasianism; on the contrary, he attempts to inscribe Eurasian geopolitical unity into the strategy of militant and eschatological communism. Kurginian's worldview is neither evolutionary nor revolutionary, but rather catastrophic and apocalyptic: the contemporary world, it assumes, is on the brink of collapse, and the only way to save it from chaos is to disseminate communist ideals across the globe and promote Russia's reassertion of its communist identity.[106]

Unlike Eurasianists, Kurginian is extremely eclectic in his religious orientations: Orthodox Christianity, ancient Russian paganism, Islam, anthroposophy, Fedorov's doctrine of "the common cause," Nietzsche's vision of the superman, and Bogdanov's collective voluntarism and God-building are equally acceptable to him insofar as they all inspire a communist unification of humanity. The common denominator of all these religious and quasi-religious systems and views could be identified as Zoroastrianism or Manichaeism, the religion of struggle between light and darkness. The Manichean tendencies that some critics find in Marxism's concept of class struggle are fully realized in Kurginian's revision of communism as a dualistic religion of light.

Kurginian's ideas are also eclectic from a philosophical or purely logical standpoint. On the one hand, he recognizes capitalism as a valid model of economic development, on a par with communism; on the other, he condemns it as a force of evil that must be vanquished. One of his favorite ideas is that of the "cognitariat" (modeled etymologically on "proletariat"), the consolidation of all scientific, technological, and intellectual resources of the nation into one huge enterprise producing the greatest proportion of national wealth—something akin to Moore's Utopia or Hesse's Castalia, only based on the most advanced computer technologies. At the same time, the value of knowledge for Kurginian is subordinated to the imperatives of universal struggle and religious exaltation of collectivism, which, as the Soviet experience attests, is detrimental to the pursuit of objective and effective knowledge.

It is precisely this eclecticism that makes Kurginian's views so representative of the post-Soviet intellectual atmosphere. His project could easily be categorized under the rubric of "esoterism," "radical traditionalism," or "the philosophy of national spirit." In fact, it incorporates all these components, and could be generally characterized as a "messianic Eurasian communism" or "Russian eschatological postcommunism." The unifying thread linking all of these teachings is their apocalyptic and messianic character: the catastrophic experience of the complete dissolution of the Russian imperial identity requires that history's course be ruptured by the revitalization of national eschatological forces. What makes Kurginian's views distinct within this rather conventional paradigm of catastrophic consciousness is his emphasis on communism *after communism*—in a way, reminiscent of the "life after death" model elaborated within religious teachings.

* * *

In the course of Marxism's evolution in the period under consideration, with the unlikely combination of Stalin and Kurginian marking its boundaries, two basic tendencies can be identified. The first moves toward Marxism's humanization, attempting to combine Marxist historical determinism with human values; in the end, it comes to understand the incompatibility of the two doctrines, and evolves into a critique of Marxism from a humanist point of view. This tendency begins in the mid-1950s with the dissemination of Marx's early writings and concludes in the late 1980s with the dismantling of Marxism by Communist Party leaders, particularly such initiators of perestroika as Gorbachev and Iakovlev. The second tendency, which moves toward the "nationalization" of Marxism, begins with Stalin's work on linguistics and culminates with the consolidation of communist and Eurasianist doctrines as embodied in ideas like "mystical communism" and the numerous other extreme-right movements.

It is worth noting that the aspect of Marxism most appealing to Western thinkers—its emphasis on the historical and economic conditions of society as structural determinants of human consciousness—proved to be equally alien to both vectors of Soviet Marxism's development. From the humanist standpoint, Marxism indeed equals economic determinism; this is why, however, it should be ultimately rejected as a prison of spirit, a dead-end of history. From the nationalist point of view, Marxism is acceptable as a mystical and moral doctrine promoting social unity and collectivist ideals, inspiring the Russian (or Eurasian) people to take up the role of world's messiah. The humanist and nationalist approaches may seem antithetical, but together they comprise the specificity of the Russian (as well as Soviet and post-Soviet) reception of Marxism. Marxism is either condemned for its soulless materialism or extolled for its messianic spiritualism. These two approaches differ in their identification of Marxism as a primarily materialist or religious teaching, but are unanimous in their evaluation of the materialist and determinist components of Marxism as "bad," and of its spiritual and moral components as "good." A third approach, characteristic of such Western Marxists as Lukács, Althusser, and Jameson, springs from a structuralist and post-structuralist interpretation of Marxist determinism identified as "good" in contradistinction to the ideological illusions and utopianism of false consciousness.[107] By stark contrast, polemics over Marx's legacy in late-Soviet Russia focused mainly on the problem of defining Marxism in terms of either its materialist or salvationist potential, and the acceptance or rejection of Marxism as a whole is based on these definitions.

Part II

Neo-Rationalism, Structuralism, and General Methodology

1.	From Formalism to Structuralism. The Fate of the Formal School	78
2.	General Premises and Particular Features of Russian Structuralism	81
3.	The Philosophy of the Semiosphere. Iurii Lotman	83
4.	General Methodology and the System of Thought-Activity. Georgii Shchedrovitsky	92
5.	Reflective Analysis. Vladimir Lefebvre	97
6.	Probabilistic Philosophy of Nature and Language. Vasilii Nalimov	99
7.	Phenomenology and the Theory of Consciousness. Merab Mamardashvili	103

A number of new methodological approaches appearing in the early 1960s may be united under the title of *neo-rationalism*. Rationalism, simply speaking, is "the position that reason has precedence over other ways of acquiring knowledge";[1] it is belief in reason's capacity to understand things adequately to their essence and to reflect the objective laws of the world. Neo-rationalism complicates this position, asserting that reason itself is part of physical, biological, and social reality, and must therefore consider the many existential and historical prisms through which the essence is refracted before it reaches rational understanding. Nevertheless, neo-rationalism is still guided by the ideal of cognitive rigor; it inherits René Descartes's principle of rationality as the chief source and test of knowledge and attempts to relate it to the development of a contemporary scientific worldview.

Although Marxism retained its nominal predominance in the Soviet Union until perestroika in the late 1980s, already in the late 1950s there began to emerge rival neo-rationalist schools, such as Iurii Lotman's structuralism, Georgii Shchedrovitsky's general methodology, Merab Mamardashvili's theory of consciousness, and the probabilistic philosophy of Vasilii Nalimov. As the official label "philosophy" was reserved for Marxism only, these alternative trends often occupied other disciplinary niches within the sciences and humanities, including the studies of language, literature, and culture.

The most consolidated and influential of these schools was structuralism. Its rapid ascendency can be attributed to its inheritance of methodologies from Russian formalism, the last independent intellectual movement to be eradicated by Marxist ideological pressure (a process that was completed in the late 1920s). Structuralism was seen as a kind of neo-formalism, and its claim to scientific rigor made it relatively more acceptable to official Soviet philosophy than other trends with religious, nationalist, or existentialist orientations.

1. From Formalism to Structuralism. The Fate of the Formal School

Formalism was a school of literary criticism originating in the late 1910s with the work of Viktor Shklovsky, Boris Eikhenbaum, Iurii Tynianov, Vladimir Propp, and Roman Jakobson. Although its influence was considerable in Russia before the Stalinist cultural purge in the 1930s, formalism's greatest impact came on the international scene, as it was absorbed by French and American structuralism in the 1950s and the 1960s. After the ideological suppression of formalist methodology in the USSR, its proponents continued scholarly work, but were forced to adopt a more traditional cultural-historical approach, associated with the Marxist analysis of social and biographical influences in the creation of literature. Abandoning his formalist trajectory, Propp occupied himself with investigations of the historical roots of fairy tales. Eikhenbaum wrote abundantly on the evolution of the prose of Lev Tolstoy. Shklovsky (1893–1984) proved the most prolific of the bunch, continuing to produce books right up until his death; these are of an essayistic nature, mixing critical analysis of prose and cinema with autobiographical musings and lyrical digressions. However, almost none of the signature paradoxical incisiveness and theoretical boldness that characterized his early work survived in his twilight contributions, which, despite a certain stylistic playfulness, do not offer much in the way of intellectual insight.

In his formalist period, Shklovsky insisted on the purely relativistic nature of literary forms:

> A literary work is pure form; it is not a thing, not a material, but the relation of materials.... The scale of the work—the arithmetic value of the numerator and denominator—does not matter; what matters is their relation. Jocular, tragic, world-wide and room-wide works; a world juxtaposed to a world, a cat juxtaposed to a stone—they are equal.[2]

Formalism defined the goal of art as "defamiliarization," or "deautomatization": everyday perception is limited to the identification of things already known, while the artistic image makes them unrecognizable, focusing our attention on them as if we were encountering them for the first time. This transition, from automatic recognition to perceiving a thing as a unique, "strange" phenomenon, determined formalism's critical strategy, which anticipated the concept of structure advanced in the 1950s and the 1960s by structuralism.

In retrospect, however, Shklovsky solidarizes with the critique of formalism. In it, he considers, looking back from the vantage point of 1969, "we separate[d] form and content. This provocative formula [concerning the relational rather than substantial nature of art—ME] is, in fact, a formula of capitulation; it cuts up the sphere of art, destroying the unity of experience."[3] Shklovsky implies that formalism, with its emphasis on the relational, ignored the content or the substance of what is related in art. Significantly, some structuralists, for example Claude Lévi-Strauss and Iurii Lotman, lodged similar critiques of formalism as neglectful of the semantic aspects of structure, as overdrawing purely syntactic aspects: the exploration of structure, they believed, should not stop at the relationships between signs, but must proceed further to the meanings derived from their differential qualities. Structuralism claimed to transcend the formalist obsession with syntax and return to the problem of content from the opposite side, from the semantic interpretation of syntactic relations. Shklovsky's self-criticism, however, pursues a far more traditional goal: to restore the cognitive and mimetic aspect of art, to refrain from reducing it to relational or formal structure. The content Shklovsky seeks to re-enfranchise is a pre-structural content, a historical or ideological one, rather than the semiotic aspects analyzed by structuralists.

In the 1950s to the 1980s, Shklovsky never shows any focused interest in structuralist or semiotic revisions of his early theories. Rather, he resorts to certain concepts from Heraclitean and Hegelian dialectics, approved by official Soviet Marxism, in order to substantiate his late methodology, which remains implicitly formalist, albeit eclectically mixed with clichés from dialectical materialism and historicism. Thus he insists: "In art we think through rejection.... In antireligious pronouncements, we still use religious words. This can be easily seen in Esenin and Maiakovsky. The high revolutionary style adopted biblicisms in their rejected form."[4] This passage could have been written by the early Shklovsky, but now instead of formalist proclamations, he refers to the Heraclitean concept of harmony proceeding from contradiction.

Symptomatic of the strained relationship between formalism and structuralism were the polemics between Claude Lévi-Strauss (1908–2009) and Vladimir Propp (1895–1970). In his essay "Structure and Form: Reflections on a Work by Vladimir Propp," which originally appeared as chapter thirteen of *Structural Anthropology* (1958), Lévi-Strauss begins by crediting Propp's pioneering research *Morphology of the Fairy Tale* (1929), often considered the earliest precedent of structuralist interpretation of literary narratives (narratology). He goes on, however, to demonstrate the difference between mature structuralism and its early formalist predecessor by indicating the absence of semiotic aspects in Propp's research. From Lévi-Strauss's standpoint, Propp tends to abstract form from the specific narrative material; as if, for example, he had analyzed the function of a tree without attending to the functional difference between plum trees and apple trees.[5] It would be wrong to classify textual elements only according to their most general functions (such as "interdiction" or "violation"), and to reduce the material to arbitrary and secondary operators. Structuralism, by contrast, allows for a far more detailed and multileveled analysis of the text, since each level reveals its own structural organization, including phonetic, morphological, and grammatical levels, levels of events and levels of objects (including trees in general, and as considered species by species). Formalism had been interested only in the level of forms, as opposed to the level of content; it ascribed artistic relevance to the former, dismissing the latter as a superfluous reflection of the external world. For structuralism, nothing in a text is arbitrary and nonstructured, not even the most trivial details or ideological impositions.

> Contrary to formalism, structuralism refuses to set the concrete against the abstract and to ascribe greater significance to the latter.... For formalism, the two areas must be absolutely separate, as form alone is intelligible, and content is only a residual deprived of any significant value. For structuralism, this opposition does not exist; structuralism does not treat one as abstract and the other as concrete. Form and content are of the same nature, amenable to the same type of analysis.[6]

Those elements of the text that seem, on one level, to be nonfunctional, purely thematic or ideological, acquire functional meaning on a deeper level. For example, the image of spiders in Dostoevsky's *Crime and Punishment*, as employed by Svidrigailov in his description of eternity, might seem arbitrary on a philosophical level, replaceable by any other insect, but if we analyze the structural level of insects in Dostoevsky's novels, we find a clear opposition between laboring insects, like ants, who symbolize the rational kingdom of socialism, and insects of prey, like spiders or scorpions, who symbolize the existential and irrational cruelty and vice inherent to human nature.

In his answer to Lévi-Strauss (published only in 1966), Propp claims that there is no essential difference between formalism and structuralism. Both methods aspire to an objective and rigorous investigation of literary texts; however, they are applicable only to those phenomena, like language or folklore that are based on the repetition and reproduction of the same elements. "But where art becomes the field of a unique genius's creativity, the application of rigorous methods will give positive results only if the study of literary repetition is combined with the study of singularity, before which we stand as before the manifestation of an incomprehensible miracle."[7] The reservation Propp expresses here became a typical argument in moderate critiques of structuralism, which recognized its relative validity with respect to formal elements of language and mythology, but insisted on its limitations with respect to unique works of art. This argument could hardly be acceptable for structuralism itself, insofar as the uniqueness of a literary work is constituted by particular configurations of repeatable elements, such as lexical and grammatical units; it is precisely the generality of the code that makes the singularity of a given message possible. Propp himself espoused a combined structural and historical approach to folkloric studies: synchronic analysis, in this view, is a necessary stage in the transition to diachronic investigation. Thus in his later works, such as *The Historical Roots of the Fairy Tale* (1946), *The Russian Heroic Epic* (1955), and *Russian Agrarian Feasts (An Experiment in Historical-Ethnographic Investigation)* (1963), Propp emphasized the historical aspects of folklore and its relationship with social reality, as opposed to his earlier focus on the fairy tale's morphology. But unlike Shklovsky, Propp never renounced the formalist or morphological approach; he continued to regard it as valid, and complementary to the historical one.

Overall, throughout the 1950s to the 1980s, the former formalists, even if some were still present on the theoretical scene, did not return to their previous position of influence, although their earlier (strictly formalist) works received considerable attention both in Russia and the West.

2. General Premises and Particular Features of Russian Structuralism

Aside from the legacy of domestic formalists, Russian structuralism owed much to the influence of international theorists like Ferdinand de Saussure, Claude Lévi-Strauss, and Roman Jakobson (1896–1982), one of the original formalists, whose emigration in 1920 enabled the dissemination of the formalist methodology in the West. From the mid-1950s on, Jakobson regularly visited Eastern Europe and the USSR to deliver papers at linguistics conferences—one of the essential channels by which Western structuralism was imported to Russia (even as Jakobson was himself the most important vehicle of Russian formalism's exportation to the West). In Russia, Jakobson's most influential theory was that of the six functions of language, one of which was the poetic function, defined as the self-referentiality of language. This definition was, on the one hand, close to the formalist vision of form as self-sufficient artistic design; on the other, it grounded poetic creativity, and literature as a whole, in the structures of language, which was close to the structuralist approach. Actually, Jakobson had simply rephrased one famous formalist assumption: that of poetry as a specific use of language for its own sake, but he included this principle within a broader set of language's functions, and thus made it more acceptable to structuralism, which holds all definitions to be meaningful insofar as they are differential.

One specific trait of Russian structuralism was its concentration on the organization of texts rather than the status of signs. According to one of Soviet structuralism's leaders, Viacheslav V. Ivanov (1929–2017):

> As distinct from the direction taken in semiotic research, which, beginning with Peirce and Saussure, was oriented toward the particular sign, for the late M. M. Bakhtin and other of our scholars, the center of attention was the sequence of signs, the cohesive text; abroad, the investigation thereof has been recognized as a main task only in recent years by the "second-generation semioticians," first and foremost due to recent articles of Émile Benveniste and research devoted to the linguistics of the text.[8]

Ivanov's observation here may be seen in the context of the Russian humanities' traditional preference for a holistic approach: the text appears a primary reality, only in the final analysis reducible to such abstract and isolated units as signs. Western thought, according to this point of view, was more disposed to inductive approaches, which proceed from "single individuals"—the atomic units of signification—to their organizing principles within textual structures.

One of the first public appearances of Russian structuralism came at the Conference on the Application of Mathematical Methods to the Study of the Language of Imaginative Literature, held in Gorky (Nizhnii Novgorod) in 1961.[9] This was followed by the Symposium on the Structural Study of Sign Systems (Moscow, 1962). The official rationale for the introduction of the new methodology was the need to accommodate the humanities, and first of all linguistics, to the needs of cybernetic systems. The basic question was: can computers be programmed to translate languages? This task presupposed that natural language, in the process of its translation, must be mediated by the artificial language of computerized commands and mathematical formulas. In this view, computerizing language entailed eliminating its ideological and evaluative meanings—an attractive prospect to Soviet scholars, who for decades had been forced to follow the ideological vagaries of the state. Computerization and mathematization of the humanities became a pretext for their de-ideologization. From the very start, this second aspect of the methodology in question became predominant: the focus was not so much on accommodating the humanities to computer science, but rather on applying new rigorous methods to studies in the humanities.

Thus for instance, the great Soviet mathematician Andrei Kolmogorov subjected Aleksandr Pushkin's verse to mathematical analysis and calculated that their regular and predictable rhythmic structures diminished their informative potential by approximately fifty percent. The basic notions of structuralist analysis at this stage were information and entropy, calculated along the lines of a given message's predictability: the less predictable, the more informative. However, this criterion proved problematic, since absolute unpredictability constitutes nonsense, zero information. The optimal amount of information is determined by a combination of predictable and unpredictable elements of the text, in such a way that there exist strict rules for the text's organization and, at the same time, the possibility of deviation from these rules. From this standpoint, poetic structures prove to be the least entropic and the most informative, since they are far more regular than ordinary speech, and thus particularly susceptible to meaningful deviations from patterns—unlike prosaic discourse, where such patterns are absent.

Poetry was thus the primary focus of early structuralist research, as the ideal model for the generation of new information presenting an optimal, albeit unattainable, strategy for computerized thinking. Poetry is more convenient for mathematical analysis than prose because, like music, it contains rhythmic and melodic patterns amenable to formal and even algorithmic description. Later, however, the focus shifted to narrative and prosaic structures, which yielded regularities that were far less evident, hence more intriguing. Poetic structure basically coincides with the organization of language units, which is determined by rules of rhyming and accentual patterns, while in prose it is actions and events that comprise a specific language, corresponding to the patterns of human behavior rather than to purely linguistic signs. The prevailing concept in later structuralist works became that of "secondary modeling systems," with the understanding that the only primary modeling system was natural language, while all other levels of culture—literature, cinema, fashion, historical narratives, and so on—should be united under the category of secondary systems.

Russian structuralism was less philosophically oriented than its French counterpart. The tradition of philosophical rationalism, which determined the methodological significance of structuralism in the West, had no substantial grounding in Russia. Here structuralism was perceived as a means to liberate one's thinking, to free it from metaphysical assumptions; as a phenomenon of scientific rationality rather than of philosophical rationalism. However, in its later developments in the 1970s to the 1990s, structuralism, as a form of neo-rationalism, came to be more deeply connected with traditional Russian intellectual currents, which at the same time led to its transformation into looser post-structuralist paradigms. It might be said that structuralism in Russia became increasingly philosophical as it lost its purely structuralist identity and merged with certain historical and intellectual trends more organic to the traditions of Russian thought.

Structuralism arose in the Soviet Union in two separate geographical locations, Tartu (Estonia) and Moscow, and despite the considerable interaction between them, certain local idiosyncrasies arose. The Tartu school, headed by Iurii Lotman, was more explicitly philosophical and methodologically self-conscious. Moscow structuralism, represented by Viacheslav Ivanov, Vladimir Toporov, Boris Uspensky, Eleazar Meletinsky, Aleksandr Zholkovsky, and Iurii Shcheglov, was more empirically oriented, and made significant contributions to the fields of comparative linguistics and mythology.

3. The Philosophy of the Semiosphere. Iurii Lotman

Iurii Mikhailovich Lotman (1922–1993) was the most significant and influential Soviet structuralist, semiotician, and literary thinker. He was the founder of the Tartu-Moscow semiotic school and a professor at the University of Tartu from 1954 to 1993. Originally a specialist in the literature of the late eighteenth and early nineteenth centuries, Lotman began to elaborate a structuralist methodology in his lectures between 1958 and 1962 that would comprise the material for his first book, *Lectures on Structuralist Poetics* (1964). Its publication was a major event in the Soviet humanities, laying the groundwork for a new school of thought that would be at the center of methodological debates for the next twenty years.[10]

Lotman's stated purpose was the establishment of a truly objective approach to literature based on a rigorous scientific methodology, as opposed to traditional—ideological or impressionistic—approaches. Structuralism was often accused by orthodox Soviet Marxists of amounting to a neo-formalist approach. For his part, Lotman gave formalism its due, but saw structuralism as a more comprehensive methodology. While formalism focuses on the formal aspects of the literary text, structuralism explores the content embodied within the form, understood as the semiotic structure of language imbued with meanings. "The investigation of any sign

Figure 2.1 Iurii Lotman.

system brings into crucial focus the question of what is signified, of the *content* of a discrete sign, and of the structure of the content of the sign system as a whole."[11] At the same time, Lotman seeks to justify the structuralist approach from a Marxist standpoint, citing Paul Lafargue's "Reminiscences of Marx" (1890): Marx "saw in higher mathematics the most logical and at the same time the simplest form of dialectical movement. He held the view that science is not really developed until it has learned to make use of mathematics."[12] Lotman attempts to make the case, moreover, that the relationship between the structure and its elements is compatible with the Marxist dialectical law regarding the unity of the whole and its parts.

Model, Text, and Code

Lotman's key concept is the "model," a system of signs that reflects a specific fragment of reality while remaining essentially distinct from it. Thus he implicitly ranges beyond the naive simplicity of Lenin's canonical theory of reflection, which postulates the full similarity between the object and its cognitive model. In light of language's communicative dimension, Lotman rejects a strictly mimetic approach to literature, which functions, he argues, not merely as a reflection of reality, but also as a communication between an author and a reader. Lotman proposes a critical method based on the notions of "text" and "code" as complementary aspects of literature, where "text" is the work itself, and "code" the system of rules by which the work is produced by the author and deciphered by the reader. This division explains the multiplicity of meanings contained in a given text, since it can be read according to a variety of codes based on intercultural or historical differences. Even members of the same family interpret texts according to different codes; moreover, several codes will coexist within one individual consciousness.

Lotman pays particular attention to such "autocommunicative" genres as diaries and personal journals. What leads an author to address him- or herself, given that the "message" would seem to contain no new information? For Lotman, culture is Heraclitus's "self-generating Logos"[13]—its codes, that is, are in a constant state of flux and modification. Thus is a diary addressed not to the same authorial self, but to a series of future selves whose codes will change the meaning of the initial writing. For this very reason, according to Lotman, an author likes to reread a piece of writing after its publication: the anticipation of a readership invites him or her to sample the text anew, according to the projected codes of others. Further, Lotman extends his semiotic model to larger "texts," like literature, art, or even culture as a whole; the latter, says Lotman, is autocommunication on a grand scale: the "text" of culture, that is, is addressed to its "author" (humanity), who is also the creator of its codes.[14] To this we might add that nature, not being manmade, can be interpreted in semiotic terms as a text addressed to humanity by some supernatural Author, while religion would be the reverse—a text composed by humanity and addressed to a transcendental Reader. Only in the communication of culture do Author and Reader coincide.

Specific cultures, in Lotman's terms, may also be classified according to the text/code distinction. He identifies two cultural types that he calls "book" and "manual" cultures. Book culture, typified for Lotman by Russia, is "textual": it understands itself as an aggregate of "correct texts," or such canonical works as give expression to its norms and ideals. Manual cultures, like those of Western Europe, structure their self-reflective understanding by a system of rules; their texts are thus not normative, but instead illustrative of the principles of the governing semiotic organization. In the West, then, the basic dichotomy is between organized and unorganized texts, which explains the Western colonial impetus as a will to organize the alien "material" of marginal cultures. Whereas Russia is marked by a dichotomy between correct texts and incorrect texts, which explains its isolationist tendency (the "Iron Curtain"): alien cultures are perceived as simply wrong.[15]

Semiotics and the Typology of Cultures

The typology of cultures is one of Lotman's decisive contributions. Aside from the dichotomy of text and code, he also applies to culture a distinction couched in terms of "semioticity" and "non-semioticity." A "semiotic" culture, such as existed during the European Middle Ages, considers all objects, manmade or natural, as interrelated signs: "In order to have social value, an object had to be a sign, that is, had to substitute for something more significant of which it was merely a part."[16] "Non-semiotic" cultures, like that of the Enlightenment, base value on the quality of "naturalness." "Signs become a symbol of falsehood, and the highest criterion of truth is sincerity, emancipation from the use of signs."[17] Whereas for medieval culture, words were considered to be prior to things (since God created the universe with words, and God himself was "the Word"), in the Enlightenment, words were thought to be artificial substitutes for reality, obscurers of true experience.

For Lotman, culture is a secondary modeling system insofar as it uses primary language to articulate itself. This explains the diversity of cultural codes, such as poetic and artistic styles, within the domain of a given national language. Communication must comprise both equivalence and difference: equivalence, because without this, exchange is not even possible; and difference, so that the information exchanged should actually inform, that is, should contain newness. Historically, Lotman identifies a shift in the aesthetic proportionality of equivalence and difference. Ancient folk culture, in his view, was characterized by an aesthetics of equivalence, and valued the art of repetition (just as children enjoy hearing the same story again and again). As folklore evolves into literature, aesthetics begins to stress the value of originality. Subsequently, as literature diversifies into myriad genres, movements, and styles, difference becomes the main criterion for the judgement of artistic merit. Interestingly, Lotman interprets freedom through the lens of this diversification, defining the concept in semiotic rather than moral or religious terms. In his view, freedom is commensurate with the multiplicity of codes in one's cultural repertoire, and, historically, the degree of this freedom has been increasing, a notion that offers a new insight on the hoary concept of "progress": "This outcome results from progressive growth in the combinatory possibilities of semiotic systems, and also from the continuous abolition of prohibitions against combining them."[18]

However, this process would, if left unchecked, result in such diversity that a lack of equivalence would undermine the very possibility of communication. Lotman sees a tendency at work which counteracts this progressive diversification: generalization orchestrates the variegated subcultural codes by means of "meta-codes," or semiotic systems that organize subcultural languages on the level of meta-linguistic descriptions. For example, it is only in the twentieth century, with the proliferation of nonrepresentational trends in art, that criticism (and critical theory) become a crucial bridge between artistic difference and the need for equivalence. In the contemporary art scene, the diversity of codes has come to such innumerable branchings that individual artists—rather than periods or movements or styles—determine the codes by which they create. In response, critics have developed general abstract meta-codes, which make communication between these solipsistic worlds possible. With the increasing individualization of codes comes a corresponding need for meta-codes, which explains the explosion of critical discourse in the twentieth century.

Semiosphere

Lotman's later works are characterized by two principal shifts. Whereas initially he had been preoccupied with the more technical aspects of semiotics (especially with regard to literature, poetics, and film), his later writings are far more philosophically and historically oriented. One offshoot of his philosophical thinking is the notion of the "semiosphere," which is conceived of as a semiotic space that precedes any specific linguistic or cultural systems. "The unit of semiosis, the smallest functioning mechanism, is not the separate language but the whole semiotic space of the culture in question. This is the space we term the *semiosphere*."[19] Echoing Vernadsky's "biosphere" and "noosphere," Lotman's "semiosphere" marks a new "organicist" turn in his thought. More importantly, "semiosphere" resonates with certain post-structuralist theories in the West.[20] In order for communication to occur, a person must already have some experience of communication. In much the same way as Derrida's concept of the *arche-ecriture*, the semiosphere must exist prior to any specific system of signs; nor can it be fixed to any historical moment of origin. In a certain sense it even escapes our attempts to rationalize it, because rationalization presumes a semiotic system.

Lotman proposes some basic concepts of the semiosphere, among them its asymmetry and boundary. "Asymmetry" in this context means that different languages existing in the semiosphere have no mutual semantic correspondences; thus the semiosphere becomes the generator of new information. For example, the fact that literary language cannot be adequately translated into the language of film or ethics, and so on, means that any attempt at such a translation must produce new information not conveyed in the literary original. Moreover, for Lotman, translation is the basic semiotic procedure that accompanies all acts of consciousness: to think means to translate from one language into another. Therefore, thinking is the most powerful generator of new information. However, since thinking is translation, "in order to produce texts, one must already have a text."[21] Thinking, then, addresses previous thinking, which in turn addresses thinking from further back, and so on, ad infinitum. Just as an archeologist must presuppose that beneath the excavations of one cultural layer there lies the layer of a preceding culture, thinking cannot be traced to its origin, since it has no other foundation than thinking itself. This view can be compared with Mikhail Bakhtin's notion of infinite dialogue (every utterance having another utterance as its presumption) and Merab Mamardashvili's idea that the purpose of thinking is the expansion of thinking itself.

Another important feature of the semiosphere is the concept of "boundary," which is defined as the "outer limit of a first-person form."[22] In Lotman's view, culture defines itself in terms of a boundary dividing it from what it is not, which articulates an "internal" space in opposition to an "external" one. Boundary makes difference possible and may be paralleled with the post-structuralist notion of *différance*. If classical structuralism proceeds from the concept of binary opposition—for example, living/dead, civilization/barbarism—Lotman's later work approximates the post-structuralist view according to which each oppositional pole contains and depends upon its correspondent. Moreover, when one pole of an opposition is conceived of as historically primary—making its counterpart derivative—it proves to be semiotically secondary. According to Lotman, "culture creates not only its own type of internal organization but also its own type of external 'disorganization.' In this sense we can say that the 'barbarian' is created by civilization and needs it as much as it needs him."[23] Thus the presumptions included in the semiosphere harbor a paradox: although barbarism is claimed to be historically prior to civilization, the conception of what barbarism means is generated by civilization itself. In the same manner, nature, ostensibly prior to culture, is semiotically derivative of culture as its external space.

Semiotics and History

Along with an increasingly philosophical approach to semiotics, the later Lotman begins to elaborate its historical dimension, moving away from the synchronic model of classical structuralism. Lotman sees history as "one of the products of the emergence of writing."[24] Beginning in the late 1960s, his articles (some coauthored with Boris Uspensky) reflect an increasing preoccupation with Russian history, as he attempts to build a model that might account for temporal transformations. Whereas previously his models stressed a stable typology of cultures, now he seeks to accommodate a diachronic dimension in semiotic terms. Lotman and Uspensky define culture as "the nonhereditary memory of the community, a memory expressing itself in a system of constraints and prescriptions."[25] This explains both the continuity of culture, its connection with the past ("memory") and its dynamics in the process of self-regulation as opposed to the "hereditary," conservative mechanisms of nature. If organic creatures strive to stabilize their surroundings, culture has built-in mechanisms of change that de-automatize existing codes and increase the amount of new information. Cultural memory is normally geared to remember exceptional events, anomalous and unusual occurrences, of the sort recorded in chronicles and in newspapers. Only relatively unexpected or improbable events generate a significant amount of information. Thus, culture is an apparatus of innovation and constantly multiplies the number of texts.

The dynamics of culture, like its typology, is built around binary oppositions specific to Western and Russian traditions. In Lotman's view, the West is inclined to mediate between opposing tendencies by finding a middle ground, whereas Russian history has progressed by a series of value reversals, so that each succeeding period attempts to overturn the semiotic opposition of its predecessor. Such dualities as "Russia versus the West," "Christianity versus paganism," or "upper classes versus lower classes" lacked any intermediate neutral zone that might have created a structural reserve for peaceful, gradual evolution. "Change occurs as a radical negation of the preceding state.... [T]his explains why, over various historical periods, Russia has been characterized by reactionary and progressive tendencies and not by conservatism."[26]

With his increasing interest in the diachronic dimension of culture, Lotman begins to question the semiotic foundations of historical description. In particular, he problematizes the notion of the historical *fact*, arguing that a historian deals only with texts, and "creates facts by extracting non-textual reality from the text, and an event from a story about it."[27] The traditional historian, in addressing a text according to his own semiotic code, offers only a selective interpretation of it, not a presentation of the "real facts" contained in the chronicle. Moreover, the chronicle itself must not be taken as a presentation of facts, since it too was constructed according to a certain semiotic code. Therefore, the historian must begin by reconstructing the code by which the chronicler mediated historical facts. Lotman writes of the historian's need to understand semiotic conventions; for example, one must be aware that the pictorial depiction of an Egyptian queen as a boy has nothing to do with her actual gender, but reflects the cultural code of the genre of the fresco. Every epoch, moreover, employs codes that condition the selection of "facts"; thus many events that later generations would consider relevant, such as intellectual and artistic achievements, are omitted by the original chronicler as "non-facts," since his code may dictate a "factuality" based, for example, solely on political and military realities.

In addition, Lotman's historian must be aware that his own cultural and disciplinary codes mediate his reception and interpretation of the chronicle. Arguing against the widely accepted notion, promulgated in particular by R. G. Collingwood, of the historian's practice as "thinking of the past as it really was," Lotman insists that such an approach is impossible, since a historian is limited by his or her own cultural code. While Collingwood argues that the historian must perform a "reenactment," leaving his own world behind and transferring himself mentally to the world of his historical subject—"thinking for himself what Caesar thought"—Lotman prescribes a different methodology: "Semiotics takes the opposite way, which entails completely exposing the differences between the structures of these worlds."[28] Thus for Lotman, the self-description of the historian's semiotic code is as crucial to the practice of history as the investigation of the codes that conditioned the texts under consideration. History, then, may be defined as a double translation: "facts" are decoded through two levels of selection—first the code of the chronicler, then the historian's code. However, translation can never be perfectly "faithful" to the original (recall Lotman's notion of the asymmetry of the semiosphere); thus, echoing Benedetto Croce, Lotman asserts that history cannot be a rigorous science.

Contingency and Creativity

Another of Lotman's departures from his early structuralist methodology centers on the notion of contingency in history. Whereas traditional structuralism generally assumes a rigidity of its models, attributable to a deterministic mechanism of semiotic processes, Lotman's later work advances the role of arbitrariness as allowing for a host of unpredictable variations. Just as biological mutation is the creative principle in nature, arbitrariness is the engine of cultural variation, although its role differs among cultural domains. In the sciences, arbitrariness relates to the process of discovery, not to its result. That is to say, Newton's discoveries were arbitrarily (mythically) attributable to the chance of a fallen apple, but had Newton not discovered his laws, someone else would have, since they correspond to an objective order of nature. Artistic creation, on the other hand, incorporates arbitrariness in both its processes and results. The "infinite monkey theorem" notwithstanding, Shakespeare's plays could not have been written in another period or by another author. "In order that a given text be articulated, what is necessary is the manifestation of a speaker completely arbitrary from the point of view of the structure of the language."[29] Speech, in Lotman's terms, is preceded by the semiosphere, but a speaker inhabits a multiplicity of spheres (including the biosphere and noosphere) whose relation to the semiosphere is arbitrary.

Creativity, in Lotman's view, occurs most typically on the margins of different spheres, and of cultural and temporal sub-spheres within the larger semiosphere. For example, in ancient Rome, the empire's geographic periphery generated more vital cultural innovations (such as Christianity[30]) than did its center. Cultural margins provide the opportunity for arbitrary interplay and combinations between codes, which give rise to the production of new codes. By contrast, the structural rigidity of the center limits its creative capacity. By the same logic, argues Lotman, the early drafts of an artistic work contain a greater measure of arbitrariness than the polished final version, and thus may anticipate nascent cultural codes that will be articulated in the future. "Drafts predict the next stages on the trajectory of art."[31]

Post-Structuralism: Language and Reality

Lotman's later theories of art move away from the scientific motivations of his early structuralist models by admitting arbitrariness as the decisive factor in the development of history and art. Historical progress proceeds by a multiplication and fluctuation of alternative codes, thus engendering possibilities of greater freedom. The implication of greater freedom, moreover, is greater responsibility, since, in Lotman's words, arbitrariness "introduces into the historical process such factors as the personal responsibility and moral behavior of its participants."[32] In the dynamics of Lotman's thought, structuralist models are gradually transformed in the direction of post-structuralism.

The plurality of semiotic codes, including the theoretical languages of their description, is essential for Lotman's approach to the concept of reality. Post-structuralist theory is inclined to denigrate the very notion of reality as a mere consequence of the metaphysics of presence. According to Lotman, the concept of reality can be both preserved and radically transformed by the adoption of such semiotic mechanisms as appear to negate it. Reality would be unapproachable and transcendental, in the Kantian sense, if there existed only one language of its description. But since languages vary immensely, each of them presumably describes those aspects of reality that are transcendental for other languages. For example, the language of gestures touches upon dimensions of reality that are unattainable to verbal language; the language of cinema reveals aspects of reality that are concealed from literary and musical languages. Thus can reality be located in the gaps between existing languages as the place of their *mutual transcendence*. Since one language is never fully translated into another, reality can be defined as this very zone of untranslatability, as "beyond" any particular language and translatable only by the totality of all existing and potential languages:

> [T]he relationships between the translatable and the untranslatable are so complex that possibilities for a breakthrough into the space beyond [language] … are created.… Thus, the world of semiosis is not fatally locked in on itself: it forms a complex structure, which always "plays" with the space external to it, first drawing

it into itself, then throwing into it those elements of its own which have already been used and which have lost their semiotic activity.[33]

Reality, then, is alternately incorporated into semiotic systems and estranged from them, and it is the extralinguistic character of reality that gives rise to the variability of languages. Lotman's solution to the problem of reality is different both from the naive assumption of its primary and self-evident presence, and, on the other hand, from the hypercritical negation of its cognitive relevance from the deconstructionist standpoint. Lotman suggests that the place for non-semiotic reality can be defined in strictly semiotic terms, and even more, that the assumption of such a reality is indispensable for the construction of semiotic systems. In semiotic terms, reality can be defined as the cause of the proliferation of languages, and of their mutual untranslatability.

Cultural Dynamics and Explosion

In his final book, *Culture and Explosion*, Lotman further emphasizes the "explosive" nature of structural dynamics, and critiques the claims of earlier structuralism: "Traditional structuralism was based on a principle previously espoused by the Russian formalists: the text was considered to be a closed, self-sufficient, synchronically organized system."[34] Structural-semiotic analysis, in its renovated form, focuses on the interaction between textual and extratextual reality, and also on the interaction between the present and the future. Since the future is not predetermined or fully predictable, the choice of any one possibility is always arbitrary, so that it contains the greatest quantity of information. The future, with its definitive uncertainty, functions as a generator of information.

The very category of "explosion" becomes the center of Lotman's thought since, in contrast to gradual progress or evolution, it presupposes the utmost uncertainty: "The moment of explosion is also the place were a sharp increase in the informativity of the entire system takes place."[35] However, Lotman believes that explosive processes in culture must be moderated and mediated by accumulative and conservative factors. In keeping with his previous works on dual patterns in Russian history, he discriminates between binary and ternary models of culture, the former peculiar to Russia, the latter, to the West. In the ternary system, even the most powerful explosion does not shake the deepest layers of culture. For example, the French Revolution, despite all its radicalism, did not disrupt the day-to-day functioning of theaters and restaurants; while in the Russian Revolution, all this detritus of "corrupt bourgeois culture" was washed away. Similarly, even as the downfall of the Napoleonic Empire represented the exploding of a political structure, the landownership laws established during the revolutionary period would be preserved. This would have been impossible in Russian society, where an explosion encompasses all spheres and structures. The failure of Russian democratic reforms in the last third of the nineteenth century was a direct result of the inability to establish a middle ground in negotiations between the government and oppositional movements, which drove both sides to the adoption of terrorism, and ultimately led to the catastrophe of the Russian Revolutions of 1905 and October 1917.

Further, Lotman explains the poignant difficulties of Russia's post-Soviet transition to democracy in terms of the inner contradiction between the desired evolutionary model and the explosive means of its realization: "Even when we are talking of gradual development, we want to accomplish this using explosive techniques. This, however, is not the result of some lack of thought, but rather the severe dictates of a binary historical structure."[36] The evolutionary manner of reform attempted by Mikhail Gorbachev in the late 1980s degraded into a drawn-out series of palliatives and bureaucratic prescriptions, losing contact with reality. On the other hand, the revolutionary means employed by Boris Yeltsin, including the instantaneous, shock-therapy method of introducing marketization and privatization, endangered the very goal of evolutionism, and brought the country, at the time of Lotman's writing, to the brink of civil war. As an inveterate Westernizer, Lotman urged Russian society to join "the ternary, Pan-European system and forego the ideal of destroying 'the old world to its very foundations, and then' constructing a new one on its ruins."[37] But as a rigorous scholar of Russian history, Lotman understood, better than many politicians, the near-impossibility of this evolutionary change of cultural paradigms.

Lotman's legacy will definitely remain a cornerstone of the Russian humanities, however the methodological approaches to his work might continue to develop in the twenty-first century. Despite his faithfulness to the criteria of methodological rigor, he never adhered to any particular theoretical dogma, and would flexibly accommodate his conceptual model to the particular features of the material at hand. He began as an acute critic of traditional, amorphous, or dogmatically Marxist methodology, which indiscriminately conflates ideological, sociological, biographical, and cultural-historical strategies. But his evolution allowed him to reincorporate many of these traditional elements, which a conservative version of structuralism would have likely eliminated. In Lotman's later thinking, we see how he integrated elements of biographical, historical, and philosophical approaches together with structuralism and semiotics, forming his own version of a consciously pluralistic post-structuralist methodology. Regardless of which element of this amalgam might take precedence in the future study of his work, Lotman's corpus will remain a model of methodological synthesis based on the rigorous analysis of and discrimination among various levels of cultural systems.

4. General Methodology and the System of Thought-Activity. Georgii Shchedrovitsky

Along with theoretical structuralism, which manifested itself mostly in cultural, literary, and linguistic studies, there developed another influential movement, originating with a group called the Moscow Logical (later Methodological) Circle. This emerged in 1952 among graduate students at Moscow State University, including Georgii Shchedrovitsky, Merab Mamardashvili, Aleksandr Zinoviev, and Boris Grushin.[38]

These founding participants subsequently left the Circle to pursue their own philosophical projects, but in the early 1960s, Georgii Shchedrovitsky (1929–1994)

Figure 2.2 Georgii Shchedrovitsky.

became the leader of what could be called the "general methodology" movement, or, as it was often referred to by its representatives, "systematic thought-activity" theory (*sistemo-mysledeiatel'nost'*, three words in one).[39] Shchedrovitsky's contribution to this movement, as its founder and indisputable leader, cannot be understood solely in terms of his publications, which are rather sparse; the crucial influence was, rather, his personality and oral "teachings." As Vladimir Lefebvre put it: "Undoubtedly, Shchedrovitsky is the brightest personality, an important phenomenon in Soviet philosophy. His intellectual influence in Soviet culture would seem to be paralleled only by that of Bertrand Russell in English-speaking culture."[40]

The activity of this group, which included Lefebvre, N. G. Alekseev, A. I. Moskaeva, N. I. Nepomniashchaia, N. S. Pantina, V. M. Rozin, and S. G. Iakobson, resulted in a collective monograph titled *Pedagogy and Logic* (1968), which went unpublished due to the ideological pressures of that period. In the 1970s and the 1980s, the school attracted many new members among such younger philosophers as O. I. Genisaretsky, Iu. B. Gromyko, S. V. Popov, and P. G. Shchedrovitsky (the founder's son). Some members remained formally affiliated with the group, while for others it served as a laboratory of their early intellectual formation. Thus for instance, Lefebvre would go on to elaborate his own theory of "reflective" analysis; Oleg Genisaretsky later became a Russian Orthodox religious philosopher; while Vadim Rozin formally divorced himself from the group, albeit retaining its principal methodological orientation.

General methodology is concerned first and foremost with the structural foundations of human activity and the practical forms of its organization. Unlike the Tartu and Moscow structuralist schools, general methodology is not so much interested in analyzing texts as in exploring the structures determining meaningful and purposive behavior, especially professional activity. The central concept of *thought-activity* theory presupposes, first, that thought is not a set of static ideas, but a process of mental activity; and, second, that human activity is determined not by biological instinct or spontaneous impulses, but by acts of reflection and self-reflection. According to Georgii Shchedrovitsky, "in the real world of social life, activity and action can exist only together with thinking and communication. Hence the term 'thought-activity' [*mysledeiatel'nost'*] is more in line with reality, and should thus replace and displace the term 'activity' in both research and practical organization."[41]

Some of the group's members, such as Oleg Genisaretsky, identified themselves as philosophical idealists, but idealism to them meant neither the Platonic idealism of transcendental and immutable essences, nor the Hegelian idealism of a historically developing absolute spirit. From the general-methodological viewpoint, the idea is contained not so much in human thoughts or in the laws of the universe as in the practical matrices of human interactions and professional activity. General methodologists distinguish between "action" (*aktsiia*) as a spontaneous and amorphous aspect of human activity, and "act" (*akt*) as action's internal form or rational algorithm, which can be consciously mastered. Action is arbitrary and improvisational, whereas act is a scheme of actions that can be prescribed and reproduced. According to Petr Shchedrovitsky (b. 1958)—Georgii Shchedrovitsky's son, and the movement's most active proponent after the death of its founder: "The sphere and the concept of action fixes the plan of the action's actual fulfillment. The sphere of the act, by contrast, fixes each action's preform, prototype, and model, which exist beyond any current action and independently of it."[42] The act, then, is action's ideal form, and the whole world of ideas, in a methodological sense, is the structured totality of acts underlying multifarious and apparently chaotic human actions.

General methodologists divide the act into several necessary components, or structural units, the combination of which constitutes its purposive scheme. Each act includes the *material* acted upon; the *instruments* applied to the material; the *knowledge*, manifested in semiotic forms, that this application entails; the *capacities* or talents necessary for the implementation of this knowledge; the *problems* that arise in the process of acting and are solved by it; the *product*, which is the result of the transformative operations; and so forth. General methodologists attempt to analyze various spheres of professional activity (e.g., engineering or management) according to such a scheme, seeking to expose irrational elements that contaminate each professional domain as a result of habit, routine, error, and inertia. In this respect, they oppose themselves to specialists (for whom they adopt the neologism "objectists" [*predmetniki*]), who are so preoccupied with the specific subject matter of their fields that they cannot rationalize the general schemes underlying the totality of their actions.

The most exemplary field of the general methodology movement was what its practitioners called "organizational-activity games" (*organizatsionno-deiatel'nostnye igry*). From 1979 to the early 1990s, members of the group, under the direction of Shchedrovitsky and in cooperation with various administrative, industrial, research, and educational institutions, undertook practical experiments in the analysis and optimization of certain professional activities, such as urban planning or university administration. This involved a redistribution of roles among managers, employees, and methodologists—a kind of intellectual "carnival" that for a week or two took the place of actual work. By removing professionals from their conventional roles, the game redefined the job's rational components and the worker's organizational predispositions and capacities. The task was to deconstruct the conventional, automatic forms of work and expose their inadequacy, with the purpose of establishing a rational scheme of action for each employee. This interdisciplinary organizational activity had to come in the "reduced" form of game-playing, since the real structure of Soviet society could hardly be deeply transformed in this way. Characteristically, for a period of more than ten years, Shchedrovitsky virtually ceased writing research papers, insofar as *game* itself had become his preferred mode of performative collective reflection.

With its emphasis on reproducible acts, it is not surprising that general methodologists focus on pedagogy as the most authentic application of philosophical knowledge. As Petr Shchedrovitsky puts it, "pedagogy is the practice of philosophical idealism."[43] Pedagogy presupposes the existence of some ideal world of rational norms different from the practical or phenomenal world of experience. General methodologists criticize the traditional system of education, worked out in the nineteenth century and oriented toward the notion of stable professional and cultural norms that can be assimilated in childhood and applied for the rest of one's life. In the twentieth century, norms themselves evolved so rapidly that education must become an ongoing process, incorporated into professional activity as its permanent self-reflective and self-critical aspect. The task of self-education is to subject any human action to the test of reflectivity, so that it will expose its deep structure, suitable for elaboration and transmission to other people. According to Georgii Shchedrovitsky: "A new specialty has appeared in the system of pedagogy—that of the teacher-designer, who develops a model-project of the human being in the society of the future."[44]

The practice of thought-activity is an *onto-practice*; it no longer follows the existing stereotyped modes of behavior, but "demythologizes the thought-act and leads to the formation of a reflective position and the possibility of resisting the manipulations organically inherent in all meta-systems of thought-act, first of all pedagogy and politics."[45] Pedagogy, as the transference of ready norms from adults to children, must give way to a higher type of discipline, a sort of *anthropotechnics*, which deals with more general methodological aspects of self-reflective humanity. "The pedagogical thought-act is connected with such entities as 'educational course,' 'educational discipline,' 'knowledge,' 'concept,' and 'mode of activity'; [by contrast], anthropotechnic experimentation is oriented on 'frames,' 'topoi,' 'space of reflection (understanding),' 'summa,' and so on."[46] The principal difference is that pedagogy presupposes the preparation of specialists and *reproduction* of knowledge, while anthropotechnics aims at more general methodological devices designed for the *development* of human capacities. While the traditional theory of development includes the concept of the end or goal, *onto-practice* is development without any predetermined end.

There are several points of similarity between general methodology theory and Marxist thought, from which the former evolved in the 1950s and the 1960s. Development without a preestablished goal is a characteristic formula in Marx's early writings. Another common feature is the emphasis on collective mechanisms of thought-activity that override the autonomous actions of an individual. "From our point of view, in a human being and his psyche, there is not and cannot be an 'activity'.... The concept of 'activity' appeals to a broader cultural and historical reality, to the processes of communication of cultural norms, forms, and prototypes of thought and behavior."[47] What is active in reality are acts themselves, algorithms of action that are preestablished by cultural forms and assimilated in the process of education. Some general methodologists go so far as to deny the validity of psychology and to affirm logic as the only reliable foundation for education.

This points to the deep internal contradiction of the general methodology project: how can a thinking individual demythologize preestablished cultural norms, if these constitute his or her very identity? Self-reflection presupposes the activity of the subject, which otherwise would be just an instrument for manipulation by metasystems of politics and pedagogy.

The general methodology school is more deeply connected with Marxism than any other branch of Soviet neo-rationalism, precisely because it underscores the ideal aspects of *practice*, which may be identified as a generic or collectivist model of behavior. Idealism of action, as distinct from idealism of thought, logically presupposes such general schemes of repetition and reproduction as are manifested in collectivist practices. "A human being is formed, and masters activity and thinking, first of all in a collective and through collectivity."[48] General methodology is a kind of practical, idealistic collectivism: the very principle of activity derives from social mechanisms that predetermine the behavior of an individual, whose own activity is thus reduced to transitions between various social machines. According to Petr Shchedrovitsky, "the freedom of a particular individual is manifested when he 'enters' intellectually and culturally organized machines of thought-activity, occupies a certain functional place in them.... A particular individual's freedom consists in his liberation from one machine of thought-activity through the construction of other machines of thought-activity and their subsequent assimilation."[49] But a crucial question remains unanswered: how can a person construct machines, if it is machines that construct people? Where is the source of human activity and self-development if "a human being by itself, a human as a biological entity and even as an individual incorporated in certain specific systems of activity, on the contrary, cannot be recognized as developing"?[50] This paradox would seem to stem from the contradiction inherent in Marxism itself, wherein a historical determinism still allows the proletariat to pull itself out of the historical conditioning of bourgeois society and construct the new machine of communist society. This same paradox applies to the theory of general methodology, which denies human activity and at the same time presupposes it. This also explains why adherents of this theory prioritize logic over psychology as the foundation of pedagogy: logic excludes the individual differences that constitute the central focus of psychological research.

One might ask, why are general methodologists so keen to emphasize the derivative or even illusory nature of human activity? "[T]he main conclusion of our work: the source of activity cannot be found in the human being itself."[51] To postulate free human activity as an independent source of thinking and behavior would cause a breach in the very foundations of the general-methodological project, which rests on the premise of superdetermination, to cite Louis Althusser's coinage for the common ground of Marxism and structuralism. A variety of machines can "superdetermine" human behavior—not just industrial-economic machines, but also political, ideological, or semiotic ones, but the only freedom left to the human is to change the order and source of this determination.

The circle of interests and scope of Georgii Shchedrovitsky's work was extremely broad and varied: pedagogy and logic; the general theory of activity and the logic and methodology of system-structural research and development; the philosophy of science and technology; design and organization; psychology and sociology; linguistics and semiotics—everywhere he left his original mark. During his lifetime, Georgii Shchedrovitsky published only two pamphlets, two collective monographs with his participation, and about 150 separate articles written alone or in coauthorship. After his death, more than twenty books were published, in particular in the series "From the Archive of G. P. Shchedrovitsky," containing previously unknown texts, as well as transcripts of his reports, lectures, and speeches. Along with Iurii Lotman and Vladimir Bibler, Georgii Shchedrovitsky can be considered one of the most influential thinkers of his generation, having succeeded in founding a whole school of disciples and followers who creatively develop his legacy. The Institute of Development and the G. P. Shchedrovitsky Research Foundation conduct regular conferences, seminars, book presentations, and discussions guided by the founder's motto: "Methodology is not just a doctrine of the method and means of thinking and activity, but a form of organizing the entire life-activity of people."[52]

5. Reflective Analysis. Vladimir Lefebvre

Vladimir Lefebvre (b. 1936) is the founder of *reflective analysis*, one of the branches of general methodology and systems theory. In the early 1960s, he was a member of the Moscow Methodological Circle headed by Georgii Shchedrovitsky, but the two then went their separate philosophical ways, insofar as Shchedrovitsky's orientation was more pedagogical and organizational, in terms of practical management, whereas Lefebvre was more interested in mathematical models of consciousness and self-consciousness. In the Soviet Union, he worked on reflective game theory, as an alternative to the game theory that had been adopted by the American defense establishment. In 1974, Lefebvre emigrated to the United States and, as a professor at the University of California, Irvine, continued his work on the mathematical conceptualization of psychological and ethical models.

In general terms, reflection can be defined as "the orientation of the human soul onto itself."[53] Lefebvre is interested in the multiple reflective relationships between human minds. For example, consider a reflective interaction between persons A and B, both of whom have internal images of one another (the first level of reflection), but also images of themselves as reflected in the mind of the other (the second level). Lefebvre offers the mathematical apparatus of Boolean algebra in order to formalize the multiple levels of reflection. These calculations are utilized in cybernetic systems, including military technology, to predict the strategic behavior of two or several systems in situations of conflict. Another application of Lefebvre's methodology helps to explain the enigma of the golden ratio, the proportion cherished by artists throughout time, in which the relationship of the smaller part to the larger part is proportional to the relationship of the larger part to the sum of the two parts.

The best-known aspect of Lefebvre's study is his formulation of two ethical systems relating to the normative rules of behavior in Western (liberal) and Soviet (totalitarian) societies. According to the former system, the confrontation between good and evil is good, and compromise between them is bad. The latter system follows the opposite model—the confrontation between good and evil is evil, and compromise between them is good. However, Lefebvre demonstrates that the first system leads inevitably to attempts at compromise between opposing parties, whereas the second system initiates confrontation. "[T]he theory predicts the existence of a kind of a paradox: ethical 'compromiselessness' is connected with a compromise in human relationships, and ethical compromise is connected with 'compromiselessness' in human relationships."[54] To illustrate this paradox, we might note that the American president who identified the Soviet Union as the "evil empire" was, especially during the perestroika period, in practice far more interested in reaching a compromise with this rival system than had been Brezhnev-era Soviet leaders, who invariably proclaimed the principle of peaceful coexistence, but in reality sought further confrontation.

According to the first system, evil means must be forbidden absolutely, even if they claim to promote good goals; just as Judeo-Christian morality in general is built on negative commandments that condemn sins rather than proclaim positive values. By contrast, the moral codex of communism is built on positive prescriptions, such as the glorification of labor and heroism, submission of individuality to the collective, the friendship of peoples, love for the socialist motherland, etc. Precisely because these behavioral codes are positive in themselves, they do not preclude any means for attaining them. Thus "positive" morality easily justifies "negative" actions, such that the struggle for "world peace" requires the bloody suppression of all "bourgeois" elements both inside and outside the country. Non-prescriptive morality, which limits itself only to the formulation of taboos, thereby presupposes positive behavior, though never commanding it. Lefebvre's mathematical explication of this apparatus is not provided here, as it goes beyond the scope of this study.

Lefebvre assumes that his models bridge the traditional gap between experimental and mathematical sciences on the one hand, and the psychological research of consciousness on the other. This does not mean that the two approaches are synthesized; rather, Lefebvre finds the concept of complementarity, elaborated by Niels Bohr in quantum mechanics, useful in describing the relationship between them: "The more we know about the brain activity of a certain subject, the less information we can obtain about his psychological state. And vice versa; the better we know the psychological state of a human, the less information we can obtain about the processes in his brain."[55] Thus, in extending mathematical models to ethical and psychological issues, Lefebvre's theory stumbles upon the limits of its own verification: what is modeled, in the words of Lefebvre himself, is not so much the internal life of an individual as self-reflective models of this life, so it can never verify itself through the reality of internal life per se.

6. Probabilistic Philosophy of Nature and Language. Vasilii Nalimov

Vasilii Nalimov (1910–1997) represents a very particular branch of philosophical neo-rationalism that relies on probabilistic methods in the natural and social sciences and applies them to the study of language and consciousness. Trained in sciences, Nalimov was a professor of statistics and headed Moscow State University's Laboratory of Mathematical Experimentation. His main interests lay in the field of mathematical models of language and living organisms; however, Nalimov was concerned not so

Figure 2.3 Vasilii Nalimov.

much with particular issues in mathematics as with its interplay with philosophy. His probabilistic theory of the universe converges closely with views developed in Eastern mysticism. The esoteric subtexts of rigorous sciences are the hallmark of Nalimov's thought.

Nalimov is among those rare Russian thinkers whose work has been well represented in English translation.[56] In Russia, his best-known and most influential book remains *The Probabilistic Model of Language* (1974).[57] The author's central concern is the relationship of language and consciousness. "The great interest of philosophers in language problems can be easily explained: the study of language is a way of studying thinking."[58] Thus does epistemology have the opportunity to become a "hard" science, insofar as language is susceptible to mathematical exploration. However, according to Nalimov, it is essentially only one branch of mathematics that can be applied to language: the theory of probability, especially Bayesian modeling in mathematical statistics. From this viewpoint, a semiotic system is not a deterministic mechanism, but rather encompasses a broad range of statistical probabilities. Every sign can have an infinite number of meanings, but some meanings are more probable than others: standard dictionary definitions are the most probable; figurative, metaphorical usages are at the opposite pole.

Nalimov suggests classifications of languages on a scale ranging from "hard" to "soft," depending on the probability of determinant meaning embodied therein. Scientific terminology is "hard" inasmuch as each term has a fixed, conventional meaning, which suggests only one interpretation. On this scale, poetry occupies the opposite pole; with its multitude of possible interpretations, its designations are "soft." Since "[t]he semantic field of word meanings is infinitely divisible,"[59] deeper penetration into this field reveals that there are no discrete meanings, only the fluctuation of possible meanings—pure semantic potentiality, or what Nalimov calls "semantic vacuum." Departing from the mathematical apparatus of the theory of probability, Nalimov describes meaning as a "wave-like" continuum that no "discrete" concept can match. He reinterprets all verbal units of natural languages in terms of their ultimate "fuzziness," which can be related to the Derridean notion of "trace." "Statements made in a discrete language are constantly interpreted on a continuous level."[60]

Nalimov analyzes nature and language using similar methods, since both present "continuous fields of probabilities" misconstrued in the sciences and humanities (respectively) as discrete configurations: "[B]oth the concept of discrete subatomic particles in physics and that of discrete words of our language are but a conventional denotation."[61] Much of Nalimov's work deals with the methodology of contemporary sciences and is aimed at synthesizing various disciplines based on "probabilistic ontology." Thus for instance he seeks an analogue, in the field of biology, of quantum mechanics' uncertainty principle, advancing the idea of "interspecific uncertainty," that is, the deformities of organisms that express the transgression of a species's boundaries.[62]

On a grander scale, and of great philosophical potential, is that probabilistic models prompt us to see the universe as the magnificent play of chance, and to revive Taoist and Zen-Buddhist paradoxes of the primordial, all-definitive unity as "something blurred and indistinct," or even as the "non-existence of the entity in its spontaneously unpackable unpackability."[63] On the basis of probabilistic methods, Nalimov comes to a myth-like view of the world as pure spontaneity, to which no "discrete" scientific concept can be properly applied. Nalimov rejects not only the Newtonian, but also the monotheistic universe generally; the very idea of creationism mechanistically opposes creator to creation. He finds traditional evolutionism likewise deficient, still too bound up with the creationist model, albeit diluting its rigid determinism with the play of chance. Amid his explanations, still more questions arise, which Nalimov himself does not hesitate to leave unanswered: "What do we know of the ontology of chance? Where is the random generator located?... Are we not trying to wed the Old Testament Demiurge with the dancing Shiva by softening the Laws with Chance?"[64]

Finally, Nalimov offers his own formulation: "evolutionism as spontaneity," whose goals cannot be detached from the very process of evolution. He summarizes this concept in the following way:

> Indeed, making use of a probabilistic ontology, we revive the ancient myth.... My attitude toward a Cartesian-Newtonian mechanistic background on which evolutionary ideas keep developing is, indeed, acutely critical. But the major point is the positive aspect, the possibility to show the legitimacy of the probabilistic, or, actually, geometric ontology of the World, whose motive power is not a law, but a spontaneity.... Spontaneity becomes the fundamental principle of the World. We cannot reduce the nature of spontaneity to other scientific notions.[65]

For Nalimov, probability is not just the result of incomplete human knowledge of the world, but the essence of the world itself: "We mean the probabilistic ontology of the probabilistic world, not the probabilistic epistemology of a deterministic world."[66] There are no general laws, even in such areas as have been considered the most rigidly deterministic, such as the physical motion of atoms and particles; there are rather only certain probabilities of events, which may very approximately be described as laws. Probability in Nalimov's view is related to *potentiality*—in his usage, an ontological concept presupposing that the primary foundation of the world is not something, but Nothing, which has only the potential of becoming. Nalimov utilizes the existing notion of physical vacuum—a space in which virtual particles constantly emerge and disappear—in order to elaborate the concept of *semantic* vacuum, where it is *meanings* that emerge and disappear. Even personality can be regarded, from this point of view, as one of the possible states of the semantic vacuum, as a "constant fluctuation of the probability distribution function determining a person's individuality on the semantic field."[67]

In his youth, Nalimov was close to the "mystical anarchism" movement, and in the late 1920s even joined the Order of the Knights Templar in Moscow, for which he was subsequently arrested and spent eighteen years in the Gulag (1936–53).[68] Nalimov sees the Judaic notion of a personal and omnipotent God as the foundational flaw of the whole tradition of Western determinism and rationalism; he seeks an alternative in Christian apocrypha, in European gnostic wisdom, and in the ancient teachings of the East, such as Buddhism and Taoism, which are radically atheistic, that is, which depersonalize spiritual reality and interpret it as pure potentiality. A substantial portion of Nalimov's writings are devoted to methods for entering the primordial Nothing, which may be identified on various levels as emptiness, the unconscious, or silence. All modes of approach to this fundamental (non)reality are based on what can be called the continuum of our conceptual and verbal activity, which cannot be reduced to discrete units of meaning. The idea that each word has a definite meaning, and each concept a definite referent, prevents us from penetrating the fluctuations of the semantic field, discoverable only through meditation and silence. Unlike rational thinking, meditation deals not with separate concepts but with the unceasing flow of consciousness and its dissolution into the fluctuations of the unconscious, no longer isolated from it. "A call for silence as the means of knowing oneself and the world ... is an appeal for direct access to continuous thinking in its pure form. The technique of meditation is a skill to govern continuous thinking without resorting to language."[69] Symbols and questioning are semiotic devices that penetrate the depth of the Nothing, since they have an unlimited range of probable meanings, and call every univocal assertion and judgement into question.

The same semantic fuzziness can be found in abstract as opposed to figurative or realistic painting, since the former is aimed at the reproduction not of discrete objects, but rather of the continuous energy fields of relations between objects. In biology, Nalimov critiques existing taxonomic systems for classifying plants and animals, arguing that the recognized taxons are constructed and contingent concepts, since in reality a living entity exemplifies a form of transition from one taxon to the next; continuity and "uncertainty" are thus characteristic also of the variety of lifeforms.[70] Probabilistic theory potentially revolutionizes all spheres of knowledge, including physics, biology, linguistics, and psychoanalysis, divorcing them from monotheistic and deterministic conceptions and reformulating them in terms of the fuzzy language that the foundational Nothing uses to describe itself.

Thus in Vasilii Nalimov, like in Iurii Lotman, we observe the gradual transition from the methodological concepts of structuralism, with its claims to rigorous scientific knowledge in the humanities, toward a quintessentially humanistic approach to the sciences, where such "unscientific" concepts as freedom, indeterminacy, silence, and intuition can be applied. Nalimov even uses the notions of the "semantic universe" and the "semantic continuum,"[71] which are quite close to Lotman's concept of the "semiosphere," encompassing as they do not only the variety of semiotic codes and languages, but also those "black holes" of meaning that lie between languages and render them mutually untranslatable.

Structuralism developed an atomistic approach to semiotic systems as composed from discrete units, each endowed with a definite meaning in the network of signs. Post-structuralism demonstrates the principal ambiguity of each sign, which manifests the qualities of a wave rather than a particle. This dilution and undulation of discrete units acquires, with Lotman, an historical dimension; with Nalimov, a probabilistic one, which is, in a sense, ahistorical, since it aspires to the pure potentiality of the vacuum—conceivable as a space without time. Lotman and Nalimov exemplify two polar orientations of early Russian theoretical post-structuralism that may be described roughly as Westernist and historical vs. Eastern and mystical. For Lotman, historical dynamics present the continuous aspect of the semiosphere, which generates arbitrariness and spontaneity as modes of the evolution—even the explosion—of semiotic systems. For Nalimov, history is, rather, a rationalization and analytical dissection of the continua simultaneously present in the probabilistic universe: "The incessant desire to split the continuum gives rise to conflicts which are the moving force of history."[72]

With Nalimov, the ultimate reality behind all historical divisions and conflicts is most eloquently described in the visions of great mystics, such as Buddha and Laozi, Jacob Boehme and Meister Eckhart. Nalimov's works, though replete with mathematical formulas and probabilistic calculations, deliberately avoid teleological reasoning and instead utilize a variety of citations from the thinkers of different epochs, from Socrates and Confucius to Wittgenstein and Carnap. His thought is a mosaic of various insights into the nature of the Continuum; being, themselves, part of this continuum, these insights do not develop in time.

Thus, Nalimov can exemplify a curious paradox of Russian "scientific" philosophy: even proceeding from the most rigorous modes of knowledge, in this case mathematics or cybernetics, it evolves into the valorization of the suprarational reality of chance, and almost imperceptibly converges with its opposite: the philosophy of personality and freedom.

7. Phenomenology and the Theory of Consciousness. Merab Mamardashvili

The reception of phenomenology in Russia was cut short when all philosophical teachings other than Marxism were branded as "bourgeois" and "reactionary" after the October Revolution. The work of such early exponents of phenomenology as Gustav Shpet and Aleksei Losev was suppressed in the 1920s, and it was not until the philosophical awakening of the 1960s and 1970s that some elements of phenomenology were reincorporated into intellectual life. And it was high time; as Merab Mamardashvili was fond of saying: "Phenomenology is an accompanying moment of any philosophy."[73]

Merab Mamardashvili (1930–1990) was the most creative Soviet phenomenological thinker of this period, although he never explicitly identified himself as a phenomenologist. In his youth he was associated with a group of young neo-Marxist thinkers at Moscow State University (including Ilyenkov and Georgii Shchedrovitsky) and focused on logical and historical issues in Marx's *Capital*. Mamardashvili joined the Communist Party in 1961, and until the mid-1970s made a successful official career. From 1961 to 1966, he lived in Prague, working in the editorial office of the international journal *Problems of Peace and Socialism* as deputy department head. He had the opportunity to travel to the countries of Western Europe; in particular, he frequently visited France, communicated with Jean-Paul Sartre, and became friends

Figure 2.4 Merab Mamardashvili.

with Louis Althusser; both would have a significant impact on Mamardashvili's growing interest in existentialism and his turn toward new, structuralist readings of Marx. Later, Mamardashvili worked as a department head at Moscow's Institute of the International Labor Movement and as deputy editor in chief of the leading Soviet philosophy journal *Voprosy filosofii* (Questions of Philosophy). Mamardashvili's reputation initially rested on his rather orthodox Marxist publications in this journal, in which he critiqued idealism, existentialism, and other strains of "bourgeois" Western thought. From the mid-1970s on, however, his work led him further and further to the margins of the officially acceptable, and eventually caused him to be regarded as an intellectual outsider. In the 1980s, he returned to his native republic of Georgia to work at the Institute of Philosophy of the Academy of Sciences in Tbilisi.

Mamardashvili's central concern is the problem of consciousness and thinking, a process that remains distinct from all other kinds of human activity. For Mamardashvili, thinking must be understood solely as a continuum, not a series of discrete thought-acts claiming some relation to truth. Thinking is an end in itself, rather than an instrument of achieving a purpose, just as a human being cannot be considered in terms of his or her instrumentality. Consciousness, in this view, should not be judged by any external standards; it can only be evaluated in terms of its potential for self-concentration and self-expansion. "Consciousness, like thought, may be defined as the possibility of a larger consciousness."[74] There is no consciousness without self-consciousness, which constantly addresses itself in its ongoing self-processing, such that the specific object of consciousness can only be consciousness itself. However, consciousness can never authentically understand itself, because, being in a state of perpetual flux, whenever it attempts to fix itself in time, it is no longer the same consciousness in question. Mamardashvili identifies misunderstanding (the failure or inability to understand, rather than incorrect understanding) as the engine of consciousness, and defines the philosopher as an expert and connoisseur of misunderstanding. If ordinary thinking aims to understand, then philosophy is an exercise in misunderstanding—an approach that resonates with Socrates's and Aristotle's view of wonder as the beginning of philosophy. Since consciousness cannot be perceived in terms of its relation to external reality, its expansion must be located in a realm of emptiness. Paradoxically, the growth of consciousness requires the elimination of thought's cognitive content, leading to a meditative state identifiable with nothingness.

Unlike the Sartrean concept of nothingness as the vehicle for an existential challenge to the world of positive objects, Mamardashvili's emptiness is more akin to the apophatic tradition of Eastern Orthodoxy, or the Buddhist notion of enlightenment as undifferentiated oneness. This tendency in his thought was concomitant with his fruitful collaboration with the Buddhologist (and influential philosopher in his own right) Aleksandr Piatigorsky (1929-2009). Together, they worked to formulate certain aspects of human cognition common to Western and Eastern philosophy.[75] Taking the Cartesian *cogito ergo sum* as the foundation for the European rationalist tradition, Mamardashvili argues that it parallels the Buddhist assumption that reality exists only as a projection of consciousness. If Descartes's declaration is taken to express the foundational certainty of self-consciousness, then external referents lose all basis for naturalistic claims. What appeals to Mamardashvili in Buddhist practice is the process by which consciousness moves toward emptiness as a series of reflective acts, each circumscribing its predecessor as an illusory entity. Thus it is a process of disillusionment—what Mamardashvili calls "thinking about thinking"— as consciousness strips away layers of contingent reality to arrive at a transcendental realm that cannot be objectified, which corresponds to Buddhist enlightenment.

Given his emphasis on consciousness as a fuzzy, continuous process, it is perhaps unsurprising that death plays a central role in Mamardashvili's thought. For him, death means the end of duality, since it is a state of consciousness devoid of any content aside from consciousness itself. "In this sense, a man who lives entirely in yoga or in the asceticism of permanent prayer is completely equivalent to a dead man ... because his individual psychological mechanism no longer begets any content different from the content of the consciousness in which he abides."[76] Since death is a state of pure consciousness, Mamardashvili in fact echoes Plato's definition of philosophy as the preparation for death.

Another important aspect of Mamardashvili's thought is his preoccupation with symbols, although he uses the term quite differently than do the semioticians of his time. Some of Mamardashvili and Piatigorsky's works were published under the auspices of the Tartu semiotic school, though their approach remained distinct from that of Lotman, as it was phenomenological rather than structuralist. Unlike structuralists, Mamardashvili and Piatigorsky espouse a non-dualistic model of the symbol, indivisible into sign and referent. "In essence, when we speak of symbol in its proper sense, we mean something that cannot be separated from the act of consciousness. It is precisely for this reason that symbol (as distinct from the general concept of the sign) cannot be posited as having some *signified* different from it."[77] "Symbol (not sign!) is always something that we do not fully understand, but that we are ourselves, as understanding and existing beings."[78] If objects exist as sensuous impressions, symbols are the traces they leave as consciousness moves through successive levels of self-reflection. Unlike objects, whose meanings depend on external context, symbols retain their meaning on all successive levels of consciousness. This theory of consciousness is *symbology*, insofar as it explores concrete phenomena as they are given directly to consciousness, estranged from any physical referent.

Mamardashvili also devoted considerable attention to the analysis of Western philosophical thinking, especially the work of Plato, Descartes, and Kant. He understood the history of philosophy as a process of liberation, whereby human consciousness frees itself from the world of objects and from the political and economic dependencies based on such cognitive attachments. He praises Plato for depriveleging the world of things in favor of a realm of ideas, but objects to these transcendent entities' reobjectification as ideal entities, models constituting a separate "world of ideas." For Mamardashvili, transcendence does not require the postulate of a transcendental world; such a move means merely substituting one dependency for another. For example, instead of human subjugation to the forces of nature, we come under the dominion of the laws of an ideal state. Thus does Mamardashvili's thinking owe much to Descartes and Kant, whose notions of transcendence did not subscribe to a stable set of ideas as ontological entities, but rather allowed for the exercise of human cognitive freedom. For Mamardashvili, it is crucial to keep the external world distinct from the world of human consciousness. In this view, human moral sovereignty is guaranteed by the Kantian idea of *a priori* faculties. Envisioning the thing-in-itself as inaccessible to the human mind, Kant by the same token placed the human will beyond the governance of external reality. Mamardashvili stresses the root correspondence, in many languages, of "consciousness" and "conscience"—which implies the possibility of deriving moral principles from epistemological categories and vice versa.

The principal goal of Mamardashvili's philosophical enterprise is to undermine the naive identification or correspondence between being and thinking. His credo might be formulated thus: Being cannot be reduced to what we think about it, and correspondingly, thinking cannot be reduced to how we apply or realize it; cannot be embodied as or transformed into any kind of real existence. This principle of the mutual irreducibility of being and thought is elaborated in both the Marxist and post-Marxist tendencies of Mamardashvili's philosophy. In critiquing the idealist reduction of being to thinking, he allies himself with Marx: "[N]o 'pure consciousness,' presupposed by classical philosophy, can reproduce reality.... Marx quite definitely formulates the principle of the irreducibility of being (including the being of consciousness) to knowledge. In this sense, consciousness, if one can put it this way, became 'existential' in Marxism long before the appearance of any kind of existentialism and phenomenology."[79] Thus Mamardashvili is willing to accept Marxism on the same terms that he accepts existentialism and phenomenology. He is uninterested in the social doctrines of Marxism, and even reinterprets the principle of social determinism such that it is an objectified form of consciousness that determines the subjective form of consciousness. As a philosophical construct, social determinism would be too naive and crudely rationalistic for Mamardashvili's theory of irreducibility, since the latter assumes that consciousness cannot explain the source of its determination by analyzing itself as a product.

Bearing in mind all these reservations, we might identify Mamardashvili as a Marxist, but another aspect of his theory of irreducibility distinguishes him from Marx, even making him an anti-Marxist. Just as being is irreducible to consciousness, consciousness is irreducible to being; that is, it cannot be explained or determined by a social milieu, nor can it be actualized in any tangible product or object. The entire project of Marxism was based on two assumptions antithetical to Mamardashvili's theory: that consciousness is determined by being, and that it can transform being. The construction of communism in the Soviet Union aimed to implement the most general concepts prescribed for realization in Marxism, such as freedom, equality, collectivism, the end of alienation. In Mamardashvili's view, both communism and fascism "proceed from the assumption that all the concepts we use in principle are susceptible to real implementation.... What the Bolsheviks implemented in reality were precisely absolute concepts; otherwise there wouldn't have been such intolerance to everything else. They considered themselves monopolists of truth."[80] According to Mamardashvili, concepts are potentialities of human thought that can never be fully actualized, made tangible. Mamardashvili might have reformulated Marx's famous eleventh thesis on Feuerbach thus: Philosophers cannot explain the world, but neither can they change it. Thinking cannot be brought into full alignment with reality, and this Cartesian dualism is the source of inalienable human freedom. Thought is not subject to reality and the laws of nature, but neither is reality subject to the dictates of thought and to intellectual constructs.

Mamardashvili's best-known works published in his lifetime discuss the differences between classical and postclassical rationality. Mamardashvili identifies a revolution in philosophy with Kierkegaard, Schopenhauer, Marx, and Nietzsche. For a Soviet philosopher to contextualize Marx among such "bourgeois" thinkers (traditionally regarded as his opponents) was of course unusual. What Mamardashvili proposed as a common denominator among these thinkers was their abandonment of traditional rationalism in favor of complicity with hidden engines of motivation. The implication for Mamardashvili is that thought is a second-order process, as it is generated by underlying primary mechanisms that are unavailable to thought itself. Thus thinking finds its ground in something *unthinkable*, be it existential uniqueness (Kierkegaard), material forces of production (Marx), primordial will (Schopenhauer), or vital instinct (Nietzsche). For Mamardashvili, this is a tragic situation for consciousness: unable to grasp its own roots, it must continuously strive to step outside of thinking in order to reappraise its own content. Thus *suspicion* becomes the methodological engine of self-consciousness, since thinking can never trust its own testimony and must constantly interrogate itself for potential subterranean determinants. Rather than proclaiming reflection's impotence, then, the *neo-rationalist* paradigm ensures a dynamism of self-critique, promoting a process of cognitive enlightenment and militating against the objectification and alienation characteristic of Platonic idealism and contemporary ideocratic political systems. Mamardashvili implicitly uses this notion of neo-rationalist or even post-rational opaqueness to challenge the primacy of ideology, which in a totalitarian system serves to subjugate reality to the activity of ideas.

In his book *Classical and Nonclassical Ideals of Rationality*, Mamardashvili describes a special type of consciousness that is contained in the structure of material artifacts and is fundamentally distinct from Descartes's *cogito*. Classical rationality proceeds from the assumption that intelligibility and rationality apply only to what a person has made for him- or herself. Mamardashvili's nonclassical principle assumes: "We understand not the made but *through* the made. What we have made, we understand least of all, and still less can we reproduce in our reflection and get control of what we have made. In other words, we understand and see the world through objects ... even as we may not understand these very objects."[81] In some respects, Mamardashvili's insights anticipate contemporary discussions of artificial intelligence, which is created by humans but is not transparent to their consciousness. Mamardashvili compares nonclassical rationality with bodily organs, which accomplish rational material acts independently of our understanding of their mechanics. "The organ acts on its own; that is why it is called an organ. Therefore, it can be said of such things that they presumably understand themselves.... [T]he movement of understanding proceeds and spreads from within these things."[82] In the same manner, Cezanne did not paint apples in his still lifes: he painted something *through* the apples, the possibility of seeing apples, or rather, apples' capacity to present themselves in a painting.

Mamardashvili calls the nonclassical rationality that lies beyond human subjective reasoning "physical metaphysics" or "third things." These are neither ideal essences, abstract laws, nor merely physical bodies, but constitute a third realm comprising the "acting material mechanisms of consciousness."[83] As an example, Mamardashvili cites the wheel, which belongs neither to nature nor to consciousness. Mamardashvili parallels "third things" to Plato's ideas, but refutes the tradition of classical rationality that understood these ideas as general concepts. In reality, these "third things" exist independently of our consciousness in the material world, but at the same time they are endowed with their own rationality. Mamardashvili sees this new type of rationality as originating with Marx, who postulated the primordial role of the material world as determining human consciousness. For example, Marx considered that an agent may act effectively within a capitalist system without knowing its laws, because the rationale of such a system escapes his rational mind, which might even be destroyed by the attempt at complete comprehension.[84] Mamardashvili is not an apologist for Marxist materialism, but he attempts to identify an objective rationality that is engrained in material culture and is constitutive of human consciousness without being transparent to it.

In this notion of the objectivity of the ideal, Mamardashvili demonstrates a clear affinity with Evald Ilyenkov (see Part I, Chapter 4), who asserted, contrary to orthodox Marxism, that the ideal is not only a subjective capacity of the human mind, but exists objectively in the outside world as a system of cultural artifacts and values. However, if Ilyenkov attempts to remain faithful to classical Marxism, Mamardashvili emphasizes those features that bring Marx closer to post-Marxist and in particular phenomenological thought: the phenomenon of interpersonal rationality, which cannot be focused in an individual mind, but is indispensable to the material structures of the cultural world. Mamardashvili's "third things," like the wheel, might be compared to Husserl's *eidoi* in terms of their absolute objectivity, which nevertheless is non-transcendental but immanent to things themselves.

However, Mamardashvili underscores not so much the cognitive but the constructive nature of these *eidoi*, whose rationality is not a matter of human intentionality, but proceeds from their own cultural being, which is beyond the capacity of human understanding. "One cannot understand the laws of the world without situating in this very world some conscious and sensitive being who understands these laws. The understanding of the laws of the world is simultaneously an element of the world whose laws are being understood."[85] Classical rationality presupposes that the world is located within our understanding, while the nonclassical principle situates the understanding inside the world, as a part of it that itself cannot be understood. Thus we are unable to understand our own understanding, which, acting rationally as an organic part of our thinking body, is for this very reason unable to examine itself.

The transindividual and opaque character of the rationality that Mamardashvili posits as nonclassical does not keep him from attempting, as an individual thinker, to theorize such a rationality. Admittedly, this project is self-contradictory, since it proposes to understand what cannot, by definition, be understood. However, according to Mamardashvili, such contradictions not only cannot be avoided, but in fact enable philosophy to be what it is—a discipline propelled by *non-understanding*. As he puts it: "Thoughts happen with us [*s nami sluchaiutsia*] but are not elaborated by us."[86] Thought itself is an event of the world that cannot be fully understood but engenders other events, that is, other thoughts, which attempt but fail to understand their predecessors. Conventional theories usually relate to stable, recurrent, and reversible phenomena, and introduce innovations only as a supplement to these fundamental and immutable regularities. For Mamardashvili, since thinking is a progressive series of misunderstandings, or the proliferation of differences among successive thoughts, then theory must begin with the mechanism of innovation, and regard any regularity or identity as a special case of deviation from the incessant process of self-diversification.[87]

Mamardashvili's own mode of discourse exemplified the processual nature of his philosophy. His contributions were primarily lectures and talks, manifesting his theoretical predisposition to regard consciousness as something that cannot be finalized in fixed doctrines and/or systems. "A philosopher deals with something that in principle cannot be known beforehand, cannot be presupposed, or imagined possible, or introduced by definition.... Philosophy is consciousness aloud."[88] Although Mamardashvili published a handful of written works during his lifetime, he admitted an inability to couch his ideas within the spatial structure of the text, preferring instead the temporal mode of oral improvisation. He is best remembered for his lectures, which combined linguistic and performative aspects in ways that defy encapsulation.

By this dynamics of here-and-now reasoning, Mamardashvili was able to create an atmosphere of expectation, as his thinking unfolded unpredictably and inspired in his listeners a similar spontaneity of response. His talks were made without recourse to prepared materials, but they were recorded and then transcribed. The texts were distributed in limited circles, before being published posthumously, edited mainly by Mamardashvili's disciple and friend Iurii Senokosov (b. 1938).[89]

In the years of Gorbachev's perestroika and in view of the imminent end of communism, Mamardashvili was increasingly perceived in the intelligentsia milieu as a philosopher of freedom, including the individual's freedom from the constraints of his or her own ethnic identity and cultural heritage. A Georgian by birth and upbringing, Mamardashvili resisted being identified as a representative of Georgian or even more broadly Soviet culture. He sympathized with what would later become known as multiculturalism, viewing it as a mode of liberation from a monolithic cultural canon, but he objected to the glorification of multiplicity for its own sake. Citing a typical argument he sums up thus: "Each culture is valuable in itself. People should be allowed to live within their cultures"[90]—Mamardashvili objects that "the defense of native culture sometimes proves to be a denial of the right to live in a different world." He refers to Georgian nationalism, which strikes him as increasingly narrow and despotic. "What if I am suffocating within this very original, complicated, and developed culture?"[91] What must be preserved, then, is the right to live beyond one's culture, on the borders of cultures, "to transcend the surrounding, native, proper culture and milieu for the sake of nothing. Not for the sake of another culture, but for the sake of nothing. Transcendence into nothing. In reality, this is the living, pulsating center of the entire human universe ... a primordial metaphysical act."[92] To transcend the limits of one's native culture does not constitute a betrayal, because the limits of any culture are too narrow for a human in the entirety of his or her potentials. Transculturalism, to follow Mamardashvili's logic, does not mean adding yet another culture to the existing array; it is rather a special mode of existence spanning cultural boundaries, a transcendence into "no culture," which is indicative, ultimately, of how the human being exceeds all natural and cultural definitions.[93]

Despite the relative paucity of his written contributions and their extremely complicated, sometimes cumbersome style, Mamardashvili's influence cannot be overstated, as his inspirational depth and charisma invited the participation of students from many varied fields, including education, psychology, and theater. Not merely a professor of philosophy, Mamardashvili was admired as a philosopher—a "Moscow Socrates"—which meant that his lifestyle was characterized by the practice of sustained self-reflection. Moreover, the theme of his reflection was philosophy itself, which he regarded as a moral imperative to question the identity of all values and to contribute the value of non-understanding to the world of total and conventional understanding. His philosophical views dictated for him a curious status within the intellectual community as neither conformist nor political dissident. In later years, he was regarded as an outsider, a challenger of established positions of every kind, and espouser only of "otherness." He used to say that "the philosopher feels as if he belongs to some unknown country and understands himself as its citizen; so his society will hardly treat him favorably."⁹⁴ As if to symbolize his non-belonging, he died at Moscow's Vnukovo airport while waiting to board a flight back to his homeland, Georgia, from which he had been previously banished by its authoritarian and nationalist ruler. Thus, otherness proved, not just the theme of his thought, but also the final resolution of his life.

After his death, Mamardashvili was quickly recognized as one of the most significant philosophers of his generation—a philosopher in the strict sense of this word, not just a thinker or cultural scholar.⁹⁵ Since 1992, conferences dedicated to his memory and legacy have periodically been held in Moscow.⁹⁶ The Mamardashvili Foundation plans to publish critical editions of nineteen volumes of his works, mostly transcribed from his talks.⁹⁷ And in May 2001, a monument to Mamardashvili was unveiled in his native Tbilisi.

Part III

The Philosophy of Personality and of Freedom

A.	**Personalism**	
1.	Personalist and Existentialist Trends in Russian Thought	114
2.	Nature and Personality. The Writer Mikhail Prishvin as Thinker	115
3.	The Religious Existentialism of Iakov Druskin	118
4.	Between Historicism and Personalism. Lidiia Ginzburg	123
5.	Personalism, Pluralism, and Spiritual Universalism. Grigorii Pomerants	126
6.	Russian-Jewish Personalism. Boris Khazanov	133
7.	Personal Freedom and Planetary Consciousness. Mihajlo Mihajlov	136
8.	The Paradoxalist Boris Paramonov. Sexual Liberation against Nationalism	142
9.	Joseph Brodsky as Thinker. Privacy as the Ultimate Value	148
B.	**Liberalism and Westernism**	
1.	Liberalism, Conservatism, and Religiosity	151
2.	Freedom and Solidarity in Émigré Thought	153
3.	Skepticism and Pluralism. Aleksandr Esenin-Volpin	156
4.	Liberal Dissident Scholars. Arkadii Belinkov and Andrei Amalrik	158
5.	Liberalism and Science in Political Thought. Andrei Sakharov	162
6.	Liberal Historians. Natan Eidelman and Aleksandr Ianov	167
7.	The Paradoxes of Late-Soviet Westernism	171

A. Personalism

1. Personalist and Existentialist Trends in Russian Thought

Personalist and existentialist trends were significant in Russian thought even prior to the October Revolution. Along with Blaise Pascal and Soren Kierkegaard, Fedor Dostoevsky is considered a founding member of this tradition. Owing to Dostoevsky's overwhelming influence, Russian philosophy began on the existentialist path sooner than its Western counterparts. The originator of this trend, Vasilii Rozanov (1856–1919), initiated a philosophy of everyday life, which included intimately autobiographical musings. In the framework of Russian philosophy, Rozanov's insistence on the uniqueness of individual human experience opposed the monumental idealism of Vladimir Solovyov, in much the same way as Kierkegaard's existentialism defied Hegelian idealism in European philosophy. One example of Rozanov's eccentric challenge to the idealist and rationalist tradition was his famous claim that nose-picking is a more profound and eternal truth than the lofty products of civilizations, which inevitably rise and fall while humanity continues the eternal practices of ordinary life. Rozanov was thus proclaiming the priority of existence over essence, and exemplifying it in his provocatively frank and "shameless" diary prose, before such thinking became prominent in the West (with the work of Karl Jaspers, Martin Heidegger, Gabriel Marcel, Emmanuel Mounier, and Jean-Paul Sartre). His legacy influenced such important Russian thinkers as Lev Shestov (1866–1938) and Nikolai Berdiaev (1874–1948), whose work after their emigration in the early 1920s directly impacted the existentialism movement in the West. In the Soviet Union, existentialism was disparaged as an expression of bourgeois individualistic despair in the face of historical reality; however, the existentialist tradition survived, mainly in the form of philosophical diaries. Reminiscent of Rozanov's "rough drafts of the soul," these writings by Mikhail Prishvin, Iakov Druskin, Lidiia Ginzburg, and others abandoned speculative discourse in favor of personalistic self-exploration.

Personalism and existentialism are closely related in intellectual history, sharing a philosophical commitment to human personality and its inherent freedom as the primary value. Both movements are critically opposed to any depersonalizing trends of thought in Enlightenment rationalism, Hegelian idealism, Marxist materialism, scientific determinism, evolutionism, socialism and collectivism, and other systems that reduce personality and freedom to the manifestation of some general laws (of nature, mind, or society). However, there are some key distinctions. Existentialism is the more metaphysically grounded of the two currents, whereas personalism is more ethically oriented. Existentialism often views the surrounding world as meaningless, irrational, and hostile, whereas personalism tends to see the world as fundamentally meaningful. For personalism, "other people" are not a "hell" of objectification and alienation, but rather allies open for cooperation and solidarity. Existentialism is more tragic in its view of human nature and its fate in the world; personalism, more affirmative and optimistic. Existentialism is politically more radical, sometimes tending to support extreme leftist and rightist movements (Sartre, Heidegger), while personalism is more associated with democratic and liberal approaches.

If we follow this distinction, the philosophy of personality, freedom, and human rights as extant in the late Soviet period has a more personalist than existentialist orientation, which explains my preference for the former term throughout the book. However, in many contexts, these terms can be used virtually as synonyms. Some of the thinkers described in this part evince a more existentialist stance (e.g., Iakov Druskin) but most clearly gravitate toward what can be characterized as the philosophy of personality in the broad sense. Also influencing my choice of the term is the important consideration that personalism is a more diffuse worldview than existentialism. It may be even better to speak of many *personalisms* precisely because it is the uniqueness of each personality, rather than the common foundational property of existence, that motivates the naming of this category.

2. Nature and Personality. The Writer Mikhail Prishvin as Thinker

The most outstanding example of the genre of philosophical diary is that of Mikhail Prishvin (1873–1954), who coincidentally had studied history and geography under Rozanov as a schoolboy. Even before the revolution, Prishvin had gained prominence as an author of ethnographic and naturalistic stories, and by keeping to this niche,

Figure 3.1 Mikhail Prishvin.

he was able to survive the Soviet ideological regime. His published work during this period, though well received, is comparatively sterile, and is often addressed to a young audience; whereas he invested the better part of his talent in his diary. For fifty years, almost without interruption, Prishvin meditated in his diaries on the fate of the individual in nature and society.[1] Unlike Rozanov, Prishvin's perspective is not provocative but is characterized by a quiet resistance to the aggressive dehumanization of postrevolutionary society. His epiphanies often proceed from certain incidents in nature that cast new light on the roots of his individual existence. In one episode, he is led to redefine the Cartesian *cogito ergo sum* in response to an observation he makes of his dog: if my dog can distinguish my odor from an infinity of smells, then it means that I exist. Thus, the evidence of existence is not limited to human consciousness, but depends on interaction with other entities, whether endowed with human consciousness or not.

"I was born with this theme of the unrepeatable and irreplaceable nature of living units, as others are born with an irrepressible aspiration to generalize and substitute one unit for another"[2]—these words of Prishvin could serve as an epigraph to his entire thought, which is directed first and foremost against patterns of "totalistic" reasoning that reduce all the variety of existence to certain preconceived schemas. The "general line" (*general'naia liniia*) was a favorite idiom of this epoch, presupposing the priority of the general over the particular, and the social over the personal. Prishvin's method of survival was to flee these oppressive oppositions and take refuge in the life of nature; succeeding in this escape, he became the Soviet Union's best-known naturalist writer.

Though Prishvin is routinely considered a "singer of nature," it would be wrong to locate him in the philosophy of cosmic mysticism, which attempts to eliminate the uniqueness of human personality. On the contrary, nature is for Prishvin a world of uniqueness, where no one thing is identical to another. Generalization is a kind of original sin peculiar to the human mind and ultimately leading to violence.

> Nature is all personal: every seed, every leaf has its own separate fate. Man is distinct from nature by his ability to make a generalization and furthermore to withdraw himself from the usual personal laws of nature. Of course, generalization, by the same token, must be a murder, and a murder on principle, not an arbitrary one, as in nature. Cain killed Abel out of principle.[3]

For Prishvin, the private, the particular, has ontological priority over the general, which is a purely logical abstraction. But since Prishvin is mostly concerned with ethics, he restores this "general" as a criterion for moral action. A person can find self-fulfillment in work for others, but this initiative must originate from the personality itself. "The highest morality is the sacrifice of one's personality for the sake of the collective. The highest immorality is when a collective sacrifices a personality for its own sake (e.g., the death of Socrates, not to mention Christ)."[4] Thus, ethics arises from an individual's relationship to the collective whereby the individual actively asserts his or her own self through self-denial. Two deviations from this Prishvinian "golden rule" may be formulated as individualism, whereby an individual asserts his or her own self at the expense of the collective; and collectivism, which affirms the benefit of "all" at the expense of the individual.

Prishvin is sometimes interpreted as a philosopher of cosmism, as a follower of Nikolai Fedorov (1828–1903), the Russian thinker who proclaimed the "common cause" of transforming the universe via the human intellect and its technological extensions and applications.[5] In such a prolific and multifaceted writer as Prishvin, one can certainly find echoes of many philosophical systems. Fedorov's idea of universal resurrection is not absolutely alien to Prishvin, although in the latter this is not a matter of scientific progress; instead, Prishvin's notion of immortality proceeds from a faith in the absolute uniqueness and indestructibility of individuality. Immortality is not something that needs to be attained—whether biologically or technologically; it is already an ineffable quality of individuality, inasmuch as it exists for itself through consciousness, and to others through love. "[L]ove is the human attempt to affirm the irreplaceable in eternity.... Thus 'irreplaceability' is the foundation for the tremendous edifice of love."[6] In Fedorov, the universal dimension of humanity takes priority over the "egoism" of a particular human personality, which must be subjected to the "common cause." In Prishvin, a complex relationship may be observed between the notions of the universal and the unique; he believes that a reconciliation of this duality will prove to be humanity's greatest moral achievement, but also that absolute balance is hardly attainable. For the abundance of life to prevail over the unitary order of death, "each" must take precedence over "all."

> The time is coming when the law of similarity demands, for the sake of truth, a [complementary] law of difference. And this will be a valid difference in meaning: God loves all people, but still more does he love each person....[7] The great sun, too, loves all boughs, all branches, all needles. It is as if it loves all of them equally, but it loves each needle more, and this is why no single needle is identical to another.... We, too, ought to settle ourselves in life like that—what could be better!—but when *we* love all, we forget about each; and when we remember each, we forget all.[8]

Prishvin does not like "all" as a logical construct. This *priority of each over all* propels the dynamic of life toward progressive personalization; what we call nature may be understood as "depersonalized complexes of beings who have forgotten about their personality."[9] Thus the human task is not to transform nature, but to restore her individuality, to remind her what she is.

> My friend, grow ever stronger with the force of kindred attention [*rodstvennoe vnimanie*] addressed to earthly creatures, peer into each detail separately, and distinguish one from another, recognizing personalities even in each tiniest entity, abandoning the general; reveal and gather millions of them, and lead all of this great council of the living ahead into the struggle against the average obligatory [*srednee dolzhnoe*].[10]

Other categories of Prishvin's personalist ethics include "the road to a friend" (*doroga k drugu*) and "creative behavior" (*tvorcheskoe povedenie*). In Russian, the word for "friend" (*drug*) has the same root as "other" (*drugoi*), and one of Prishvin's key thoughts is that human life constitutes a search for another, with whom one might mutually merge. "Creative behavior" is a concept stating that the most profound artistic act is not the fashioning of some aesthetic object, but the dynamic modification of one's own life. Attention, concentrated on something particular and unique, is the primary force of creativity. One must frame what one looks at. "Thus, attention is placing the whole into a part, the Universe into the sparkling dewdrop of a morning iris."[11] The concept of attention presupposes that a given single thing is crucially intensified in its meaning, without being transformed into a symbol with obligatory reference to some other world. Prishvin's *attention* is akin to Walter Benjamin's concept of "immanent epiphany"—the aura of holiness devoid of its transcendental attributes or supernatural sources.

For Prishvin, reality is endowed with absolute meaning, independent of its relationship to either transcendental ideas or human subjectivity. Wisdom, according to Prishvin, is the ability to move beyond the boundaries of one's ego.

> The wisdom of a human consists in the art of using one small interval of life; for a moment, one must be able to imagine that the same life goes on even without him. "Where were you?" a sage is asked. He gives a slight smile and says nothing. He was where life flows without his participation, as it is by itself.[12]

Prishvin's attitude toward life can be compared with the famous principles of Albert Schweitzer's ethics of "reverence for life." But the striking difference is that Prishvin did not proscribe the killing of animals and was himself an avid hunter (like Turgenev and the pre-conversion Tolstoy). Hunting and fishing was a vital necessity for many people during the mass Soviet starvations of the 1920s to the 1940s (most notably, the Holodomor) caused by government persecution of the peasantry. Life for Prishvin was defined not so much in biological terms as in terms of personal relationships with its creations. His commandment would not be couched in the negative—"Thou shalt not kill"—but rather, positively; perhaps: "Personalize your relationship with all living beings." Prishvin's personalism arose in a Christian tradition, rather than in a Jainist or Buddhist one, in which physical violence against animals would be strictly forbidden. For Prishvin, the notion of sin is connected first and foremost not with physical action, but with the loss of one's own soul; and this is brought about by failing to recognize the souls of other beings.

3. The Religious Existentialism of Iakov Druskin

Iakov Semenovich Druskin (1902–1980) was the longest-living member of the informal avant-garde literary-intellectual group *Chinari* (the "titled ones," or "rankists"), which

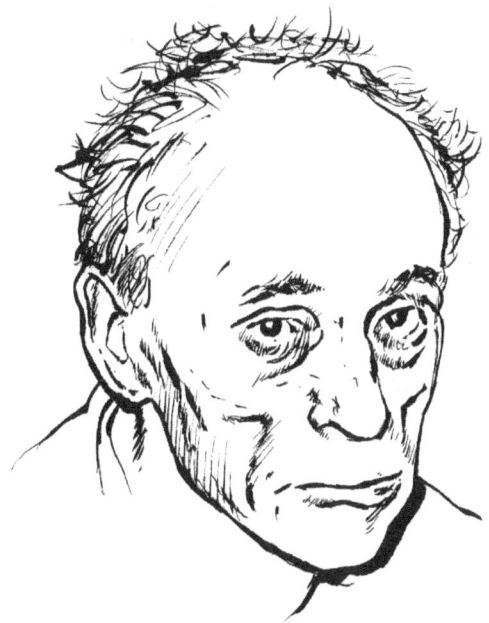

Figure 3.2 Iakov Druskin.

in the late 1920s and the early 1930s included the poets Daniil Kharms and Aleksandr Vvedensky and the philosopher Leonid Lipavsky, all of whom died young in the late 1930s and the early 1940s. In spite of Druskin's illustrious education in sciences, the humanities, and music, he lived the modest life of a Leningrad evening school teacher. Although Druskin's views developed over the course of six decades, none of his writings were published in his lifetime. His legacy includes *Near the Messengers*, *Before Accessories of Something*, *Jacob's Ladder. Essays, Treatises, and Letters*, and *Diaries*.

Druskin's thought is profoundly personalistic, both in content and form. We may view a note he made in 1969, "I've thought through my life and lived through my thought," as his motto.[13] Druskin's diary, which he wrote over half a century (1928 to 1979) and which was published posthumously by his younger sister Lidiia Druskina, is titled *Before Accessories of Something*, which suggests the existential position of man as thrown into a prefabricated world. This means that the objects before him belong not to him, but to some unknown and likely inanimate possessor, which he can only refer to as "something." Druskin's thought is religious in nature, though apophatic, insofar as he identifies God by his absence: "God is farther [*Bog dal'she*]. God has no distances. He is not having [*ne est' imeiushchii*]. God, as a bearer [*kak nositel'*], is beyond any definite place. But close to myself, in my own place, I noticed the bearer: it is a kind of absence."[14] This absence, however, is defined only in relation to the author's self; it may not be identified as a realm of things or ideas. Druskin writes:

> I used to begin with numbers and trees, but now I've found a solid and reliable foundation: what has a relation to me, this is the beginning. Having a relation to me is a kind of absence. Events do not have a relation to me; I avoid them.... Views and convictions do not interest me; I have no thoughts.[15]

This entry was written in 1932, at the very dawn of the existentialist tradition in the West, and Druskin anticipated its foundational precept that human existence is posited not in terms of ideas and thoughts, but instead in relation to some radical emptiness of meaning, which Druskin calls "absence."

Though Druskin was a specialist in philosophy, mathematics, and music, he did not earn his living by these professions and resisted professional status in any field, preferring the position of the dilettante. Druskin refused to make universal claims, and instead focused his philosophy on the uniqueness of his own existence. Not unexpectedly, there were several personal events in his life that left a decisive imprint on his thinking. The most important among them, in his own view, was his awakening to thinking itself in May of 1911, at the age of nine. Among others of importance, he cites his 1928 conversion to Christianity (under the impact of Bach's music), the death of his father in 1934, and his mother's death in 1964. He called this last event his Jacob's ladder, because it showed him the way to another world.

Druskin's views may be characterized as *religious existentialism*, in which both components are equally important and practically indivisible. Space and time are the essential categories of his philosophy, and he specifies the *touch* as the basic unit of space and the *moment* as the indivisible unit of time. These are genuine "beginnings," since they mark the relation of space and time to the individual. "Touch is the beginning. Where reasoning suddenly stops, where the system is broken, there a last remainder is present—there is touch."[16] In his terms, touch is the ultimate evidence of a reality that cannot be otherwise generalized. Similarly, Druskin considers the *moment* to be the irreducible unit of time, a time that kills the authenticity of existence by dissolving the moment of now in the flow of temporality.

> I look at the world as does a newborn. I am born all the time, but time kills me and I drift into the past. I want to live *now*, but now I'm only emerging; having emerged, I cease to exist now, because time carries me into the past. I accuse time: time created the boundary, time killed the feeling, time separated me from life, time destroyed the now, time brings death.[17]

Thus the relativity of space and time, with the multiplicity of its physical manifestations, must be permanently overcome through the effort of the human being to be born anew every moment and to directly touch other beings. This is what it means to strive for complete authenticity in a world of substitutions and similitudes.

In Druskin's view, only faith is capable of transgressing time and space and attaining the permanent "now." Faith for Druskin is not a state of quiet bliss but rather a torment, since faith makes blasphemy possible, even inevitable. The nonbeliever, by contrast, cannot fall into sin because he does not know God. "Whosoever does not know God cannot deny Him. A nonbeliever cannot blaspheme. He who does not know Christ cannot crucify him. Only he who believes in God blasphemes, only he who believes in Christ crucifies him.... I blaspheme and I crucify Christ. When I am not crucified together with Christ, I crucify him."[18] Faith is thus an unbearable burden for the soul, since to live in faith is also to live in perpetual consciousness of one's own sinfulness. Druskin's philosophical diaries are full of self-denunciations: for him, every step of faith led him deeper into self-denial.

In Druskin's conception, guilt is an absolutely personal state of being that cannot be shared with anyone else. Druskin could not accept the conventional Christian view, expressed so powerfully in Dostoevsky's *The Brothers Karamazov*, that everyone in this world is guilty. He argued that since the "I" cannot be generalized and transferred to another, the only pronoun compatible with being guilty is one's own "I."

> I cannot generalize this proposition; I cannot say that this I is every I. If I say that each of us must consider ourselves guilty for everybody, then this proposition will lose its radical and existential character. If I am guilty for all, then the guilt is removed from all others. This proposition is not only singular but unique, the most personal.... Logic knows three kinds of propositions: general, particular, and singular. But there are still other propositions which are not known to logic: they are absolutely subjective and unique. Such propositions relate only to myself.[19]

This is the basis of Druskin's "methodology," if this term can be applied to his principally anti-methodological stance: the idea that all of his judgements are applicable only to himself.

Druskin's existentialism, however, refutes solipsistic self-concentration, the multiplying stages of self-reflection that lead to the hell of selfness. In one of his works, "The Vision of Non-Vision," Druskin examines the multiplicity of selves that are opened in the process of looking at oneself in the mirror: "I, close to myself—alien to myself," "I, close to my own self—alien to my own self."[20] He identifies nine successive selves, which are reminiscent of the circles of hell not only in quantity: "Here I have analyzed my own self, my 'I's' and 'anti-I's,' all my possibilities, and I have come to the last one, the most terrible: to the fiery Gehenna in my own self."[21] The way out of this hell is through profound and truly religious communication with "the other." The I-Thou relationship is one of the principal axes of Druskin's world, which was revealed to him independently of Martin Buber's and Mikhail Bakhtin's dialogic philosophies and Karl Jaspers's views on existential communication. Special meaning is given to the Thou, who becomes the center of intercommunion. For Druskin, communication does not mean opening one's heart and speaking to another, but rather listening with one's heart. Listening is a state of active silence.

> To be capable of listening noumenally is often more important than speaking. I must listen and, while simply listening, remain silent, but in such a way that my silence is not just a simple fixation with a speaker's words but an answer to his

question.... The ability to listen is a gift from God, and if I don't possess it I am guilty.[22]

Druskin uses the term "neighboring world" (*sosednii mir*), which was initially proposed by his friend, the philosopher Leonid Lipavsky (1904–1941). Lipavsky was also a member of the *Chinari* group, which often created and used its own intellectual jargon. The category of the "neighboring world" is applicable to the worlds of other entities, be they people, animals, or inanimate objects.

> We see and hear them, but sometimes understand nothing, and still want to feel at least something of their world.... How does the semiliquid jellyfish residing in the water feel? Is it possible to conceive a world in which there are differences only within one quality, for example, a world of differences only in temperature? What are the feelings and qualities of entities living in other, remote neighboring worlds, which may even be nonexistent and only imaginable? I too might contain a neighboring world.[23]

This notion of the neighboring world may be compared with the formalist idea of defamiliarization, or estrangement (*ostranenie*), which was introduced into literary theory by Viktor Shklovsky; and also with Bakhtin's concept of "being beyond," or "outsideness" (*vnenakhodimost'*). Lipavsky and Druskin establish the category of otherness as essential for philosophy in general, not only for the comprehension of the outside world, but for self-knowledge as well. By treating any world as neighboring, one may come to the experience of the nature of one's own world as a neighboring world. Any act of thinking objectifies its contents and at the same time attempts to reveal them from within. In the next move, Lipavsky and Druskin introduce the concept of the "messenger" (*vestnik*), or a representative of a neighboring world. Messengers are different from humans, but embody the capacity for subjectivity and self-expression in such a way as to resist objectification by the philosopher. Thus, the neighboring world of the jellyfish might be represented to the thinker by a messenger—the bearer and conveyor of jellyfishness. This is not the "what" of the Platonic idea, but rather the "who" of post-Christian personalism. In the context of the European philosophical scene of the late 1920s and the 1930s, the concepts of neighboring worlds and their messengers represent one of the earliest attempts to extend existential contemplation beyond human subjectivity. By establishing the neighboring worlds of other creatures as alternative existential positions, the members of *Chinari* sought to allow Being to speak on its own behalf through its messengers.

The presence of a personal messenger, someone like an "alter-Druskin," inspired Druskin and allowed him to see the world differently and more creatively. The departure of his messenger, however, threw him into a state of emptiness, which he called *ignavia* (Latin for "apathy," "sloth"). In this state, he compared himself to a speck of dust lost in infinity, and could find nothing about which to think or write. We can draw parallels between *ignavia* and the absurd in French existentialism, but what is characteristic of Russian existentialism is how it offered a way out of such a state. Whereas French existentialism (e.g., that of Sartre) posits freedom as a mode of self-determination that overcomes absurdity, the way out of *ignavia* is through other-expression, via the messenger. Druskin in fact rejects the very concept of "free will," which in his view is counter to the Bible and the Gospels and was justly debunked by Augustine and Martin Luther, but which has retained its grip on philosophy and found its zenith in the concept of autonomous choice. His point is that "freedom of choice is formally determined by choice itself"[24]—that is, insofar as choice itself is a matter of necessity, it cannot be free, which is echoed by Sartre's famous proclamation that man is "condemned to be free." In being obligated to choose moment by moment, the individual's determination of one alternative condemns him to exclude every other possibility. Thus freedom, in practice, becomes a chain of necessary limitations. This fallen freedom

> is determined by my passions and caprices, by my reason and will.... By natural means, I cannot liberate myself from this freedom of choice which is slavery.... But: "What is impossible for man is possible for God." The slavery of the freedom of choice is overcome not through the denial of one of the offered possibilities, but through the denial of the very situation of choice.[25]

Druskin finds that this situation of false choice may only be transcended in a supernatural way—through prayer, self-denial, and active love. When the human will embraces the infinity of God's will, it alleviates the necessity of choice by behaving in the only way possible, meaning it now contains a freedom that is complete and not divided into alternatives. Individual freedom may only be substantiated by the transcendence of self.

Druskin finds the philosophical foundation of religious belief in Husserl's idea that "the boundaries of the empirical 'I' are broken by God, 'I' comes to 'Thou' through God."[26] In Druskin's view, "every 'Thou' can become for me an appropriate assistant—'Thou' for 'I'. Then there is God between us even if we are not aware of it."[27]

Such a relationship constitutes the foundation of a genuine church, which he believed could not be identified with any existing denomination. Druskin never joined any church or associated himself with a particular tradition, as he believed that all existing churches were in fact Judaic synagogues or heathen temples only pretending to be Christian. A real church is formed of personal relations between people, he argued. Druskin recalls Christ's saying: "Where two or three gather for the sake of my name, there I will be with them."[28] He adds, however, that he cannot find a second person with whom he might taste the body and blood of Christ. Druskin's entire body of thought is an attempt to create a Christian church on a purely existential foundation of loneliness, an attempt that never succeeded, thus imparting a tragic tone to his lifelong spiritual quest.

4. Between Historicism and Personalism. Lidiia Ginzburg

Lidiia Ginzburg (1902–1990) as a thinker should be placed within the framework of personalism, despite coming to public attention as a literary scholar and disciple of

Figure 3.3 Lidiia Ginzburg.

the Russian formalists. Her immediate teacher was Boris Eikhenbaum, under whose guidance she wrote her dissertation on Aleksandr Herzen, who may be regarded as one of the founders of Russian philosophical personalism (in his autobiography *My Past and Thoughts* [1852–1870]).

Ginzburg's best-known books of criticism comprise an informal trilogy: *On Psychological Prose*, *On Lyricism*, and *On the Literary Hero*. Published when she was in her sixties and seventies, they brought her the reputation of a fresh and original scholar who combined the subtlety of formal analysis with a deep insight into the human dimension of literary characters, something not typical for a formalist. All three works focus on the variety of poetic and prosaic manifestations of human personality—likewise the central concern of Ginzburg's philosophical notebooks, diaries, essays, and fragments, which she began writing in the 1920s and continued until her death.

If Prishvin's basic theme is the personality in its relationship with nature, and Druskin's, its relationship with God, then Ginzburg concentrates on its relationship with history. She examines the various kinds of pressures a given historical moment exerts on an individual to shape his or her philosophical self-understanding. Focusing her attention on particularly dire circumstances, such as the Nazis' siege of Leningrad (1941–4), Ginzburg elaborates the existential implications of such overwhelming pressure especially on life within a totalitarian regime.[29] Karl Jaspers's concept of the "boundary situation," where a person is pushed out of routine experience to the borders of death, guilt, fear, despair, passion, sickness, or loneliness, may apply to the entire mode of existence in the communist state. Thus Ginzburg is interested in the metaphysical consequences of oppression, the kind of experience brutally historicized in the Soviet Union, and foregrounding the existential dimension of human tragedy. If in Western democracies, such boundary situations occur mainly in the form of personal hardships, in a totalitarian state one's entire self-understanding arises in a situation of permanent existence on the border of nothingness, which enforces a life of unrelenting intensity. "My topic: how a person of a particular historical formation calculates his or her substance in the face of nonbeing."[30]

Unlike Prishvin or Druskin in their diaries, Ginzburg tends to discuss her intimate experience in an estranged manner, not directly in the first person, but as if she and her friends and contemporaries were literary characters subject to deep ethical and psychological examination. Thus, Ginzburg uses the formalist technique of defamiliarization for the purpose of *self*-defamiliarization. More broadly, she applies her methods of historical and psychological analysis primarily to members of the Soviet intelligentsia—a cohort that constituted both totalitarian's first victim, and its initial culprit. Pasternak's formula "A fool, a hero, an *intelligent*"[31] encapsulates the topic of Ginzburg's philosophical meditations. That is to say, her theme is the Soviet historical subject who paradoxically combines these three distinct characters. In the face of nonbeing, the Soviet intellectual was forced to determine his or her life's meaning after being robbed of the possibility of authentic expression or the application of personal talent by a society that turned thinkers into cogs of the ideological machine. In Ginzburg's terms, "meaning is a structural connection by which a phenomenon is included in a higher and more general order."[32] This position presupposes that a personality must look for meaning beyond itself in those higher orders in which it finds itself embedded—and ultimately destroyed, which makes the *intelligent* both heroic and foolish. Hence, the phrase "the meaning of life" (*smysl zhizni*) becomes ambivalent: on the one hand, life gives meaning to everything a person may experience or accomplish; on the other, this individual life is part of a larger order of historical events that may deprive it of meaning. "What a strange word 'meaning' is when it becomes the 'meaning of life.'"[33]

Ginzburg classifies individual existential orientation into two basic categories: immanent and transcendent. The immanent personality equates the meaning of life with life itself. This type was common among the Soviet intelligentsia from the 1920s through the 1960s, because not only was atheism a cornerstone of official ideology, but such a circumstance also engendered a generation of people keen to avoid any and all metaphysical, transcendental concerns. Marx's notion of immanent historical progress cannot impart meaning to personal life, which, from this point of view, terminates with death and becomes meaningful only as a member of a class, society, or the human species. Soviet intellectuals thus found themselves in a metaphysical interval between religious transcendence and the historical immanence of Marxism—neither of which is compelling enough to win one's wholehearted acceptance. But as Ginzburg notes, the paradox of finding the meaning of life within life itself leads the consciously immanent personality to the inevitable violation of its own foundational principle. "A human being seeks within herself something that is higher than herself." Although death negates life's meaning, the immanent personality lives as if such meaning might transcend life's cessation. "Existential practice demands that a transitory human being live as if her actions were designed for an infinite historical succession."[34]

Noting that, in practice, immanence gives rise to a paradoxical relationship with meaning, Ginzburg argues that there are two modes of existence that lead beyond immanence and depend upon neither Marxist historicism nor religious transcendence: love and creativity. These are two modes of *existential transcendence*, which for her are interrelated. "If the principle of love is that what is beyond me becomes me, then the principle of creative activity is that I become something that is beyond me."[35] In a sense, love and creativity may be compared with inhaling and exhaling: in the first case, I subjectify what is outside myself; and in the second, I objectify what is within. From a purely egocentric point of view, either of these modes would be essentially meaningless, but they are a variety of transcendence to which even the most skeptical intellectual is susceptible in practice.

In the worst case, even in denying these meanings, the skeptic attempts to make such denials as meaningful as possible. "Reason repeats again and again that there's no sense in writing, and at the same time tries to solve the problem of how to write better about how writing makes no sense. Oh, damned insular circle of egocentric consciousness!"[36] These insular and paradoxical circles comprise Ginzburg's favorite philosophical topic; one of her best-known works is titled *The Thought That Has Traced a Circle*. In describing the immanent position, Ginzburg attends to the inevitably circular nature of existential practice. Although she never attempts to make an explicit description of transcendental or "otherworldly" values, they comprise the implicit trajectory of her critique of both individualism and totalitarianism. Overall, her position might be summarized as "critical personalism," since first and foremost it addresses inauthentic states of personality that have arrived at the dead end of solipsistic self-reliance.

5. Personalism, Pluralism, and Spiritual Universalism. Grigorii Pomerants

In the quaking bog of reflection, there is only one solid point—personality. Personality integrates in itself everything that reason splits.[37]

One cannot know truth without being the Truth.[38]

Of all Russian personalist thinkers, Grigorii Pomerants (1918–2013) was the most persistently engaged in the social debate about the value of personality and the threats posed by totalitarian and post-totalitarian society. Pomerants was a philosopher and Orientalist by education. He graduated from the literature department of the Moscow Institute of Philosophy, Literature, and History (IFLI) in 1940. In 1941–5, during the Soviet-German War, he served in the army. Arrested in 1949 on a political charge, he spent four years in labor camps. Upon his return to Moscow, he served as a librarian at the Fundamental Library of Social Sciences. In the 1960s, Pomerants began to publish articles about culture and religion, and at the same time became a very active samizdat

Figure 3.4 Grigorii Pomerants.

and tamizdat author, which prevented him from receiving an academic position; in particular, he was denied the opportunity to defend his dissertation on Zen Buddhism because of his involvement in the human rights movement. He remained a freelance writer and commentator, and was among the first to speak publicly on the dangers of reemergent nationalism and conservatism as early as the late 1960s.

Pomerants's writings belong to the genre of philosophical *publitsistika*—sociocultural essays and commentary that were the characteristic mode of discourse in the Russian intellectual tradition, beginning with Petr Chaadaev, Vissarion Belinsky, and Aleksandr Herzen. His philosophical views resist systematization, because their core is a notion of the personal character of truth; hence his writings make no claim to universal validity, tending rather to constitute free meditations replete with autobiographical reminiscences and painful confessions. Irony is also important for Pomerants, since it liberates thought from false generalization and fanaticism. "Irony helps me to understand: everything that is said cannot be the perfect truth; everything that exists cannot be a perfect lie."[39] Via irony, the thinker clears the way to a multiplicity of ideas, each of which must abandon its claim to absolute truth. Pluralism and personalism, then, are two sides of the same coin, since a "truth" that is contingent upon personality gives each individual an equal stake in Truth. To a degree, this position can be paralleled with Bakhtin's notion of dialogic truth, but Pomerants is interested more in the ethical and political implications of pluralism. For him, intolerance is the main cause of evil in the world: "The devil begins with the foam on the lips of the angel who joins the struggle for good, truth, justice, and so on, until, step by step, he comes to the fire of Gehenna and Kolyma."[40] "The merciless struggle against evil fosters cruelty and feeds on this new evil."[41] Thus, evil usually comes in the guise of good intentions, founded on the feverish faith in some absolute or universal truth.

Pomerants defines religion as "the system of communication of socially important mystical experience,"[42] and argues that religion is at least as necessary a condition for human existence as is the state. The state acts by external force, while religion enlightens the human soul; they are thus complementary in maintaining balance in the social structure. "[T]he active immorality of the State is supplemented with the passive morality of religion."[43] Pomerants is sharply critical of institutionalized, "degenerated" religion, which merges with the state and loses its rebellious spiritual mission or even claims to become a state of its own, a theocracy. In his view, the worldwide crisis of religion, especially under communist regimes during most of his lifetime, has been to the good—because persecution and the threat of extermination reinforced religion's original spirit of opposition to the state and preoccupation with the inner self-determination of the human personality. This opposition to all forms of authoritarianism, especially such as acquire the status of spiritual dogma, is typical for Pomerants.

Despite the centrality of religion to Pomerants's work, his religiosity is nondenominational, and his thinking cannot be characterized as a "religious philosophy." Unlike the thinkers usually categorized thus, Pomerants is not affiliated with a specific religious tradition or dogma, and, moreover, his philosophy leads to religion only in the final analysis, instead of taking it as a starting point.

> I was seeking myself for so long that it became the habit of my entire life. Perhaps for this reason, I am not drawn to any single denomination. I am grateful to the keepers of the sacred fire, but am more fascinated with the people who are able to ignite this fire anew; people who begin from zero.... You're welcome to choose the faith of your fathers—or any other faith—but one that you have chosen, not that someone else chose for you. This is my utopia, my project to find the way out of the present impersonal world.[44]

Among world religions, Pomerants most often cites Christianity, Buddhism (especially Zen Buddhism), and Taoism, primarily because he sees these as the least authoritarian and most paradoxical. He was among the first to introduce the profundity of Eastern wisdom to the Soviet intelligentsia, which had traditionally been oriented toward the West. Following Hakuin Ekaku, a major representative of Japanese Zen, he repeats the three requirements for salvation: great faith, great persistence, and great doubt, stressing the last, since it is only by doubt that one can move beyond the signs of God to God himself.

This is the lesson of the East that Pomerants sought to introduce to traditional believers and nonbelievers alike, insofar as they adhered to some systems of signs: in order to experience the signified, one must have doubts about the meaning of the sign.

The word "God" may have no meaning in itself, like all other words used to express supreme values, such as "love" or "wisdom." When one compares one's beloved to "a star" or the "sun," one is not expressing the wish that this significant other should transform into a celestial body. By the same token, "God" does not signify a supernatural entity, it is a word of love addressed to life, to its infinite value.[45]

Because of his anti-fanaticism, Pomerants felt an affinity with the Eastern traditions, which tend to be less inclined to change the world from some dogmatic platform, preferring to discover modes of genuine existence within the world. For example, in comparing the Bible prophet with the Buddhist bodhisattva, Pomerants emphasizes the relative ethical risks of either position.

> The bodhisattva leaves the epoch as it is, and shows that in *any* epoch, one can live in the most profound silence and light. The prophet tries to introduce a particle of eternal truth into the life of society. Hence, he collides with evil and flares up with holy fury; he is turned away and often subjected to stoning, but sometimes he achieves victory and lays the foundation of a new kingdom. The bodhisattva never becomes furious and doesn't found any kingdoms. His kingdom is not of this world.[46]

Thus, the Bible prophet, in promoting change, runs the risk of falling into a new absolutism, whereas the bodhisattva, with no dogma to impart, avoids the ethical pitfalls of authoritarianism.

Pomerants's position may be identified as religious personalism, which eschews any church affiliation. No religious tradition may be favored over another, because faith is born out of nothing and excludes any stable historical foundation. "God is revealed fully only in personality; and personality is revealed fully only in God.... The personality that is strongly developed ... like a good swimmer, seeks the deepest place, where there is nothing under one's legs. It is there, above the abyss of nothingness, that it is easiest for her to swim."[47]

Another tendency of Pomerants's personalist religiosity is ecumenism. Pluralism of faiths presupposes their interaction and convergence. Between the Hinduism of Rabindranath Tagore, the Judaism of Martin Buber, and the Catholicism of Heinrich Böll there is far more in common than between two versions of medieval Catholicism, those of St. Ignatius of Loyola and Dominic of Caleruega and the orders they founded. The former kinds of religiosity are open and transparent, the latter intolerant and self-enclosed. For Pomerants, what is important is not what people believe in but how they believe; whether their faith promotes understanding or serves as an instrument of power.

In the ideological arena, Pomerants finds similar risks, most expressly in the "prophetic" person of Aleksandr Solzhenitsyn. Despite admiring him as the author of *The Gulag Archipelago*, as an unmasker of the insidious nature of communism, Pomerants recognizes the implicit danger in Solzhenitsyn's subsequent program of political reform. In offering a different—but equally absolutist—foundation for social change based on the priority of national interests,[48] Solzhenitsyn threatens to usher in a mere changing of the guard—a revitalized authoritarian state, fueled by genuine inspiration and moralistic enthusiasm, but authoritarian nonetheless. In identifying the evils of the totalitarian state, Solzhenitsyn fails to understand the risk implicit in substituting one foundational truth for another, a risk intensified by the enthusiasm for political change in Russia, which might easily drift into a new totalitarianism based on nationalist ideals. What Pomerants finds most threatening in Solzhenitsyn's polemic is the absolute seriousness and lack of irony, which remind him of the traditions of the Bolshevik ideocracy and prerevolutionary Russian autocracy, which considered any doubt, joke, or criticism to be inherently subversive. For Pomerants, "irony is a companion of democracy,"[49] since it prevents the crystallization of absolute truths.

Pomerants's debate with Solzhenitsyn was initiated in the early 1970s with the latter's critique of the former's daring views on the role of the intelligentsia in Russia. Most notably, Solzhenitsyn took issue with Pomerants's essay "The Person from Nowhere" (1967–9), which explicates his views on the relationship between the intelligentsia and "the people." The Russian word for this latter concept, *narod*, can be translated as "folk," "people," or "nation," but in Russia it has a special meaning: the vast majority of the simple, working people who comprise an organic whole, one with its own will, spirit, and fate. Pomerants criticizes both the official notion of "the toiling masses" as the moving force of historical progress, and also the romantic and neo-Slavophile view of the people as the repository of spiritual purity and authenticity. The concept is threadbare even from a strictly economic standpoint: the peasantry—the canonical understanding of *narod*, the "truth and strength of the land"—has ceased to be a productive force. "Nations where peasantry prevails are starving, while in the nations where peasantry disappears, hunger disappears as well."[50]

For Pomerants, the very term *narod* has ceased to refer to any actual community, since both the working classes and the peasantry have succumbed to a process of physical and spiritual degradation. It is not only the Soviet regime that has sapped the people of their creative vitality, but also the inevitable course of history, which has undermined the integrity of nations by dissolving the aesthetic values of folklore and the moral values of collectivism. To the extent these archaic values still survive, they serve mainly to enforce authoritarianism and suppress the freedom of individuals. The *narod*, therefore, in its passive indifference, should be held accountable for the silent acceptance of the terror and repression engendered by the communist regime.

Pomerants holds that the highest values, such as the contemplation of the universe, the creation of art, or spiritual love, are not produced by the *narod* and are beyond its understanding. Pomerants thus turns instead to the intelligentsia (the people "from nowhere"), whose moral and religious autonomy make society's progression toward freedom possible. In the Soviet period, the term *intelligentsia* officially referred to "persons of mental labor," which encompassed the bureaucratic elite, teachers, doctors, and educated members of all professions. For Pomerants, by contrast, the intelligentsia is "a very narrow circle of men and women capable of independently discovering the sacred values of culture."[51] The intelligentsia always comprises the minority of a nation; accordingly, in Pomerants's view, "everything great has always originated with a minority, and even more, with one lone person … It is on this lone person that

I rely."⁵² He compares the intelligentsia with the Jewish diaspora, "the people of air," who lost touch with their native soil. Anguish, fear, loneliness, confusion, anxiety—all these categories of existential philosophy come from the psychology of the ghetto, as expressed by Franz Kafka. For Pomerants, this situation of diaspora, including both ghetto and the perspective of assimilation, is characteristic not only of Jews but all thinking humanity.

Assimilation means that an intelligent person potentially finds him- or herself participating simultaneously in many religious and national traditions. "To unite through loneliness,"⁵³ to spread solidarity among those who are solitary—this is what Pomerants identifies as his personal duty. One can view him as a prophet not of the *narod* (like Solzhenitsyn), but of the intelligentsia, like Camus, who claimed to speak on behalf of "millions of solitary individuals."⁵⁴ But while the relationship of Camusian existentialism to pessimism remains an open question, we can at least say that Pomerants's existentialism is an optimistic one, hinging as it does not on absurdity but faith. The intelligentsia is called to give meaning to life while keeping life free from any obligatory and uniform meaning.

Pomerants was well aware that the victory of the intelligentsia and the destruction of traditional society creates the possibility both for a new, expanded freedom—and for new, horrific oppression. "Intellectual freedom is similar to atomic energy. It can serve good and evil, can save the world and destroy it."⁵⁵ The intelligentsia may be blamed for the elaboration of monstrous ideologies that brought not peace but the sword to suffering humanity. However, Pomerants defends the freedom of thinking, even if it ultimately commits suicide and generates totalitarian censorship. "My chosen people is bad. I know this. But, like Jehovah, I have no choice: the others are even worse."⁵⁶

Ironically, Pomerants's praise of the intelligentsia proved provocative for the intelligentsia itself, since he challenged its conventional self-conception as the debtor and handmaiden of the people. Solzhenitsyn was among those most provoked and irritated, since Pomerants had anticipated many of his sublime ideas about the soil and people—even before Solzhenitsyn himself had the chance to express them publicly. From the very beginning of Solzhenitsyn's journalistic endeavors, he identified Pomerants and those of a like ideological cast as his main antagonists. Solzhenitsyn categorizes liberals and pluralists as *obrazovanshchina*—his coinage to designate Soviet society's conformist, superficially educated elite (from *obrazovanie*—education). Solzhenitsyn demotes them to the status of self-important philistines and pharisees who deny their debt to the people and, in the final analysis, end up supporting a regime that educated them for its own benefit. Whereas Solzhenitsyn is eager to place blame with the regime (and by extension the intelligentsia), Pomerants is less inclined to apportion praise or blame.

> Solzhenitsyn has a firm grasp of which heroes were right and which were wrong. He enthrones the right and dethrones the wrong, while in my view all heroes are somewhat wrong. I recognize that both reds and whites, grandfather-revolutionaries and grandson-dissidents, are heroes, but in my judgements

about them, irony is integrated and I attempt to go beyond their heroic goals and characters.[57]

Pomerants continues on this ethically conciliatory note: "One should dream not of some tribunal that will render the surviving executioners their due, an eye for an eye, but of one's own ability to forgive at least one executioner. Because the end of executions comes about not through execution, but through forgiveness."[58]

Thus Pomerants's response to Solzhenitsyn is based also on religious views, though principally different from those of the latter. For Solzhenitsyn, faith means a loyalty to exclusive and absolute values, so its political equivalent is enlightened authoritarianism. For Pomerants, faith should be grounded in a humility that rejects all claims of absolute truth; pluralism, then, justifies secular democracy, but also each person's God-given freedom, which forbids the restriction of the freedom of others. This is perhaps the most common personalistic feature of liberalism and pluralism in the Russia of the 1970s and the 1980s: not an old-fashioned positivism that opposes religion, but rather an extension of the religious values of tolerance and nonviolence.

One illustrative example of Pomerants's disagreement with Solzhenitsyn concerns the latter's celebrated motto: "To live without lies" (*zhit' ne po lzhi*). Intended to decry the hypocrisy on which the regime had depended for decades, this was perhaps the single most influential moral imperative of the late Soviet period. Solzhenitsyn made allowances for timorous rank-and-file Soviet citizens, summoning them not to express the full truth out loud, but only to abstain from direct falsehood. However, even this imperative finds a convincing opponent in Pomerants. In reality, the refusal to lie would mean that a teacher of literature must resign from her classes, because she was obliged to teach the "masterpieces" of socialist realism. A gifted student would have to leave the university and never become a physicist or mathematician, because doing so meant having to pass exams in Marxism-Leninism. With professional prospects ruined, such a person would moreover have to depend materially on his or her parents, or, in order to survive, to emigrate, leave family behind, betray one's friends. Yes, it is immoral to lie, but is it not equally immoral to live at others' expense or bury one's talent? "The most poignant moral difficulties arise when commandments collide with each other. For example, not to lie—and not to live at someone else's expense; not to lie—and not to abandon one's friends, one's mother tongue."[59] Thus for Pomerants, even the simplest truth reveals its ambiguity as soon as one discovers the plurality of truths.

There is no way to eliminate the tragic split in the process of personal self-determination, to separate absolute truth from absolute falsity. No impeccable behavior or moral perfection is possible in this world, and this is the beginning of faith. For Pomerants, like for Iakov Druskin, "God and sin are indivisible. The abyss of God opens a view on the abyss of sin. From the abyss of sin, the yearning for God is born."[60]

Pomerants's philosophy may be defined as personalism in search of God. The two elements of this definition are inseparable, since personalism without God degenerates into complacent, egoistic self-will, while religion without personalism turns into conservative ritualism. Pomerants's favorite writer and thinker is Dostoevsky, the founder of Russian religious existentialism. However, for Pomerants, even Dostoevsky tends to smother the existential component of faith, especially in his novel *The Devils*[61] and in his journalism (*The Diary of a Writer*), professing the national rather than personal way to God. Dostoevsky's *pochvennichestvo*, his native-soil ideology, was his metaphysical treason, an attempt to escape the loneliness of a human relationship with God. Pomerants attempts to critique Dostoevsky with Dostoevsky's own words, to oppose the religious existentialism of his novels to the religious conservatism of his articles. For Pomerants, "no amount of soil could fill the abyss of existence (or, in Dostoevsky's terms, the abyss of God), the abyss a human being confronts, always face to face, without any external support."[62]

Pomerants calls upon the liberal intelligentsia to elaborate a religious outlook that might constitute a compelling alternative to the Dostoevskian, conservative ideal of "the God-bearing nation" (*narod-bogonosets*). He finds the truth of personalism in the very nature of Christianity. "The promise of eternal life is given to a personality, not to a nation.... Christianity does not deny nation, but situates it in the transient world, secondary to the personality, with its eternal soul."[63] Following the path of Nikolai Berdiaev and Georgii Fedotov, the two outstanding Russian religious personalists of the first half of the twentieth century, Pomerants formulates the goal of contemporary spiritual seeking as a synthesis of freedom and faith: "Russian liberalism must acquire a religious depth."[64]

6. Russian-Jewish Personalism. Boris Khazanov

Personalist thinking in Russia incorporates a strong Jewish component, introduced by one of its principal founders, Lev Shestov (1866–1938). It would be interesting to compare the two mainstreams of Russian personalism, one deriving from a purely Russian source, Vasilii Rozanov, and a Jewish trend originating with Shestov. Personalism as such presupposes a challenge to the dictatorship of generalities grounded in reason and proceeds from the uniqueness of the human personality. However, the source of this uniqueness may be conceived in different ways. Rozanov, much like his successor Mikhail Prishvin, was oriented toward the organic relationship of personality and corporeality, which for Rozanov expressed itself as sexuality and marriage and for Prishvin, as the natural world. For Shestov and his successors, Russian-Jewish thinkers like Druskin, Pomerants, and Khazanov, the antithesis of reason is faith rather than nature, and the source of human uniqueness is found in one's complicated and contradictory relationship with God.

Like Pomerants, Boris Khazanov (a pseudonym of Gennadii Faibusovich, b. 1928) came from a Jewish background. He was educated in classical philology at Moscow State University and was arrested in 1949 for "anti-Soviet" activity. Upon his release in 1955, Khazanov became a medical doctor and worked for many years as a physician. In 1982, he emigrated to Germany and settled in Munich, where he edited (together with Kronid Liubarsky) a Russian-language political-philosophical journal, *Strana i mir* (The Country and the World). He is the author of several books of philosophical fiction and essays, which concentrate on existentialist and national themes.

As in the case of other personalists, Khazanov's polemics are directed against nationalism, including its most refined philosophical premises, which tend to identify nation with a single personality and to extrapolate onto a whole people such categories as "will," "destiny," "fear," and "hope." As soon as a nation is viewed as a personality with its own soul and fate, a real personality becomes a mere supplement to this enormous collectivist entity. "Russia is a huge body, a warm female body. To sink into it completely, to dissolve in it.... This is, properly speaking, whence comes the concept of nation as a higher existentiality, embracing individual existences, all of us without exclusion; and contemporary Russian nationalism has added nothing new to this concept."[65]

Khazanov embodies the Jewish personalist tenet quite explicitly as he focuses much of his work on the problem of Russian Jewry. Russia, in his definition, is the country where absurdity is not just a metaphysical principle but a constant condition of everyday existence. What German and French existentialists managed to express in concise philosophical formulas, Russians experience as a daily routine. "The feeling of the absurd is not abstract. It may dominate the entire life, it may become a mass feeling.... This, I would say, is a Russian feeling."[66] For Khazanov, it is absurdity that is the antithesis of religion, not materiality, since materiality is not opposed to meaning and reason. Soviet materialism, despite its avowed hostility to traditional religious faith, relies on a faith in objective laws of matter and on a historical telos, and thus is quite compatible with spirituality. Absurdity, on the other hand, is inimical to both materialism and spiritualism, since it denies meaning on all levels of existence.

In Khazanov's view, being a Jew in Russia intensifies this feeling of absurdity, since the Jew has not even the solace of being organic to the place that engenders the absurd. He is alien even to absurdity, hence exponentially aware of his parlous existential condition. "You will say, What about the ground, how could one live with an abyss under one's feet instead of native soil? But the fate of Russian Jews is to walk on water."[67] This metaphor of walking on water gave the title to one of Khazanov's most significant philosophical books, which features the problem of ungroundedness as its central concern. The core of this work is Khazanov's correspondence with two religious friends that addresses the problem of belief. Khazanov's own position is far from the confidence of either the believer or the atheist. His starting point is the uncertainty of the human being, who is forced to rely solely on the uniqueness of his or her own existence. "The world is devoid of meaning, and a person imposes meaning on it. Heaven is empty but is reflected in mortal, human eyes, which lend it value and justification by the very fact that they see it."[68] At this point, Khazanov's position is close to Sartre's atheistic existentialism, but without the idea of the political *engagé*. For him, meaning cannot be supported by practical changes in society, a polity typically too absurd to be substantively changed; and thus remains a purely personal spiritual challenge to the emptiness of life. A person is like a sailor on a sinking ship: it is not in his power to save the ship; "but which flag flies from the mast is determined by this man, and this is the meaning and the justification of his life."[69] The flag on a sinking ship is the symbol of Khazanov's heroic pessimism, reminiscent of Camus's Sisyphus, who finds happiness in the absurdity of his existence. This dignified atheism ("atheism may become a formula of high human dignity"[70]) allows one to preserve meaning in a world of silence and indifference. A person's only destiny is "to determine his destiny for himself, because nobody else will make it for him."[71] Khazanov pessimistically calls this position "the morality of crying in the wilderness," since nobody, not even God, will respond to this cry. Thus the fate of human freedom in this world is never victory but only resistance.

Disagreeing with his religious interlocutors,[72] Khazanov argues that atheism does not preclude spiritual greatness and moral righteousness. He likewise disputes Pascal's famous wager as an argument for belief in God; the bet, in Khazanov's view, presupposes a lack of value in earthly life. For Pascal, wagering on God's existence promises an infinite reward (eternal life, a higher good) if one wins, but costs nothing substantial for the loser, since this world is viewed as transient and empty. Khazanov objects that the Pascalian gambler has already written off his or her life on earth even before the game begins. As an alternative to Pascal, he proposes that, in the face of the uncertainty of God's existence, we choose to live with the assumption that He does *not* exist. In such a situation, "we are that which must fulfill in this world the function of God,"[73] thus maximizing the meaning of worldly life, rather than, as does Pascal, discounting it.

Atheism has the moral advantage of refusing to justify human sins with claims of demonic temptation, and avoids the religious paradox of needing to sin in order to repent. Khazanov defends atheism against the charge of engendering the totalitarian systems of communism and fascism by arguing that Lenin and Hitler were not secular atheists at all but quasi-religious visionaries; thus it is the mentality of religious fanaticism that may be charged with the atrocities of the twentieth century. For Khazanov, atheism is not so much an opponent of religion but one of its necessary, though long-neglected, components. Atheism, as a kind of iconoclasm, supplements religion by distinguishing between God and his false images and names. Khazanov revives the old monotheistic tradition forbidding the creation of God's likeness or taking his name in vain. While proposing to live *as if* there is no God, he means to emphasize the real existence of God beyond human comprehension. "There is a feeling that forbids proclaiming God. There is no God, because He is. God exists in such a way that he does not exist."[74]

Khazanov cites the story of Moses, who wants but is forbidden to see the face of God.

> God stands behind one's back, never before one's eyes. Let us resist, then, the temptation to turn around, since if you look back you will find nobody.... God does not want to be seen, he does not require declarations of faith, does not want icons, statues, prayers, glorifications. God must feel disdain for all attempts to violate the natural course of things; that is why, as one Hassidic teacher said, God is not generous with miracles.[75]

Khazanov's atheism thus becomes an instrument of negative theology, which he compares to the dialectical theology of Karl Barth and Paul Tillich, but prefers to call "border [*pogranichnaia*] theology": "it refuses to talk about divinity because divinity is always on the border of comprehension, of vision, on the border of existence."[76] To support the theological importance of atheism, Khazanov notes that, even from the standpoint of belief, it must be granted that God gave humanity the freedom to doubt his existence, and that He blesses those that struggle against him, like He blessed Jacob.

Khazanov is well aware of the shakiness of his position, which remains "somewhere between the assertion that God created man and the assertion that man created God."[77] But he sees this uncertainty not only as a sign of the religious crisis of the epoch of secularization, but as a hint of a new religious consciousness nascent in our time. Atheism and theism will comprise two complementary aspects of this consciousness, which "neither denies the meaning of the world in the name of the world itself, nor denies the world in the name of eternal meaning."[78] He foresees a perspective from which the traditional antinomies of scientific knowledge and religious revelation will seem absurd. Following Dietrich Bonhoeffer, the outstanding Protestant German theologian of the twentieth century, Khazanov explains this vision as the outcome of the "maturation" of humanity, which can return neither to its childhood belief in God nor to its adolescent nihilism. Like the teenager who abandons his childlike notion that babies come from the mutual sympathy of parents in favor of a belief in the purely material process of sex, humanity has transitioned from its mythological conception of God to a scientific rejection of religion. But a mature person understands that love and sex are compatible explanations of birth, in the same way that religion and science are compatible explanations of the world.

7. Personal Freedom and Planetary Consciousness. Mihajlo Mihajlov

Personalism of the second postrevolutionary generation, as represented by Pomerants, Khazanov, and Mihajlo Mihajlov, is far more closely connected with political liberalism than was that of the first generation. Prishvin, Druskin, and Ginzburg had established their worldviews during the Stalin era, when political liberalism could only exist in the abstract, but under Khrushchev and Brezhnev, personalist thinking acquired a more focused political dimension, allying itself with the growing human rights movement in the Soviet Union and other socialist countries.

Having grown up in Yugoslavia as the son of Russian émigrés who had fled after the revolution, Mihajlo Mihajlov (1934–2010) would be one of the initiators of the human rights movement in the socialist world. He was the first, as early as 1964, to draw the attention of the West to the growing dissident mood in Russia—the topic of his first major book, *Moscow Summer* (1965). A literary scholar by training, Mihajlov spent seven years in prison under the Tito regime for his criticism of the Soviet system and his attempt to create an independent literary journal in Yugoslavia. From 1978 on, Mihajlov resided in the United States, where he taught Russian literature and philosophy at several universities; he was also an editor at Radio Liberty in Washington, DC. He returned to Serbia in 2001, after the ouster of President Slobodan Milosevic.

Mihajlov's philosophical views are presented in his books *Russian Themes* (1968), *Global Consciousness* (published in an English translation as *Underground Notes*, 1976), and *Unscientific Thoughts* (1979). The central concern of his philosophy is a revolution of spirit envisioned as leading to the formation of a new global consciousness. Mihajlov's personalism is bipolar, concerned both with the individual and the whole of humanity. It is only by laying bare the unique core of human personality that international unity can be achieved, since the artificial boundaries imposed by national, class, and religious differences only serve to isolate people, and all attempts to unify them on the basis of such partial commonalities result only in their growing discord and enmity. "Planetary consciousness, the birth of which can soon be expected, leads to the existential questions, which in their turn, are decided by each man separately, depending on his feeling of the link between his own existence and the whole life of the planet, the life of the universe."[79] Thus, in Mihajlov's view, personality must come into direct relationship with universality—a secular projection of Kierkegaard's idea of a singular person communing with a singular God.

Mihajlov's political struggle for democracy also proceeds from his personalistic position: it is only at the level of "individuality," not of larger collectivist units, that the basic value of freedom may be substantiated both for oneself and for others. "Only when through the depth of one's 'I' one feels the reality of other 'I's' is political democracy possible and vice versa: When man is cut off from his deep roots he does not feel the reality of somebody else's 'I,' and he easily initiates violence toward others."[80]

For Mihajlov, the meaning of modernity is the progressive dissolution of national, class, and religious cohesions to produce a global community founded on a common existential experience. He formulates several paradoxes, according to which the historical processes that tend to divide and depersonalize the world, in reality lead to its unification and to an increase in the role of personality. Although the process of specialization has been accelerating in professional spheres, the outcomes of specialized labor and research have become increasingly important on a global scale. Furthermore, moral laws that previously seemed to be merely abstract acquire physical tangibility, since actions in one part of the world immediately influence conditions elsewhere, and commandments formerly pertaining to one's relations with one's neighbors are now applicable to entire nations and global actors. Even the rise of totalitarianism, which suppresses the rights of the individual, paradoxically increases the potential moral impact of individual action, since any part of the collectivist organism is directly connected with the whole. This is why the globalization of humanity provokes existential questions: as humanity becomes unified, as if it were a single individual, a single individual becomes a microcosm of the entirety of humanity.

Mihajlov vehemently criticizes communism, but concentrates still more on the dangers of those reform movements that proceed from nationalist or special-interest ideologies. In his view, communism's successful expansion was due to its internationalism; and the only viable weapon against communist internationalism is not nationalism, but an anticommunist internationalism. Mihajlov was thus one of the earliest critics of Solzhenitsyn's program of national revival. In Solzhenitsyn's emphasis on national roots and traditions as the sole basis for resistance to communism, Mihajlov sees the threat of a new spiritual oppression.

> A person's homeland is freedom, and not a geographical, state, or national identity. In the struggle against communist totalitarianism, it is only the rights of the individual person and the spiritual freedom thereof that have real meaning, and this struggle is absolutely impossible without a spiritual and religious revival that restores the supreme value, the value of each separate human personality.[81]

Mihajlov distinguishes between Solzhenitsyn the writer, who deeply sympathizes with oppressed personalities, and Solzhenitsyn the thinker, who avoids the subject of personality and subjugates the individual to a new will of national identity. Mihajlov likewise critiques Solzhenitsyn's recommendation of autocracy as the best successor for totalitarianism rather than democracy. The point is that democracy is not compatible with nationalism, since "[d]emocracy itself is based on the equality of rights, regardless of a person's national, religious, ideological, racial, or political identity. This is why *democracy is always international.*"[82]

Internationalism is the aspect of Soviet ideology that Mihajlov considers the most appealing. Like Solzhenitsyn, Mihajlov is critical of Western democracy, but for the opposite reason—for being too oriented toward national interests and too centered on private property rights. While he admires the many freedoms granted to citizens of Western democracies, he objects to such capitalist priorities as private ownership, even going so far as to claim that "[t]he possibilities for democracy in a socialist society (but not one-party, of course) are much greater than in a capitalist society."[83] This statement is characteristic of the early works of Mihajlov, who believed that public ownership of the means of production as an economic principle could be combined with individual freedom as a political principle. This is the project of democratic socialism in the truest sense of the term, which rejects the idea that freedom is necessarily connected to private property. But even this adherence to socialist ideals is inspired by Mihajlov's internationalist project for a united humanity, which is better accomplished through a collectivist economy.

Besides Solzhenitsyn's nationalism, Mihajlov raises objections to his identification of religious faith and patriotism. For Solzhenitsyn, such expressions as "national revival," "Orthodox revival," and "religious revival" are synonyms. Mihajlov compares Solzhenitsyn to Dostoevsky's Grand Inquisitor, who predicts that after the people become disillusioned with the atheistic social system, they will return to the old authority, that of the Church, relinquishing their freedom in order to be fed, crying: "Save us from ourselves!" Mihajlov suspects that Solzhenitsyn's autocracy, based in Russian Orthodoxy, is nothing but the Grand Inquisitor's project of theocracy, which will strip people of their freedom even more convincingly than the supplanted atheism.[84] Mihajlov cites Hegel's idea that before Christ there existed nations and after Christ there exist only personalities. As soon as religion becomes a national institution, it works as a force of spiritual oppression by denying the existential freedom of faith.

"The confusion of the religious and the national is especially dangerous. This confusion, seen all the time in Solzhenitsyn, is the fertile soil of Russian messianism."[85]

However, despite Mihajlov's suspicion of Solzhenitsyn's messianic leanings, he does not wish to do away with religion altogether; in fact, it is on the point of religion that he disagrees with another prominent dissident, Andrei Sakharov.[86] Despite sympathizing with Sakharov's democratic aspirations, he doubts that a purely scientific outlook can provide a foundation for human liberation. Sakharov, in contrast with Solzhenitsyn, espoused a technocratic, Westernist opposition to the Soviet regime. Mihajlov believes that scientific and technological progress cannot by itself guarantee freedom; on the contrary, he cites numerous examples of such progress producing only more sophisticated means of oppression. "No so-called highly developed scientific-industrial society can resist totalitarianism, because such a society, by its very structure, prepares the ground for totalitarian movements by enslaving man with an external rational-mechanical and technological structure of life."[87] Mihajlov also critiques Sakharov's "theory of convergence," which aspires to reconcile capitalist technocracy and socialist egalitarianism into a harmonious unity. Such hybrids are not automatically democratic, but may even produce the sort of absolute totalitarianism that George Orwell depicts in *1984* under the name of Ingsoc (English socialism). Sakharov's argument, that the imperative of scientific progress may compel the Soviet regime to liberalize society, is thus unsound. Freedom must not become a means of advancing technical progress, but should be the goal of progress in general. "Freedom of men and society is not a scientific-technical problem, but an existential one. That means *first of all a religious problem*."[88] Thus is Mihajlov's *religious liberalism* opposed both to Solzhenitsyn's religious nationalism and Sakharov's secular liberalism.

The tendency of Pomerants, Khazanov, and Mihajlov to connect personalism with a religious outlook may appear strange from the Western viewpoint. In Western democracies of the twentieth century, political freedom is largely a secular principle, presupposing a latitude of religious or nonreligious convictions. The key difference is that, in the USSR, official atheism as an extremist and oppressive form of secularism came to be associated with political despotism, while religion appeared as a way of transcending the ideology of the State. Hence the ease with which liberalism and religion join forces here as a new foundation for democratic society. Certainly religion in this context is interpreted not in narrowly denominational or dogmatic terms, but as a reservoir of freedom that exceeds the limits of social institutions. In order to be free on this earth, a person must not feel bound to earth; thus, for Mihajlov religion becomes a necessary foundation of liberalism in its broadest conception, including but not limited to the political dimension.

> The connection between freedom and religion is not so obvious to the people in the West. In totalitarian societies where a man's true impulse toward freedom leads to the concentration camp or the psychiatric hospital, the link between freedom and religion fully manifests itself. Only when man feels that by submitting to oppression he is losing his soul, his "I," himself forever—and that this loss is

worse than any physical torture or even death—only then can man rise against totalitarian dictatorship.[89]

Thus, despite Russia's near lack of liberal tradition, Mihajlov believes that the country contains a strong impetus for democratic reform, located within totalitarianism itself. "[T]here appeared in Soviet reality a new and very firm foundation for democracy, of which many other cultures with longstanding liberal traditions are actually devoid. This foundation is the experience of totalitarianism, of ideological demagogy and common sufferings."[90] This negative lesson of Russian history may strengthen a commitment to future democracy, since its alternative has already proven so oppressive to human dignity.

In general, Mihajlov is deeply concerned with explicating the lessons of totalitarianism, not only political but spiritual. In his article "The Mystical Experience of Captivity," based on the recollections of writers such as Solzhenitsyn and Andrei Siniavsky (Abram Terts), Mihajlov argues that the prison is an ideal model for human subjection to the laws of physical necessity, including illness, suffering, and death; thus the Soviet system of political repression initiated a gigantic metaphysical experiment on the human soul, modeling, in the concentration camp, the oppressive condition of life itself. The result of this experiment, in Mihajlov's view, is absolutely positive and optimistic: amid external bondage, the human soul is revealed as harboring inexhaustible resources of spiritual liberation. What is more, "*the physical world is subject to the spiritual forces of the human soul.*"[91] "Occurrences in the physical world depend on occurrences in the spiritual world—not the other way around."[92] Mihajlov calls this the "basic law of the dependence of the external world on the internal world," which "changes the entire construction of human thinking, and explodes the foundations on which the principles of science rest."[93] Among numerous examples, he tells the story of an astrophysicist who, to save his sanity in solitary confinement, engaged in theoretical work but needed some specific, factual knowledge in order to complete the formulation of his theory. By chance, a guard appeared with a book containing the necessary information, and the prisoner was able to copy the data before the prison administration realized he had mistakenly been allowed access to a book. Thus, in the very circumstances where personality is most oppressed, it asserts its power to transform its circumstances: this imparts a mystical dimension to Mihajlov's personalism.

Mihajlov's spiritualism also has a karmic dimension, since all seeming injustices of personal destiny have underlying explanations in an individual's history. For example, most of the people imprisoned during Stalin's repressions were personally innocent of the crimes for which they were sentenced, but after the experience of imprisonment, they came to understand, he asserts, that they had undergone punishment in a deeper sense, since they—the generation of "Old Bolsheviks" decimated by Stalin—had been guilty of crimes against humanity by their earlier support of violent revolutionary methods. By becoming instruments of an oppressive regime, these people betrayed their inner selves; thus imprisonment was the vehicle for restoring their integrity.

Mihajlov's personalism is close to the views of Kierkegaard, Dostoevsky, Shestov, and Emmanuel Mounier—critics of the so-called "scientific" consciousness, which asserts the dependency of human experience on objective laws. According to the scientific paradigm advanced by Baruch Spinoza, the Red Sea was parted not by God but by strong winds. For Mihajlov, this is tantamount to saying that Pushkin was killed in a duel not by d'Anthès, but by a lead bullet. Mihajlov wants to revive a magical relationship between human beings and the world, whereby the world proves to be not just a collection of inanimate things but the scene of interaction between a myriad of animate wills (human and nonhuman). In Mihajlov's view, scientific refutations of magical occurrences succeed only because magic cannot be reproduced from the standpoint of skepticism, but only through faith. Contrary to Marx, faith does not alienate a person from their essence, but constitutes a reappropriation of the human essence from all surrounding things, which prove to be manifestations of soul.

Mihajlov's philosophy is religious, but anticlerical. For him, priests and atheists are two sides of the same coin, since they deny the miracle of individual belief. "Both destroy: those who throw away earthly life destroy eternal life; those who don't recognize eternal life destroy earthly life."[94] For socialists, the other world is empty; for priests, this one is. But for Mihajlov, the essence of faith is the link between the two worlds, which makes them both alive. In his earlier writings, he prophesies a new revolution unlike either the French or Russian, one that will be "the revolution of the spirit in the name of life. It is a revolution that will shatter not only 'the spirit of scientific knowledge' but also historical Christianity, which has done so much to bring mankind to the 'reign of science.'"[95] Mihajlov suggests that this revolution will most likely take place in a post-socialist and post-atheist society, one that has already buried the dead God of the Church and has matured spiritually enough to revere the living God. Again, totalitarian experience, though negative in itself, proves to be a crucial step in humanity's spiritual ascension.

> After atheism's fiery purge, mankind is returning to God. But not to the God of Catholicism or of any other religion, not to the God of the "holy Mass" and "Virgin Mary," not to the God of death and the quiet killing of all life which marked historical Christianity, but to the God who said: 'I am the living God,' ... to a religion of laughter, life, vitality, a religion embattled and perhaps even bloody, as was Christianity when it began.[96]

Mihajlov predicts that historical churches will be as inimical to this new fiery faith as was Marxist atheism, and will probably unite with their old enemy to combat the change. This new religion will embrace an internationalism cleansed of its totalitarian component. Thus will humanity's global unification derive its energy from a spiritual foundation that will be personalistic and nondogmatic. Mihajlov's project is rather vague and idealistic, but its core remains the conviction that the enormous sufferings of Russians and other peoples under atheistic totalitarianism can provide a springboard for a new consciousness. Atheism smashed the walls of religious denominationalism, thus clearing the way for a trans-denominational religiosity. In the same way that humanity evolved from polytheism to monotheism, it will gravitate from many faiths to one "global" faith.

Mihajlov's corpus is composed largely of journalistic pieces and aphoristic musings. Though he never wrote any extensive or systematized philosophical studies, his contribution to Russian intellectual history is original in two respects. First, as concerns the dispute between nationalistic and technocratic outlooks (Solzhenitsyn versus Sakharov), Mihajlov advances a third, divergent position which presents religious personalism as the only possible foundation for political democracy. Such a combination of religiosity and liberalism was rare in the tradition of Russian thought, and Mihajlov (along with Pomerants) was the first and foremost exponent of this position in the generation that grew up in the totalitarian climate. He had one well-known predecessor, Georgii Fedotov (1886–1951), the most prominent religious liberal thinker among the first generation of postrevolutionary Russian émigrés. However, in the case of Fedotov, as well as that of Berdiaev and Semyon Frank, the ideal of free religiosity remained closely connected with the Orthodox Christian tradition and was elaborated in terms set by the prerevolutionary religious revival. In contrast, Mihajlov derives his idea of religious reformation from the lessons of totalitarianism and projects it on a post-totalitarian future; his vision is thus not a revival of Christianity, but a new religious consciousness growing from the very soil of mass atheism. Mihajlov was probably the first to conceptualize philosophically the positive spiritual aspects of the oppression of the personality under communism. These thoughts, expressed as early as the 1960s, were later developed by the liberal and humanist wing of Orthodox thinkers that included Evgenii Barabanov and Mikhail Meerson-Aksenov.

8. The Paradoxalist Boris Paramonov. Sexual Liberation against Nationalism

Boris Paramonov (born 1937) is probably the most exemplary manifestation of Vasilii Rozanov's tradition of philosophical extravagance in late- and post-Soviet thought. He returns to several themes raised by Rozanov and subsequently suppressed as "indecent" by all schools of Russian philosophy for half a century, particularly sexuality and Jewishness. Paramonov taught courses on the history of philosophy at Leningrad State University until his emigration to the United States in 1978. The author of numerous controversial articles, Paramonov has been best known as a philosophical commentator for Radio Liberty in New York, where he hosted a program called "The Russian Idea," later retitled "Russian Questions." This program was widely discussed in Russian intellectual circles as one of the most provocative forums for theorizing the fates of Russian culture.

Like other personalists, Paramonov formulates his own views via a critique of Russian intellectual traditions based on the tendencies of collectivism and utopianism. He argues that communism was the natural successor of Russian Orthodoxy—both emphasized a collectivist spirituality, *sobornost'* ("togetherness") at the expense of individuality. The originality of Paramonov's criticism is its reliance on psychoanalytic theory, which he applies to the "collective unconscious" of the entire Russian nation. In his view, Russians have not yet reached the stage where the ego, or self, becomes differentiated from the id of the national soul. This is why Russian culture is so rich in mythical and artistic creations but so poor in the capacity for rational self-reflection. Collective archetypes still dominate the Russian imagination, which prevents the country from developing a technological and democratic mentality.

Paramonov critiques Russian culture for its "logocentrism" and even the specific literary obsessiveness that inspired its revolutionary movements—communism itself amounting to a literary utopia that places the idea before reality. In Paramonov's view, great tyrants and great artists appear in the same social climate, where mystery and imagination are sanctified, while the material aspects of reality are largely ignored. Essentially, a great tyrant is nothing but an artist who succeeds in molding his country according to an inspired vision.[97] "The emotions of the repressed society are projected on the genius, and this process, properly speaking, institutes this very genius. In our country, a person of genius is compensation for society's deficiency."[98] Paramonov notes that as social conditions in Russia improved, the type of the genius withered away proportionally; then revived with the emergence of a new oppressive regime. Only by abandoning her visionary impulses, then, will Russia ever succeed in entering the circle of pragmatic Western civilization. Russia must sacrifice her ideological and prophetic ambitions, give up her claims of spiritual superiority over the "cynical" West, in order to meet the practical needs of her suffering population.

Paramonov generally prefers Freud's version of psychoanalysis to Jung's because the former deals with individuals and does not romanticize the archetypal images of the collective unconscious. At the same time, Freud's rationalism, aimed at the desublimation of unconscious impulses, appeals to Paramonov as a kind of therapy that should be applied to the whole of Russian society. He sees political oppression in Russia as deeply rooted in the psychological repressions specific to a culture governed by the ascetic ideals of Orthodoxy. In overwhelming the Russian libido, the Orthodox superego forced it to seek expression via sublimated channels, either through art or by the political neuroses that took the form of autocratic and totalitarian violence. In Paramonov's view, the most effective cure for the Russian complex is a radical desublimation of its repressed libido, a process which will lead to the loss of both its artistic genius and its political perversions.

A basic paradox of Paramonov's thinking is that moral aspirations produce immoral actions, and vice versa, the less we care about morality as such, pursuing instead the goals of effectiveness and productivity, the higher are the objective moral results of our actions. From this point of view, Henry Ford, with his invention of the assembly line, did more for the moral advancement of humanity than Lev Tolstoy, who demanded that all human activity be judged on the basis of moral criteria, and held up the peasant lifestyle as the most righteous. Societies that are guided by the highest ideals usually end up with human oppression, whereas the most egoistic and formalist criteria for a social structure result in a harmonious combination of private interests. "[H]istorical experience shows that societies that took utilitarian or eudaemonist morals as a guide for action succeeded in creating a way of life of greater human dignity than those societies whose moral culture was built on idealist premises and inspired by sublime ideas."[99] The point is that a person should never assume a divine role in arbitrating the true, the beautiful, and the good. Individuals must be responsible only for themselves and by the same token must not idealize their fellow people as exemplary human beings. Authentic democracy does not idealize humanity, but proceeds from the assumption of its egoism. "[C]ontemporary democracy, powerfully supported by psychoanalysis, is not under the delusion of humanism. It has ceased attempting to construct a humanistic myth, which does not prevent it from accepting human beings just as they are. It is inclined to forgive and not to condemn and punish. And what better corresponds to the religious approach to humanity: forgiveness or punishment?"[100]

Paramonov understands that his position might easily be criticized as atheistic and materialistic, and so he devotes several of his major articles to what he calls the "religious justification of democracy." Paramonov's attitude toward religion is rather ambiguous, though it invariably defends the values of tolerance and humility. His quintessential article on democracy is titled "Pantheon" and proposes that social pluralism may be based on religious pluralism, which itself might even be characterized as polytheism.[101] Paramonov never formally declares himself a polyteist, but his interpretation of Christianity makes it a version of existential loneliness, as opposed to all kinds of religious and secular dogmatism and collectivism. In this context, Christianity's sole feature is its individualist foundation, which allows one to identify all personalistic enterprises as implicitly or explicitly Christian. "[T]he contemporary historical-cultural situation enables the synthesis of the existential positions of the artist, the Christian, and the bourgeois."[102] Thus the alienation of the artist and the private interest of the capitalist both prove to be extensions of a "Christian" spirituality that gives supreme precedence to personality. "History may be defined as the birth of personality, as the emergence of quality from quantities, and ultimately as an overall individualization, a transformation of the masses into individuals.... Christianity in history: this is the conversion of history into biography, the privatization of history, not the perturbations of various 'churches.'"[103]

In the Russian intellectual tradition, Western democracy is usually counterposed to religiosity as a purely secular and potentially agnostic or even atheistic worldview. For Paramonov, agnosticism is closer to genuine spirituality than the dogmatism of institutionalized religion, since it expresses the humility of the human mind, which does not pretend to know God, his designs and intentions. Among Christian traditions, Paramonov praises the Protestant Reformation, and especially Calvinism, as a rediscovery of a pure Christianity addressed to the individual. The Reformation was valuable if only because it gave rise to capitalism; an individual could only arrive at salvation through his personal faith and worldly initiative rather than by ritualistic observances and obedience to Church authority.

In Russia, Protestant innovations (with an attendant capitalism) were initiated by Old Believers in the seventeenth century, only to be suppressed by Patriarch Nikon and once again 250 years later by the Bolsheviks. Curiously, Paramonov characterizes Solzhenitsyn as representative of a Protestant spirituality—a figure who, like the Old Believers, appears as a dissident in the eyes of both the communist and Orthodox establishments. "We had the same type of religiously concerned bourgeois-capitalist as existed in the West ... Now this type is powerfully revived in Solzhenitsyn, who is our European."[104] In Paramonov's interpretation, Solzhenitsyn expresses those aspects of an emerging Russian capitalism that correspond not to the mature stage of contemporary secularized Western democracy, but to its earliest religious origins in the seventeenth and eighteenth centuries; hence his vehement criticism of the contemporary West as having lost those spiritual ideals that centuries prior had inspired the birth of capitalism. Even Solzhenitsyn's nationalism can be interpreted in the context of the Protestant Reformation, which tended to galvanize European nations against the dominance of the cosmopolitan Catholic Church. Capitalism and nationalism coincided at the time of their historical emergence, which explains Solzhenitsyn's quarrel with contemporary Western capitalism and liberalism, which have exhausted their explicit religious impetus and now tend to homogenize nations with an emphasis on purely materialistic values. But for Paramonov, the pluralism and skepticism Solzhenitsyn so fiercely opposes in fact attests to the implicit religiosity of Western, capitalist democracy. "In short, American pluralism has a deep religious meaning. 'Skeptical social ontology,' as Berdiaev called democracy, becomes an analogue of apophatic [negative] theology—the only method of religious gnosis. Agnosticism turns out to be the way to know God."[105]

Paramonov seeks the religious foundations of democracy in such varied sources as William James's religious pluralism and pragmatism, Shestov's agnostic existentialism, and Solzhenitsyn's conservative dissidentism. Though he often refers to the historical experience of Western Europe, Paramonov is far more sympathetic to the American version of democracy, since it was constructed on purely Protestant principles and remained unscathed by those autocratic and totalitarian movements that arose in European areas dominated by Orthodoxy and Catholicism. Amid contemporary Russia's search for some spiritual foundation for a new social and economic freedom, Paramonov would prefer his homeland take up American individualist democracy, based on the religious tradition of Puritanism.

The convergence of religion and democracy is complemented in Paramonov's philosophy by an exploration of the relationship between totalitarianism and sexuality. In his view, the totalitarian project began with Plato's *Republic*, based on a latent homosexuality, which demanded the repression of procreative sexual drives and thus led to the decline of the nuclear family. By promoting a strict collectivist organization, where the emphasis was placed on same-sex solidarity, the totalitarian state downplays the importance of intergender relationships. According to Paramonov, the cult of comradeship, which was typical of Russian revolutionary groups of the nineteenth century, is a sublimated form of homosexuality that prevailed in Bolshevism and molded the political structure of Soviet society. He analyzes several works by Soviet writers, such as Andrei Platonov and Solzhenitsyn, disclosing hidden homoerotic subtexts in their depictions of the revolutionary beginnings of communist society. Thus for the heroes of Platonov's novel *Chevengur*, "the love of woman and procreation with her was ... an alien and natural matter, not human and communist. Chepurnyi recognized so far only class caresses, not feminine ones; he felt these class caresses as a close attraction to the homogeneous proletarian man."[106] Paramonov views communism as a gnostic rebellion against the laws of nature, in an attempt to create an absolutely homogeneous society where a woman is as inimical to the idea of comradeship as is the bourgeois. "Thus is a woman a natural, in the direct meaning of this word, counterweight to communism—'the naked order of comradeship.'"[107]

Following the collapse of the Soviet Union, Paramonov greeted new legislation decriminalizing homosexuality with the hope that the resulting desublimation would destroy the latent wellspring of totalitarianism.

> The homosexual who directly sees his problems as simply homosexual problems will not build a metaphysical concept of some "impossible Eros".... He will demand not a new heaven and new earth, but a lover and a municipal marriage certificate. And this is for the best, because humanity, devoid of Berdiaev's philosophy of creativity and of gnostic strivings in general, simultaneously rids itself of Bolshevism, extremism, and poisonous activism. This is the way from "culture" to "civilization" ... from the creative ecstasies of extraordinary geniuses to the rights of ordinary men.[108]

Paramonov also raises the question of Christianity's relationship to sexuality, citing Rozanov's contention that Christian brotherly love is a kind of sexual abnormality. But Paramonov is not as certain as his predecessor. Although he finds similarities in the asceticism of Christian and revolutionary creeds, he ultimately draws a distinction between Christianity, which sanctifies earthly life and promotes marriage, and the "gnostic heresy" that gives rise to all revolutionary movements and is uncompromising in its hatred of life. Bolshevism appears to Paramonov as a kind of metaphysical (not merely physiological or psychological) homosexuality; he takes it as a metaphor of the rejection of "nature" and the "natural" order of things, as the motive and cause of a total rebellion and gnostic challenge to being. Gnosticism, in Paramonov's usage, refers not only to the famous mystical sect of the early Christian era, but to any system that proceeds from the assumption that the natural world is evil and must be destroyed in order to liberate humanity from the chains of earthly oppression. The Bolsheviks were only the latest modification of this gnostic model, which Paramonov believes to have originated in Russia with the religious philosophers of the late nineteenth and early twentieth centuries, like Fedorov, Solovyov, and Berdiaev. Each of these thinkers professed that the procreative impulse renders the human a slave of nature and ought to be eradicated or radically transformed into spiritual creativity. Fedorov, in particular, envisioned humanity's ultimate goal as the resurrection of the world's dead, which presupposed the replacement of romantic/sexual love with love toward one's progenitors and ancestors. These projects had religious foundations, and it is no coincidence that Paramonov views Bolshevism too as a kind of religion, whose alleged materialism was only an extension of its idealistic presumptions. Silver Age religious philosophy and the ideology of Bolshevism share a fervent idealism that, amid the utopian project for a radical transformation of the world, neglects the small, practical needs of society. Both ideologies, moreover, draw associations between the bourgeois mentality and a certain conceptualization of the feminine, and thus endeavor to suppress both. From this point of view, capitalist civilization, with its emphasis on conspicuous consumption, is generated by heterosexual impulses whose gratification demands that women be seduced by material abundance. The alternative civilizations proposed by Silver Age philosophers and Bolsheviks alike would be reoriented along masculine lines, suppressing the natural hedonistic impulses in favor of heroic spirituality. Thus, in spite of their proclaimed opposition to socialist ideals, Paramonov names Fedorov, Solovyov, and Berdiaev as the true fathers of Bolshevism.

Historically, the idealism the latter figures espoused was opposed by the existentialism of Rozanov and Shestov, which Paramonov posits as the philosophical foundation of future democratic reform in Russia. Shestov appeals to Paramonov in his challenge of the notion of absolute truth and his demystification of idealistic illusions, but Paramonov is especially sympathetic to Rozanov's positive assessment of sex as a religious center of human life. Like Rozanov, Paramonov evaluates the spiritual vitality of a given religion by the degree of its sexual emphasis. Both thinkers place Judaism at the forefront of world religions, on account of its promotion of marriage and family life as the sacred duties of God's children. Thus Jews are more in tune with the logic of nature and will therefore succeed in dominating the world. For Rozanov, this prospect was frightening; hence the inseparability of his Judeophilia from his Judeophobia. For Paramonov, the Judaization of the world is rather a positive possibility, since he views Jewishness as the bearer of individualism rather than messianic nationalism. The Jews, having existed for two millennia without a homeland, embody for him the ideal of a human individuality stripped of national allegiances. The Wandering Jew as a symbol of pure personality and "diasporic being" is the existential model of future humanity, when national interests will be superseded by a world democracy based on the rights of the individual.

In Paramonov's view, the Russian Empire's demise gave a people that had been confined to a collectivist existence for centuries an opportunity for diasporic dispersion. Emigration is a positive spiritual experience, since the loss of one's homeland means the discovery of one's own self.

> Paradoxical as it may seem, the "challenge" created by democracy appeals to a person's existential depth, to his capacity to survive in solitude.... The experience of Russian emigration must be understood in this context.... So far, the Russian has lacked the experience of loneliness.... Russian life was always too crowded for a man to find his own fate in it, or to realize the necessity of such a fate. Democracy, if it is to be established in Russia, will be an experiment in comprehensive emigration from Russian reality and Russian myths.[109]

Like the Wandering Jew, the Wandering Russian may serve as a catalyst for the radical individualization of the world, which will ultimately constitute a single "nation" of immigrants (or emigres). Paramonov's "Americanism" grows here into a philosophical apology of immigration as the desirable future of humanity.

Not surprisingly, Paramonov's individualism leads him to an antagonism with Russian nationalists. Like Bolsheviks, contemporary nationalists tend toward repressive sexuality and often depict women as a source of moral corruption. Paramonov analyzes the works of several representatives of the nationalist "village prose" trend of the 1970s and the 1980s, like Vasilii Belov and Valentin Rasputin, who portray young women in a very negative light, blaming them for their susceptibility to Western consumerism and excessively liberal, even libertine, inclinations. Only old women find favor with nationalists, since they are the vessels of traditional morality. Paramonov argues that the nationalist's fear of women is correlated with his fascination with the images of soil, roots, and native land. As with communism, Paramonov offers a psychoanalytic interpretation, identifying nationalism with the Freudian anal stage of infantile development. Thus the nationalist love of earth is paralleled with a fixation on excrement typical of pre-genital sexuality; the title of the article in which Paramonov elaborates this theory—"Shit"—thus denotes more than just his evaluative position.

Paramonov's manner of treating metaphysical questions is rather ludic, leading one commentator to remark that "Paramonov plays in contemporary Russian culture the role of buffoon, or God's fool."[110] This role, consciously assumed, allows him, as it did Rozanov, to radically alter his views from one period to the next. For example, Paramonov's early articles praise Slavophilism as "not only a reminiscence but a program, since humanity, including Russia, is bound to return, in all its historical and cultural dimensions, to the sources of being."[111] At this point, Slavophilism represents to him an organic and existential kind of religiosity, and he even equates it with "a Judaic type of thinking, as opposed to Greek rationalist gnosis."[112] Later, he contrasts Jewishness, as individualism, to Slavophilism, as a religious collectivism responsible for the messianic and totalitarian seductions of Russia.

Having assumed the role of *enfant terrible*, Paramonov has managed to make enemies in practically every ideological camp, including the liberal faction, which dislikes his intellectual radicalism, his "extremist" propensity for criticizing the entire Russian cultural tradition as a conscious or unconscious seedbed of totalitarianism. Indeed, Paramonov seems to propose that the construction of a new Russia begin with the jettisoning of everything Russian, up to and including Orthodoxy itself, which he sees as a perverse form of Christianity. There was likely no more overtly "Russophobic," pro-American, and pro-capitalist thinker among Russian intellectuals of the 1980s and the 1990s. It may be that Paramonov's status as one of the few non-Jewish Russians among contemporary personalists affords him the luxury of such a radical critique of the Russian national tradition, since his is also a kind of self-criticism that includes a psychoanalytic demystification of the philosopher's own identity.

9. Joseph Brodsky as Thinker. Privacy as the Ultimate Value

Personalist trends can be found not only in the realm of philosophy but in that of literature as well. Particularly prominent among literary representatives of personalism is Joseph Brodsky (1940–1996). He is best known for his poetry, which won him a Nobel prize in 1987. However, his essayism was no less considerable, both in terms of volume and intellectual profundity. Brodsky, along with the novelist Andrei Bitov and poet Aleksandr Kushner (the latter two also being talented essayists), belong to the Petersburg cultural tradition, which unlike the Moscow scene has a distinctly Westernist cast. Thus, his personalism may be attributable in part to his intellectual background as an inheritor of St. Petersburg's cosmopolitan orientation. After his emigration to the United States in 1972, Brodsky composed almost all of his essays in English; these are collected in two volumes: *Less Than One* (1986) and *On Grief and Reason* (1995).

The prevailing theme of Brodsky's reflections is art and literature, which for him is not merely a specific sphere of culture but is the embodiment of individual freedom. Brodsky's favorite term is *privacy* (which incidentally does not have an exact Russian equivalent), with artistic creation being the quintessentially private act.

> If art teaches anything—to the artist, in the first place—it is the privateness of the human condition. Being the most ancient as well as the most literal form of private enterprise, it fosters in a man, knowingly or unwittingly, a sense of his uniqueness, of individuality, of separateness—thus turning him from a social animal into an autonomous "I." Lots of things can be shared: a bed, a piece of bread, convictions, a mistress, but not a poem.[113]

Thus literature's contribution to social life is not the promotion of specific social ideals or initiatives; literature is social insofar as it is *antisocial*, as it preserves the sense of human uniqueness. Brodsky argues that aesthetic categories take precedence over ethical or political ones. One likes or dislikes something before one categorizes it as good or evil or useful or harmful. Therefore, the refinement of aesthetic taste can foster a fairer ethical sense and provide a liberal orientation for society. This does not mean that moral virtue is by itself capable of producing a literary masterpiece, but as Brodsky puts it, "evil, especially political evil, is always a bad stylist."[114] The experience of Soviet and Nazi regimes confirms that stylistic poverty and crudeness is inevitable in totalitarian ideological production. Thus, aesthetic criteria could be used for the promotion of democracy in society insofar as they exemplify individual freedom. This is why antidemocratic political movements inevitably tend to suppress artistic freedom, which is the truest indicator of a free society.

Another favorite theme in Brodsky's philosophy is time and history. He regards time as more important than space, since it contains the dimension of thought, while space is purely physical. "[S]pace to me is, indeed, both lesser and less dear than time. Not because it is lesser but because it is a thing, while time is an idea about a thing. In choosing between a thing and an idea, the latter is always to be preferred, say I."[115] Time is what allows an individual to differentiate itself from the homogeneity of space; it is a way to escape the external world and transcend the facticity of being. Reflection, as existence in time, allows one to reproduce the same object in continuous modifications from moment to moment. It is not by chance that the totalitarian state strives for expansion in space, while it attempts to freeze the flow of history. And vice versa, when an empire crumbles, the speed of historical changes is greatly accelerated in its fragmentary parts.

The philosophy of history is at the center of one of Brodsky's lengthiest essays, "Flight from Byzantium." Here he discusses the complicated relationship between Western and Eastern cultures, focusing on the concept of personality. In his view, Eastern culture is inimical to this concept, as it emphasizes collectivity rather than individuality. Byzantium, which was the greatest Christian empire of the medieval world, symbolizes for Brodsky the defeat of Christianity. Geographically, it was overrun by Muslim civilization; historically, it gave birth to Russian Orthodox Christianity, which in turn engendered a devastating atheism and totalitarianism. Hence for Brodsky, Byzantium becomes the symbolic site of the East's conquest of the West, of the triumph of the state and mass consciousness over individualism. He uses the metaphor of dust, so ubiquitous on the streets of Istanbul, to convey the process of depersonalization, whereby individual elements lose their contours and merge into meaningless conglomerations.

Brodsky's critique of the Eastern spirit of impersonality goes so far as to identify all monotheistic religions, including institutional Christianity, as the inspirational source of nondemocratic institutions. On one level, Christianity appears to have fallen victim to Eastern expansion in Byzantium—both externally, with its defeat by Islam, and internally, through its evolution into Orthodoxy, with its spirit of state domination and communalism. But on another level, Christianity itself may be regarded as an invader from the East, since it broke the cultural legacy of Greek and Roman antiquity. Thus one wave of Easternization was subsumed by a second, making Byzantium the site of the progressive elimination of the Western tradition, which for Brodsky is rooted in antiquity. His impression of the East is sharply negative and leads him to the provocative conclusion that the whole history of Byzantium represents a flight from the positive values of classical culture, a culture built on a polytheistic religious foundation.

For Brodsky, culture, polytheism, and democracy are interdependent.

> [P]olytheism was synonymous with democracy. Absolute power—autocracy—was synonymous, alas, with monotheism. If one can imagine an unprejudiced man, then polytheism must seem far more attractive to him than monotheism, if only because of the instinct of self-preservation.... [T]he longer I live the more this idol worship appeals to me, and the more dangerous seems to me monotheism in its pure form.... [T]he democratic state is in fact the historical triumph of idolatry over Christianity.[116]

This is perhaps the most extreme expression of the conviction common to many personalists that no system of truth should be given precedence over any other. Thus polytheism becomes the religious equivalent of pluralism, and together they guarantee the individual's privacy and freedom of choice.

Certainly, Brodsky's provocative conclusions make him an easy target for conservative criticism. Ironically, however, the most extreme factions of Russian nationalism also gravitate toward polytheism, although their renunciation of the Christian tradition is motivated by a consideration diametrically opposed to that of Brodsky: they view it as too liberal and individualistic. Polytheism is a seductive idea for a contemporary thinker, insofar as it is the most radical alternative to the dominant religious institutions. Thus we should not be surprised to see radical nationalism and programmatic personalism, albeit vociferously opposed to one another, at times arriving at similarly polytheistic positions.

For Brodsky, the importance of polytheism is in its relationship to individualism, which is his guiding philosophical and political principle, and the basic value of education, as he argued in his Williams College commencement address in 1984: "[T]he surest defense against Evil is extreme individualism, originality of thinking, whimsicality, even—if you will—eccentricity.... Something, in other words, that can't be shared, like your own skin: not even by a minority. Evil is a sucker for solidity. It always goes for big numbers, for confident granite, for ideological purity."[117] To Brodsky, eccentricity has merit in and of itself, since it allows one to escape all centralized systems of determination. In fact, eccentricity may be the purest expression of personalism—not only guaranteeing the freedom to distinguish oneself from others, but also the freedom not to be limited by a cohesive and stable self-identity.

B. Liberalism and Westernism

1. Liberalism, Conservatism, and Religiosity

The history of late-Soviet liberalism includes several names that are well known in the West for their affiliation with the dissident movement, such as Andrei Sakharov and, to a lesser extent, Andrei Amalrik and Aleksandr Esenin-Volpin. Overall, liberalism was the prevailing political position among members of the Russian intelligentsia in the 1970s and the 1980s, including such major writers (many of whom were forced to emigrate) as Vasilii Aksenov, Lidiia Chukovskaia, Iulii Daniel, Aleksandr Galich, Natalia Gorbanevskaia, Naum Korzhavin, Viktor Nekrasov, Bulat Okudzhava, Irina Ratushinskaia, Andrei Siniavsky, Tomas Venclova, and Vladimir Voinovich; and also the literary critics and political writers Valerii Chalidze, Aleksandr Ginzburg, Efim Etkind, Lev Kopelev, Lev Timofeev, and many others. Liberalism was the major intellectual force behind the entire dissident movement in the late Soviet period, far more influential than Russian nationalism (as represented by Aleksandr Solzhenitsyn and Igor Shafarevich).

Rather than address liberal political views, which have been treated extensively in the context of Russian social history, we will focus on the general philosophical premises of this movement, which is inherently connected with personalism and often constitutes its political extension. To offer a concise formula, liberalism may be defined as an intellectual defense of personal freedoms that are independent of class, racial, sexual, religious, and other differences. With their emphasis on the individual and the moral and political rights thereof, liberalism and personalism are closely linked, which is why they are presented here in the same part of the book. Nearly every thinker identified here as a personalist has tended toward liberalism in their political views.

However, not every kind of liberalism can be attributed to a personalist worldview. The difference is that personalism offers a specific philosophical understanding of personality, while liberalism, though concerned with individual rights, may be derived from various philosophical dispositions, such as skepticism, rationalism, idealism, empiricism, and so on. This is not to say that liberalism could have been included with any of the other philosophical schools under discussion; rather, in the late Soviet period, it shares with personalism an emphasis on individual action and practical self-determination as opposed to a purely theoretical orientation.

In prerevolutionary Russia, the personalist or existentialist position was often connected with political conservatism. Dostoevsky and Rozanov, the two greatest Russian existentialist thinkers, vehemently polemicized against liberal views. The Western type of democracy was interpreted as a degradation and leveling of personality that tends to merge with socialist movements. Counterposing the sovereign personality to the socialist anthill, these thinkers appealed to the Russian national tradition and to the spiritual communalism of the Church as an organic soil that nurtures the blossoming of the personality. But the historical experience of the twentieth century—Soviet communism, German Nazism, Italian fascism—bespoke a view of socialism far closer to nationalism (in terms of totalitarian tendencies) than to the democracy of the European type. Thus the personalism of the late Soviet period lost its conservative association and was increasingly allied with liberal thinking. Though Dostoevsky remained a quite popular figure among liberals and conservatives alike, each party emphasized different aspects of his legacy, with liberals focusing on the existentialist strivings of his literary characters, and conservatives valorizing the nationalist ideals of his journalistic writings. Of course, such a strict dichotomy would leave untouched those characters, central in *The Brothers Karamazov*, such as Zosima and Alesha, and also Prince Myshkin in *The Idiot*, in whom religious and existentialist, traditionalist and personalist aspects of Dostoevsky's Christianity are merged. However, in the late Soviet period, these two aspects lost whatever organic connection they may have had for Dostoevsky himself: there is hardly anyone to be found in the conservative camp who might be interested in developing Dostoevsky's existential metaphysics; just as no one in the liberal camp shares Dostoevsky's nationalist convictions.

Another new feature of late-Soviet personalism and liberalism is their striking affinity with various kinds of religious outlook, which was unusual in prior historical epochs, when liberalism was conventionally associated with secular, even atheistic, philosophy, while religious thought gravitated toward fundamentalist and conservative positions. In the 1970s and the 1980s, most Russian personalist and liberal thinkers sought, in one form or another, an ultimately religious justification for their views, and the most significant Orthodox thinkers (like Aleksandr Men or Sergei Averintsev) distinctly gravitated toward liberalism in their political and ethical orientations. This tendency is different from the previous revival of Russian liberalism in the late 1950s and early the 1960s (Arkadii Belinkov, Aleksandr Esenin-Volpin), which was more closely connected with prerevolutionary secular liberalism than was the liberalism of the 1970s and the 1980s.

One might suggest that the conjunction of liberalism and religiosity can be most definitively traced to the mid-1970s, as evidenced by such publications as the *Self-Awareness* collection (New York, 1976), with contributions from Lev Kopelev, Mikhail Meerson-Aksenov, Georgii Pomerants, Boris Shragin, and others. This work may be compared with *Landmarks*, the well-known collection of philosophical essays published in 1909, not in terms of its importance and impact, but inasmuch as it too represented a call to the Russian liberal intelligentsia to abandon its antireligious prejudices; and, at the same time, a call to the Orthodox Church to reconsider its negative attitude toward liberal humanism and the freethinking intelligentsia. Significantly, *Self-Awareness* arrived two years after another collection—*From Under the Rubble*, compiled by Solzhenitsyn, Shafarevich, and associates[118]—likewise intended to revive the spirit of *Landmarks* in its critique of the atheistic bias of the Russian intelligentsia. The crucial difference was that Solzhenitsyn's collection condemned liberalism in favor of a nationalist platform. Arguing that only nationalist and conservative views are compatible with religious faith, this collection implicitly equates liberalism, secularism, and atheism. The goal of *Self-Awareness* was, by contrast, to correct this bias by seeking to ground liberalism in a religious worldview, following in the footsteps of the Russian émigré philosopher, historian, and liberal theologian Georgii Fedotov (1886-1951).

2. Freedom and Solidarity in Émigré Thought

Due to political constraints within the Soviet Union, it fell to émigré thinkers to take the historical initiative in elaborating such topics as political and religious freedom. The political orientation of the philosophers of the first emigration—such thinkers as Berdiaev, Frank, and Sergei Bulgakov—was diverse, but was generally marked by an interest in avoiding two extremes: on the one hand, totalitarianism, which in the interwar period was exemplified by Soviet communism and German Nazism; on the other, the liberal democracy of the West, which seemed too weak and unreliable in its opposition to totalitarianism. Russian thinkers had special reason to fear the excesses of bourgeois democracy, since the historical manifestation of such a system in their own country, in the short period between February and October 1917, had been unable to withstand the aggressive policies of Bolshevism. They sought a middle way, one that would not diminish personal freedom, but would also appeal to social justice, solidarity, and collectivist economic forms.

In the period under consideration, this tendency was continued in the work of several émigré thinkers who called themselves "solidarists." Formally, they belonged to the People's Labor Union of Russian Solidarists organized in 1930, the only political party of Russian émigrés to have elaborated its own practical strategy to combat Soviet communism. The leading thinkers of this party, and also the major intellectual representatives of solidarism, were Sergei Levitsy and Roman Redlikh.

Sergei Levitsky (1908-1983) wrote several philosophical treatises in which he appeared as an heir of Nikolai Lossky and Semyon Frank. In his book *The Tragedy of Freedom* (1958), freedom is theorized as the highest value but, paradoxically, a not autonomous one: it cannot, that is, constitute an end in itself, but must presuppose a goal attainable only through the exercise of freedom. For Levitsky, freedom is a condition for creativity, which approaches reality with the transformative goal of overcoming material constraints. In order to be meaningful, then, the concept of freedom requires the existence of necessity. Though it would seem that freedom and necessity are complementary concepts with the same metaphysical status, their relationship is not symmetrical. Necessity does not require freedom, and one can imagine a world—or solar system, for that matter—that is entirely subordinated to the laws of necessity. But freedom cannot exist without necessity, against which action is applied. Thus the concept of necessity may be deduced from the concept of freedom, which therefore claims its ontological priority. The idea that freedom is a broader concept that essentially incorporates necessity accounts for the solidarist vision of political freedom. Pure liberalism is a utopian concept, bordering on anarchism, since freedom is contingent on its own limitations.

The social theory of solidarism was most clearly elaborated in the works of Roman Redlikh. His best-known books, written in the late 1940s and early the 1950s, are devoted to the critique of Stalinism and Soviet society; here he appears as one of the pioneers of "Sovietology." His positive views are explicated most concisely in his small book *Solidarity and Freedom* (1984). In it, Redlikh attempts to summarize the ideas of Russian philosophy that constitute the premises for the philosophy of solidarity, including Solovyov's vision of all-encompassing unity. Redlikh also cites the philosopher Evgenii Trubetskoi (1863–1920), who argued that morality proceeds from the criterion of community and therefore the good becomes everything conducive to solidarity, while evil is everything that drives people apart. Another source of solidarism is Frank's conception of *Us* as comprising a solidarity of *I* and *You* as opposed to an agglomeration of *I*'s. For Redlikh, solidarity rather than individuality is the basic concept of social organization. He proceeds from the idea of society as an organic whole, composed not of individuals but of a myriad of lesser communities, such as families, parties, professional organizations, and so on. "[E]ach social body (e.g., the family) lives a triple life: its own life (the common life of the family), the life of the individuals that comprise it (father, mother, children), and finally, the life of the higher order in which it is included (e.g., the nation)."[119] Thus society as a whole is "the union of unions," with the solidarity peculiar to human individuals expanding to ever broader units. Redlikh contrasts this organic conception of society with the mechanistic opposition between individual and society. Liberalism and socialism are two polar versions of this concept of social atomism. For the founders of liberalism, only separate individuals exist in reality, which renders "society" merely a conventional name for their interaction. For socialists, it is the opposite: society as a whole is the primary reality, determining the behavior and even consciousness of its members. "Theoretical thought grounded in the social and state structures of our time, both in democratic and socialist countries, has seemed to be enchanted with this antinomy and opposition between personality and society."[120]

In reality, an individual is not assimilated directly into some vague all-encompassing institution called society; instead, he or she participates in several smaller social units, including circles of friends, professional groups, political and cultural associations, church parishes, and so on, which in turn participate in larger units that, taken all together, make up what we think of as society. Thus the opposition between the individual and society is mediated and neutralized in each link and section of social life and exists only in the abstract, theoretical imagination. It is on the level of small collectives that the solidarist foundation of society is expressed most clearly: people unite into families, schools, factories, and trade unions because of common goals and interests. Redlikh calls these units the "closest collectives," since they best approximate the freedom of the individual and at the same time harmonize this freedom with that of other individuals. Any improvement to society must begin, therefore, on the level of spontaneous associations, whose freedom is the best guarantor of society's democratic evolution. Since the solidarist program was mostly addressed to the needs of transforming communist society, it stressed the right of self-government for collective enterprises, which was a more realistic program for the USSR than supporting free elections and private ownership.

In general, the idea of a middle way was probably most influential in Russian social philosophy abroad, where émigrés had experienced the disadvantages of two competing systems. Within the Soviet Union, where oppressive conditions made capitalist democracy seem ideal by comparison, pure liberalism held a greater attraction. Émigrés, having fled communism to find themselves alienated within Western society, elaborated theories that allowed them to critique communism from a liberal perspective, and critique Western individualism from a solidarist one.

The theory of the middle way was influential not only among the first generation of émigrés, but found renewed favor in the 1970s and the 1980s with such political thinkers as Vadim Belotserkovsky (1928–2017), who after his emigration to the West in 1972 joined the European movement called the "third position," which was substantially supported by the German anthroposophy movement and by many Czech intellectuals who emigrated after 1968. In his book *Freedom, Power, and Property* (1977), Belotserkovsky praises the democratic freedoms of the West, especially the freedom of association for the collective promotion of special interests, but at the same time critiques the aggressive competition ingrained in the capitalist system. He uses Hegelian terms to explicate the phases of economic development: private ownership is the thesis, and state ownership, the antithesis, but what is needed is the synthesis of these two forms.[121] The foundation for this synthesis is contained in smaller collectives and enterprises, which must be given full freedom of self-government. Corporate property should prevail over both private and state property. Belotserkovsky finds that the most progressive developments in the contemporary West deviate from the model of pure liberal capitalism and incorporate some collectivist concepts, including strong administration and planning on the level of economic micro-collectives (corporations).

Thus, in summarizing the political theories of Russian émigré thinkers, one can conclude that liberalism was only one component of their integrative efforts to reconcile freedom with solidarity and the rights of the individual with the values of collectivism. In the Soviet Union, the theory of the "third position" also had some influence, as we shall see in Sakharov's concept of convergence, but among dissident intellectuals within Russia, the pure liberal orientation was more pervasive.

3. Skepticism and Pluralism. Aleksandr Esenin-Volpin

The earliest manifestations of Soviet philosophical liberalism came from radical doubt in the possibility of a single truth and from a rationalist analysis of the predominant ideology. This critique rarely culminated in the creation of some positive philosophical doctrine and thus may be characterized as essentially a form of intellectual skepticism.

Aleksandr Esenin-Volpin (1924–2016) is particularly known for having authored what was probably the first original philosophical treatise written in Soviet Russia after the 1930s. Entitled "A Free Philosophical Treatise, or An Instantaneous Exposition of My Philosophical Views," this work was composed in one sitting during the span of several hours on July 2, 1959 (so that it could be given to a departing foreigner, who smuggled it out of the country). The spontaneous, "seat-of-the-pants" circumstances of the treatise's creation made a fitting match for the precariousness of any philosophical enterprise in the Soviet Union, and reflected the author's principal tenet that "philosophy is not really obliged to be a system ... [and perhaps] ... it cannot become a system."[122]

Naturally enough, Esenin-Volpin's sharpest criticism is addressed to the system of which he was an intellectual (and for a time, an actual) prisoner. His analysis begins by identifying a paradox implicit in the materialist worldview: though all phenomena are reduced to their materiality, "this very reduction is unthinkable without the aid of the intellect."[123] This contradiction, so far from being a "merely" epistemological issue, is reflected in the whole scope of Soviet civilization, in which, contrary to Marx's theory of the primacy of base over superstructure, economic development is in reality determined by ideological constructions; that is, the superstructure rules the base.[124]

Esenin-Volpin's views must be characterized as complete skepticism, a position he believes to be the only philosophical path to real freedom. He criticizes all monistic systems that claim to arrive at a single truth and/or foreground a single principle from which to derive all else—a variety of systems that includes Christianity and Marxism. "Religions—consciously or instinctively—have propagated monism, and materialism has inherited this from other religions."[125] He even goes so far as to deny the reality of the human ego: "I do not imagine myself at all as something unitary! There is within me an entire chain of experiences which are unrelated to each other. They so little resemble each other that no philosophical desire arises to consolidate them into a single *ego*."[126] Thus, claims Esenin-Volpin, there is no reason to fear death: the person who will die in some unknowable future has nothing to do with myself as I presently am, because the ego dies every minute. The same critique relates to all Christian ethics, which discourages sin with the threat of hell: the creature that may find itself tormented in those fires is not identical to the earthly being whose actions decreed such a fate.

Politically, Esenin-Volpin tends toward anarchism, but he believes that this ideal cannot be realized in our time, since it would lead to crude demagogy and the dissolution of society. In general, the "role of ideals does not lie in their realization"[127]—this is one of the most unexpected and promising turns of Esenin-Volpin's skepticism, since it recognizes the validity of spiritual values without insisting on their practical enactment. A given concept may be justified on an ideal level, but morally intolerable in reality (e.g., communism). The relationship between thinking and reality cannot be posited in terms of truth/falsity, but must include a variety of modal "operators." In particular, he suggests, "it is useful to regard the phrase 'it seems to me' as a logical operator, and then to develop a corresponding formal logic."[128] Thus the ideal can be related to reality not in terms of necessity (the imperative of realization), but in terms of possibility, so that the realms of ideality and reality are never obliged to correspond on either an epistemological or ontological level. The harmony between them—a harmony on which both materialism and idealism are founded—can never be logically substantiated. Esenin-Volpin abrogates both imperatives: that thinking should reflect reality, and that ideals ought to be actuated. "Thought consists in a search for truth; life, in a search for advantage. These two ideals represent opposite poles to anyone who must choose between them."[129]

This choice, however, itself includes a logical problem, because in reality there are no definitely opposite things. As a professional mathematician and logician, Esenin-Volpin rejects formal logic's "law of the excluded middle" ("tertium non datur"). The point is that a clear distinction between concepts is a prejudice rather than a predicate of reality. "Actually, both reality and ideas are amorphous; i.e., they are diffuse and (in general) have no defined limits.... In view of the diffuseness of the majority of concepts, modal logic should be developed without the law of the excluded middle."[130] Thus our convictions can only approach a degree of probability, but never ground themselves in "the nonexistent area where we should like to draw the boundary line."[131] For example, such concepts as freedom and necessity are derived from verbal signs rather than reality—where they continually blend into each other. In Esenin-Volpin's view, most of our philosophical problems are linguistic problems, but he does not believe that language may be rendered absolutely intelligible. His emphasis on modal factors anticipates the philosophy of probability later developed by Vasilii Nalimov. But while Esenin-Volpin stresses the skeptical aspect of probability, as denying any positive or truthful judgement, Nalimov attempts to build a positive ontology of the probabilistic universe.

The implications of Esenin-Volpin's brief philosophical foray are mostly negative and critical. "I reject an orderly system; but what do I propose in its place? Nothing, for the present: in fact, I want nothing but freedom of opinion on this question. Freedom does not tolerate dogma. Freedom is a vacuity."[132] This confession probably explains why Esenin-Volpin's philosophical endeavors did not develop much after his first treatise.[133] In rejecting system as such, he was concerned to avoid lapsing into dogmatism in presenting his own thoughts. In this respect, his spontaneous philosophical treatise must be considered logically irreproachable.

Esenin-Volpin paved the way toward a libertarian tendency, integrating elements of liberalism and anarchism and supporting the legal defense of individual rights in a totalitarian state. Furthermore, in his critique of every sort of philosophical and religious monism and of the concept of the stable, self-identical ego, Esenin-Volpin can be viewed, along with Andrei Siniavsky, as an early precursor of Russian postmodernist theory.

4. Liberal Dissident Scholars. Arkadii Belinkov and Andrei Amalrik

Russian liberalism was a versatile phenomenon developed by authors from various fields. Arkadii Belinkov (1921–1970) and Andrei Amalrik (1938–1980) were professional scholars whose greatest contributions were in-depth critical assessments of totalitarian ideology as a historical and psychological phenomenon. Both were among the earliest liberal opponents of the Soviet regime, Belinkov as a literary critic and Amalrik as a historian. As a result, both suffered persecution: Belinkov spent thirteen years in Stalin's Gulag, Amalrik, six years in Brezhnev's camps. Both managed to emigrate to the West, in 1968 and 1976 respectively, but neither had much time to enjoy his newly acquired intellectual freedom, as each met with an untimely death shortly after leaving the Soviet Union.

Among Soviet dissidents, Belinkov and Amalrik were the staunchest Westernists, as is reflected in their relentless criticism of prerevolutionary Russian history. One hears echoes of Chaadaev, the founder of Russian Westernism, in their invectives against a historical "progress" achieved by the enslavement of citizens by the state. In their assessment, even Westernism became a tool of violence and domination in the hands of such leaders as Peter the Great and Lenin, who imported technological and intellectual advancements, which in the West had been used in the cause of freedom, in order to strengthen the grip of the state. As Belinkov puts it: "[T]he main task of Russian history was always an attempt to stifle freedom—with the Russian intelligentsia always willing to help."[134] Amalrik agrees: "As a people, we have not benefited from Europe's humanist tradition. In Russian history man has always been a means and never in any sense an end."[135]

Arkadii Belinkov was among the first consciously outspoken liberals of the Soviet epoch born after the revolution. Already by the age of twenty-three, after graduating from the Literary Institute (Moscow) and Moscow State University, he found himself imprisoned for composing a novel titled *A Draft of Feelings. An Anti-Soviet Novel* (1944). During his thirteen-year imprisonment, he repeatedly returned to creative work, most notably writing another novel called *Anti-Fascist Novel*. After his return to Moscow in 1956, he resumed his philological studies and published a book titled *Iurii Tynianov* (1960), devoted to the prominent Soviet literary scholar and historical novelist (1894–1943). The book received wide critical acclaim and became the first published manifesto of liberalism in the Soviet humanities. Proceeding from Tynianov's novels, *Kiukhlia* and *The Death of Vazir-Mukhtar*, which describe the fate of Russia's aristocratic intelligentsia in the 1820s (as represented by the Decembrists and Griboedov respectively), Belinkov argues that a conflict between the intelligentsia and the dominant authority is inevitable in any society. There are three ways for the intelligentsia to comport themselves vis-à-vis this conflict: neutrality, conformity, and resistance. For each category, Belinkov planned to write a critical exposition of a corresponding author: the first, on neutrality, was his book on Tynianov; the second, called *The Surrender and Demise of a Soviet Intelligent* (1958–68), was devoted to the talented Soviet writer Iurii Olesha; the third, not completed because of Belinkov's untimely death, was to be about Aleksandr Solzhenitsyn.

The book on Tynianov was designated for official publication and thus still follows certain "obligatory" rules of Soviet rhetoric, such as praising the October Revolution for allegedly managing to accomplish what the Decembrists in 1825 failed to do. However, Belinkov's view of Russian history is sober and merciless: "[B]eginning with Ivan the Terrible, the State systematically ate society up."[136] The book on Olesha, albeit published posthumously, would be Belinkov's most significant critical accomplishment; it was written regardless of censorship. Belinkov demonstrates the "insolubility of the inevitable struggle between an artist and society, unceasing for centuries";[137] when this struggle *is* "resolved," it is usually artistry that falls victim. Any compromise with authority or dedication of one's talent to the service of the dominant ideology gradually destroys this talent.

Although Belinkov's major works are devoted to literature, he approaches this subject from the standpoint of intellectual history rather than in terms of literary criticism. "More than in literary scholarship … I am interested in the history of the hopeless traditional baseness [*podlost'*] of the Russian intelligentsia, which has invariably remained, through all historical conditions."[138] The fate of the intelligentsia is Belinkov's central theoretical concern, because this thin layer of Russian society, with which he himself identifies, is the only one to have maintained a vital interest in the freedom of spirit. He attempts to explain why the Russian intelligentsia so often betrays its own liberal ideals, concluding that it is this tiny class's utter alienation from its own people that makes it so corrupt. This corruption takes two distinct forms. In the face of failure, the intelligentsia repeatedly demonstrates a tendency for self-blame and the betrayal of its own cause, as was the case with the Decembrists and the Bolshevik "old guard" that repented its sins in Stalin's show trials. In victory, the intelligentsia is likely to become even more oppressive than the regime it unseats, as would have been the case had the Decembrists proved successful, and was the case with Lenin and his Bolshevik followers. "The dictatorship of the [Decembrist leader] Pestel would have suppressed Pushkin no less vigorously than [Emperor] Alexander, and the poet who 'would not bow his proud head' would have resisted Pestel even more than he did Alexander."[139]

Whereas the main bulk of Belinkov's work is sharply critical and mordant, his positive theses may be summarized with the concept of spiritual freedom, which is always opposed to the establishment. He cites Lenin's famous dictum, "One cannot live in society and be free from society," and suggests a compelling refutation of this determinist Marxist stance. "Then from which society come those who destroy it? …

All remarkable personalities, protestants, genuine artists, thinkers, and spiritual leaders are free of society, and whoever is free of society is hostile to it.... Only independence from society has historical meaning."[140] This is one of the purest formulations of the liberal position, which recognizes no other meaning of history than the progressive development of human freedom.

One of the key interpretive issues for Russian liberalism is the relationship between the pre- and postrevolutionary periods of Russian history. If conservative nationalism mostly denied the connection between Soviet totalitarianism and the traditional Russian autocracy, the liberal position was to find much more continuity in Russian history, attributing various social configurations to some underlying and constant patterns. Belinkov's interpretation attempts both to connect the Russian and Soviet polities and to distinguish between them. "Soviet history is Russian history, but it has chosen from Russian history only the most reactionary, loathsome, chauvinistic, and bloody, while forgetting all that is noble, high, pure, and beautiful."[141] Belinkov's thinking is broad enough to look for the roots of such a disposition in the character of the entire nation. Why should we think that only positive cultural phenomena derive from the depth of national spirit? Why should *Faust* be called quintessentially German and not *Mein Kampf*? It is a historicist illusion to attribute the best cultural products to the nation as a whole while blaming the worst on individual "bad apples." Belinkov's thinking presupposes that the entire society bears responsibility for the criminal events of its history.

Belinkov's younger contemporary, Andrei Amalrik, was likewise interested in the implications of prerevolutionary history in determining the Soviet epoch. Trained as a professional historian, Amalrik initially specialized in the earliest period of Russian history and wrote a term paper defending the "Norman theory" (of the Scandinavian origins of Russian statehood), which was considered so unpatriotic that he was expelled from Moscow State University in 1963. Exiled to Siberia and the Urals several times for his participation in the human rights movement (1965–6, 1970–5), he produced, in a short interval, his most famous work, *Will the Soviet Union Survive until 1984?* (1969). The title was inspired by George Orwell's novel *1984*, but the book offers the opposite viewpoint, suggesting that socialism would collapse at the very moment where Orwell's fictional anti-utopia triumphs.

Amalrik was probably the first Soviet analyst to approach the phenomenon of the Soviet Union from an objective standpoint, as a historian and not a polemicist. In spite of the seeming might of the Soviet system, Amalrik penetrates to its internal tensions, predicting that these will eventually lead to its disintegration. At the time of his writing, during the Soviet invasion of Czechoslovakia in 1968, his predictions seemed quite fantastic, and his words in the introduction perhaps almost comical: "I was forced to interrupt my researches on the origin of the Imperial Russian State; now, as an historian, I hope to be compensated for that loss by being a witness to the end of that state."[142] Now we see that almost all of Amalrik's insights came true (except for his prediction of a major war with China).

Amalrik's analysis centers on what might be called the "Russian ideology" in its extension from prerevolutionary times into the Soviet epoch. This ideology values the categories of "force" and "justice" as opposed to the idea of individual freedom, which for the Russian imagination has only negative associations. "[T]he idea of self-government, of equality before the law and of personal freedom—and the responsibility that goes with these—are almost completely incomprehensible to the Russian people.... To the majority of the people the very word 'freedom' is synonymous with 'disorder' or the opportunity to indulge with impunity in some kind of antisocial or dangerous activity."[143] It is tellingly ironic, he notes, that, even in its condemnation, the Stalinist tyranny in Russia came to be euphemized as the "cult of personality" (or "individual," *lichnost'*—i.e., the cult of the specific person of Stalin), when in reality the personality was most cruelly humiliated and oppressed in this period. Instead of freedom, Russians are driven by a desire for justice, but this too is understood in problematic terms, since it "involves the desire that 'nobody should live better than I do'.... In general, when the average Russian sees that he is living less well than his neighbor, he will concentrate not on trying to do better for himself but rather on trying to bring his neighbor down to his own level."[144]

Amalrik concludes: "Thus two ideas that the masses understand and accept—the idea of force and the idea of justice—are equally inimical to democratic ideas, which are based on individualism."[145] Amalrik argues that this disposition toward force and the justice of leveling occurs most frequently among the lower classes, and thus he locates the source of possible reform within the middle class, which opposes the dominant ideology with three alternatives: "authentic" Marxism-Leninism, which criticizes the official Soviet Marxism for its bureaucratic and totalitarian distortions; Christian faith, which promotes the ideals of a religious morality as a foundation for social reform; and liberal ideology, which is oriented toward Western democracy. However, all of these oppositional factions may stumble against an increasing nationalist movement, where the interests of the governing bureaucracy are easily wed to the psychological predispositions (the "Russian ideology") of the lower classes.

It is characteristic that in Amalrik's later article "Ideology in Soviet Society" (1975–6), the triangle of potentially influential ideologies has changed to reflect the new distribution of forces within the Soviet political scene: nationalism has replaced Christianity. In Amalrik's assessment, any political crisis, whether caused by economic instability or military conflict, will lead to the ascendency of a "neo-Stalinist nationalism" that fulfills all the criteria of a strong ideology, which Amalrik formulates thus: "It must be totalitarian and non-pluralistic, homegrown and not heterogeneously Western, and purely political rather than ethically political."[146] The advantage of neo-Stalinist nationalism is that it synthesizes the Marxist orientation toward social "justice" and the traditions of Slavophilic patriotism. However, its chances for victory are not strong in a Soviet empire where Russians are a minority. The country's fate will more likely be determined by the clash of two forces already undermining the empire: "the constructive movement of the 'middle classes' (rather weak) and the destructive movement of the 'lower classes,' which will take the form of extremely damaging, violent and irresponsible action."[147] In ideological terms, this will be a clash between a liberal minority, which will rely on Western technological aid, and a violent majority, which will be susceptible to various kinds of fascist extremism.

Amalrik goes so far as to predict that Russia's inevitable deimperialization may in the best case lead to the independence of Soviet ethnic minorities and to "some sort of federation ... similar to the British Commonwealth or the European Economic Community."[148] This liberal variant of deimperialization indeed took place as a result of Gorbachev's perestroika and the disintegration of the USSR: most of the former Soviet republics initially established the so-called Commonwealth of Independent States (CIS), which in the following decades disintegrated in its turn, in part because of Russia's militarist revanchism vis-à-vis the former empire's periphery. In any case, Amalrik was prophetically convinced that the imperial state composed of many nations had become obsolete. The "Russian idea" as Amalrik interpreted it constituted a ceaseless expansion in space, and expansionist failures are invariably followed by progressive change; thus did the defeats in the Crimean, Russo-Japanese, and First World Wars give rise to the reforms and revolutions of 1861, 1905, and 1917. One could further surmise that the Soviet failure to annex Afghanistan was a factor in producing perestroika and the demise of communism.

Amalrik has nothing good to say about the history of the Russian Empire; in his view, this polity was particularly notable for having destroyed the very nations and tribes that were its true creators: Scandinavians, Byzantines, Tatars, Germans, and Jews. Now that there was nearly nowhere left on the map to expand to, he believed, the Russian (or Soviet) Empire would finally destroy itself; the adoption of a socialist, internationalist ideology had been only a vain attempt to postpone this disintegration. "Just as the adoption of Christianity postponed the fall of the Roman Empire but did not prevent its inevitable end, so Marxist doctrine has delayed the break-up of the Russian Empire—the third Rome—but it does not possess the power to prevent it."[149]

Neither Belinkov nor Amalrik produced finished philosophies of liberalism, but they showed how organically can liberal views inform the interpretation of Russian literature and history. Their liberalism features a strong moral emphasis: in a country that was overwhelmingly socialized in terms of economic relations and political order, and virtually devoid of liberal traditions of statehood, morality was the only sphere where liberal ideals could gain a foothold. It was only later, in the years of perestroika, which they did not live to see, that the value of personal freedom espoused by Belinkov and Amalrik came to be understood as a necessary motive force of economic and political change.

5. Liberalism and Science in Political Thought. Andrei Sakharov

Andrei Sakharov (1921–1990) was the most authoritative and influential political thinker and activist in the Soviet Union in the 1970s and the 1980s and the acknowledged (though not formal) leader of the dissident movement. His activity as a renowned physicist and spokesperson for human rights and democratic reforms is well known in the West, and here we will present only a short exposition of the theoretical

Figure 3.5 Andrei Sakharov.

underpinnings of his liberal position. Though Sakharov cannot be considered a philosopher, his views exerted an enormous influence on the intellectual life of the late Soviet epoch. The uniqueness of his impact is attributable to a rare combination of gifts. Not only did he possess a brilliant analytic mind, but his absolute moral integrity informed a consistent commitment to the humanist cause, even to the point of extreme self-sacrifice, which earned him worldwide recognition, as epitomized by his winning the Nobel Peace Prize in 1975.

Even in his earliest works, "Reflections on Progress, Peaceful Coexistence, and Intellectual Freedom" (1968) and "Memorandum" (1971), Sakharov espoused the "theory of convergence" that credited both socialism and capitalism with specific advantages that should be combined in a unified social system of the future. "[O]vercoming the tragic contradictions and dangers of our epoch is possible only through the rapprochement and mutual deformation of capitalism and socialism."[150] According to the conventional communist view, capitalism had exhausted its potential and was fit to be overthrown in socialist revolution. Sakharov refutes this Marxist assumption and calls not merely for the peaceful coexistence of the two systems—which was in any case the official position of the Soviet regime—but for their creative integration into a new comprehensive world order that would employ the best features of both. The economic advantages of capitalism, as well as its democratic political system providing for individual freedoms, and its judicial system serving the cause of human rights, would be joined with the advantages of such socialist moral principles as collectivism, equality, internationalism, full employment, free education and healthcare, and so on.

Sakharov's criticism of the Soviet Union focused on its corrupt bureaucratic structure, its aggressively expansionist foreign policy, and its continual attempts to revive Stalinist totalitarianism, but in his earliest works he defended, albeit in part out of tactical necessity, "the principal conclusion as to the moral-ethical advantages of the socialist way of social development."[151] Some of Sakharov's assumptions of this period—for example, his praise for the "socialist principle of payment according to the quality and quantity of the labor,"[152] or his acceptance of the socialist myth of the heroic and morally superior worker—may seem naive from the standpoint of subsequent liberal thought, but for their time, Sakharov's writings were dangerously radical and provoked the wrath and condemnation of the authorities. Sakharov would subsequently come to believe that even those positive transformations he had attributed to socialism were accomplished despite rather than because of it, since nonsocialist countries had also made the same, or even greater, advances, which Sakharov explains as manifestations of a humanist impulse implicit in the logic of historical progress.

Another example of the evolution of Sakharov's views may be seen in his revised estimation of the potential for convergence between capitalism and socialism. In 1968, he appealed to the generosity of socialism, which "must not destroy, through armed violence, the [capitalist] soil that gave birth to it—this would be humanity's suicide.... Socialism must ennoble this soil by its example."[153] But in his next major treatise, *My Country and the World* (1975), socialist society is viewed in an extremely negative light, as an example of what humanity should never attempt to do. "Heretofore socialism has always meant a one-party system, power in the hands of a grasping and incompetent bureaucracy, the expropriation of all private property, terrorism on the part of the Cheka or its counterparts, the destruction of productive forces ... and violence done to free consciences and convictions."[154] Over time, Sakharov not only loses all faith in socialism but gives a definite priority to the capitalist system, which, Marxist condemnations notwithstanding, "has proved its capacity for development and transformation ... and provided a level and quality of life unprecedented in the history of humanity," by becoming "capitalism with a human face."[155] Thus does the theory of convergence now lose its symmetrical structure, since it is much easier for a capitalist society to assimilate socialist ideas in their pluralistic, anti-totalitarian modification than for a socialist society to approach the democracy and openness of the Western world.

The distinctiveness of Sakharov's liberalism is best seen by way of comparison with the political thought of another leader of the Soviet dissident movement, Aleksandr Solzhenitsyn. Both were influential in their criticism of the regime, but Sakharov's solution was liberal democracy, whereas Solzhenitsyn espoused national self-preservation. Sakharov found fault with Solzhenitsyn's program as outlined in his "Letter to the Soviet Leaders" (1973), in which the writer suggests that the authoritarian system based on Orthodoxy and law had not really been so bad, since under such a system Russia preserved her national wellbeing right up to the early twentieth century.[156] Sakharov counters this assertion with a sharp critique of the prerevolutionary Russia idealized by Solzhenitsyn. "The servile, slavish spirit which existed in Russia for centuries, combined with a scorn for people of other countries, other races, and other beliefs, was in my view the greatest of misfortunes."[157]

The differences between these two anticommunist ideologies hinge first and foremost on the relationship between leaders and the people, and between the Russian people and other nations. For Solzhenitsyn, authority is vested through religious and moral criteria, while Sakharov emphasizes the necessity of democratic procedures and free elections. Furthermore, Solzhenitsyn views Soviet totalitarianism as an interruption of the tradition of Russian autocracy, caused by the intrusion of Western ideas, which should be blamed for establishing a weak democracy (in 1917) incapable of resisting aggressive communism.[158] Sakharov, on the other hand, sees the Soviet period as resulting from the organic evolution of Russian autocracy, which fostered the spirit of servility that allowed the Bolsheviks to seize power without challenge.

Another aspect of the same controversy centers on the two thinkers' relative positions on international relations. According to Solzhenitsyn, Russia requires a period of self-isolation so as to recover spiritually from communism and "proletarian internationalism." In Sakharov's view, Solzhenitsyn's aspiration to base a thriving economy on the simplest technology—in effect, manual labor—is a pipe dream: the idea

> appears on the whole to be impractical, and in the difficult conditions of the Northeast it is doomed to failure from the start. His program is more the creation of myths than a realistic project. But the creation of myths is not always harmless, particularly in the 20th century, which thirsts for them. The myth of an "outpost-preserve" for the Russian nation could turn out to be a tragedy.[159]

Sakharov not only rejects Solzhenitsyn's "religious-patriarchal romanticism," but finds striking parallels between it and official Soviet propaganda, especially that of the later Stalin era and Brezhnev's time, when Russian nationalism, "military-patriotic education," and a "domesticated" Orthodoxy served to stir the ideological enthusiasm of people who had been sorely disillusioned by the internationalist slogans of communism.[160]

Interestingly, Sakharov's critique of Solzhenitsyn can be viewed as an attack on the rightist principles contained in communist ideology, while Solzhenitsyn's critique of Sakharov targets the leftist principles contained in the same system. The paradox of totalitarian logic is that it combines polar elements such as left and right, internationalism and nationalism, revolutionary and conservative attitudes, Westernism and Slavophilism, atheism and fanaticism. Thus it contains two perspectives, one of which is inevitably employed to attack the other—thereby eliciting a criticism that implicitly argues *for* some aspects of communism even as it argues against others. If Solzhenitsyn can easily decry Sakharov's belief in "scientific and democratic regulation of economics" and his "utopian" dream of convergence, then Sakharov can just as easily find fault with the "nationalist and isolationist direction of [Solzhenitsyn's] thoughts" and his patriarchal mythology. The point is that the regime the two criticize from opposite sides was both materialistic and utopian, pragmatic and mythological, in such a way that it managed to transform its opponents into opponents of one another. Thus the antagonistic relationship between Sakharov and Solzhenitsyn, the most outstanding and influential critics of totalitarianism, was the ironic outcome of the treacherous, "doublethink" logic of totalitarianism itself.

In spite of their many disagreements, Sakharov and Solzhenitsyn were united not only in their criticism of the Soviet regime, but also their vehement condemnation of Western leftism and liberalism. This would seem to be natural in the case of Solzhenitsyn because of his overt conservatism, but Sakharov's position needs clarification. There is a distinction to be made between Soviet and Western versions of liberalism. In the West, liberalism has come to denote a political position supporting greater government involvement in ensuring (even enforcing) the well-being of citizens (via welfare, healthcare, public works, etc.) as democracy incorporates some socialist ideals. In Russia, where these socialist ideals dominated for most of the twentieth century, the term liberalism has more typically retained its original meaning ("classical liberalism") of opposition to governmental intervention of any sort. The Russian liberal is inspired by the same ideals that accompanied the capitalist revolution against absolutist monarchy. From this point of view, all leftist movements are regarded as adversarial to human freedom, since they explicitly or implicitly support communist regimes, like the Soviet or Chinese. Sakharov wrote: "I am deeply convinced that the thoughtless, frivolous pursuit of leftist-liberal faddishness is fraught with great dangers. On the international level, one danger is the loss of Western unity and of a clear understanding of the ever-constant global threat posed by the totalitarian nations."[161]

Sakharov's criticism of Western liberalism reflects his association of leftism with the danger of totalitarianism; it is another irony of Soviet ideology that its dissidents quarreled not only among themselves, but also with those freethinking Westerners who might have been most sympathetic to the dissident cause. Soviet ideology not only combined leftist and rightist views, but inverted them in such a way that what was leftist for the West became rightist for the Soviets and vice versa. By the standards of Western terminology, Sakharov's positions could be characterized as conservative, because he adhered to the traditional values of bourgeois democracy, such as laissez-faire economics and free technological advancement.

At the center of Sakharov's liberalism is the concept of progress. He is well aware that the experience of the twentieth century has rendered this concept ever more dubious and unfashionable, but contrary to all nostalgic ideologies demanding that a balance be struck between ecological conservation and technological development by bridling the latter, Sakharov insists that it is impossible to turn industrial progress back. Instead, he believes that all of the problems created by technological advancement may be solved only by technology itself. "Population growth, the depletion of natural resources—these factors make it impossible for humanity to return to the so-called 'healthy' life of the past (which in reality was quite hard, often cruel and joyless)."[162] The point is that various aspects of scientific and technological progress are so organically interconnected that one cannot, for example, eliminate the processes of urbanization, industrialization, and automatization without threatening human health and longevity. "[I]t would be impossible to abolish some directions of progress without destroying civilization as a whole."[163] An environment that has been polluted in the name of progress, then, must be cleansed via the application of technologies wedded to true progress—a progress that includes the imperative to address its own shortcomings. Ideally, progress itself will heal the wounds it has inflicted. Rephrasing Francis Bacon's famous aphorism, one could express Sakharov's position thus: "A little technology destroys nature; a lot of technology restores it."

Surprisingly, Sakharov's belief in historical progress is combined with a vision of a recurring universe.

> I support the cosmological hypothesis which states that the development of the universe is repeated in its basic features an infinite number of times. In accordance with this, other civilizations, including more "successful" ones, should exist an infinite number of times on the "preceding" and the "following" pages of the Book of the Universe. Yet this should not minimize our sacred endeavors in this world of ours, where, like faint glimmers of light in the dark, we have emerged for a moment from the nothingness of dark unconsciousness of material existence. We must make good the demands of reason and create a life worthy of ourselves and of the goals we only dimly perceive.[164]

Thus, Sakharov's commitment to the idea of progress is not only an apology for technological advancement, but can be understood as a moral challenge to the natural order of eternal recurrence. His liberalism, therefore, acquires an existential dimension, since it defies the fatalism suggested by the universe's inevitable repetition.

Although many of his ancestors were Orthodox priests, Sakharov himself abandoned religion at the age of thirteen. However, at the end of his life he acknowledged that his position had over the years become vague. While remaining personally averse to the intolerance and ritualism of organized religion, he confesses in his memoirs that he cannot imagine a universe devoid of the "spiritual warmth whose source lies beyond matter and its laws. Such a feeling can probably be called religious."[165] This style of religiosity can be compared with the attitude of many great scientists of the twentieth century (including Albert Einstein) who disclaimed any institutional or denominational ties but were inclined to accept notions of an underlying spiritual foundation for being.

6. Liberal Historians. Natan Eidelman and Aleksandr Ianov

Whereas Amalrik was primarily a historian of the contemporary USSR, or perhaps even a "historian" of a future, post-Soviet Russia, in this chapter we shall examine two figures who were historians "proper"; that is, who engaged exclusively with the past and did not act as political dissidents. Insofar as Russian history largely excluded liberal traditions, it leaves a great deal of room for liberal criticism. Natan Eidelman (1930–1989) was by far the most popular Soviet historian from the 1960s to the 1980s, read by millions of devotees. Conventionally, the historical scholarship of the Soviet period was composed of dry Marxist analyses of economic and social processes, and Eidelman was the first scholar to revive popular interest in history by focusing on personalities rather than depersonalized forces. He wrote primarily about individuals who expressed themselves in literature and culture, approaching their life-stories as if these were imaginative works, engaging in their own right. This reflects a Russian tradition for mythologizing creative personalities, who by virtue of their vocation create interest in their own lives as literary texts. "Possibly nowhere else but in Russia is the biography of a writer or thinker interwoven so tightly with his creations, and sometimes it even becomes one of his principal masterpieces."[166] Eidelman used this biographical predisposition of Russian intellectual history to personalize history itself, to transform it into a scene of dynamic individual relationships where love, friendship, and creativity united with politics.

Eidelman's specialization covered approximately seventy years, from the late eighteenth to the mid-nineteenth century, beginning with the enigmatic Russian tsar Paul I, and ending with the Russian liberal opposition leader Aleksandr Herzen. At the center of this period stand such figures as Aleksandr Pushkin and the Decembrists, who are the heroes of Eidelman's numerous books. In spite of the diversity of these subjects, one finds a thematic common denominator: the fate of freedom under the Russian autocracy. Eidelman's narratives appeal to the broad audience of the intelligentsia, who could easily identify with the heroes of his books. In them, the rise of the intelligentsia in Russia is presented as a complicated and somewhat mysterious phenomenon, since the autocratic state that relied on a polar social stratification of nobility and peasantry had no room for an intermediary layer. The paradox of the intelligentsia in the nineteenth century was that it came from the nobility, which was the main ideological and social bulwark of the autocracy. "These were people who had long strengthened the regime with their support and participation, but gradually withdrew to the opposition, becoming superfluous people or revolutionaries."[167] Of course, the same could be said of the Soviet intelligentsia—among which many, educated as ardent communists, became dissatisfied with the disparity between Soviet reality and the Marxist ideal, thus falling into opposition with the state.

One reason for the popularity of Eidelman's books was thus the implicit parallel between the fate of the intellectual in the first half of the nineteenth century and the latter half of the twentieth, when the Soviet intelligentsia found itself similarly superfluous as it surfaced in the wake of Khrushchev's liberal reforms. This parallelism partly explains the reason for Eidelman's chosen period of specialization: prior to the late eighteenth century, there was no Russian intelligentsia; and after the mid-nineteenth century and the reforms of Alexander II, it was no longer an alienated and suppressed class. Another factor in Eidelman's influence was the general public's familiarity with the psychological and social types of this time, known through works of Pushkin and Lermontov that were integral to the core Russian literary education.

The intelligentsia always stood in opposition to the authorities, but Eidelman distinguishes between two kinds of opposition, political and spiritual, embodied by the Decembrists and Pushkin respectively. While initially Pushkin supported the Decembrists in their rebellion against serfdom and bureaucratic tyranny, his position gradually changed, especially after the defeat of the Decembrist revolt, in favor of a spiritual opposition which does not require violent uprising, but instead aspires to an internal freedom of the creative spirit. From the official Soviet viewpoint, the Decembrists represented a more radical challenge to the autocracy than did Pushkin, but Eidelman was one of the first to argue that "in certain essential respects, Pushkin's insight was deeper, broader, and farther-reaching than that of the Decembrists."[168] Eidelman emphasizes the legacy of the later Pushkin, whose growing attraction to religious and moral values led him away from the uncomplicated, Voltairian atheism of his youth. Pushkin comes to understand history not as a direct collision between freedom and despotism, but as a tragic knot of contradictions whereby yesterday's revolutionaries become tomorrow's tyrants. "One can say that from a starry-eyed attitude toward revolutionary upheaval, he passed to an inspired insight into the meaning of history."[169] "[Pushkin's] experience and historical and artistic intuition increasingly singles out, in the historical mechanism, the problem of personality, the meaning of personal freedom."[170] Such passages from Eidelman's *Pushkin and the Decembrists* (1979) and *Pushkin: History and the Present in the Artistic Consciousness of the Poet* (1984) were clearly understood by a Soviet audience in the context of the contemporary dissident movement, which in specifically this period—the late 1970s and the early 1980s—was suffering the regime's ratcheted-up persecution and was on the brink of extinction. Eidelman demonstrated that another form of dissidence was possible, a spiritual rather than political resistance, and his work itself exemplified precisely the kind of intellectual challenge he portrayed.

Aleksandr Ianov (b. 1930) represents another type of liberal historian. From his dissertation *The Slavophiles and Konstantin Leontiev: The Degeneration of Russian Nationalism 1839–1891* (1970) on, he has devoted himself to investigating Russian nationalism, both in its historical evolution and its contemporary potentials. Since emigrating to the United States in 1974, Ianov has published a number of books meant to sound the alarm and warn Westerners of the growing danger of a nationalist ascendancy in Russia. Unlike Eidelman, who focused on positive, liberal heroes of the Russian intelligentsia, Ianov concentrates on those figures who are portrayed by the liberal tradition in a negative light. If Eidelman made use of such Westernist and "leftist" elements of official Soviet ideology as allowed him to celebrate liberal dissidents of the past, Ianov overtly criticizes those elements of official ideology that are sympathetic to nationalist dissidence, both past and present. The traditional Russian ideological milieu can be viewed as a tripartite division between Westernist (liberal), nationalist (conservative), and official state ideologies, the latter attempting to maintain an equilibrium between the first two. The difference between Eidelman's and Ianov's approaches reflects the changing vector of Soviet ideology itself, which in the course of the 1960s to the 1980s took an increasingly nationalistic turn.

The primary issue in Ianov's thought is the relationship between the Soviet and pre-Soviet periods of Russian history. Four logical viewpoints on this relationship may be outlined, comprising the main ground of divergence among ideologies of the 1970s and the 1980s. The *official Soviet* perspective was to oppose the glorious Soviet period to a dark, brutal, ignorant, and oppressive epoch of Russian autocracy and serfdom.

This counterposing of the Soviet and the Russian is also supported from the standpoint of *romantic conservatism* (expressed, e.g., by Solzhenitsyn), but this position interprets the Soviet period as a degradation of the glorious Russian past, perpetrated in the name of imported leftist ideologies. The other two approaches seek, by contrast, to attribute continuity to Russian history and to find common factors uniting Soviet and prerevolutionary Russia. The first of these may be called a *critical liberal* perspective, since it finds in Russian/Soviet history an authoritarian and imperialist impulse that evolved from autocracy into communism. The fourth interpretation, the *patriotic-nationalist* one, considers the same continuity in positive terms, valorizing the Soviet period as an advancement of Russia's role of great world power. Thus, Stalin is regarded as the heroic heir to the majesty of the Russian tsardom. This approach was originally promoted by Eurasianists—Russian émigrés of the 1920s who soon after the October Revolution pledged allegiance to the Soviet regime, which seemed to represent the growing potential for Russian expansion—and could also be called "national-socialism," since it integrates Russian nationalism and Soviet communism.

It is important to recognize the difference between the nationalist-conservative (neoromantic) and national-socialist (neofascist) perspectives, especially in the context of Ianov's critique. The romantic nationalism of Solzhenitsyn's type was a form of dissidence, since it was sharply opposed to the ideology of Soviet Marxism. National-socialism (or national-communism, as Ianov puts it), to the contrary, embraced Soviet ideology in its most hardcore Stalinist modification. This makes it the target of Ianov's sharpest critiques: having long opposed a discredited Soviet Marxism, he now turns to national-socialism as the greatest threat to the development of Russian democracy.

Ianov's writing, although highly critical of the imperialist and authoritarian tendencies in Russian history, also identifies several encouraging precedents for reform. In his view, Russian history has progressed in a kind of zigzag, with alternating periods of reform and reaction. In fact, his characterization is distinctly cyclical; for example, Ianov identifies periods of "perestroika" that were invariably succeeded by counter-reformist backlashes and periods of "stagnation." In the 1550s, the reforms of Aleksei Adashev were reversed by Ivan the Terrible; in the 1680s, Vasilii Golitsyn's liberalism was crushed by Peter the Great; in the 1820s, the Decembrist revolt was defeated by Nicholas I and was followed by a long epoch of stagnation; in 1917, the democratic policies of the Provisional Government were overturned by Lenin's military communism of 1918–21, which was somewhat alleviated in the 1920s with Bukharin's NEP, itself in turn rescinded with Stalin's rise; and lastly, Stalinism was succeeded in the late 1950s and the early 1960s by Khrushchev's Thaw, which "iced over" once more in the period of Brezhnev's "stagnation." Notably, the periods that official Soviet discourse usually characterized as revolutionary and innovative, such as the epochs of Ivan the Terrible, Peter the Great, and Lenin, are interpreted by Ianov as transitions to periods of stagnation, since from a liberal point of view, those policies that Marxists call "progressive" are seen as, to the contrary, violent and despotic interruptions of a peaceful reformist process.

The implication of Ianov's cyclical, or rather pendulum-like model of history for contemporary Russia is the uncertainty produced by the perestroika period and the ensuing democratization. Should the pendulum continue to swing, the democratic turn would inevitably be followed by counterreform—which has indeed occurred under Putin's rule with an escalating pace of internal authoritarianism and external aggression and revanchism. According to Ianov's predictive judgment: "The evolution of the 'Russian idea' goes through three main phases: from liberal nationalism, which confronts the regime, to isolationist nationalism, which strives to cooperate with the nationalist part of the establishment, and finally to a militarist and imperialist Black Hundred nationalism, which, in the process of counter-reform, merges with official ideology."[171] In Ianov's estimation, the antidemocratic backlash would take the form of a fascist coup d'etat, which would make a certain version of militant national-socialism the new state ideology of the Russian "empire."

Thus the collapse of the Soviet Union turned out to be a crucial point of historical uncertainty and bifurcation. Even as it seemed that the process of democratization had firmly taken root, its claim has been disputed by the inertial forces of tradition, where counterreform has *always* prevailed. Hence, to make democratic reform irreversible would be to reverse the enormous momentum of Russian history and to break the chain of its repetition with a noncyclical model of progress.

7. The Paradoxes of Late-Soviet Westernism

The roots of contemporary liberalism are certainly found in nineteenth-century Westernist ideology. However, this original Westernism was paradoxical, insofar as the West itself was approached as the source of both individualism and socialism, which were viewed as equally desirable without recognition of their contradictory natures. This is why the thought of the most influential Westernists of the nineteenth century, Belinsky and Herzen, was inevitably strangled by inner contradictions: they admired the Western valuation of the freedom of the personality and at the same time were fascinated by revolutionary and socialist utopias.

The postrevolutionary experience of the twentieth century disentangled Russian liberalism from all associations with socialism, now interpreted as a disastrous delusion. The classical liberal of the nineteenth century, like Stepan Verkhovensky in Dostoevsky's *The Devils*, is also famous for his "religion of beauty" and indifference to properly religious values. In the twentieth century, atheism, as an epiphenomenon of classical liberalism, became compromised by its ideological alliance with the communist regime. Therefore, late-twentieth-century liberalism, purged of its former materialist, socialist, and atheist "temptations," gravitated toward religious personalism or existentialism as its philosophical foundation. To a certain degree, this viewpoint may seem anachronistic to a contemporary Western observer, appealing as it does to those religious freedoms of individuality that inspired the emergence of European liberalism in the seventeenth century, as a consequence of the Protestant Reformation. However, the very concept of anachronism cuts both ways, since for many Russians, it is contemporary Western liberalism that seems anachronistic—reminiscent, that is, of their own nineteenth-century past, when liberalism was associated with secularization and positivist doctrines in philosophy.

Postcommunist Russia, therefore, has a dual historical identity: in economic terms, it lags behind the West, abiding in something like the early capitalist past, but ideologically, it has already suffered the consequences of socialist and materialist theories perceived as progressive in the West (at least in some political and intellectual quarters). Paradoxically, then, the late-Soviet and early post-Soviet mentality (1980s and the 1990s) was both younger and older than the contemporary West; this mixture of *precapitalist* and *postcommunist* features accounts for the uniqueness of Russian thought. Certainly, one can find in Russia examples both of classical secular liberalism, as in Sakharov, and pure religious personalism, indifferent to liberal aspirations, as in Druskin. But the mainstream of liberal thinking converges with personalist philosophy and, to a certain degree, religious (albeit nontraditional and nondenominational) views.

This is not to say that personalism and liberalism are the only contemporary representatives of Westernism in Russia; structuralism and culturology, in their own ways, share the same legacy of nineteenth-century ideology. Structuralism is inspired by the ideal of rigorous science, relating to another aspect of nineteenth-century liberalism: its cult of positive knowledge. Culturology has a more complex origin, relating to organicist theories of the German Enlightenment and romanticism, with their concepts of *Volksgeist* and *Zeitgeist*, rather than to English empiricism and French rationalism. Paradoxically, Russian Westernists, despite their fascination with an essentialized West qua West, demonstrate most convincingly the actual variety of "Wests," as embodied in different national-philosophical traditions. Each Westernist trend employs its own model of the West: structuralism is oriented to the "West" of French rationalism, while culturology has in mind the "West" of German *kulturgeschichte*, and liberalism is inspired primarily by the "West" of English secularism and empiricism.

One of the most popular arguments against Westernism among later Soviet intellectuals had to do with the radical self-criticism operant in the West itself, and its progressive orientation toward multiculturalism. From this critical point of view, it was only in the nineteenth century that the West was considered the repository of all cultural achievements and values; thus while the position of classical nineteenth-century Russian Westernism may still be justified, it is absurd to apply these anachronistic standards to contemporary circumstances, in which the West itself has renounced its cultural supremacy in an effort to embrace the heterogeneity of non-Western cultures. This Russian nationalist critique of Westernism paradoxically adopts many standard arguments employed by contemporary Western cultural critics, who by their denunciation of Western exclusionism, provide fuel for anti-Western sentiments and nationalism in non-Western cultures.

Liberal Westernists respond with the assertion that this tendency for self-criticism constitutes the very essence of the West, which does not undermine itself through multiculturalism, but rather extends its characteristic receptivity to encompass new cultural perspectives. Leonid Batkin (1932–2016), a historian of the Italian Renaissance and one of the most persuasive Westernists on the late-Soviet intellectual scene, argues that Western culture is not just a distinct entity, but constitutes the very space where dialogue between East and West becomes possible.

Eurocentrism ... became obsolete only in the sense that it began to spread everywhere and grew into polycentrism. Each dynamic society was infused with the aroma of Europe. Eventually, old Europe in its turn had to receive some lessons of meta-Europeanism from other parts of the world.... Even the very dispute between West and East becomes possible and acquires meaning only on European ground.[172]

The more sophisticated of Russian Westernists, like Batkin, tend to become "meta-Europeanists" in the sense that they do not pledge allegiance to some limited, ideal set of European values, but view Westernism as a mode of the progressive self-transcendence of values. The West, as seen from this angle, is not just a place or a tradition, but a possibility to overcome national and cultural limitations through continual self-criticism. This *meta-Western* perspective might be illuminating for those critics who counterpose a multicultural dimension to a traditional canon while ignoring the fact that their criticism is itself the most vital part of this canon, which is Western precisely because it is capable of revising and expanding itself. Paradoxically, it is through Western perception and assimilation of these non-Western phenomena that their value is revealed. For example, the cultural value of pre-Petrine Orthodox icons was only "unearthed"—after being buried for nearly two centuries of intense Westernization (in the narrow sense)—at the turn of the twentieth century, by scholars and painters who had received European training. One cannot transcend Westernism, since Westernism itself means the continuity of self-transcendence. This meta-Westernism should be clearly distinguished both from the narrow Westernism of the classical canon and from the multiculturalist refutation of this canon, since what is considered to be the canon is precisely its capacity for radical self-denial.

Part IV

Culturology, or, the Philosophy of Culture

1. The Concept of Culture in Culturology 175
2. Dialogism and the Methodology of the Humanities. Mikhail Bakhtin 178
3. Dialectical Idealism and the Phenomenology of Culture. Aleksei Losev 185
4. Culture, Myth, and Imagination. Olga Freidenberg and Iakov Golosovker 192
5. Philosophy and Philology. East and West. Dmitrii Likhachev and Nikolai Konrad 197
6. Dialogical Logic in the Interaction of Philosophies and Cultures. Vladimir Bibler 204
7. The Philosophy of Culture and Christianity. Problems of Hermeneutics. Sergei Averintsev 211
8. Living-Thinking through the Diversity of Cultures. Georgii Gachev 222

1. The Concept of Culture in Culturology

The concept of culture proved to be central for many important thinkers in post-Stalinist Russia as an alternative to the concept of society dominant in Marxist theory. While society is divided into classes and parties, each fighting for power and supremacy, culture has the potential to unite people and transcend social and political divisions. From a culturological standpoint, culture can be defined as a symbolic network: any new artistic work or philosophical theory introduced into the system of culture changes the meaning of all other elements, and in this way not only does the past influence the present, but the present gives shape to the past. The model of history as a unidirectional vector, which long held sway over the Soviet mentality, was challenged by the concept of culture as a multidimensional continuum wherein epochs are not successive steps in humanity's progress, but coexist on equal terms and give meaning to one another.

Culturology, as a meta-discipline within the humanities, investigates the diversity of cultures and their modes of interaction. Its aim is to encompass and connect the variety of cultural phenomena studied separately by philosophical disciplines, philology, history, psychology, literary theory, art criticism, linguistics, and so on. The philosophy underlying culturology may be traced to the German intellectual tradition, particularly the views of Johann Wolfgang von Goethe, Johann Gottfried Herder,[1] Wilhelm von Humboldt, Wilhelm Windelband, Georg Simmel, and Oswald Spengler on culture as an integral organism.[2] From this standpoint, culture embraces various kinds of cognitive and creative activities, including politics, economics, science, the arts, literature, philosophy, and religion. All these fields find their roots in the primordial intuition, the "ur-phenomenon" (Spengler's *Urphänomen*) of a given culture.

In Russia, this organicist concept of culture found its earliest expression in the work of Nikolai Danilevsky (1822–1885), a Slavophile thinker who in his *Russia and Europe* (1869) outlined, half a century before Oswald Spengler's (1880–1936) *The Decline of the West* (1918, 1922), a certain number of cultural-historical types, including "European" and "Slavic." For Danilevsky, culture is the broadest concept encompassing four kinds of activities: religious, political, socioeconomic, and cultural in the narrow sense (art, science, and technology).[3] Danilevsky and Konstantin Leontiev (1831–1891) pioneered the use of biological and morphological analogies in the comparison of cultures. Culturological topics were further discussed in prerevolutionary Russian philosophy, with Nikolai Berdiaev, Dmitrii Merezhkovsky, and Pavel Florensky speculating on culture as a complementary aspect of *cult*, that is, as humanity's free creative response to God's act of creation. According to Berdiaev, "in social life, spiritual primacy belongs to culture. The goals of society are fulfilled in culture, not in politics and economics."[4] Culturology as a specific branch of the Russian humanities culminated in the 1960s–80s with works by Mikhail Bakhtin (1895–1975), Aleksei Losev (1893–1988), Vladimir Bibler (1918–2000), Sergei Averintsev (1937–2004), and Georgii Gachev (1929–2008).[5]

A strong challenge to Marxism in the 1960s came also from structuralism, the methodology that must be credited with propelling the concept of culture to the forefront of the humanities. Though both structuralism and culturology consciously opposed themselves to orthodox Marxism, there are clear methodological distinctions between them. The structuralist project is predominantly scientific, attempting to introduce the standards of mathematics and natural sciences into the core of humanistic research, whereas culturology, as influenced by neo-Kantian and hermeneutic traditions, is careful to emphasize the specificity of cultural phenomena as inaccessible to rigorous analysis and calculation. According to such major representatives of culturology as Bakhtin and Averintsev, the humanities' nonattainment of formal rigor is to their advantage rather than detriment. The humanities have, as their very object, a human subject endowed with free will and spiritual activity eluding mathematical or naturalistic definition; the humanities therefore elaborate their own criteria of precision, and challenge scientific approaches to culture as a system of informational codes. Culturology thus emerged in the USSR as a kind of "third force" in the methodological dispute between Marxism and structuralism: abandoning social and ideological bias in its approach to culture, culturology also attempted to overcome scientific and technological bias as another form of reductionism. The formation of culturology as a single disciplinary field occurred at the turn of the 1970s, with the waning of the initial enthusiasm for structuralist rigor and the publication of the last works of Bakhtin and the first works of Averintsev, which were internally polemical with respect to technological rationalism. In notes made in 1970–1, Bakhtin called for "[t]he study of culture (or some area of it) at the level of system and at the higher level of organic unity: open, becoming, unresolved and unpredetermined, capable of death and renewal, transcending itself, that is, exceeding its own boundaries."[6]

The advancement of culturology in the post-Stalin period proved to be in consonance both with national traditions of universalism and with pluralistic and liberal modes of thinking. In culturology, "culture" is treated as a descriptive rather than a normative concept, the term itself being used both in the singular and in the plural. *Culture* as an integrity of disciplinary spheres presupposes the diversity of *cultures* as multiple national and historical types, each with its own formative principle, irreducible to others. While culturology is concerned with culture as a whole, it also recognizes the diversity of these "wholes," and is reluctant to discriminate among them in terms of value.

Thus the methodology of culturological research necessarily combines two procedures. First, it seeks to identify the broader underpinnings of diverse disciplines, to go beyond the specificity of any professional sphere. Bakhtin, for example, in his meditations on the tasks of literary scholarship, insists that literature

> is an inseparable part of culture and ... cannot be understood outside the total context of the entire culture of a given epoch.... In our enthusiasm for specification we have ignored questions of the interconnection and interdependence of various areas of culture ... and we have not taken into account that the most intense and productive life of culture takes place on the boundaries of its individual areas and not in places where these areas have become enclosed in their own specificity.[7]

The second procedure presupposes a definition of cultural phenomena in terms of their historical and national specificity. If, within a given culture, various disciplinary and professional spheres are linked by a common intuition, then the uniqueness of this intuition serves to distinguish one culture from another on a global scale. This aspect of culturology was most thoroughly developed by Aleksei Losev in his extensive investigations of classical aesthetics, which demonstrate that Hellenistic antiquity as a cultural phenomenon preserves its individuality on all levels of interpretation. Analyzing the most abstract theories of the dialectics of sameness and difference in Plato and the neo-Platonic school, Losev shows that behind these abstractions, and "permeating all antiquity ... , lies the powerful and inescapable intuition of a *universal organism*, or the intuition of all reality as a living organism."[8] For Losev, the principal goal of culturological research is to perceive the uniqueness of a given phenomenon as an "expressive countenance of being" (*vyrazitel'nyi lik bytiia*). "In exploring any fact from the culture of classical antiquity, I did not rest until I found in it a quality that sharply distinguished it from everything that is not classical.... 'Style' and 'worldview' must be integrated by any means; they must necessarily reflect one another."[9]

These two aspects of culturology, "diversity" and "integrity," are inseparable, but certainly their respective significance may vary within the works of a given thinker. Russian culturology, as it formed in the late 1960s, found great living proponents for each aspect of the discipline in Bakhtin and Losev, both of whom had already laid the groundwork for this methodology in their earlier works of the 1920s. While Bakhtin stresses the dialogic nature of a specific culture in its internal and external differentiations, Losev is more inclined to theorize cultural identity as a multifaceted manifestation of one basic, primordial intuition.[10]

2. Dialogism and the Methodology of the Humanities. Mikhail Bakhtin

Given the wide critical acclaim of Bakhtin both in the West and Russia, it would be redundant to undertake here a broad survey of his life and work, which has already been admirably performed by many notable scholars.[11] Instead, it will be useful to focus on Bakhtin's later writings, which are relatively brief and mostly represent works in progress, although, in all probability, they were not even meant to be completed. These present a specific "late-Bakhtinian" genre of "drafts," "summaries," or "synopses," where thought is postulated in the form of direct thesis, without supporting analysis or documentation. Many sentences are elliptical, missing verbs or other parts of speech. One may suggest that "unfinalizability," that principal category of Bakhtin's philosophy,

Figure 4.1 Mikhail Bakhtin.

becomes the intended stylistic device of his later writings. These pieces demonstrate thought in the process of its generation, at the stage of a rough draft that does not conceal its "roughness."

As compared with his major monographs about Dostoevsky and Rabelais, Bakhtin's later fragments concentrate more specifically on the methodology of the humanities. In the relatively free atmosphere of the 1950s–70s, Bakhtin attempts to make up for the enforced silence regarding general methodological questions that, out of political necessity, had marked his major works of the middle period (1930s to the 1940s). In the early works that did have explicit methodological orientation, such as *Freudianism: A Critical Sketch* (1927), *The Formal Method in Literary Scholarship* (1928), and *Marxism and the Philosophy of Language* (1930), Bakhtin had to conform to the official Soviet version of Marxism and, perhaps for this reason, published them under the names of his friends and collaborators Pavel Medvedev and Valentin Voloshinov.

Bakhtin's later writings deal with the themes of his previous thought, albeit quite selectively. Of the two most elaborated concepts of his mature period—dialogism, developed in his book on Dostoevsky, and the carnivalesque, introduced in his book on Rabelais—only the first survives, while the second is mostly ignored. This may be explained in part by the fact that all revisions and elaborations on the concept of carnival had to be absorbed into the preparation of his book on Rabelais, which was not published until 1965. In any case, "carnival" fell out of the network of Bakhtin's later reflections on the nature of text and the methodology of the humanities, even as, in the late 1960s and the 1970s, Bakhtin's popularity in Russian intellectual circles was primarily due precisely to his ideas on laughter, ambivalence, and the grotesque, all derivatives of his notion of carnival. This enthusiasm for Bakhtin's book on Rabelais paralleled the booming success of Mikhail Bulgakov's novel *The Master and Margarita*, a work likewise written in the 1930s but not published till 1966. These two books, by Bulgakov and Bakhtin, were perceived as manifestations of the same carnivalesque spirit shattering the rigidly stratified official culture of the Stalin and Brezhnev decades. Nevertheless, later, in the 1980s, both books were reevaluated not so much as challenging the dogmatism and stagnation of the Soviet social system, but rather as generated by the spirit of incessant structural-political reversals and upheavals that triumphed in postrevolutionary Russia, especially in the "carnivalesque" atmosphere of Stalin's purges and repressions. The essential deficiencies of Bakhtin's understanding of the Middle Ages and of Bulgakov's understanding of early Christianity were criticized by later thinkers, such as Sergei Averintsev, who was particularly attuned to the "seriousness" of the ongoing process of Russian religious revival and thus not inclined to encourage a liberal-humanistic rearticulation or revolutionary-carnivalesque reversal of Christian values.[12] In fact, Bakhtin himself wrote of the "seriousification of the world" (*oser'eznenie mira*) and breakdown of the carnival vision in his notes "On the Philosophical Bases of Scholarship in the Humanities" (1940–3; published posthumously).[13] Although direct evidence of religious orientation is scarce in Bakhtin's work, the near-total absence of the notion of carnival and its derivatives in his later methodological meditations may be an oblique indication of his growing acceptance of the ultimate seriousness of Christianity. If so, then in the 1960s and the early 1970s, Bakhtin is once again "ahead" of his contemporaries, who continue to deploy and celebrate conceptions he elaborated in the 1930s and the 1940s.

The numerous notes and fragments of his later scholarship may be divided into two often overlapping categories: one concerning language/speech relationships and dialogic approaches to textuality ("The Problem of Speech Genres," "The Problem of the Text in Linguistics, Philology, and Other Human Sciences: An Experiment in Philosophical Analysis"); the other addressing the deep philosophical and moral questions of the humanities, in particular philology ("From Notes Made in 1970–71," "Toward a Methodology for the Human Sciences," and other series of fragments). The fundamental methodological problem underlying all these works is Bakhtin's relationship with such major intellectual movements in the humanities as existentialism, philosophical anthropology, structuralism, and emergent post-structuralism.

In particular, Bakhtin critiques Ferdinand de Saussure and, through him, the entire structuralist movement, for a preoccupation with "language" as a self-enclosed sign system, and a neglect of "speech" as the sphere of allegedly spontaneous and individual acts. From a strictly structuralist point of view, speech cannot be analyzed and generalized in semiotic terms, since it presupposes a personal dialogic relationship between the participants of communication. Bakhtin, however, finds that the purely linguistic approach, based on such formal units as sentence and word, syllable and phoneme, mystifies the process of communication, which in reality consists of *utterances* as distinct from *sentences*. An utterance may comprise a single syllable or many thousands of sentences, as in a novel or treatise, but what makes it an organic unity is the expression of a definite authorial position and the anticipation of a response from the interlocutor, be it a person, society, or God. An utterance is a unit of existential communication, as opposed to the objectified and mechanical structure of language as studied in grammar, lexicography, rhetoric, and stylistics.

At this point, Bakhtin's polemic with structuralism (continuing his 1920s polemic with formalism) seems to be articulated from an existentialist or broadly humanistic position and marked by a mistrust for any formal generalization. However, Bakhtin gives priority to utterance over sentence only in order to advance the task of systematization as applied to utterances themselves. This recurring pattern underlying the variety of seemingly spontaneous utterances is what Bakhtin calls "speech genre," and it preexists any individual act of speech: "We speak only in definite speech genres, that is, all our utterances have definite and relatively stable typical *forms of construction of the whole*.... [W]e speak in diverse genres without suspecting that they exist."[14] Bakhtin pays special attention to such quotidian genres as greetings, farewells, congratulations, wishes, and the sharing of information about health and business, which are far less recognized and described than genres of scientific or literary discourse. Bakhtin does not offer any systematic classification of speech genres, though he presupposes the feasibility of such a project. But what is methodologically most important is Bakhtin's strategy of the "dialogistic" refutation of structuralism, followed by the generalization of dialogic experience itself. This rather unexpectedly brings him into the paradigm of the post-structuralist theory of text that in the late 1960s and the early 1970s made its initial advances in the works of Jacques Derrida. Genres, as formulated by Bakhtin, are "much more flexible, plastic, and free"[15] than the grammatical forms of language or algorithms of semiotic codes. Nevertheless, they organize the multiplicity of speech acts, which are thus not absolutely free and arbitrary, as would be imagined from a purely existentialist point of view. As distinguished from classical structuralism, Bakhtin looks for structures not where they can be found in their most rigid and finalized forms, as in language, but in the fluid and spontaneous realms of existence and speech where they are least expected, and furthest from conscious conceptualization. Bakhtinian *speech genres* can be paralleled with such post-structuralist notions as Michel Foucault's *episteme* and Thomas Kuhn's *paradigm*.

The concept of genre systematizes all the deviations and ruptures that speech utterances introduce into the system of language, which makes Bakhtin a uniquely lonely figure in the intellectual climate of the 1930s or the 1950s, but increasingly influential in the 1960s to the 1980s. If "genre," as a non-structuralist type of structure, is Bakhtin's favorite theoretical concept, it is no wonder that his favorite genre is the "novel," which is alien to any strict genre definitions and accumulates whatever features might deviate from the purity of other genres, such as epic (Bakhtin explored these paradoxes of the novel in his works of the 1930s and the 1940s). Bakhtin is at the height of his methodological powers when he deconstructs the existing "structural" modes of description and reconstructs a new totality of the elements he himself has just deconstructed, that is, when he pinpoints the exceptions within the existing rules and then formulates the flexible, "probabilistic" rules for these very exceptions.

This is why it is so difficult to include Bakhtin in any single methodological school, for the same reason that it is difficult to include the novel in any existing genre order. The deconstructionists would criticize Bakhtin for his belief in the objective meaning of utterances; structuralists reproach him for the denial of purely scientific and rigorous methods in the humanities; existentialists find him too inclined toward scientific generalization and classification. It might be said that the phenomenon of Bakhtinianism arises only at the intersection of various methodologies, in the field of their dialogic interpenetration. Bakhtin emphasized that "the most intensive and productive life of culture takes place on the boundaries of its individual areas."[16] In the same way, one might suggest that the most intense and productive manifestations of Bakhtin's methodology take place on the boundaries of other methodologies, not in their isolated interior spaces.

In the Soviet Union in the 1960s, structuralists like Iurii Lotman and Viacheslav V. Ivanov, and their opponents, conservative and nationalist critics like Vadim Kozhinov and Petr Palievsky, alike claimed Bakhtin as one of their own. But an attentive reader will find, even within the same works of Bakhtin, assertions that substantiate both these opposing claims, even as they undermine them. For example, in "The Problem of the Text in Linguistics, Philology, and Other Human Sciences: An Experiment in Philosophical Analysis" (1959–61), Bakhtin advances the concept of text in a mode very similar to the structuralists and, obviously, immediately inspired by them: "a human action is a potential text"; "text is the primary reality and starting point for any humanistic discipline."[17] On the other hand, Bakhtin criticizes the very concept of text as alien to the properly human dimension of the humanities, as a purely linguistic object divorced from dialogic relationships between its producers and recipients: "The term 'text' is not at all adequate to the essence of the entire utterance."[18] Thus Bakhtin's attitude toward structuralism was as ambivalent as had been his attitude toward formalism in his early career. On the one hand, he held structuralist scholars' scientific erudition and ideological neutrality in high regard and shared their infatuation with textuality.[19] On the other hand, he criticized structuralism for its depersonalized and formalized interpretation of the text, which eliminates its dialogic dimension.

> My attitude toward structuralism: I am against enclosure in a text. Mechanical categories: "opposition," "change of codes".... Sequential formalization and depersonalization: all relations are logical (in the broad sense of the word). But I hear *voices* in everything and relations among them.... Contextual meaning is personalistic; it always includes a question, an address, and the anticipation of a response, it always includes two (as a dialogic minimum). This personalism is not psychological, but semantic.[20]

The topics of structuralist research are intentionally void of any subjectivity and are understood as mere objects, as a set of elements susceptible to objective knowledge. But, according to Bakhtin, meaning exists only between two persons. Such an approach inspired the renunciation of structuralism undertaken by "traditionalists" and "organicists" like Kozhinov and Palievsky, who in the early 1970s established the annual theoretical collection *Context*, which explicitly opposed the structuralist emphasis on *text*.

In the worst case, these incompatible interpretations reflect terminological inconsistencies and logical contradictions in the later Bakhtin, but on a deeper level, they reveal the very phenomenon of Bakhtinianism as the conscious interaction of different methodologies. "This is not a question of mere eclecticism: the merging of all trends into one and only one would be fatal to science (if science were mortal). The more demarcation the better, but benevolent demarcation. Without border disputes. Cooperation. The existence of border zones (new trends and disciplines usually originate in them)."[21]

It is this "inconsistency" that made Bakhtinianism such a welcome participant in the 1980s and the 1990s Western theoretical discourse, torn between a playful deconstructionist relativity of meaning and, inherent in any scholarly research, an aspiration for objective and definite signification. Dale Peterson explains Bakhtin's popularity in the West precisely as a result of his mediation between the extremes of semantic relativism and structuralist dogmatism:

> [A] Bakhtinian analysis of verbal signification insists on freeing cultural signs from that prison-house of language constructed by doctrines that maintain either the autonomy of texts or the "deadlock of dyads." Yet, and this is crucial, despite Bakhtin's partiality toward 'unfinalized' signification in actual communication, there is not the least trace of sympathy for the radical Deconstructionist move toward the "endless play of signifiers." Bakhtin manages to rein in the infinite

deferrals of signification by insisting that any utterance, at any given moment of enunciation and/or reception, is projected into a delimited "field of answerability."[22]

Bakhtin is only partly responsible for the far-reaching postmodern repercussions of his ideas. If we try to reconstruct his own philosophical project, it will seem far more traditional and organically connected with the neo-Kantianism of his earliest writings. This project, which was never fully realized by Bakhtin, but for which all of his works constituted preliminary stages, could be given the general title of *Philosophical Anthropology*. Max Scheler, the founder of the discipline of that name in Germany, was among Bakhtin's favorite thinkers, and toward the end of his life Bakhtin intended to write a book titled *Essays in Philosophical Anthropology*.[23] This anthropological dimension is the most evident point of difference between Bakhtin and structuralist and post-structuralist thinkers who are unanimous in their attempts to "dehumanize" the humanities. For Bakhtin, the very term "humanities" (*gumanitarnye nauki*, literally "the humanistic sciences") was especially precious, because it indicated not only the theme, but also the criterion and methodology of investigation: "Everything in this world acquires meaning, significance, and value only in relation to the human, as the human. All possible being and all possible significance are located around the human as the center and the only value; everything—and here, aesthetic vision knows no boundaries—must be related to humanity, and become human."[24]

Incidentally, Bakhtin's definition of the novel is also purely anthropological: in the novel, "a human being is either greater than their fate or less than their humanity."[25] The peculiarity of the novel consists in the representation of those potentials of humanity that cannot be realized in a given social status or role: "[T]he human cannot be completely embodied in any existing sociohistorical body."[26]

Bakhtin clearly demarcates the humanities from all other sciences on the basis of a distinction between "thing" and "personality." A thing is devoid of subjectivity and therefore can be cognized unilaterally, from the outside. A personality, as itself a subjective source of cognition, cannot be objectified in the same way, but must instead be engaged in knowledge intersubjectively, dialogically. Thus the humanities not only address dialogue as a principal dimension of textuality, but are dialogic in themselves. "The object of the humanities is an *expressive* and *articulate* existence [*bytie*]. This existence never coincides with itself and is thus inexhaustible in its sense and meaning."[27] Whereas the natural sciences ask questions and furnish their own answers, the humanities arrive at answers only through internal dialogue with their subjects. The criterion of truth in the humanities, then, is not the accuracy of knowledge but the depth of understanding, the dialogic penetration.

However, Bakhtin is not a "pure" personalist: his "dialogic imagination" is refracted through multiple cultural prisms. For Bakhtin, understanding hinges on the key perspective of "outsideness" or "being beyond" (*vnenakhodimost'*). "In order to understand, it is immensely important for the person who understands to be located outside the object of his or her creative understanding—in time, in space, in culture."[28] A subject cannot know itself authentically from its own perspective, not even in a mirror or photograph. It is only other people who can provide an image of one's self.

Bakhtin applies the requisite of "being beyond" to larger-scale investigations, specifically to culturology. Just as individual subjects come to self-understanding dialogically, individual cultures can be understood deeply only through the eyes of other cultures. For example, "antiquity itself didn't know the antiquity that we know now. There used to be a school joke: the ancient Greeks didn't know the main thing about themselves, that they were *ancient* Greeks."[29] Bakhtin criticizes Spengler for envisioning "closed and finalized cultural worlds" incapable of transcending their particular intuitions. "We raise new questions for a foreign culture, ones that it did not raise itself.... Such a dialogic encounter of two cultures does not result in merging or mixing. Each retains its own unity and *open* totality, but they are mutually enriched."[30]

Bakhtin extends his critique to Hegelian and Marxist dialectics, which appear to him as schematic reductions of the dialogic relationship. Dialectics destroys the relationship between multifarious living voices, reducing them to abstract "opposites" and confining them to the framework of one comprehensive consciousness. Thus a *dialectic* philosopher pretends to work with objective oppositions, claiming to be above them in some privileged zone of omniscience. A *dialogic* philosopher participates in the relationship between opposing voices and poses open questions to them—questions whose answers he or she does not know beforehand.

Despite his attraction to such philosophical tendencies as neo-Kantianism, existentialism, and phenomenology, Bakhtin refuses to identify himself with a particular intellectual trend. He emphasizes his love for variations of terms and multiplicities of perspectives even as they pertain to the same concept. He would prefer to be, not just a philosopher of dialogue, but a dialogist in the realm of philosophy. To a certain degree his position may be described as oscillating or rather mediating between existentialism and post-structuralism. His treatment of texts as unfinalizable networks of meaning that arise at the intersections of various consciousnesses, on the one hand, echoes Martin Buber's "I-Thou" relationship and, on the other, anticipates Derrida's deconstruction.

In an interesting way, Bakhtin prefigures the post-structuralist "death of the author" with his description of the author as occupying the zone of silence and always appearing in a mask, producing speech acts on behalf of multiple others. "It is customary to speak about the authorial mask. But in which utterances (speech acts) is there a *face* and not a mask?"[31] Bakhtin's ideas about silence and ubiquitous invisible quotation marks are ways of escaping the metaphysics of logos, which identifies language with a monologic subject. If the primary subject is silent, then what's written is always someone else's voice and exists only in the mode of quotation, though the degree of alienation from the author's speech may vary infinitely. "The word of the primary author cannot be *his own* word. It must be consecrated by something higher and impersonal.... Therefore, the primary author clothes himself in *silence*."[32] Bakhtin means that utterances in the literary text do not belong to the real, "biographical" author, but only characterize the image of the author created artistically by the writer. The paradox is that although the writer him- or herself is silent, s/he produces "citations" not only on behalf of characters but also on behalf of the "author" (who is only a conventional image, introduced into a text equally with other images). The real author has no words of his or her own, but only various modes of silence, including "irony as a special kind of substitute for silence."[33] This "erasure" of the author from the substance of the text anticipates typically post-structuralist eliminations of "authorship" as an individual presence.

However, Bakhtin's compatibility with post-structuralism should not be overstated. As mentioned, his principal interest is with anthropological questions, with the humanness of knowledge. If Bakhtin critiques metaphysics, he does not want to do away altogether with the notion of the "human." Though his anthropology is relational, not substantialist, it is still anthropology, not semiotics, grammatology, the politics of power, or a general economy of language. The human is "the witness and the judge" of the world and gives a different meaning to the world even if the world remains physically what it is.

> A stone is still stony and the sun still sunny, but the event of existence as a whole becomes completely different because a new and major character in this event [the human being] appears for the first time on the scene of earthly existence—the witness and the judge. And the sun, while remaining physically the same, has changed ... because it has been reflected in the consciousness of the other.... (This has nothing to do with "other existence").[34]

Bakhtin is careful to renounce a transcendental realm of "being," emphasizing instead by this term the new relationship made possible by consciousness confronting otherness. Thus *humanness* has no substance, but is a mode of relation that grants the possibility of meaning and cultural dimension for everything that exists in the world.

3. Dialectical Idealism and the Phenomenology of Culture. Aleksei Losev

Whereas most thinkers in the area of cultural studies are identified with some specific subfield (typically philology, literary theory, history, or linguistics), Aleksei Losev (1893–1988) belongs among the rare species of "pure" philosopher. He is the rightful heir to the metaphysical tradition of Russian thought founded by Vladimir Solovyov and continued by Pavel Florensky, Nikolai Berdiaev, and Sergei Bulgakov. So fertile were even his earliest contributions that his work was featured in Vasilii Zenkovsky's and Nikolai Lossky's late 1940s and the early 1950s histories of Russian philosophy, in which he was regarded as the latest representative of Russian Hegelianism and phenomenology.[35] Among his most important influences were also Plato, the subject of his first published article, "Eros in Plato" (1916), and Schelling, who had a significant impact on his theory of symbol and mythology. His philosophical work can be clearly divided into two major periods: the first dating from approximately 1916 to 1930, and the second from 1956 until his death in 1988.

During the first period, he published eight volumes (from 1927–30) developing a comprehensive project of "constructive dialectics," by which he endeavored both to

Figure 4.2 Aleksei Losev.

describe different modes of culture (such as music, language, and mythology) and to derive them logically from their eidetic origins. These volumes may be divided into two subgroups, one concerning general philosophical issues (*The Philosophy of the Name*, *The Dialectics of Artistic Form*, *Music as an Object of Logic*, and *The Dialectics of Myth*[36]), the other addressing the culture of antiquity (*Ancient Cosmos and Contemporary Science*, *Outlines of Ancient Symbolism and Mythology*, *The Dialectics of Number in Plotinus*, and *The Critique of Platonism in Aristotle*). In all of these texts, Losev proceeds from the concept of *eidos*, which he understands as a form directly posited in consciousness and substantialized in cultural creation. Methodologically, Losev owes much to Husserl, but finds Husserl's phenomenology too abstract, concerned predominantly with the procedures of perception rather than with the things perceived.

For Losev, *eidos* is the self-displaying integrity of an object, its "countenance" (*lik*), which is both visual and meaningful at the same time. This explains why his phenomenology so readily applies to cultural studies; instead of being inclined inward, toward mental processes, it points outward, to objects as they are shaped in culture. The first step of Losev's method is to elaborate the set of attributes distinguishing a given *eidos* from all others, then to synthesize the distinctions into a comprehensive, concise definition of the object. For instance, in his book *The Dialectics of Myth*, he undertakes to define myth by discussing what myth is not: myth is not fiction or fantasy, is not a scientific or metaphysical construction; it is not allegory or poetry, not religious dogma, and so on. After several negative examples, he finally posits a short assertive definition: "Myth is a wondrous personal history given in words."[37] The simplicity of this formula is deceptive; it represents the synthesis of an extensive analysis of myth's distinctive features. But even this definition can be further compressed: after several more analytic dissections, Losev arrives at the irreducible core: "Myth is the unfolded Magical Name."[38]

This definition is not surprising in light of another Losev work, *The Philosophy of the Name*, which represents his response to the ongoing Russian Orthodox preoccupation with names as modes of supreme revelation. Prior to the revolution, Orthodox theologians had been divided into two antagonistic factions; the first, called *imiaslavtsy* ("name-glorifiers"), held that, since the name of God is tantamount to God himself, the best means of spiritual ascension was the repetition of this sacred name. The second group accused the first of heresy, since the attribution of the divine to a mere word elides God's mystery and constitutes a form of idolatry. In this dispute, Losev prefers the side of the "name-glorifiers" and exhibits a deeply religious understanding of the divine nature of the name, but puts a dialectical spin on the theological controversy, proposing that, while the name of an entity is identical with this entity, the reverse is not true: the entity is not identical with its name. "a) The name of God is God's energy, indissoluble from the very essence of God and therefore is God Himself. b) However, God is different from his energies and his name, and therefore God is neither his name, nor any name in general."[39]

For Losev, it is the name that animates an entity, so that a world without names would be a collection of dead matter. Furthermore, Losev conceives of entities as mythic: "Every inanimate thing or phenomenon, if taken not as a purely abstract, isolated object, but as an object of living human experience, is necessarily a myth."[40] For example, in Losev's words, "the sun that shows itself in winter after a long procession of overcast days is not the same sun as that of astronomy, but has a cheering, exhilarating element that allows one to breathe more easily, to feel one's soul rejuvenated and one's potencies revived."[41] Thus, in dialectical terms, no object exists distinctly as an abstraction, but all objects have a mythic meaning that imbues them with human significance.

Losev's brand of dialectics left him at odds with the official Soviet philosophy of dialectical materialism. In *The Dialectics of Myth* (1930), he suggests a coherent refutation of dialectical materialism, which is astounding considering his intended audience in the USSR of that time. For Losev, materiality is an abstract concept that cannot be perceived by our senses, just as roundness cannot exist independently of round objects. "Materialism is an absolutization of an abstract concept, i.e., a typical abstract metaphysics.... From the standpoint of pure dialectics, one cannot absolutize the concept of matter as a privileged abstraction among so many others.... 'Dialectical materialism' is a scandalous absurdity, an utter mockery of all kinds of dialectics, and a most typical bourgeois abstract metaphysics."[42] Furthermore, dialectical materialism is also a mythology, or rather a dogma of some satanic religion. "Matter becomes an eyeless, black, dead, heavy monster which, despite its deadness, rules the entire world.... In this case, everything is governed by a corpse."[43] This is an example of Losev's method of interpreting philosophical and scientific ideas in terms of their mythic underpinnings. The "corpse" metaphor implicitly refers to the Lenin mausoleum in Red Square, which was the sacred center of Soviet civilization, and illustrates Losev's point regarding the quasi-religious nature of dialectical materialism. In its rejection of Christianity, this worldview nevertheless does not constitute a return to paganism—which, Losev argues, would be a celebration of the life-giving forces of nature—but is rather concerned only with the stark mechanics of matter.

Given the provocative tone of these works, it is not surprising that in 1930 Losev was exiled to a labor camp at the White Sea Canal (Belomorkanal), where he spent three years. Upon his return, he was permitted to resume his scholarly activities but was banned from publishing original works. Thus he remained silent for twenty-three years, returning to print only after Stalin's death. But the Losev of this later period was not the brash, defiant thinker of his youth; instead, his work now self-consciously conformed to Marxist-Leninist precepts. So concerned was he to qualify his original insights in the light of explicit loyalty to the dominant ideology that he often seemed to abandon his earlier phenomenological approach in favor of reductive readings of philosophy as the "mere" superstructure of an economic base—for instance, attributing the cultural productivity of the ancient world to the prevalence of slavery: "This inhuman economics produced remarkable examples of philosophy, art, and science.... This tragic dialectics of the general historical process can be understood and explained popularly in the present time only by Marxist-Leninist theory."[44]

But despite its doctrinaire shell, the true pith of Losev's later work was his further dialectical elaboration of the eidetic essences of culture, primarily of antiquity. His principal work of this period was *The History of Ancient Aesthetics* in eight volumes. Totaling approximately eight thousand pages, this work appeared between 1963 and 1991, proceeding sequentially from mythic prehistory through the late Hellenistic period, with major sections devoted to Plato, Aristotle, and Plotinus. The title of the work is narrower than its contents, insofar as, for Losev, "aesthetics" meant the eidetic essence of all Greek antiquity, and not—as it came to be understood in the eighteenth century (with the German philosopher Alexander Baumgarten)—a merely sensuous faculty inferior to reason and responsible for the perception of beauty. For example, in ancient cosmology, the universe was viewed as a work of architecture, which observed such rules of aesthetic harmony as the golden section. Ancient scientists compared the interaction of atoms with the dramatic plot in tragedy and comedy. "Rhythm, symmetry, and proportion are such popular philosophical categories of antiquity because the living, animated, and thinking human body did not set out for some limitless horizon, but found its principle in itself."[45] In Losev's view, the ancient emphasis on corporeal form derived in part from the practice of slavery, which imparted a sculptural intuition to all branches of culture.

A slave owner knew well each of his slaves by face and had only a negligible quantity of slaves. Proceeding from the physical immediateness of human potentials, which also created a primitive mode of production, an ancient Greek of the early classical period understood all things, the entire universe, as a well-organized, animated, and entirely sensuous substance; this cosmic organization led to the categories of harmony, symmetry, rhythm, and other purely corporeal categories.[46]

According to Losev, fate, too, is a concept that derives from slaveholding: the master/slave relationship is an analogue for that of fate/human being, which in turn corresponds to the relationship of the sculptor and his statue. Thus corporeality, as a self-sufficient and aesthetically perfect form, is the unifying *eidos* of ancient culture, accounting not only for specifically artistic modes of expression, but also for economic practices and philosophical and scientific speculations. Summarizing the overarching meaning of his masterwork, Losev writes: "It may be said that in antiquity, philosophy and aesthetics appeared to be the same thing.... [A]ncient aesthetics was nothing other than the teaching of the expressive forms of universal wholeness ... and from this point of view, the history of ancient aesthetics can be regarded as the history of ancient philosophy in its extreme totality."[47]

Losev's philosophical interests also led him to consider other historical periods, perhaps most provocatively in *The Aesthetics of the Renaissance*. The Renaissance was usually exalted in Soviet philosophy as an awakening from the dogmatic slumber of the theocentric Middle Ages into a revolutionary celebration of human immanence. Losev, however, highlights what he considers the negative aspects of Renaissance ideology, specifically its proclivity for titanism, which transgresses all moral boundaries in its glorification of human self-deification. The reader would have heard echoes with the ideology of the Russian Revolution, which claimed its struggle against tsarism and the Orthodox Church as kindred in spirit to the Renaissance rebellion against medieval superstition and clerical dominance. Friedrich Engels glorified the titanism of the Renaissance as leading to the full expression of human capacities, and viewed such figures as Leonardo da Vinci as prototypes of the new communist personality—true "Renaissance men" who would overcome the division of labor with their breadth of universal creativity. Mikhail Bakhtin also valorized the Renaissance sensibility, specifically the inclination toward the inversion of moral and social hierarchies, which he demonstrates in the carnivalistic aesthetic of François Rabelais. Bakhtin viewed the carnivalesque as enabling the reversal of values, the undermining of all sacred and hegemonic systems. Implicitly, then, Losev's critique of the Renaissance represents both a response to his philosophical predecessors and a challenge to the Soviet fascination with atheistic titanism. In Losev's terms, the practical application of such an ideology leads to the sanctioning of large-scale massacres for the sake of heroic self-aggrandizement, as the will of one giant trumps consideration of a multitude of "ordinary" people. Countering Bakhtin, Losev attacks the Rabelaisian wisdom as all-permissiveness, summed up in the motto of the Abbey of Theleme: "Do what you will."

Another principal interest of Losev was modern mythology and music, the brightest expression of which he found in Wagner and Skriabin. While in his discussions of ancient mythology, Losev focused on the Apollonian aspects of classical sculptural intuition, in his philosophy of music, he concentrates on the Dionysian elements underlying Wagner's *Ring* cycle and Skriabin's *The Poem of Ecstasy*. He equates philosophy with the music of thinking and identifies in the musical myths of Wagner and Skriabin the same spirit that girds the revolutionary destruction of Western civilization, as exemplified in Aleksandr Blok's call to the intelligentsia: "Listen to the music of Revolution." Having originally shared this enthusiasm, Losev had come to recognize, in the revolution's bacchanalian fervor, the same force that destroyed Orpheus; and he saw the best minds of Russian culture (including his own) likewise victimized, silenced and annihilated. To his last days, Losev remained an admirer of Wagner and Skriabin, but his attitude toward Dionysian elements in mythology and music grew increasingly negative.

Losev's overall philosophical project is directed toward criticizing abstract idealism and materialism in favor of a notion of the concrete embodiment of the idea. He blames modern European metaphysics for the idea's abstraction from the realm of visuality and corporeality. "Under the influence of modern European abstract metaphysics, it has been long since forgotten that the very word 'idea' is derived from the root *eidos*, meaning 'visual image' ... This essence of the thing seen by the intellect (or as the Greeks used to say, 'intelligible'), the internal and external countenance of the thing, is its idea."[48] Losev wants to return from the metaphysical separation between idea and matter to their primal unity; this is why he is critical even of the triadic dialectic often attributed to Hegel and adopted by Marx: *thesis, antithesis, synthesis*. In Losev's view, this type of dialectic misses the *fourth* stage, when the synthesized idea fuses with reality. Thus there are two stages of synthesis, one internal to the idea, the other incorporating it into material being; hence Losev's aspiration to establish dialectics as a *tetradic* rather than triadic process.

One of Losev's last books, *Vladimir Solovyov and His Time* (published posthumously in 1990), sums up his own philosophical career by paying homage to the founder of the Russian philosophical tradition, thus consummating the hundred-year cycle of its development. The conventional Marxist interpretation of Solovyov brands him as an idealist, but Losev argues that his work in fact constitutes a reconciliation of the ideal and the material, accomplished via his emphasis on Sophiology. According to the Christian theological tradition, as well as Gnostic teachings, Sophia is the feminine figure of divine wisdom; Vladimir Solovyov understands Sophia as the soul of the universe, which imparts spiritual depth to the material world and is revealed first of all in the love between a man and a woman. Losev interprets Solovyov's Sophiology from the perspective of his favorite philosophical conception, that of the reconciliation of pure idealism with pure materialism. "Sophia is the aspect of reality's depth who, by remaining an ideal being, is maximally addressed to the real and material.... Of all types of idealism that exist in the history of philosophy, Sophiological idealism is the most saturated with materiality."[49] Losev's characterization of Solovyov may also serve as the best explication of his own philosophical goals: "[T]he essence of the Sophiological idealism of Vladimir Solovyov consisted in critiquing the isolation of ideas, their hypostatization in abstract form."[50] Both Losev's critique of the triadic dialectic and his sympathetic analysis of Solovyov consistently aim at the reconciliation of the ideal and the material.

Losev was perhaps the most systematic philosopher of the Soviet epoch; as the last representative of the prerevolutionary religious and cultural heyday, he preserved the spirit of the Russian Silver Age initiated by Solovyov's visionary thinking. Characteristically, in his discussion of Solovyov, Losev underscores the pessimistic conclusion of the philosopher's life: Plato, according to Solovyov, had failed to see his idealism embodied in the historical progress of humanity, and, as Losev notes, the same was true of Solovyov himself. Just as the unification of philosophy and politics outlined in Plato's *Republic* proved unattainable, so too did Solovyov's vision for the unification of Eastern and Western Christianity under an ecumenical theocracy co-governed by the Russian tsar and Roman pope. The tragedy, however, lay not just in this failure, but in the recognition that success itself would have been disastrous for humanity, since, as Solovyov acknowledged in his last work, a unified state would have easily fallen under the sway of the Antichrist.

The broad picture of Losev's own philosophical career may be explicated in similarly tragic terms. Compelled to subscribe to the very version of materialist dialectics he had so fervently denied, and to abandon his religious commitments and devote his life to the study of an ancient philosophical tradition he found "impersonal" and insufficient for his own Christian vision, Losev never fully realized his creative potential. In a letter addressed to his wife from exile, he wrote: "How loathe I am to die! I'm standing like a sculptor in a studio filled with plans and models and materials, and containing not a single completely finished statue."[51] This was written in 1932; but even fifty years later, as the author of numerous philosophical volumes, he might have expressed the same sentiment, since the statues with which he had surrounded himself were all stylizations in their forced accommodation to the Soviet style of materialist scholasticism.

Losev's intellectual significance, however, remains enormous, comparable, among all his contemporaries, only with that of Bakhtin. These two together were the founders and brightest exponents of Soviet culturology as a synthetic poetics and aesthetics of culture. Though not as original as Bakhtin in his philosophical intuitions, Losev was far more prolific and multifaceted in his juxtaposition of various cultural layers and traditions. If Bakhtin emphasized the dialogue between different cultures, then Losev presented the eidetic unity of culture as expressed in diverse artistic and intellectual systems. Through the complexity of his dialectical distinctions, we see his aspiration to unify abstract categories into a primordial archetype, *eidos*, rooted in the basic intuition of a given culture. In this, Losev can be categorized as a follower of Oswald Spengler, with his vision of world cultures as structured into a system of distinctive gestalts. Upon reading Spengler in his youth, Losev commented on the omission of Christianity as a potentially unifying and continuous current between isolated cultures. Ironically, Losev himself would be forced to make the same omission, though not because he had overlooked it. Losev's philosophical contributions represent only a fragmented realization of his virtually encyclopedic mind.

The later Losev's strangely apologetic inclination toward Marxism, seemingly so inconsistent with his eidetic approach to culture, can nevertheless be explained on the basis of this very approach. Losev insisted on the integrity of the primordial *eidos*, which determines all aspects of the cultural whole, in particular the unity of its material and spiritual levels. In order to maintain the correspondence between a primordial *eidos* and its stylistic manifestations in his own time, Losev had to become a Marxist— not because he shared Marxist views, but because his eidetic philosophy obligated him to exemplify the *eidos* of his own epoch. Sergei Averintsev, himself a longtime disciple of Losev, points to this aesthetic rationale for Losev's Marxism:

> Losev's thought, precisely as thought, beyond all external circumstances, was obsessed with the imperative of rigid, inexorable unity; according to this law, the minutest features of the "integrative countenance" [*tselostnyi lik*] and "worldview style" [*mirovozzrencheskii stil'*] must be dialectically deduced from some initial principle, with the same measure of obligation and compulsoriness that is standard for Euclidian geometry.... The early Losev, with exceptional ardor, insisted that Platonism "dialectically requires" slavery, and Orthodox Christianity ... "dialectically requires" medieval types of social relationships.[52]

Paradoxically, this is the origin of the later Losev's Marxism: his non-Marxist, rather Platonic and Spenglerian theory of *eidos*. In other words, Losev was a Marxist out of allegiance not to Marx, but to himself. For him, it would be aesthetically unbearable to remain an "old-school" idealist or phenomenologist during the dictatorship of the proletariat. Losev had never been a liberal, and in one of his early writings he proclaimed that the Russian Revolution, with all its terror, was not only just but even insufficiently oppressive with regard to the loathsome bourgeois society of "petty and cold egoists." Thus he can be counted among those Russian intellectuals who philosophically justified their own extinction at the hands of the fresh forces of a new barbarism. Losev's tragedy was greater than that of one individual thinker caught in history's meat grinder; it was the tragedy of thought itself, which found itself compelled to a self-undermining complicity. Alongside such martyred Marxists as Bukharin or Trotsky, who fell victim to the very triumph of their theories, one can mention the tragedy of such non-Marxists as Losev, who had to suffer the intellectual catastrophe of rigorously conforming to the *eidos* of their epoch.

4. Culture, Myth, and Imagination. Olga Freidenberg and Iakov Golosovker

From the 1920s on, the field of the humanities in the Soviet Union was as preoccupied with the concept of myth as in the West, and for similar reasons. Such movements in art as Symbolism and surrealism, and such trends in philosophy and psychology as Nietzscheanism, psychoanalysis, and existentialism, were attracted to myth as a means of challenging outmoded European rationalism. In Russia, this opposition was manifested in the formation of a postrevolutionary, "new" society based on the values of collectivist consciousness, which inevitably revived mythological patterns of archaic societies. Though the abovementioned Western trends were condemned in the Soviet Union as bourgeois and irrationalist, the focus on folklore and myth was one of the predominant directions of early Soviet scholarship. Along with Losev, two other major theorists are well known for their significant contributions in the philosophical and philological exploration of myth.

Olga Freidenberg (1890–1955) is best remembered by general readers for her almost lifelong correspondence with her cousin Boris Pasternak. She was a leading scholar of classical philology, chairing the first department established in this field during the Soviet period, at Leningrad University (1932–50, with several breaks). In the 1920s and the 1930s, she was a follower of Nikolai Marr (1864–1934), the founder of Soviet Marxist linguistics, later severely criticized by Stalin for "vulgar sociologism." Freidenberg's interests extended far beyond philology; her project encompassed the whole nexus of literature, mythology, folklore, ritual, primitive thinking, language, religion, and theater. This range is typical for what would later come to be known as culturology.

Freidenberg sought to find unifying patterns of different cultural fields in "semantic complexes," which can be compared to Jungian archetypes but are devoid of any psychological implications. She argued against the theory of primitive syncretism developed by the prominent nineteenth-century Russian comparativist Aleksandr Veselovsky, who believed that literature, art, religion, and theater proceed from an initially undifferentiated ritual. In Freidenberg's view, these spheres are all united, but semantically rather than "genetically"; not through common origin, that is, but through overarching units of meaning—semantic complexes that are simultaneously manifested on the levels of language, myth, and religion. This conception can be related to Ernst Cassirer's theory of symbolic forms, though she developed it independently in the 1920s and the 1930s and presented it in 1936 in her well-known book *The Poetics of Plot and Genre (The Period of Ancient Literature)*, which became the target of harsh criticism and was removed from circulation. In her analysis, *eating*, *dying*, and *revival* constitute the three basic semantic complexes determining the variety of mythological plots, including the cycles of Jason and Oedipus.

Freidenberg formulates a "great law of semanticization," according to which semantics precedes the reality of the things it designates. For example, the Russian words *tsar'* and *rab* ("slave") existed before the corresponding phenomena of tsarism and slavery. This theory anticipates by half a century the post-structuralist theories that prioritize the signifier in its capacity to engender the possibility of the signified. For Freidenberg, the genre of literary discourse predetermines and even produces its message.

In her last book, *Image and Concept*, written in 1945–54 but published only in 1978, Freidenberg elaborates an epistemological analysis of ancient imagery, arguing that the concept, as the vehicle of philosophical and scientific thinking, developed historically from poetic metaphor. "[A]ncient abstract concepts, in spite of their novelty and restructurings of meanings, not only derived from concrete images, but even continued to preserve these images within themselves and to be supported by their semantics."[53] An image grows into a concept in proportion to its metaphorization, by which its figurative meaning is distanced from its initial literal meaning. For example, the concept of suffering derived from the specific image of childbirth and was referred to by the same designation of "labor pains."[54] Thus, conceptualization and metaphorization of the image are the same process, which progressively leads to the formation of philosophy and literature as distinct from history, which preserved the literal, factual meaning of the image. This explains the generation of various spheres of consciousness from the same combinations of words, and the equivalence of the semantics of all of them. Freidenberg's *The Poetics of Plot and Genre* was almost completely forgotten after her death, and it was only in the late 1970s, with the appearance of writings unpublished in her lifetime, that her legacy was evaluated as an original culturological contribution, made decades ahead of its time.

Another prominent representative of the Russian humanities who managed to survive despite the tremendous pressures of Stalin's epoch was Iakov Golosovker (1890–1967).

Many of his works were destroyed in two house fires, including a philosophical novel titled *The Indestructible Inscription*, which was later reconstructed from memory under the name *Burned Novel*.[55] The fire claimed other works as well, including a large

Figure 4.3 Iakov Golosovker.

treatise on Nietzsche and his mystery trilogy *A Great Romanticist*. Golosovker spent six years in the Gulag and internal exile (1936–42), and was only in a position to begin reconstructing some of his lost works in the 1950s.

Golosovker's areas of specialization were ancient Greece and Germany of the eighteenth and nineteenth centuries. What connects these topics is Golosovker's preoccupation with mythology, which he elaborates in his book *The Logic of Ancient Myth* (completed in the late 1940s, published in 1987). Like Freidenberg, Golosovker regards myth as the common denominator of various cultural fields and disciplines that came to be differentiated only over the course of historical evolution. However, his treatment of mythology is less linguistic and more philosophical than that of Freidenberg. Proceeding from the theories of myth developed in German idealism, and anticipating the structuralist theories of Lévi-Strauss, Golosovker explores myth not just as a poetic fantasy, but as a special kind of logic where the formal "law of the excluded middle" ("tertium non datur") does not apply. "Along with the structure of knowledge, there exists a structure of error and ignorance ... the structure of the miraculous."[56] Myth embraces a logic of the illogical. Thus in Greek myths, the immortal Scylla is killed by Heracles in spite of her immortality. Another law of mytho-logic is the coincidence of the ideal and the material. For example, since Athena is a goddess of wisdom, she must be born from the head of her father, Zeus.

These laws of mythology led Golosovker to outline a broader field of philosophical investigation, namely, a theory of imagination. Critical of narrow formulations of the imagination as the site of fantasy, with fantasy standing as merely the arbitrary combination of images, he posits imagination, to the contrary, as the highest cognitive faculty. Golosovker's major philosophical contribution is his treatise *The Imaginative Absolute*, though it too remains not quite complete, having been burned twice and twice reconstructed. In it, Golosovker defines his task as that of "constructing an imaginative epistemology such that the role of imagination in culture may be disclosed to the eyes of thinkers and touch the conscience of science."[57] Golosovker condemns the traditional neglect of imagination by scientists and philosophers, which has resulted in imagination's enforced confinement to the realm of the arts and elementary education. In Golosovker's view, imagination deals not only with concrete sensuous images but also with general ideas. Philosophers and scientists consistently employ imagination, albeit applying it to ideas rather than to images and pictures. "[T]he highest activity of imagination occurs in the realm of ideas."[58]

Thus Golosovker attempts to bring together two poles of culture, the mythic and the scientific. Demonstrating the presence of logic in myth, and that of imagination in science, he ultimately argues that culture itself, as a whole, is not opposed to nature, but grows from the most basic of natural human drives. Traditionally, culture is considered to override the instinctual, but for Golosovker it is only civilization— and especially technology—that is hostile to nature, while "the instinct of culture is innate and elaborated in humans."[59] Spirit and thought, according to this theory, are the highest instincts, which explains why humanity in its drive for cultural creativity and moral perfection can suppress other, lower instincts. Golosovker develops a conception of "spirit as the impulse toward symbolic immortality in all hypostases of its incarnation, as the stimulus to perfection, to eternity, to the ideal; that is, as the stimulus to culture."[60] Whereas Nietzsche attempted to glorify instinct as a higher morality, Golosovker glorifies morality as the highest instinct.

Along with Losev and Bakhtin, Golosovker can be considered one of the founders of Russian culturology. While Losev focuses on the primordial eidetic unity of culture, and Bakhtin on the dialogic interaction of cultures, Golosovker's theme is the instinctual foundations of culture and its imaginative potentials. Golosovker has much in common with Losev, especially with regard to the synthetic capacity of human consciousness, which Losev defines in phenomenological terms as *eidos*, and Golosovker conceptualizes with his own formulation of the "meaning-image" (*smysloobraz*). The principal difference between the two thinkers is that Losev's *eidos* is a preexisting, determinative model of culture (like Spengler's ur-phenomenon, or Jung's archetype), while Golosovker's "meaning-image" is the free creation of imagination and thus features a greater evolutionary capacity.

The last and most popular of Golosovker's works is a comparative philosophical analysis of Dostoevsky and Kant, which stands as an important interdisciplinary contribution to culturology. Golosovker reveals within *The Brothers Karamazov* an underlying structure of thesis and antithesis as presented by Kant in his *Critique of Pure Reason*. Kant formulates four antinomies that cannot be resolved rationally: (1) the world as limited in space and time versus the world as infinite therein; (2) the composition of all complex substance from simple parts, versus the fundamental absence of simplicity in the world; (3) the existence of, along with laws of nature, another kind of causality, grounded in freedom, versus the subjection of everything to the laws of nature; and (4) the belonging of an unconditionally necessary entity (God) to the essence of the world as its part or cause, versus the absence of any absolutely necessary entity, either in the world or beyond it. Golosovker sees these antinomies echoed in the mentalities of Dostoevsky's characters, Alesha and Ivan Karamazov, as well as in the elder Zosima and the Grand Inquisitor. The position of Dostoevsky himself is neither thesis nor antithesis, but rather the antinomical, irresolvable character of these contradictions. The devil asserts that if God exists, then it is necessary to assert that He doesn't; the Grand Inquisitor believes that if God does not exist, then it is necessary to assert that He does; Ivan maintains that both God and the devil are human inventions. This play of antinomies relates to a "hell of the mind" which is forever tormented by Kantian antinomies. Golosovker's book, published in 1963,[61] had a considerable impact on the post-Stalin intelligentsia as the first independent philosophical-critical investigation to appear since the ideological suppression of free philosophy in the late 1920s.

For Golosovker, philosophy's status as an art rather than a science rests on its pushing the imagination to the limits of all possible worlds. However, he considered himself a systematic philosopher, not an essayist or commentator. Systematic thinking was valuable to him inasmuch as he could enrich it with non-systematic elements.

> I resort not to the incessantly consistent development of the main thought, that is to say to its lengthening; but to a deepening of the thought, taking it from various

unexpected sides—from above and from below, and drilling into it and catching it in flight—developing it, exploding it, and penetrating into it—not just logically but also psychologically, and even affecting it in a poetical-imaginative way: exposing its meaning-image.[62]

In this approach, Golosovker was a typical romanticist, following Friedrich Schlegel's view that it is as fatal for the spirit to have a system as to have none.

Golosovker's version of culturology proved less complete than Bakhtin's or Losev's, in part because of the misfortunes befalling his corpus. The texts he reconstructed in his old age probably do not reflect the vitality of their original versions. However, Golosovker is not only an important representative of the interdisciplinary approach to culture, but also stands as a link between two seemingly incompatible epochs and methods of European thought, romanticism and structuralism. Like Schelling, he finds a revelation of absolute spirit in ancient mythology, and like Lévi-Strauss, he attempts to decipher the logic of ancient mythology as an instrument for the classification and mediation of "meaning-images." It was the specific historical conditions of Russia that preserved the romantic spirit of nineteenth-century German idealism and enabled its direct injection into the realm of new scholarly endeavors in the mid-twentieth century.

5. Philosophy and Philology. East and West. Dmitrii Likhachev and Nikolai Konrad

Bakhtin, Losev, and Golosovker represent the first generation of Soviet culturologists, born in the 1890s and coming to intellectual maturity in the 1920s and the 1930s. These were the founders of culturology, before it came to understand itself as a definitive discipline or methodology. The next generation is represented by two scholars whose most influential contributions to the humanities were made in the 1960s. Both Nikolai Konrad (1891–1970) and Dmitrii Likhachev (1906–1999) had brilliant academic careers and became full members of the Soviet Academy of Sciences, the former in the field of Far Eastern studies, the latter in old Russian culture. Their books published in the mid-1960s—*West and East* (1966) and *The Poetics of Old Russian Literature* (1967) respectively—represented the first applications of culturological methods to concrete periods and issues in literary history.

Konrad and Likhachev are not as openly philosophically oriented as the theorists of the previous generation; their method is more inductive than deductive, proceeding to cultural generalizations from analysis of specific literary and historical material. This second generation, which grew up within the confines of the Stalinist ideological framework, found it could avoid accusations of methodological deviation from Marxism-Leninism by concentrating on a narrow area of specialization. Both Konrad and Likhachev underwent arrest and imprisonment in the 1930s, but this did not hinder their subsequent academic success. Though each had already published works of specialized research prior to the Second World War, it was only in the more relaxed atmosphere of the 1960s, and by relying on their established professional reputations, that they were able to publish scholarly works whose importance transcended the boundaries of their disciplines and acquired general cultural resonance.

In his *Poetics of Old Russian Literature*, Likhachev was the first to analyze the literature of the eleventh to seventeenth centuries from a perspective other than historical, ideological, religious, or linguistic. His interest lies, instead, in its use of conventional poetic forms, clichés, and topoi as vehicles for cultural patterns of this epoch. Like Ernst Robert Curtius in his well-known investigations of medieval European tropes, Likhachev approaches literature as a manifestation of broader cultural configurations. He introduces the concept of "literary etiquette," the totality of socially and morally approved forms of writing in medieval Russia. "Besides in painting, etiquette can be discovered in the architecture and decorative art of the Middle Ages, in clothing and in theology, in the attitude to nature and in political life."[63] Likhachev decries the "realist" approach to old Russian literature, based on the conventional assumption of Soviet aesthetics that realism is the highest form of art, and that the goal of art is mimesis, the reflection of reality. For Likhachev, "[a]rt not only represents life, but also gives it the forms of etiquette.... The very object of discourse requires, for its representation, certain stereotypical formulas."[64] Etiquette is not identical to ethics; it does not pursue sublime spiritual goals but aims to normalize and formalize habitual behavior. In the same way, medieval literature should be analyzed not as the revelation of religious spirit or embodiment of ideological activity, and still less as a reflection of history but, instead, as the performance of a code of verbal behavior, a handbook of correct gestures and poses distinct from raw colloquial practice. Likhachev's culturological approach to literature was praised by Bakhtin and served as a model for Averintsev's later investigations in his *Poetics of Early Byzantine Literature*.

However, according to Likhachev, "etiquette" is only an earlier stage in the development of literature, which, with the Renaissance, becomes increasingly innovative and individualistic. The main measure of literature's evolution is the decrease of its conventionality, the loosening of taboos and canons, and its rapprochement with historical reality, on the one hand, and with authorial individuality on the other. In his remarkable article "The Future of Literature as an Object of Investigation" (1969), Likhachev attempts to delineate the various parameters of the development of world literature, among them: the growth of individual self-expression, the increasing freedom of artistic vision, the broadening of the reader's social milieu(x), the intensification of cross-cultural connections and influences among national literatures, and the more active role of critical reflection and self-reflection in literary creativity. More important than the mere summary of these factors is their interaction and complementarity. For example, literary works' increased originality calls for a more active role on the part of criticism, so that artistic idiosyncrasies can be socially communicated to the general public. Since all these factors continuously influenced the development of literature in the past, Likhachev assumes the possibility of predicting its future; this was probably the first experiment in Soviet cultural prognosis to be conducted independently from Marxist ideological projections of the desired communist future.

Likhachev's investigations of old Russian literature in the 1960s and the 1970s responded to a generally heightened interest in the historical roots of Russian society. This was the period in which the so-called "village prose," extolling the patriarchal values of the disappearing past, became a major trend in Soviet literature;[65] and in fact, Likhachev would long be regarded by conservative writers as a tacit nationalist. But his search for Russian spiritual identity had a much broader cultural perspective; he was keen, not so much to assert some Russian uniqueness, as to establish links between the Russian present and the Russian past, and between Russian and Western cultures. The "villagers," by contrast, opposed the "healthy peasant" to the "rotten *intelligent*," the natural life of the village to the alleged decadence of urban civilization.

Likhachev's major aspiration can be seen in such expressions as "cultural memory" and "the ecology of culture." "Ecology should not be reduced to the task of the preservation of nature and the biological environment. For the life of humans, no less important is the environment created by the culture of their ancestors and by themselves."[66] For Likhachev, there is no essential antagonism between nature and culture. He criticizes the traditional notion of "natural goodness" as opposed to "cultural evil," a dichotomy Russian thought had borrowed from Rousseau and assimilated through Lev Tolstoy as one of its basic assumptions. There was a strong tendency in both pre- and postrevolutionary Russia to condemn culture and intellect as the deterioration of the primordial integrity of human nature—a viewpoint that, in the Soviet period, justified a suspicious attitude on the part of the "toiling masses" and their "grass-root leaders" toward the "self-reflective" intelligentsia. Countering such attitudes, Likhachev emphasizes that "education and high intellectual development are precisely the natural states of a human being, while ignorance and a lack of intelligence are abnormal."[67] According to Likhachev, the human brain has enormous resources, and even the most "backward" people still have a potential reserve of "three Oxford Universities" in their minds. Therefore, natural health presupposes the full realization of the brain's capacity; ignorance is a kind of mental illness.

If it is natural for a human being to be cultural, then, in Likhachev's view, culture itself comprises the hidden essence of nature. "Nature has its own culture. Chaos is not natural ... on the contrary, chaos is an unnatural state of nature."[68] The cultural state of nature is manifest in the order of the celestial bodies, in the interdependent organization of plant communities, in the genetic code, and the code of animal behavior. The relationship between nature and humanity is thus the relationship of two cultures that have their own forms of etiquette; their encounter should be based on the rules of politeness and mutual respect. In Likhachev's view, human culture softens the sharp and "wild" features of nature, while nature restores the equilibrium disturbed by human labor and technology. "Both cultures seem to correct one another and create humaneness and freedom."[69]

Within human culture, a balance is also called for, most of all between the past, present, and future. Likhachev objects to the prevailing future-centric orientation of Soviet culture, which led to the elimination of cultural and religious traditions and pushed the entire nation into a kind of cultural nomadism. Among the human capacities, memory is the most vital for the integration of the past into the present, for the accumulation of values. Likhachev distinguishes the multidirectional flow of time in culture from the "civil-historical" dimension—wherein the orientation toward the future is justified by the unidirectional movement of time. "As distinct from the general movement of 'civil history' [*grazhdanskaia istoriia*], the history of culture is not only the process of change, but also the process of the preservation of the past, the discovery of the new in the old."[70] This means that cultural time has two vectors: "Not only does the culture of the past influence contemporary culture … , but also the present in its turn, to a certain degree, 'influences' the past…. The contemporary permanently enriches the past and allows us to penetrate into it more deeply."[71]

However, Likhachev condemns the egocentrism of the present, which prefers to see in the past only the "narcissistic" reflection of its own interests and demands. This egocentrism functions not only as a popular prejudice, but as a methodological position in the humanities: to interpret great works of the past in accordance with topical social or moral ideas. Ecology is the discipline that preserves nature from the aggression of collective human egocentrism, but culture needs the same kind of protection. On a practical level, this implies the preservation of historical and architectural monuments, and of ancient manuscripts; and also of contemporary monuments and manuscripts, which will become antiquity for posterity. This task was especially urgent in the Soviet Union due to the barbarous destruction of the treasures of the prerevolutionary epoch. The academician Likhachev thus became the founder and leader of the movement for the conservation and restoration of the cultural heritage.

> On the theoretical level, the ecology of culture means the ability to understand and interpret works of the past on their own terms. Penetrating into the aesthetic consciousness of other epochs and other nations, we must first of all study the distinctions among them and their distinction from our own aesthetic consciousness…. To approach old art, and that of other countries, only from the standpoint of contemporary aesthetic norms, to seek only what is close to ourselves, is to greatly impoverish our aesthetic heritage.[72]

Ecology in this sense is a cognitive principle establishing the self-sufficient value of the object of our knowledge. "Human consciousness has a remarkable capacity to enter into the consciousness of other people and to understand it in spite of all differences. Furthermore, consciousness comprehends also what is not consciousness, what is different [from consciousness] by its nature."[73]

Characteristic of Likhachev's method is the use of two "old-fashioned" concepts—*historicism* and *humanism*—that prove to be complementary. Historicism presupposes the adequacy of our knowledge to the specific conditions in which a given cultural work was conceived and created. Likhachev objects to a phenomenological interpretation of art, which "brackets" its historical origin and treats it as an atemporal configuration, directly given to our consciousness as here and now. Historicism means the capacity of the researcher to perceive the otherness of a cultural creation, its rootedness in another time and space. Humanism presupposes the unity and universality of human nature, the openness of one epoch to another, and the capacity of a researcher to find new meaning in old works of art. The humanities are not only a complex of disciplines, but also represent a moral factor in the development of humanity, equivalent to the commandment "Love thy neighbor as thyself." This principle helps to reduce the distance between countries, cultures, and epochs, since "the other," the object of study, proves to be as significant as the researcher's own system of values.

The methodology of the humanities is of special interest to Likhachev, who attempts to situate his position between traditional and structuralist methods. He recognizes the enormous potential of structuralism in the investigation of literary forms, but insists that "excessive rigor may prove to be an obstacle for the development of scholarship."[74] The point is that a work of art is essentially open to the most diverse interpretations and cannot be reduced to a mathematical algorithm or a logical calculation. The criteria of truth and rigor are different: in order to be truthful, literary scholarship must deviate from the ideal of rigor peculiar to the natural sciences.

Likhachev's project for the development of the humanities presupposes the restoration of philology as a discipline unifying the literary, linguistic, and historical investigation of texts. Philology literally means "love of the word," and since the word is the most universal manifestation of human consciousness, philology should be the central discipline of the humanities. Likhachev believes that the most productive tendency in the development of scholarly disciplines is not so much their differentiation as integration, the emergence of interdisciplinary methods. "The advancement of our knowledge about the world takes place precisely in the intervals between 'traditional sciences.'"[75] Under the pressure of differentiation, philology was divided into linguistics, literary criticism, literary theory, the study of historical sources, textology, philosophical hermeneutics, and so on. The further advancement of these disciplines requires a new stage of their integration. "Philology is the highest form of humanistic education, the form unifying all the humanities.... Understanding a text means understanding the entire life of the epoch underlying the text.... The word is connected with all forms of being.... It is clear, then, that philology lies at the foundation not only of scholarship, but of all human culture."[76] Likhachev views philology as a disciplinary synthesis analogous to culturology; philology covers the variety of the *verbal manifestations* of culture. "Philology brings together humanity, its contemporaneity and its past. It brings various human cultures together, not by erasing the differences between the cultures, but through consciousness of these differences."[77]

This recognition of the diversity of cultures, along with the emphasis on human unity, is characteristic of Likhachev's position, which may be identified as *methodological tolerance*. He is not as original and profound a thinker as Bakhtin or Losev, but, on the other hand, he is free of the sort of theoretical exaggerations and one-sidedness that so often accompany innovative thinking. What Likhachev introduced into the Russian humanities, traditionally obsessed with radical, far-reaching, often utopian ideas, was a tone of intellectual sobriety and self-restraint. Tolerance as a methodology is different from eclecticism, since it clearly delimits the applicability of a given method to a given field of study, instead of applying one method to all fields (monism) or applying many methods to one field (eclecticism). For Likhachev, the new synthesis of the humanities, whether we call it philology or culturology, can be achieved only through the restoration of their initial project: to treat humanity always as a goal and not as a means for technical knowledge or socioeconomic efficacy.

A similar humanistic outlook can be found in the works of the prominent orientalist Nikolai Konrad. His major book, *West and East* (1972), seeks to establish a new level of commonality between these two great cultural traditions. One of the thorniest obstacles to the comparative study of East and West had been the apparent absence of a Renaissance in Asian literatures. Konrad received international renown for his elaboration of the concept of Renaissance as a cultural and historical paradigm common both to West and East. As early as 1955, Konrad considered the question of the Renaissance in China and found striking parallels between Vasari's concept of *rinascita* and Han Yu's concept of *fugu*, which literally means "the return to antiquity." In the same way that the Italian, and later the European-wide Renaissance was oriented toward the culture of the ancient Greek city-states, China's "Renaissance" of the eighth–twelfth centuries focused on the restoration of the Confucian and pre-Confucian legacy of the city-states. Both Renaissances sharply critiqued their preceding epoch: the "dark" ages of medieval European Christianity and the third to seventh centuries in China, when Daoism and Buddhism were predominant, with their otherworldly orientation. In both cases, the Renaissance sought the restoration of humanistic values, which in Europe were associated with Greek philosophy and Roman jurisprudence, and, in China, with the ethical and legal philosophy of Confucius and his disciples. Han Yu, like Pico de Mirandola, asserted that the human being is the master of all that exists on the earth, and valorized the human universal capacity for love and compassion for all forms of being. The Chinese ideogram *ren*, "love for a human," which Han Yu found in Confucius and made the "motto" of the Chinese Renaissance, is close to the European concept of *humanitas* that such early Italian humanists as Salutati and Bruni derived from Cicero.

Certainly one could reproach Konrad for his extension of the Renaissance model to China, Japan, and other East Asian cultures on the grounds that his methodology amounts to little more than refined Eurocentrism. If the old-style Eurocentrism would not have recognized the applicability of such specifically European categories as the Renaissance to the "obscure and backward" cultures of the East, the new-style Eurocentrism, later famously criticized by Edward Said as "orientalism," attempts, on the contrary, to impose these categories on non-European cultures with an arrogance akin to that of imperialism. One cannot, however, assess the meaning of this gesture without considering the historical background. The decade before Konrad advanced his universalist theory of Renaissance was marked, in Russia, by Stalin's chauvinistic campaign against so-called cosmopolitanism. Comparative literature as a discipline went virtually extinct, as the very idea that one national culture could influence another would be condemned as "ideologically vicious." Konrad was one of the first Russian scholars to begin, immediately after Stalin's death, to promote comparative methodology in the Russian humanities. He revived the meaning of such terms as "world literature," "literary connections," "cultural mediation," and so on. He was anxious, however, not only to restore the discipline as it was established in the Western European tradition of scholarship, but to expand its boundaries both geographically and chronologically, in particular by the inclusion of East Asian literatures in the scope of comparative research. "Therefore, by extending the boundaries of the investigation of world literature of the seventeenth to nineteenth centuries to encompass the whole cultural world of that time, we can overcome the spatial limitation of Western European comparative literary scholarship."[78]

For Konrad, the concept of the Renaissance served not to assert the hegemony of European culture, but rather to overcome the limits of Eurocentrism and to elaborate a universal language for the mutual understanding of West and East. When Eastern terms seemed most suitable to designate certain cultural universals, Konrad did not hesitate to apply them to Europe. For example, he uses an old Japanese term to designate the complex of the humanities before it divided into separate disciplines: philosophy, history, sociology, and so forth. In his letter to the Japanese publisher of *West and East*, he writes:

> In our time, along with the continuing and even increasing differentiation of knowledge, the deep connection of all sciences about man and society is revealed in all its vitality, and the need for one general term is felt. In Japanese, *dzimmon-kagaku*, in my view, is very suitable for this.... In any case, now, as to the question of which field of scholarship I work in, I will answer: in *dzimmon-kagaku*![79]

Significantly, Konrad here arrives at the same necessity of studying humanity as a whole that Likhachev expresses in his concept of philology; but the Japanese term, which includes the ideogram "human," proves to be even more adequate to the range and task of this comprehensive knowledge.

Konrad's preoccupation with universal human values led him to write his most philosophically charged essay, "On the Meaning of History" (1972), in which he argues that the concept of progress remains crucial to any meaningful interpretation of human history as a whole. In all countries, despite significant national variations, the basic events and upheavals of history—the downfall of slavery, the creation of universal religious and ethical systems, the establishment of private ownership, and so on—have occurred in a similar order of progression. "[T]he history of humanity is precisely the history of all of humanity, and not of separate, isolated nations and countries."[80] The question, however, is what to consider the criterion of this notion of progress. Konrad believes it cannot be reduced to the measurement of technological or social advancements that are compatible with the moral degradation of humanity. The concept of progress will be realized when "it is discovered how to unite the development of history with the movement of ethical categories generated by thought."[81]

Konrad and Likhachev represent the type of the second-generation Soviet scholar who exemplifies the traditional figure of humanist and philologist. The first and third generations of Soviet culturologists deviate from this balanced and tolerant mode of intellectual productivity. The first generation was caught up in the ideological storms of the early revolutionary epoch, whereas the third generation was already approaching the decay and destruction of the Soviet social system. The most outstanding representatives of this latter generation, Vladimir Bibler, Sergei Averintsev, and Georgii

Gachev, were born after the revolution and reached the peak of their creativity in the 1970s and the 1980s. Overall, they are more theoretically innovative, more selective in their philosophical predilections, and more oriented toward metaphysical or religious values ranging beyond the straightforward criterion of "humaneness."

6. Dialogical Logic in the Interaction of Philosophies and Cultures. Vladimir Bibler

Vladimir Solomonovich Bibler (1918–2000) was a prominent philosopher of culture and intellectual history. Trained as a historian, he was by vocation a philosopher, founding in particular the "dialogue of cultures" school of thought that would attract many followers from various humanistic disciplines. He worked at the department of philosophy of the Moscow Mining Institute (1959–63), the Institute of the History of Natural Science and Technology of the USSR Academy of Sciences (1963–8), the

Figure 4.4 Vladimir Bibler.

Institute of General History of the USSR Academy of Sciences (1968–80), the Institute of General and Pedagogical Psychology of the Academy of Pedagogical Sciences of the USSR (1980–91), and the Russian State University for the Humanities (1991–2000).

It was during regular seminars held at his Moscow apartment that Bibler gave expression to his most creative and seminal ideas. Having founded the seminar in the mid-1960s, he conducted it under unofficial (underground) conditions until 1991, when it achieved formal status, under the name "Arche," at the Russian State University for the Humanities (Moscow). The meetings attracted a number of prominent scholars in Moscow, among them Aron Gurevich, Vadim Rabinovich, Leonid Batkin, and Anatolii Akhutin, whose own work in cultural studies and in the history of science echoed some of Bibler's methodological insights. Prior to the collapse of the Soviet Union in 1991, Bibler published only two short books (including *Thinking as Creativity*, 1975), and his influence spread primarily through oral presentations and discussions.

Culture and Cultures

Bibler considered himself an intellectual disciple of Mikhail Bakhtin, to whom he devoted a monograph entitled *Mikhail Bakhtin, or The Poetics of Culture* (1991). This term, "the poetics of culture," is how Bibler defines Bakhtin's philosophical contribution, as distinct from the narrower applications of the word "poetics," which is usually limited to one author, work, or literary movement (e.g., "Shakespeare's poetics" or the "poetics of Symbolism"). According to Bibler, Bakhtin's achievement was to have applied poetics to culture as a whole, as the latter can be understood only dialogically. For his part, Bibler proposes taking the next step: from poetics to logic, or, more precisely, to the *dia-logic* of culture. "Thus, the first definition (interpretation) of culture: culture is a specific form of communication and simultaneous existence of the people of past, present, and future cultures (this is not 'circular' logic but the genuine meaning of the definition)."[82] Here, Bibler seems to fall into a vicious circle by defining culture in terms of multiple cultures, but for him this circular definition is not just suitable but the only one possible. Culture is an all-encompassing phenomenon, one that can be understood only from itself. Unlike such particular aspects of cultural activity as literature or science, culture cannot be defined via comparison to something that is not culture. Hence it must be characterized and derived from within, by means of internal differentiation and the communication of cultures through dialogue.

This "self-determination" of culture is the fundamental paradox upon which Bibler focuses his thinking. He finds a parallel to this paradox in the mathematician Georg Cantor's set theory. The paradox reads as follows: the set of all sets is, and at the same time is not, a member of its own class. In Bibler's terms, the same paradox of self-inclusion and self-exclusion applies to the definition of culture, a phenomenon that is composed of all cultures and is at the same time culture itself, and must be accounted for as a set that contains itself as a member.

Thus Bibler advances the concept of "a work of culture," an effort that cannot be identified with a particular species of culture since it is represents a dialogue among cultural disciplines. Nietzsche's *Thus Spake Zarathustra*, Spengler's *The Decline of the*

West, the writings of Freud and the novels of Thomas Mann, would all be examples of works of culture, not just of philosophy, history, psychology, or fiction. As cultural microcosms, they embrace the entirety of culture, but at the same time, they exist within the frameworks of specific disciplines (psychology, literature, etc.).

Arche

One of the central categories in Bibler's philosophy is the Greek *arche*, meaning "beginning," "foundation," "origin," and "first principle." Philosophers have generally found it problematic to define a concept on the basis of the concept itself; this issue arises when, for example, in tracing any phenomenon to its source, one is obliged in turn to trace the source of the source, and so on. One solution has been to impose a limit to the investigation by positing some foundation with absolute priority, such as Platonic ideas, the Thomist God, or the Cartesian *cogito*. This brings to the fore the issue of self-determination, which is central to Bibler's philosophy of *arche* and paradox. The *arche* must justify itself as both self-determining and self-determined. Bibler calls the logic of self-determination "dia-logic," since it presupposes an inner dialogue within what is considered to be an *arche*, an absolute beginning. The principle of all principles cannot be posited except as a dialogue between principles. Thus the Cartesian formula, *Cogito ergo sum*, raises the question, what kind of *ergo* precedes the *cogito*? That is to say, if existence is substantiated by the fact of thinking, what fact substantiates thinking itself? Bibler's answer would be, *Cogito ergo cogito*, which means that thinking may be substantiated by thinking itself, but only insofar as it is initiated as a *self-dialogue*, a dialogue *between thinking and thinking.*

Certain parallels can be drawn between Bibler's concept of the self-determination of *arche* through self-dialogue and Derrida's notion of the *arche* as an "always already." Derridean post-structuralism famously rejects any concept of an original or absolute beginning, on the grounds that the very proposition of beginning is a paradoxical, backward projection. Thus, Derrida attempts to eliminate the metaphysics of origins—but at the price of establishing another metaphysics, one that privileges the "trace," the secondariness of the sign. Bibler's concept avoids the trap of metaphysics by resorting to the dia-logic relationship between the self-determining and self-determined aspects of the beginning.

Thus, Bibler defines the initial or primary *cogito* as the dialogue between *cogito*es. The implications of such a conception go beyond the limits of logic. For example, Thomas Aquinas's treatment of the ontological argument ends up presupposing an Ultimate Reason that cannot be deduced from anything prior to itself. Atheists counter that such a limitation is arbitrary; if God created the universe, then who or what created God? For Bibler, neither approach adequately solves the problem. Instead of an arbitrary limitation or an unending progression, Bibler offers the concept of a self-foundation that involves dialogue. If the Word, as the Gospel of John suggests, was in the beginning, and the beginning was God, then the Word must have been dialogic in order to posit a world beyond itself.

Dia-logic

Dia-logic is a mode of thinking that operates by what Bibler calls "transduction" (*transduktsiia*), as distinct from either logical deduction or induction. "The logical foundation (and the analogue) of the idea of self-determination is the requisite *transformation of the logical principles* of our thinking ... Conventionally, this logical transformation and mutual substantiation of the principles of thinking we define as 'transduction'."[83] If deduction is reasoning from the general to the particular, and induction the drawing of a general conclusion from a number of known facts, then transduction is the interaction between different or alternative modes of generality. Thus, various philosophers postulate different ontological principles, like the Leibnizean "monad," the Fichtean "I," the Hegelian "absolute spirit," or the Nietzschean "will to power," generalizing about particular facts and then applying these general principles to a variety of specific phenomena. However, alongside these inductive and deductive operations, the *transductive* method should be deployed so as to correlate all such general principles through their dialogic relationships. By transduction, then, the Marxist "mode of production" and Nietzschean "will to power" would be understood as two voices in a philosophical dialogue extending over centuries. Transduction is not the logical relationship of the general to the particular, insofar as both these categories are contained within a single consciousness. Whereas induction and deduction are, alike, acts of objectification, the multitude of different consciousnesses, being dialogically equal, cannot generalize about one another. Bibler writes:

> Each Interlocutor, be it Plato in his *Parmenides*, or Aristotle in his *Metaphysics*, or Spinoza in his *Ethics*, etc., is absolutely irreducible, unsurpassable, capable of an infinite unfolding and deepening of his argumentation (or substantiation of his beginning)—in response to the objections, actual and possible, of all past and future philosophers. And the more interlocutors there are, the less the infinitely potential world is reducible to a single definite logic.[84]

For Bibler, the philosopher's task is nothing less than to venture a new foundation for thinking. Doing this means entering into dialogue with all existing systems of thought.

> Any philosopher begins his being of the world "anew" [*nachinaet svoe bytie mira 'zanovo'*], next to another philosopher, in response to him, and, at the same time, as if completely independently of him. As many philosophers as there are—of course, in the genuine and not in the "academic" sense of the word—there are just as many "beginnings of existence," beginnings of thinking, and just as many times the world "begins for the first time."[85]

Being and Thinking

This multiplicity of logics concerns not only the relationship between various systems of thought, but also the relationship between thinking and non-thinking (being), and between culture and non-culture (nature). The dialogue as the beginning of all beginnings, believes Bibler, makes it possible to explain how thinking posits the beginning of being and being posits the beginning of thinking, since dialogue is always addressing the other and thus evokes the coexistence of plural foundational elements. Being and thinking are mutually enabled through their dialogic orientation toward each other. "[B]eing *is* (?) *the pre-supposition of thought* (i.e., *non-*thought) ..., thinking *is* (?) *the pre-supposition of being*, that is *non-*being. Here is contained the paradoxicality of contemporary ontology."[86]

Bibler aims to explain why science or philosophy can function as cultural phenomena that are irreducible to their narrow professional domains. Inasmuch as science is concerned with the exploration of the objective world and approaches it monologically, in terms of deduction and induction, it remains science per se. However, a science that considers itself a dynamic interrelation among various cognitive minds and models, as a dialogue of consciousnesses, becomes relevant as a domain of culture. In some of his works, Bibler applies this culturological approach to such towering scientists as Galileo or Kepler, whose ideas exceed a monological relationship to the world of nature and engage in the process of self-determination through dialogue with other logics.

The Logic of Paradox and Culturology

Bibler's philosophy was instrumental in the formation of the Moscow culturological school that applies dialogic principles to the natural sciences and to philosophical and pedagogical systems. Bibler never formalizes his ideas in terms of formal logic or structural semiotics, which sets him apart from Iurii Lotman and structuralism. At the same time, his analyses are more abstract and methodologically self-conscious than Bakhtin's. It is sometimes difficult to find concrete examples to support or refute his ideas, as his work is meta-philosophical, rather than addressed to specific cultural phenomena.

Bibler defines his own contribution to culturology as complementary to that of Bakhtin: in addition to dialogic poetics, he elaborates dialogical logic, which deals not with the voices of fictional characters but with systems of thinking. The logical principles embedded in the foundation of great philosophical systems and substantiating them— these themselves require substantiation. How can Plato justify his notion of idea, Aristotle his principle of form, and Descartes his concept of rationality? Either we admit the tautological nature of these self-justifying principles, in which case our logical thinking experiences paralysis; or, we identify some new logic that might determine the interaction and interrelationship between these principles. According to Bibler's dia-logic, primary principles can be substantiated, not from themselves (which would be tautological), but from their dialogue with other principles.

Here we encounter a logical paradox: the principle that determines the relationships among other principles is at the same time one of these principles; or the whole is one of its own parts. This paradox, decisive for Bibler's thought, can be explained again by set theory, according to which "[t]he set of all sets that are not their own elements, cannot be its own element and cannot not be. *It generates itself as its own element and thereby generates itself as a set which cannot be its own element.*"[87] If the principle of dialogue is a set that contains all other sets that do not contain themselves, this means that it can and cannot contain the principle of dialogue as one of its elements. To put this another way, the culturologist is a representative of one specific culture, a participant in its dialogue with other cultures, and at the same time is the intellectual vehicle—"the set of all sets"—through which all these cultures come to mutual recognition and interaction. In this case, what would this culturologist's relationship to his or her own cultural identity be? This is the sphere of questioning in which Bibler posits his logic of paradox as a rupture in traditional logic. The culturologist simultaneously is and is not a member of any specific culture, even that to which they belong by birth and education.

> The twentieth century demonstrated the necessity for the communication (and not Hegelian *Aufhebung*) of unique, irreducible, but mutually dialogic cultures, each of which is universal and infinitely rich with potential meanings: the cultures of antiquity, the Middle Ages, modernity, the contemporary world, and of the West and East. What is necessary is the logic of thinking, insofar as the logic of communication among such historical cultures, including potential cultures, has not yet been realized.[88]

Furthermore, Bibler extends this dia-logic beyond culture itself to address the relationship of the dia-logic to non-culture. "Culture is not only where there are at minimum two cultures: *culture is more than itself through 'pre-cultural, raw being'*."[89] In the same way, thinking can be defined only in its relationship to the unthinkable. The paradox is that "one has to reproduce, invent this unthinkable (impossible for thinking), extra-conceptual being as *extra-logical—precisely through the logic of thinking*."[90] If thinking completely absorbs and assimilates its object, it becomes tautological. Such is the deficiency of Hegel's absolute idealism, which is unable to establish the being of the object as radically distinct from thinking and thus replaces this object with thinking itself, rendering the entire historical process as the progressive self-consciousness of the absolute idea. Bibler criticizes Hegel for his monological mode of thinking; rather than positing the "beginning," the initial concept, as returning to itself at a higher level of self-awareness, would it not be more appropriate to acknowledge the plurality of beginnings? One can conclude that Marx's reversal of Hegel is equally averse to the dia-logic model, since thinking proves to be only an instrument for the self-development of the material world, just as the world proves, for Hegel, an instrument for the self-development of thinking. Only by recognizing that neither thinking nor being are reducible to each other, can we establish a truly dia-logic relationship between them.

Dialogism in Bibler and Bakhtin

Bibler's important contribution to culturology consists in his logical and philosophical explication of the problems that Bakhtin analyzed—primarily in the sphere of aesthetics, poetics, and linguistics. As compared to Bakhtin, Bibler puts a greater emphasis on the dialogue between logical principles and cultural systems, rather than between personal consciousnesses. It is for this reason that he uses concepts and terms like "paradox," "self-substantiation," "set of sets," and "the origin of thinking," which do not necessarily involve verbal dialogue, but can be related to a single theoretical consciousness. His project, however, is to demonstrate the dialogic nature of such logical categories as are conventionally deployed with no mention of the concept of dialogue whatsoever. In other words, Bibler's ultimate purpose may be formulated in two complementary ways: he attempts to conceptualize dialogue in logical terms; and to interpret logical concepts dialogically. His project is to "bakhtinize" Hegel and "hegelize" Bakhtin, a unique accomplishment in the history of contemporary thought.

Another clear distinction between Bibler's and Bakhtin's varieties of dialogism is the former's focus on the phenomenon of self-consciousness. If Bakhtin presupposes the necessity of an actual other, external to me, Bibler emphasizes the presence of this other *within myself*. In the act of self-consciousness, I am the other for myself. This once more introduces a Hegelian dimension into Bibler's theory, though he insists on the dialogic relationship of oneself to oneself (as one's own other), which is different from the Hegelian model of self-consciousness. However, having done away with Bakthin's requirement that the other actually be another, Bibler shows a tendency to slip out of the dialogic model into a model of self-reflection as an expanding self–dialogue of me with Thou within my own self–consciouness. "The very definition of personality as the self-conscious *I*, to whom I relate, who is outside of me, who is whole and finished for me—this definition includes the definition of another *I*, of Thou, a Thou whose existence is coexistent with me, comprises what is more essential for me than my own being."[91]

Ethics and Pedagogy

This paradox of self-reflection, which posits the *I* as both "self" and "other" in the same act of reflection, can be further displayed on the level of ethical paradoxes. For example, the most elementary moral commandment, "Thou shalt not kill," contains a paradox that prevents it from being fully implemented. In a case, that is, in which one cannot prevent a killing except *by* killing, the situation has no satisfactory moral resolution. "However I act, my conscience will condemn me."[92] To commit a killing myself or to allow the murder of another is equally transgressive, though we cannot escape the dilemma of making a choice. The paradox of morality demonstrates the impossibility of morality as such—of some "pure" morality clearly distinct from immorality. Morality in relation to oneself proves to be immorality toward the other. Since "self" and "other" comprise a self-reflective unity, one can conclude that morality consists in a permanent dialogue with immorality, in the same way that repentance presupposes an ongoing dialogue with one's sins.

Many of Bibler's ideas did not develop into completed books and articles, but were collected posthumously in two volumes titled *Conceptions* (2002). Bibler, like Bakhtin, appreciated the genres of "draft" and "outline" as valuable in themselves; they contained openness and invited a reader to co-thinking.

An important monument to the legacy of Bibler is the periodical collection *Arkhe*, the proceedings of the "cultural-logical [*kul'turno-logicheskii*] seminar" of the same name. The seven volumes published from 1993 to the present include rich materials developing Bibler's and his disciples' methodology and the ideas of other Russian thinkers close to his circle, such as Lidiia Ginzburg and Vladimir Bibikhin.[93]

Another form of practical dialogism for Bibler was the educational process. The bulk of his later activity was devoted to "The School of the Dialogue of Cultures," which he founded as a pedagogical extension of his philosophy. Many gifted educators from various regions of Russia participated in the programming and teaching of courses that spanned from elementary to advanced levels. Bibler proposed a curriculum by which children begin to study the logic of antiquity and then medieval logic, moving up to the logic of the Enlightenment: thus, individual development incorporates the history of human reason in its multiplicity of logics and cultures.[94]

7. The Philosophy of Culture and Christianity. Problems of Hermeneutics. Sergei Averintsev

Sergei Sergeevich Averintsev (1937–2004) was an outstanding Russian cultural scholar who made essential contributions to many fields of the humanities, including philology, philosophy, theology, literary studies, and intellectual history. From 1971–91, he was a senior researcher at the Gorky Institute of World Literature of the USSR Academy of Sciences, and from 1981–91, he was head of the institute's Department of the History

Figure 4.5 Sergei Averintsev.

of Ancient Literature. From 1989–91, he served as a people's deputy of the USSR and drafted a law on the freedom of conscience. From 1989–94, he was a professor in the History and Theory of World Culture section of the Philosophy Department of Moscow State University; from 1992–2004, he headed the Department of Christian Culture of this university's Institute of World Culture. From 1994 to the end of his life, he was a professor at the Institute of Slavic Studies of the University of Vienna.

Averintsev was a man of encyclopedic erudition that encompassed Greek and Roman antiquity, the Old and New Testaments, the Middle East, Byzantium, the European Middle Ages, nineteenth-century Russian literature and philosophy, the Russian Silver Age, and twentieth-century Western literature, religious thought, and intellectual history. He was a philosopher in the deepest sense, a seeker, and lover of wisdom. A scholar with a talent for broad and original reasoning, he had a firm grounding in the humanistic and religious foundations of Russian and European culture. His approach constituted a challenge to totalistic thinking of any kind, whether of the communist or nationalist, religio-fundamentalist or technocratic-pragmatist varieties. His credo comprised a unity of faith, reason, and freedom, and in this regard he might have repeated after St. Augustine: "Believe in God and do what you want."

Averintsev was born in 1937—in a time, that is, by which Stalin had hoped to successfully carry out the aim of annihilating religion in the USSR. Tens of thousands of priests had been arrested and tens of thousands of churches destroyed or turned into warehouses. Averintsev did more than any other Russian intellectual to restore his contemporaries' connection with the spirituality of the past, thus opening the way to the spirituality of the future. Beginning in the late 1960s, with the publication of his articles in the five-volume *Philosophical Encyclopedia* and the journal *Voprosy literatury* (Questions of Literature), and then with his book *The Poetics of Early Byzantine Literature* (1977), Averintsev established himself as a *vlastitel' dum*—a "ruler of minds" of the Russian intelligentsia. In the minds of many intellectuals, he reversed the standing relationship between politics and culture. Under the Soviet regime, that is, culture was conceived as a tool of politics; whereas for Averintsev, politics was but a small segment of culture, inscribed within larger and spiritually deeper segments, such as literature and language, philosophy and theology. He can be considered, along with Mikhail Bakhtin and Aleksei Losev, a founder of Soviet and post-Soviet culturology—of an integrative, multidisciplinary approach to culture.

Given the remarkable breadth of his professional erudition, Averintsev made a brilliant philosophical commentator, one who rendered the material of his inquiries with such clarity that it is difficult to separate his own thought from his analyses of the works of others. The reader of his texts gets the impression that the mentalities of distant cultures begin to articulate themselves, with Averintsev merely playing the role of mediator. This poses certain difficulties as far as the exposition of his own views is concerned.[95]

Hermeneutics

The principal problem of culturology, as formulated by Averintsev, is the hermeneutic circle that arises between investigators and their subject matter. A scholar may pretend to be able to bracket his or her own cultural preconceptions for the purpose of complete immersion in another culture, but such a claim, in Averintsev's view, is self-deceptive. "We regard the illusion of all-inclusive understanding as a lethal threat for humanistic thought, which is always an understanding 'across the barriers' of non-understanding. In order to feel authentically even the closest subject, it is necessary to confront it and to experience the resistance of its impenetrability; only emptiness is completely penetrable."[96] This is the first precondition of humanistic knowledge: to recognize the otherness of the culture under consideration. A scholar inclined to study, for example, medieval aesthetics finds him- or herself in a paradoxical situation, insofar as the very concept of aesthetics did not even emerge until the eighteenth century. Thus, medieval authors cannot be made to conform to our own understanding of aesthetics as a separate discipline. The researcher of medieval aesthetics as aesthetics implicitly presupposes that "the thinkers of the past, instead of working on their own problems, were busy exclusively with the preparatory work on our problems as we now understand them."[97]

However, even in recognizing this paradox, it is impossible to eliminate one's contemporary conceptual framework, which means that the scholar must identify those modes of medieval sensitivity that correspond to our concept of the aesthetical. In other words, they must neither identify themselves with the subject of their study, nor estrange themselves from it. Authentic interpretation is a dialogic interpenetration of the two cultural perspectives. For example, the predicate of being means two different things for a modern philosopher, for instance Kant, and an early medieval thinker like St. Augustine. For Kant, being is not a real predicate; it adds nothing to the concept of a given thing, but serves only to attach attributes to it; it is only a linking element in a logical proposition. For Augustine, being is a real quality, comprising the thing's most important aspect. "Everything that is, participates in the good to the degree that it is."[98] Being as such becomes a good in itself, a measure of all possible perfection, and thus for medieval consciousness, being was an aesthetic rather than purely a logical or ontological category. In modern philosophy, ontology is occupied with being while aesthetics is occupied with beauty, and there is no essential intersection between them. But for the thinkers of the Middle Ages, it was the other way around: being was an aesthetic issue, beauty an ontological one. According to Averintsev, "technically, Anselm does not 'prove' anything, but proposes to closely examine the concept of being and, having found that being is the most important of all perfections, concludes that the concept of the utmost perfection greater than which one cannot conceive (i.e., God), by definition includes this perfection [of being]."[99] Another theological argument, that of the so-called "unmoved mover," can also be understood in aesthetic rather than logical terms. The succession of causes proceeding one from another must ultimately be derived from a cause that has no prior cause, or is its own cause, thus arriving at an aesthetic whole instead of the vague, irrational concept of infinity.

Cultural Forms and Their Multileveled Intersections

Averintsev assumes that culture has its own logic, one that operates independently of human intention and may even contradict it. For example, the fourth-century Roman emperor Julian the Apostate, in attempting to ban Christianity in favor of a return to paganism, actually conformed to his epoch's cultural logic, which demanded that an emperor be the defender of the true faith. The fact that Julian's theology was pagan rather than Christian was, in Averintsev's view, less significant than his conformity to the dominant paradigm of Byzantine civilization, which cast the emperor as a theologian duty-bound to instruct his subjects in matters of religion. Averintsev is interested in the interplay of meanings between the subjective intentions of historical figures and the objective consequences of their accomplishments. This tenet has nothing to do with the socioeconomic determinism of the Marxist approach to the humanities, but is reminiscent, rather, of Oswald Spengler's notion of the morphology of culture, later echoed in the works of Aleksei Losev. According to Averintsev, "[t]he main task Spengler set himself was to grasp the primary phenomenon, the internal forms of each of the eight cultures he inventoried, and then deduce eidetically from this primary phenomenon absolutely everything: the forms of politics and the types of eroticism, the juridical and the musical, mathematics and lyricism."[100] Averintsev also uses the Spenglerian method of transdisciplinary analysis among different aspects of culture, finding connections between, for example, the political ideology of the Byzantine Empire, the theory of symbol in Pseudo-Dionysius the Areopagite, and the creative use of metaphor by Byzantine poets.

Despite certain affinities, however, Averintsev argues against those aspects of Spengler's approach to culture that seem to simplify and vulgarize the eidetic mode of description. In his view, Spengler neglects to assess distinctions among levels and aspects of culture, reducing everything to a single dominant theme. Averintsev's own methodology attempts to preserve the specificity of each cultural category, not mixing philosophy and poetics or ideology and mathematics.

> One should look for the connection between different levels while keeping in mind that these levels remain different; their connection should be presented neither as a rigorous mechanical link nor as a kind of magical engagement. I assure the reader that even in a bad dream I would not imagine that metaphors or acrostics are an expression of the psycho-ideology of certain layers of early Byzantine society or the materialization of some abstract categories of philosophical or theological doctrine. A metaphor is first of all a metaphor, an acrostic is an acrostic; a literary scholar ceases to be a scholar if tautologies of this sort are not dear to him.[101]

This observance of common sense and suspicion of overgeneralization are characteristic of Averintsev's refined and balanced intellectual style.

Another objection raised to the Spenglerian approach is its reliance on static and discrete cultural forms, like the "Apollonian" or "Faustian," which, in Averintsev's view, fail to account for transitional and synthetic cultural modes. Averintsev argues that culture is always in the process of transition. It is not by chance that his methodological principles are derived from an analysis of Byzantine culture, which exemplified a transition from classical antiquity to the civilization of Christian Europe and also an interaction between Eastern and Western cultural models. One could never define

Byzantine culture according to Spengler's categories because it encompasses and blends elements of several types that he classified as incompatible, such as "Apollonian," "Magical," and "Semitic."

Averintsev is adept at locating multidimensional links among cultural phenomena, rather than reducing all phenomena to a single concept or proto-phenomenon. He elaborated a technique of what might be called culturological "allusion," whereby he places a phenomenon in relation to several (temporal and spatial) layers of cultural associations, without insisting that any of these be mandatory or privileged. Averintsev attempts to extend the sphere of possible associations rather than narrow it to one general principle. For example, in his characterization of early medieval verse, which revives the devices of Alexandrian "learned" poetry, Averintsev cites T. S. Eliot's dictum: "a degree of heterogeneity of material compelled into unity by the operation of the poet's mind is omnipresent in poetry."[102] In doing so, he does not neglect to mention that Eliot is himself an heir of Alexandrianism, referring as he does to Origen in his "Mr. Eliot's Sunday Morning Service" (1920); and that this dictum, moreover, can be related to the style of the seventeenth-century English "metaphysical poets."[103] Thus, the Alexandrian epoch, Byzantine literature, the baroque, and T. S. Eliot reveal their cultural affinities in the space of one short passage, illustrating how Averintsev's work is saturated with the articulation of cultural connections and facts. His is not simply an erudition measured by quantitative knowledge, but a deeper and more subtle talent for simultaneous analysis and synthesis of the broadest range of cultural allusions and associations.

Christianity as Intercultural Mediator

Like Aleksei Losev, Averintsev sees Spengler's omission of Christianity from his cultural typology as his principal oversight. For Averintsev, Christianity does not represent yet another cultural type, but is rather a kind of intercultural mediator that dissolves the borders between distinct cultures, like blood moving among different bodily organs. In some of his most influential contributions to the *Philosophical Encyclopedia* (vol. 5, 1970), Averintsev presents his own theological views, which, oddly enough for a Soviet publication, were explicitly those of a Christian believer. He regards Christianity as the most highly developed form of theism, and as a personalist conceptualization of the Absolute. Theism, in Averintsev's view, was favorable for the development of new sciences and technologies in Europe, since it stripped nature of its magical component and rendered it a resource for human innovation. However, Averintsev indicates a principal difference between Eastern and Western forms of Christianity, one that hinges upon their relative concern with ontological versus juridical questions.

> For Catholic theology, God and man are first of all subjects of will; for Eastern Orthodoxy, they are the objects of ontological processes. For Catholicism, it is most important to find a harmony between two wills, either in a rationalist and juridical plane (scholasticism) or through sentimental emotion oriented on individualistic

subjectivism (mysticism).... The basic theoretical problem of Orthodoxy is the ontological relationship between human and divine nature in the God-man.[104]

In Averintsev's view, Orthodoxy emphasizes the divine order of a God-created universe rather than the historical progression of mankind as a function of God's will. While Catholicism centers on the subjective, psychological relationship between man and God, Orthodoxy focuses on the divine nature of material forms, since the world was sanctified by God's incarnation in a human body. This may be one of the reasons why technological development in the Christian East lagged behind the West: nature was not seen as an object for human operations, but rather as the holy flesh, inseparable from the spirit and sanctified through the birth of Christ and his resurrection.

For the Soviet reader of Averintsev, his discussions of classical and biblical intuitions are easily extrapolated to theoretical comparisons of Western and Russian cultures. For example, the "symbolism of the warm and womb-like maternal love, which is as characteristic of Greek-Slavic Orthodox culture as it is alien to antiquity, comes from the Old Testament."[105] An insightful Russian audience could, through Averintsev's works, trace its cultural lineage back to the distant and noble roots of biblical spirituality that Soviet history had nearly succeeded in suppressing. Unlike the Western intellectual, who enjoys the luxury of freedom of expression traceable to liberal and demonstrative ancient Greek oratorical modes, a member of the Russian intelligentsia finds himself in the position of the hunched and harried scribe of the ancient Near East, who, fearing persecution for speaking freely, had to reserve his best thoughts, not to be delivered "out loud" to contemporaries, but written solely for posterity. This accounts for the gravitation of Russian culture, among others in Eastern Christianity, to the literary mode of expression—to the "mute word," while Western culture has favored the oral and visual modes.

Ethics, Art, and Cultural Synthesis

Averintsev's moral philosophy follows the same patterns of cultural differences. Thus, his interpretation of the biblical author Ben Sira, who espoused the ideals of humble dignity and the wisdom of common sense, reflects the position of a free man in an unfree society.

> If we imagine a man legally free, respected and sufficiently provided for, who is placed in the same climate of political unfreedom that had predominated in the Hellenistic East, as it had predominated in the time of the Pharaohs, and would predominate in the time of the Byzantine emperors; who realizes how little depends on him, but would nevertheless prefer to live his life in a righteous and human way...; who would prefer, most of all, to live quietly and peacefully to the end of his days, but cannot deny the [ever imminent] possibility of becoming a beggar or a prisoner; if we endeavor to see this social and ethical type, we shall understand that the didactic book of Ben Sira has ensured itself an enduring role.[106]

We would be mistaken to assume that Averintsev's descriptions are meant to convey a hidden ("Aesopian") critique of "Eastern despotism" in its Soviet manifestation; instead, their breadth invites application to many epochs and circumstances, including, but not limited to, contemporary ones.

In 1995, the well-known poet and essayist Viktor Krivulin recalled the effect of Averintsev's public lectures on Soviet intelligentsia audiences in the 1970s.

> In the overcrowded halls, the atmosphere was far from academic. The issues of medieval theological debates, the enigmas of Byzantine aesthetics, and first and foremost, the specific understanding of the form and ritual, the metaphysical spirit of civic myth-construction—all this revealed, to numerous listeners, new modes of understanding Soviet daily life. To many, medieval Byzantium began to seem closer than contemporary Europe or America. The Platonic, inhuman beauty of the State, molded into odd but stable and finished forms, was fascinating.... Averintsev's Byzantium attracted Russian intellectuals in the same way that, in the eighteenth century, the idealized Greece of Winckelmann attracted Germans.[107]

The overall goal of Averintsev's culturology, in addition to scholarly research, is to restore the missing or neglected links of cultural heritage. Russia, which has suffered most severely from a violent utopianism that suppressed her connections with humanity's collective memory, has particular need of such restoration, of recalling not just the central, but even the more or less marginal layers of world culture. "Russian culture badly needs the memory of its Syrian and Coptic origins."[108] Such directly programmatic pronouncements are rare in Averintsev, but they do illustrate one of his project's ultimate goals: to reunite Russia with the traditions of Christianity, and by the same token to reunite culture with religious consciousness.

In some of his articles, Averintsev addresses themes of twentieth-century philosophy and literature, focusing on figures most resonant with his own cultural intuitions, such as Thomas Mann, Herman Hesse, Viacheslav Ivanov, and Osip Mandelshtam. Despite their diversity, a common denominator can be found in the cosmopolitan nature of their creative endeavors, oriented as these writings are toward synthesizing Eastern and Western and classical and Christian traditions. They are as distant from the avant-gardist renouncement of tradition as from the fundamentalist reverence for one national or religious heritage. Averintsev's concern is to discover a middle road between these two extremes of militant innovation and intolerant conservatism. His cultural "heroes" are those who represent culture in the multiplicity of its dimensions and find the most cautious, tolerant, and refined ways of mediating between binary oppositions.

This relates especially to Averintsev's native culture, which was the victim of two extremes: Westernizing self-condemnation and Russophilic self-exaltation. The culturologist is concerned with presenting culture in its entirety, and thus with carefully balancing its competing tendencies. "I have before me a way between the Scylla of loveless and inattentive hypercriticism and the Charybdis of romantic, historically themed myth-making."[109] In the fierce polemic between the "neo-Slavophiles" and "neo-Westernizers," Averintsev rejected the extremes of both positions, always trying to rely on Aristotle's "golden mean," but at same time avoiding facile attempts to "neutralize" these opposites.

Averintsev's view of art finds its middle passage between theological and secular approaches. "[A]rt is an analogue of the man mystery of Christianity—the 'humanization' [*vochelovecheniia*] of the Absolute."[110] From this point of view, art is an act of objective transfiguration of matter, not a mimetic illusion of reality or the subjective self-expression of an artist. On the other hand, Averintsev acknowledges the need to maintain a distance between art and "theological principles," to provide full independence for each of these spheres. In his reasoning, he follows quite closely the neo-Thomist doctrine of the twentieth-century French theologian and philosopher of art Jacque Maritain, who insisted upon the sovereignty of art, which is truly religious insofar as it does *not* obey any theological doctrines. Thus the pretensions of artists like Wagner or some of the Russian symbolists, who claimed a vocation to the sacred mission of theurgy, the God-like creation or transfiguration of the world, not only vulgarized the messianic idea but also produced didactic and abstract forms of art. In Averintsev's view, the most appropriate position for an artist is to identify him- or herself as an artisan producing beautiful things, without claiming thereby to be transforming the world. In other words, the religious essence of art demands humility, both of the artwork and the artist.

Averintsev's primary moral concern, which is inseparable from his scholarly endeavors, centers on the overcoming of sectarianism of all kinds—political, religious, nationalist, and so on. He repeatedly warns of the danger of sectarianism, the spirit of self-righteousness and esoteric dedication to a specific code, professional jargon, or redemptive doctrine. In his view, utopianism of all kinds (including communism) is nothing but the distortion of the Judeo-Christian promise of salvation. "The most radical opposition to the theistic idea of salvation in the new European epoch appears to be the social and technological utopia which substitutes, for the transcendent existence granted by God, an earthly future that is planned by people themselves."[111] Totalitarianism is but a sectarianism that has swollen to encompass all humanity, isolated from its past and from the variety of its possible futures.

In the late 1980s, while totalitarian ideology was disintegrating, the danger of sectarianism remained real in the plurality of minor totalitarianisms (nationalist and religious dogmas) threatening to take root among the fragments of a fallen system. Averintsev feared a potential atomization of culture through the proliferation of aggressive subcultures and sectarian movements of narrow-minded "believers" who style themselves the chosen ones and condemn the representatives of other nations or denominations as "subhuman." Such a situation can be remedied only by consciousness of the unity of all human culture and the inseparability of religion and humanism. In Averintsev's view, fanaticism, which eliminates the humanist element, and atheism, which eliminates the religious, are not only perverse in themselves but tend to merge into a single doctrine of fanatical atheism, as was the case, he maintains, with both twentieth-century varieties of totalitarianism, Nazism and communism. This is why Averintsev adheres to Christian theology, which presents God as embodied in a human personality, and thus provides the necessary balance between the religious and humanistic elements of culture. Philosophically, Averintsev's views echo Vladimir Solovyov's idea of "Godmanhood" as the foundation of the growing syntheses of diverse aspects of world cultures, the ideal of the utmost freedom of parts in the utmost unity of the whole.

The Sacred and the Secular: Religion and the State

Averintsev's view on the unity of religion and humanism extends to his political thinking, which focuses on the relationship between secular and religious powers. He traces the origin of Russian statehood to the Byzantine idea of the "sacred state." "Christianity and the Caesarist idea of sacred power met in the epoch of Constantine, comprising the two poles of the Byzantine social consciousness, which necessarily complement one another."[112] The same relates to the concept of "Holy Russia," which was conceived not as a local or ethnic entity but as a world of genuine belief encompassing all geographical spaces, including even Eden. Russia began to emerge as a political power as the Byzantine Empire was disintegrating; thus did Russia borrow the attribute of holiness to become the only world power whose political claims were allegedly justified by a religious authority. Averintsev draws parallels between the Russian and Byzantine empires in terms of their Eurasian geographic dominion and their theocratic self-determination. However, he finds that in the Russian sensibility, the antinomies of sacred power are sharpened as compared with Byzantium. On the one hand, Russia's tsars were perceived as the high priests of the Church, and loyalty to them was tantamount to loyalty to God. On the other hand, power as such was considered sinful, in light of Christ's designation of his kingdom as being "not of this world" and his distinction between allegiance to God and Caesar. The point is that "power in itself, at least autocratic power, is something that abides someplace higher or lower than the human world, but in any case seems not to enter into it. It is very difficult here to separate the blessing from the curse."[113] Averintsev contrasts this duality of the Russian attitude toward power with the Western recognition of the possibility of mediation and neutralization between these two extremes. In particular, the West elaborated the rules of politeness and civility, which are neutral in terms of good and evil.

> The Catholic worldview divides being not into two parts ("light" and "dark") but three: between the celestial domain of *supernatural* grace and the infernal domain of the *antinatural* there exists, for a time, the domain of the *natural*, which proceeds according to its own laws, albeit under the authority of God. State power belongs precisely to this last domain ... Russian spirituality divides the world not into three parts but two, the realms of light and dark; and nowhere is this felt so keenly as where the issue of power is concerned. [The kingdoms of] God and the Antichrist come close to each other without any buffer zone between them.[114]

How can we extricate ourselves from this duality? Averintsev believes that Russia must escape these two extremes, neither sanctifying power nor, by renouncing it, fleeing into the "false innocence of irresponsibility."[115] Thus, power must be acknowledged as a secular necessity, rather than worshipped or resisted on religious grounds. Democracy is preferable to theocracy because it desacralizes power without subordinating the religious to the secular. It creates a zone of neutrality that must be allowed to follow its own natural law.

> I must say that in political matters I am unreservedly pro-democracy, precisely because democracy among all political forms is the most openly secular. As an advantage of democracy—its religious advantage—I see exactly the frankness of its non-mystical character. It is difficult even for a spiritually intoxicated person to confuse democracy with the kingdom of God, more difficult than the most terrible regimes, which pretended to be the likeness of God's kingdom and were accepted as such by many. This is why I believe we must feel the greatest fear before the specter of false theocracy, since this is what the revelation of John the Theologian depicts as the ultimate and fullest manifestation of evil.[116]

Averintsev's political and aesthetic views mirror one another. In each case, he argues the danger of blurred distinctions: in the former, between secular and religious power; in the latter, between secular and religious art. The danger arises with the human pretension to know and embody God's will. Thus are political theocracy and aesthetic theurgy equally guilty of substituting human intention for divine providence. Overtly nonreligious systems are preferable to quasi-religious ones insofar as the former implicitly acknowledge the transcendental aspect of divinity, which cannot be translated into human terms and imposed on the secular realm. The religious imperative of humility, then, is more adequately realized in democracy than in theocracy, by which human rulers attempt to identify, translate, and dictate God's plan. Although Averintsev proceeds from religious premises, he comes to conclusions that suggest affinities with existentialist thinkers like Grigorii Pomerants, who defended secular, pluralistic structures as humbler and more spiritually justified than any kind of moral or religious authoritarianism.

The Carnivalesque: Averintsev versus Bakhtin

Averintsev represents a new, post-Bakhtinian stage of culturology, one that is far more attentive to religious aspects of culture and more skeptical about the utopian implications of the theory of carnival. Averintsev is particularly wary of Bakhtin's valorization of laughter as a liberatory force. In his book on Rabelais, Bakhtin famously counterposed laughter to all kinds of dogmatism and authoritarianism—a framing that clearly challenged the official ideology of Stalin's time. For Averintsev, conversely, laughter may easily be used as a tool of authoritarianism, and he cites numerous examples of carnivalesque gestures by Ivan the Terrible and Stalin himself. Both tyrants were skilled in all manner of ambivalence, masters of the ritualistic crowning and uncrowning of their victims. "The terror of laughter ... successfully cooperates with the repressive terror."[117] Paradoxically, Bakhtin's concept of carnival may be interpreted as a justification of Stalinism, an equivalent to those pseudoscientific, materialist theories, like that of Lysenko, that described the continual generation of life from nonliving matter: "The biological cosmos appears truly as a Bakhtinian 'grotesque body,' bursting from continual pregnancy but alien to form, structure, logos."[118]

Averintsev proposes to distinguish noble laughter—mostly at one's own sins, fears, weaknesses—from cynical or boorish laughter, by which one becomes "liberated" from shame, pity, conscience. Liberation itself is value-neutral: "Liberation from evil is good; liberation from something indifferent is indifferent; while liberation from good is evil."[119] Thus laughter has no intrinsic moral value—that depends on whichever "serious" values the laughter liberates us from. Averintsev argues that laughter may be justified as a spontaneous transition from unfreedom to freedom, but if protracted (as idealized in the Bakhtinian concept of carnival), it becomes hysterical, even diabolical. The moment of laughter may well represent an explosion of freedom, but its continuation renders it an automatic series of convulsions that exceeds a person's self-mastery. Thus is the face of the devil often represented as a laughing mask, frozen in mockery.

This discrepancy between Averintsev's and Bakhtin's approaches to laughter is revelatory of their fundamental disagreement about the nature of totalitarianism and culture in general. For Bakhtin, totalitarianism inherits the ideological dogmatism of the Middle Ages, which should be opposed by the liberating forces of the material bottom, by nonofficial carnivalesque revelry. For Averintsev, it is this material bottom, with its licentious, literally "base" instincts, that in the Soviet period rose to the top of the totalitarian hierarchy and suppressed society's spiritual needs. Revolution itself may be understood as a great carnival that reverses the entire social structure, raising its bottom to the top and vice versa. From Averintsev's point of view, Bakhtin's concepts of carnival and ambivalence may stand as an apologia for the very sort of permanent revolution proclaimed by Trotsky and later by Mao Zedong, and performed in Stalin's purges. Looked at from a certain angle, that is, Stalinism might appear as the continual inversion of social layers so as to prevent the sedimentation of authority in bureaucracy and promote its rejuvenation with the spirit of the masses. In reality, totalitarianism would seem to combine features peculiar both to official religious cult and to the popular carnival of the Middle Ages. Laughter is united with terror.

Thus Bakhtin's apologia of the material bottom as opposed to the ideological top, and Averintsev's apologia of spiritual seriousness as opposed to carnivalesque relativity, may both have anti-totalitarian ramifications. If Bakhtin's cultural heroes are Gargantua and Pantagruel, then Averintsev's heroine is Joan of Arc, with her devotion to God's mission. But the real heroes of Stalin's epoch were *lumpen*-knights—both carnivalesque fools and pious communists, like the heroes of Andrei Platonov, the ascetics of the materialist faith. This is the ambivalence of totalitarianism: as its very name attests, it totalizes the official and carnivalesque aspects of culture, making of them a unified whole. Averintsev's emphasis on seriousness demonstrates that, as the totalitarian epoch began to recede into the past in the 1970s and the 1980s, the system of values reversed by the October Revolution was ripe for another reversal. In the 1920s and the 1930s, when Bakhtin's concept was emerging, the "bottom" was fast ascending to the "top," while in Averintsev's time, the spiritual "top" gradually restored its position, presaging the impending collapse of the whole system of communism as "frozen carnival."

Averintsev's own philosophical views are imbedded within his expositions and criticisms of other thinkers. He consciously abstains from pretensions of innovation or originality, attempting instead to contextualize his own ideas organically in the cultural matrix of a given epoch or tradition. The difficulty that arises in attempting to distill Averintsev's own ideas from his scholarship reflects his concern with the universality of culture and situates him among those Russian thinkers, like Vladimir Solovyov or Pavel Florensky, who saw their goal as building connections between the diverse ideas of other minds, disciplines, periods, and cultures on the basis of the Christian and Neoplatonic traditions. This was the ideal of "all-encompassing unity" (Solovyov's concept of *vseedinstvo*), in this case approached by an individual thinker in his attempt at intellectual and spiritual synthesis.

8. Living-Thinking through the Diversity of Cultures. Georgii Gachev

Situating Georgii Dmitrievich Gachev (1929–2008) under the rubric of culturology is somewhat conditional, insofar as his thinking integrates several trends and might also be subsumed under the heading of "philosophy of personality" or "of national spirit." However, both personality and nation, as treated by Gachev, are inscribed in a comprehensive network of cultural interdependencies and thus may be interpreted as constituents of a broadly culturological concern. Gachev's versatility is attested to by his varied institutional affiliations. He worked under the auspices of several institutions of the Academy of Sciences of the USSR, such as the Institute of World Literature, the Institute of the History of Natural Sciences and Technology, and the Institute of Slavic and Balkan Studies. Initially trained in philology and literary theory, he expanded the scope of his erudition to physics and mathematics, major European cultures, and the Hebrew and ancient Chinese languages, among other things.

Gachev was an exceptionally prolific writer; he published forty-six books in his lifetime, and many of his manuscripts still remain unpublished. His first book, *The Accelerated Development of Literature* (1964), contained the germ of his methodology, which centered on the problem of "the whole." He found a formulation for his basic principle in the saying of the ancient Greek philosopher Anaxagoras: "Everything is in everything," which suggests that each part of the world is a micro-model of the whole. The son of Bulgarian revolutionary Dmitrii Gachev, a prominent theoretician of aesthetics who died in a Stalinist concentration camp, Georgii Gachev in his first book turned to his native Bulgarian literature, arguing that it represents a small-scale reflection of the development of the entirety of world literature in the variety of its

Figure 4.6 Georgii Gachev.

genres and their historical succession. For example, in Bulgaria, the transition from poetry to prose as literary forms took place over the span of only a few years in the nineteenth century, but Gachev attempts to demonstrate that this changeover mirrored an evolutionary process that, on the scale of world literature, took several centuries. *Acceleration*, for Gachev, is a universal model, applicable not only to literature but all aspects of culture, and not only to Bulgaria, but all such nations as appeared only belatedly on the scene of world culture. In his later books, Gachev demonstrates the same condensation of various stages of world culture in the oeuvre of the well-known Kyrgyz author Chingiz Aitmatov (1928–2008).

The most influential of Gachev's books, *The Content of Artistic Forms*, was published in 1968. In it, Gachev elaborates a theory of the relationship between form and content, relying on the category of genre as developed by Bakhtin and Olga Freidenberg in her 1936 book *The Poetics of Plot and Genre* (though without references to her work). Genre, in Gachev's description, is the form that precedes and predetermines any specific artistic content produced by an individual writer. For example, Lev Tolstoy's *War and Peace* displays not only the author's original content, but first and foremost the formative volition of the epic genre itself. Thus it is Homer and all other epic authors who speak through the mouth of Tolstoy, by the very law of generic succession. How the form acts to produce each of its subsequent realizations is conditioned by the genesis of this form, which is itself nothing but the crystallization of some primordial content. For example, the epic genre formalizes such essential features of the ancient worldview as the precedence of the tribe or nation over the individual, and the idea of event as opposed to action (which characterizes the dramatic genre). These basic spiritual qualities are condensed in the generic form in order to travel through time and radiate their primordial meaning into all future actualizations of the genre.

> Shouldn't we see in this activity of the form, in the force of tradition, not only something negative, but also a blessed force of the people, reflecting the deep stability of being, the simplicity and clarity of the foundational values thereof.... In [genres], the objective life of deceased humanity survives: through genres, the reasoning of previous epochs understands, assimilates, and humanizes all [cultural] innovations.[120]

Gachev insists that "one will never succeed in finding the first birth, common for all humanity, of a given form: each new immersion in the past will entail still deeper immersion, and so forth, ad infinitum."[121] However, if it is genealogy we seek, we can easily recognize, in Gachev's early reconstructions of the spirituality of material and semiotic forms of culture, the Hegelian pattern of the self-development of absolute spirit. What Gachev calls "form" is a step in the self-alienation of the spirit, which undergoes a process of materialization and corporealization in order to reappropriate itself—in its later manifestations, already consciously. Like Bibler, but in a narrower way, Gachev "hegelizes" the Bakhtinian notion of genre, which is a purely formal structure generating and shaping the contents of actual utterances. Bakhtin's thinking is still rooted in the Marxist tradition, which prioritizes the material "body" of the artistic work over its ideological superstructure, its "mind" and "soul." For his part, Gachev, instead of formalizing content, seeks to spiritualize form, an approach reflecting the Hegelian interpretations of Marxism rather common for philosophers of his generation, such as Evald Ilyenkov, who, like Bakhtin, had a personal influence on Gachev.

What Gachev ultimately aspired to was not, however, idealism or materialism in their pure forms, but rather their organic complementarity. Already in *The Content of Artistic Forms*, he finds his model of the philosopher in pre-Socratic antiquity, when thinking and being were not estranged as subject and object. "[P]hilosophers were not merely thinkers but sages, that is, what they thought and understood about life and man was expressed not only in words, teachings, theories, and systems, but in how they built their lives, dressed themselves, behaved, talked, and so forth."[122] The entirety of Gachev's philosophical project may be viewed as a revival of this pre-Socratic union of thinking-being, its reintroduction into a contemporary world steeped, by contrast, in intellectual division and specialization.

Despite its warm reception among critics and scholars, this book was officially condemned as anti-Marxist and "formalist," and, although Gachev continued to write prolifically until the end of his life, publication of his works decreased, and it was not until the advent of perestroika that more of his volumes began to appear—with surprising frequency.

Gachev's major publications derive from his voluminous diaries, and although they are being published as individual works, they are consistent in their general philosophical worldview, which Gachev calls "living-thinking" (*zhiznemyslie*). As mentioned in part three in connection with personalism, the philosophical diary is a long-standing tradition in Russian thought, perhaps beginning with Dostoevsky's *Diary of a Writer*, and continued by Vasilii Rozanov and Mikhail Prishvin, Lidiia Ginzburg and Iakov Druskin. In the Soviet period, this genre afforded the thinker a certain measure of freedom from external pressures, but in Gachev's case its use has far more radical implications. He applies to humanistic thinking the sort of self-testing procedures required in experimental sciences, and questions the very tools of investigation themselves as potentially involving their own hindrances. "[T]he personality [of the thinker] must be introduced and his/her influence on the object of exploration must be considered in theoretical thinking, where the 'tool' is this living human being with a specific life-trajectory, a particular soul and character."[123] Thus thinking, if it is to be adequate to reality, must theorize the situation of the observer and, moreover, must take careful note of the time of observation. The results of physical and chemical experiments, after all, vary depending on their location in a definite space and time—and how much more is this true of the results of humanistic thinking, which should be registered in terms of their succession and temporality. The form of diary serves Gachev as a tool for experimentation in the field of thinking, each portion of which is rigorously dated. Gachev calls this approach "existential culturology."[124] All his voluminous works on such diverse subjects as "Travels of Europeans to India," or "French, German, and Greek Treatises on Hydraulics," invariably expose the atmosphere of his Moscow apartment or country house and his everyday relationships with his wife (the philosopher Svetlana Semenova), his two daughters, and his friends and colleagues.

By marrying his philosophical contemplations and investigations to the flow of personal experience, Gachev offers a challenge to the Western tradition of abstract thinking. This abstractness is evident not only in such explicitly metaphysical systems as those of Plato or Hegel, but even in those thinkers who attempted to refute them, like Nietzsche, Husserl, Heidegger, or Sartre. Ironically, these latter rebellions against abstract thinking are couched in abstract terms: nowhere in *Being and Time* or *Being and Nothingness* do we find anything concerning the personal, or actual, existence of the author—only speculations about general principles of being. For Gachev, "each moment of life is sacred not only in its uniqueness, but also insofar as it is full of enormous meaning."[125] He tries to articulate a philosophical language subtle enough to describe the infinitesimal elements of everyday experience. This kind of thinking he calls "attracted" (*privlechennoe myshlenie*), since it is *attracted* to life rather than *abstracted* (*otvlechennoe*) from it.

For example, in one section devoted to a summer sojourn, he meditates on the specificity of living in a wooden house as opposed to a brick one, a difference which may be exemplified by the process required to affix items to the walls.[126] In a wooden house, one uses a hammer, which functions by a striking motion; a brick house calls for a drill, which operates in a circular manner. Thus Gachev extends this operation to his general mode of being, claiming that he is a different person in each environment: in a wooden house, he is more direct—a mode appropriate to country life; in a brick house, his behavior is more conducive to city living, whose dominant social convention entails convolutedness. Therefore "drilling" is both the literal means of penetrating a brick wall, and also the way of negotiating the denser cultural complexities of a civilized milieu.

The traditional philosopher employs a quite limited repertoire of specialized terms to elaborate his thinking, and the richness of the world may thus be lost beneath the repetition of abstract concepts. For Gachev, philosophy should strive not to reduce experience to some underlying comprehensive concept—be it absolute spirit, the will-to-power, being, or différance—but to amplify the world's diversity. Rather than try to look past the particular to some overarching generality, Gachev imbeds his philosophy in the particular, such that his ideas are contingent upon the specific lived relationships between himself and the material contexts of his life. For example, during his investigations of Descartes, Gachev's daughters happened to be ill with bronchitis, a circumstance which impacted his philosophizing: "Well, why should I meditate on mechanics when my children are ill? This is what I said to myself in the morning. In this case I should meditate on medicine, anatomy. And suddenly I feel that in my contemplation, anatomy and mechanics come together, owing to Descartes."[127] Gachev goes on to describe the lungs in terms of statics and dynamics, in order to find isomorphic parallels between organism and mechanism, as well as between his life and Descartes's thought.

In addition to Kant's schematic apriorism, Gachev uncovers a figurative apriorism that underlies rational thinking generally. Beneath the logic of philosophical and scientific descriptions, Gachev identifies metaphorical visions of which the thinkers in question themselves seem unaware. Incidentally, Gachev analyzes Kant's own philosophical reasoning as a set of images, including those of a branchy tree and a tournament of knights.[128] Thus does Gachev practice a kind of deconstruction, laying bare the figurative frameworks that support abstract constructions. For example, he attributes Newton's universal gravitation—an abstraction *par excellence*—to an English metaphorical vision of the relationship between the sky and earth as informed by the predominance of fog, mist, and clouds in the English climate. Fog, understood as clouds fallen to earth, implicitly illustrates the law of gravitation, which was expanded by Newton to describe relations between celestial bodies.[129] In the same way, he compares Galileo's theory of free fall to the descending diphthongs of the Italian language.

These parallels between scientific discourse and cultural imagery enable Gachev to develop what he calls a "humanistic approach" to the natural sciences. This idea is the inverse of the structuralist method: instead of understanding art in terms of science, Gachev wants to understand science in terms of art. For instance, he envisions a mutual illumination of the waltz and Copernican cosmology as congenial formations in the culture of modernity—a double rotation of the individual (of the earth) around its axis ("I"), and around its center (the sun) on the plane/ballroom of the social or cosmic arena. Thus the dance and the cosmological model are generated by the same episteme. Gachev calls this method the "deduction of the imagination," opposing it to the logical notion of a deduction of abstract concepts. Applying it, the mind generates "thought-images" (*mysleobrazy*), which differ from the discreet thoughts by which philosophy has traditionally proceeded insofar as they are more akin to waves than particles. "Working through thought-images is a specific kind of spiritual activity where reason and imagination are combined, where the rational capacity is exercised along with the artistic capacity."[130] Gachev's reasoning and even terminology is quite close to Iakov Golosovker's "meaning-images" (*smysloobrazy*) and the core ideas of his book *The Imaginative Absolute* (written mostly in the 1920s and 1930s but published only in 1987).

Intellectual artistic prose—the genre that allows the writer-thinker both poetic frivolities and scientific insights—may be found in ancient Greek and Roman literature; for example in Plato's dialogues, or Lucretius's philosophical poem "On the Nature of Things." In Gachev's view, these syncretistic works should not be thought of as merely the products of an archaic stage of culture but rather as examples of a mode by which increasingly disparate aspects of culture may once again be unified. As culture has given rise to a trend of ever-growing specialization, Gachev sees the need to build bridges across scientific disciplines and artistic fields, so that a sense of holistic cultural identity might be retrieved. He envisions his work as a vehicle for this comprehensive interaction of diverse disciplines; it would allow, for example, a physics treatise to be read from the standpoint of a literary scholar, or a landscape poem to be considered from the standpoint of a biologist. His method is not meant to produce just "popularizations" of science, but to generate new ways of thinking across boundaries, even transcend the conventional understanding of interdisciplinary studies, insofar as such modes of thought allow for the confluence of different types of consciousness. Via translation among various disciplinary languages, new information is generated, and new meta-languages may even arise.

Gachev's own meta-language constitutes an attempt to overcome disciplinary boundaries by appealing to the deep figurative structures underlying culture. In his terms, the figurative apriori is grounded in language itself, since the terminological uses of words are already metaphorical. "Wave," "field," and "current" are all terms used by physicists in a metaphorical sense, inasmuch as they are abstracted from their literal meanings in immediately observable nature ("waves of the sea"—"electromagnetic waves").[131] Thus the language of science, though it claims to be rigorous and universal, is essentially a language of images, and is therefore subject to interpretation as a phenomenon of culture. For example, whereas Kant and Laplace developed similar theories of the origin of the earth, they proceeded in different languages, each appropriate to their national culture. In Kant, the world is comprised of dispersed particles of solid matter that respond to the laws of attraction and repulsion. This expresses a distinctly German way of thinking in terms of opposition. Laplace has *his* universe evolve from a liquidity that is distributed throughout space and crystallizes according to varying temperatures and pressures. Gachev attributes this theoretical model to a French sensibility that is far more susceptible to tactile representations, whereas the German imagination is far more inclined to abstract reasoning.

Gachev's lifelong project was to theorize the diversity of national cultures, attempting to characterize them by a meta-language derived from the ancient classification of the four elements: earth, air, fire, and water. These are the basic lexical constituents of Gachev's meta-language, whose syntax includes the relationship of attraction and repulsion.[132] In this, the Soviet scholar may be seen as echoing the philosophy of Empedocles, wherein the cosmic process is described in terms of eternal alternations of love and hate between its elements. A more recent and even closer parallel to Gachev's categories would be Gaston Bachelard's (1884–1962) theory of imagination, which is elaborated in terms of these four elements.[133] While Bachelard characterizes the varieties of imagination as corresponding to individual elements (and their sub-categories, such as "water-imagination" and "lake-fantasies," or "earth and reveries of will and repose"), Gachev considers the relationships between all these elements in the organic unity of a national culture. "The national image of the world may be treated as a system of mutual correspondences. There are almost no parameters which would be unique for a given nation, but while there is everything everywhere, it is present in various proportions. There are various accents, combinations, or hierarchies of elements."[134] Thus, in the French image of the world, the element of water predominates over the other elements; the feminine predominates over the masculine; the curve over the direct line; the horizontal over the vertical; touch and taste over vision and hearing; painting over music; and color over figure. The French image of the world is characterized by balance and symmetry. By contrast, in the German conception, opposition and antinomy predominate. Gachev's approach is partly reminiscent of Oswald Spengler's "morphology of culture," in that it attempts to elucidate the "ur-phenomenon" of each culture by bringing together its various aspects (art, philosophy, mathematics, etc.). But Gachev is interested in the description of real nations, not some broader multinational "cultural types," or "civilizations," which are artificially constructed by Spengler.

Gachev describes more than a dozen national cultures in terms of their natural imagery and peculiar modes of sensitivity and logical thinking, which he defines as the "cosmo-psycho-logos" (*kosmo-psikho-logos*) of each culture. Among these are India, Italy, England, France, Germany, the United States, Russia, Poland, Bulgaria, and several of the former republics of the Soviet Union (Armenia, Georgia, and others). His method includes a comparative examination of the most representative texts of a given culture. Thus, in his work "The American Image of the World, or, America through the Eyes of a Person Who Has Never Seen It," he examines Herman Melville's *Moby Dick*, Walt Whitman's *Leaves of Grass*, Mark Twain's *Tom Sawyer*, philosophical treatises of Charles Peirce and William James, the inventions of Edison, Henry Ford's memoirs, and even cookbooks. He pinpoints the cosmo-psycho-logos of the United States as a world of *-urgia* without *-gonia*, "that is, artificially created by immigrants, and not naturally growing from Mother Nature like all the cultures of the Eurasian peoples, where *-urgia* (labor, history) continues *–gonia* (begetting, creation) in its forms, and where culture is natural."[135] Gachev illustrates this distinction with images of plants: whereas for Eurasian cultures, the model of the "world tree" (for instance, the Old Norse Yggdrasill) is typical, America's leaves, like in Whitman's imagery, grow from the grass, not being rooted deeply in the soil. American geniuses have typically been immigrants, likewise unnurtured in that country's soil. American cultural heroes, moreover, are frequently adolescents (Tom Sawyer, Huck Finn), and concomitantly, the future is a far more important dimension of time than the past. If for Europe, the Oedipus complex is typical, then for the reality of the United States, Gachev proposes the notion of an "Orestes complex"—matricide, which is connected with the historical abandonment of one's motherland (in Europe) and the merciless pollution of one's new homeland.

Although Gachev derives his definitions of national character mostly from natural determinants, he does not rule out negation as a means for a nation to overcome the power of nature. In a profound way, the concept of negation is applied to Russia's identity, which relates to Western culture by a kind of attraction/repulsion. If Western logic proceeds from positive definitions, phrased as, "This is —," then the Russian mind, according to Gachev, is more inclined to proceed from negation: "Not this, but —." Notably, what is negated is far clearer, more distinct, than what is designated as the positive pole. "The Russian mind begins with some negation, the rejection of a ready, given [reality], taken as a 'thesis-victim,' and typically derived from the West."[136] But what follows the negation, "but —," is not clear, and remains a question hanging in the air. Russia is a kind of negative continuum, dissolving the positive values and realities of Western civilization. Gachev alludes to "nonbeing, emptiness as manufactured articles."[137] This active and ardent production of nothingness is different both from positive Western industriousness and contemplative Eastern wisdom.[138]

Gachev's project for the description of "national images of the world" is founded upon an aphorism from Heraclitus: "The universe for those who are awake is single and common, while in sleep each person turns aside into a private universe."[139] In Gachev's view, every nation conceives the wholeness of the universe in an idiosyncratic way, as a dream specific to each cultural paradigm. "Why study dreams? So as not to take them for reality, to be aware how limited and local even our most common views are."[140] Thus Gachev's exploration of national cultures offers more than just a rich philosophy of diversity. It also serves as a way to prevent the fallacy of attributing collective fantasies and myths—even if they take the guise of science or philosophy—to reality itself.

It would scarcely be possible to verify Gachev's cultural claims, but he himself does not put much stock in "truth" as a criterion of his work's value. Iurii Lotman, whose structuralist approach to culture took an opposite path, at one point wrote to Gachev: "Your thinking is artistic.... You are inspired and not persuaded by scientific ideas, and you want to inspire your reader more than persuade them."[141] This was meant as a kind of criticism, but Gachev was happy to agree with Lotman, because it was his conviction that the thinker must unite him- or herself with the artist. In the case of a writer associated with the genre of fiction, no one requires that such descriptions be factually verified. Why, then, can ideas not derive from the realm of imagination and have the same ontological or epistemological status as characters or events in fiction? What would prevent a thinker from writing "fictional philosophies"? "Ideas, problems, theories, cultural epochs, national universes: these are his characters, and they enter into imaginative collisions; plots and peripeteias are played out between them—why is such an artistic work impossible?"[142] Nobody, remarks Gachev, identifies Dostoevsky or Thomas Mann with the ideas of their characters; why, he wonders, should the drama of ideas evolved in a philosophical work be judged on the assumption that the author necessarily subscribes to them? Gachev's writing presupposes an indeterminate and changing distance between the author and his ideas; the latter should be appraised as literary characters. With such an approach, apparent contradictions need not undermine the philosophical value of a work, since they merely represent various hypothetical positions applied to the same problem. Gachev's enduring conceptual concern with *the whole* is well served by such a multiplicity of perspectives.

Despite Gachev's quite distinctive method for the interpretation of cultural phenomena, it would be difficult to systematize his numerous insights. This is a rare kind of philosophy—one that is methodical but non-systematic, or perhaps methodically non-systematic. Characteristically, Gachev never attempted to edit or polish his manuscripts; this would betray their authenticity as diaries conveying certain unrepeatable moments of living-thinking. Gachev himself recognizes his reluctance toward system, which goes hand in hand with his engagement with the whole. The whole belongs to life itself, which cannot be systematized, since any system is inserted into the life of the thinker. "My Whole, that is, what I will have understood and assimilated on my life-path, will be displayed in the end as the total of all particular insights in their mutual dependency and development. *My life = my system. Life as an epistemological ladder.* My 'Whole' will be discovered after me."[143]

Gachev is perhaps the most multidirectional figure in late-Soviet philosophy. Since his meditations are imbedded in his personal life-world, his philosophy might be identified with personalism; his preoccupation with organicist national images of the world, on the other hand, situates him in the tradition of Russian neo-Slavophilism and conservatism; and (as is obvious by his placement here), his interest in the comparison and dialogue among various cultures qualifies him as a culturologist. Furthermore, his "fictional" and "ludic" approach (presuming a distance between the author and the idea) might be said to resonate with the philosophy of postmodernism.[144]

Conclusion

Culturology opposed itself to official Marxist doctrine, but in part inherited its utopian disposition. As political utopianism faltered with the stagnation and deterioration of Soviet society in the 1970s and the 1980s, the philosophy of culture took over its role as a unifying and redemptive totality. In the 1970s, the German writer Hermann Hesse's *The Glass Bead Game*—a philosophical novel written in 1943, at the height of the Second World War, but published in Russian translation only in 1969—became a "cult" book among Russian intellectuals (mirroring, not incidentally, Hesse's countercultural status in the West). As an aesthetic challenge to political totalitarianism, the novel presents an imaginary land called Castalia where the rules of a universal game are passed down from generation to generation by a circle of cognoscenti and devotees. Chinese hieroglyphs, mathematical and logical formulas, musical notation, paintings, poems, and philosophical concepts constitute the symbolic vocabulary of this game. Implicit in this utopia of an all-encompassing game is its potential to serve as a definition for culture as a whole. Whereas Hesse displays a subtle irony in counterposing the game's artificial setting to the real world outside Castalia, late-Soviet culturology took this game model seriously, and used it as a methodological insight for the investigation of historical cultures. With the noblest of motivations, culturology absolutized and sometimes mystified the notion of culture, partly in order to ease the pressure of its dominant Soviet brand, to relativize its meaning, strip it of its fetishistic self-worship and situate it in historical and comparative context, alongside other cultures.

Soviet culturology rarely addressed issues of the Soviet system as such—this would have been fraught with grave political implications—but allusions to it abounded beneath the surface of any historical investigation. For example, when the historian Aron Gurevich (1924–2006) wrote about popular culture in medieval France,[1] it was understood by readers at large that his socio-anthropological method could be applied to the impersonal, collectivist patterns underlying the "neo-medieval" society of the Soviet Union. If the cultural scholar Leonid Batkin (1932–2016) wrote about the meaning of individuality and the aesthetics of difference in the Italian Renaissance,[2] this was meant to contrast with the cult of equality and collectivism in Soviet ideology. Culturology often functioned as an intellectual therapy, helping the Soviet intelligentsia realize its own peculiar fate within a broader historical perspective. Repressed critical impulses could be lived out in the process of reading about, say, Egyptian, Babylonian, or Byzantine civilization, which brought a kind of sophisticated consolation: yes, Soviet civilization may have alienated itself from the world, but at least it still had precedents in history and was subject to certain general laws (the predominance of the state and the suppression of human individuality, an enormous bureaucracy, militarism, etc.).

However, despite the fact that culturology promoted alternative visions of cultures and elaborated a technique of their implicit comparison, it should not be understood as a mode of political critique, or veiled dissidentism; rather, it pursued philosophical goals close to those of Oswald Spengler in his "morphological" exploration of culture. From his point of view, different cultures are natural organisms that go through similar stages of birth, ascent, and inevitable degradation. Russian culturology, however, is more optimistic than the Spenglerian variant; it underscores the continuity of culture (or, of Culture), which survives all of its transitional manifestations. Perhaps this is the most striking peculiarity of late-Soviet culturology: on the one hand, it bore a pluralistic orientation, and asserted the principal variety of cultures and their mutual irreducibility; on the other, this diversity of all cultures was considered to be a mode of the progressive cultural self-determination of humanity, as various aspects and stages in the construction of panhuman Culture.

For the same reason, late-Soviet culturology cannot be reduced to what is known in the West as "cultural studies." The British founders of cultural studies—Richard Hoggart, Raymond Williams, and Stuart Hall—were working-class intellectuals inspired by old and new left ideals, and heavily influenced by Marxism. By the late 1960s, Marxism, having lost nearly every political battle in the West, was receding into the more quiet cultural realm, attempting to transform it into a new political arena. Cultural studies emerged and continued, in effect, as political studies of culture, experiments in its social transformation. Russian culturology was similarly oriented toward a radical alterity to its surrounding system, but all to the contrary: having emerged in a socialist, totally politicized, and morally indoctrinated society, it viewed culture not as an instrument of politics (to which culture was actually reduced in the USSR), but as the horizon of liberation from the limits of politics by reaching out to other realms. For culturology, science presented an escape from politics; art, an escape from science; religion, an escape from art; philosophy, an escape from religion; and finally, culture, an escape from all of them, the capacity of humans to release themselves from all mental and symbolic prisons. Culturology attempts to approach culture on its own terms and to develop a holistic language that avoids lapsing into scientism, aestheticism, moralism, religious fundamentalism, technical utilitarianism, or the absolutization of any single aspect of culture.

Insofar as cultural studies is focused on politically invested forms of culture, or even culturally disguised forms of power, the aim of this discipline is primarily critical and deconstructive. Culturology, by contrast, is focused on the constructive potentials of culture, and aims to broaden and multiply the meanings of every cultural symbol beyond its literal and pragmatic meaning. Culturology addresses the practices and institutions of power no less critically than does cultural studies, as evidenced by the former's liberational message and explosive role in the networks of Soviet official culture. But culturology is not a form of oppositional politics, because it departs in principle from the political accentuation of culture, which is often predominant in cultural studies. Culturology does not critique one politics on behalf of another, allegedly more advanced and progressive one. Rather it critiques *politics*—as a type of discourse, as a relation of power, as a narrow pragmatism—from the standpoint of culture as a whole. Culturology is not about opposition, but about transcendence: how to transcend a given practice or theory using the symbolic capacities of other cultures, their infinitely rich, multileveled encodings and decodings of every human phenomenon.

Looking at late-Soviet culturology from the retrospective standpoint of the twenty-first century, we need to explain the paradox of its subsequent ascendency. In the wake of democratic reforms and the collapse of the Soviet Union, it was culturology that came front and center in a university system previously dominated by Marxism-Leninism. Courses on the history of world culture, cultural anthropology, and comparative culturology ousted such disciplines as "dialectical and historical materialism" and "scientific communism." Of all the philosophical trends that attempted to undermine the ideological hegemony of Soviet Marxism, culturology proved the most successful. Why?

Precisely because it had no specific political claims—liberal or conservative, socialist or capitalist, religious or nationalist—culturology was acceptable for any political force, in any ideological setting. It was also the least methodologically rigid sort of philosophy, and the most receptive to the values of "otherness," to dialogue with diverse cultures. Culturology could easily coexist with other philosophies and integrate them as components of various traditions and worldviews. For example, culturology readily adopted and combined semiotic, structural, phenomenological, hermeneutic, axiological, anthropological, cognitive, and many other methods applicable to the exploration of culture. Rather than concentrate on certain general principles and criteria, it opened up infinite horizons for the theoretical and historical study of facts and values of world cultures. Of all philosophical positions, it evinced the greatest academic potential.

In the mid-1990s, culturology was added to the Higher Attestation Commission's list of specialties for which scholarly degrees can be awarded. Thus was culturology officially ratified as an academic field and profession in its own right. In the decades that followed, it would attain the status of "supreme" humanistic discipline and principal mediator in interdisciplinary studies; culturology took the pivotal place in the academic curriculum and was established as an obligatory discipline, taught at virtually all institutions of higher education, including professional schools of health, business administration, law, and engineering and technology. Of course, this "cult of culturology," a vast industry with dozens of various textbooks, programs, and courses, is only distantly related to the creative philosophy of culture as it emerged in the 1970s and the 1980s. But some of the principles asserted by Bakhtin, Losev, Bibler, and Averintsev, including systematic and dialogic approaches to the diversity of cultures, live on in contemporary scholarship and education.[3]

* * *

Rarely in the history of thought has philosophy served as so liberating a force as in Russia from the 1950s through the 1980s. The Soviet state had generated a rigid system of "historically proven" and "logically irrefutable" ideas meant to perpetuate its mastery over individual minds. For this reason, philosophical thinking, which by its nature transcends the limits of the existing order and challenges sanctioned practices, was under permanent suspicion as a potentially subversive activity. To philosophize was an act of self-liberation via an awareness of the relativity of the dominant ideological discourse.

Philosophy comprises not only the thought, but also the fate of philosophers. The relationship between power and thought in the Soviet Union is well illustrated by the fact that of the thirty-seven thinkers to whom this book's respective chapters are devoted, fourteen were subjected to arrest and imprisonment: Amalrik, Bakhtin, Belinkov, Brodsky, Esenin-Volpin, Golosovker, Khazanov, Konrad, Likhachev, Losev, Mikhajlov, Nalimov, Pomerants, and Sakharov. If we exclude Marxists, this represents a full half of the list of prominent thinkers covered. (Even as, for that matter, the most creative of the Marxists, Ilyenkov, committed suicide.) Nine opted or were forced to emigrate to the West.

As cited in this book's introduction, Berdiaev wrote of a paradoxical combination: Russians tend to philosophize, yet "the fate of the philosopher in Russia is painful and tragic." This applies even to the relatively tranquil and "vegetarian" period of Russian history that followed Stalin's death. Indeed, even in its senility, Soviet power remained obsessed with the ruling philosophy and jealous of all its rivals—individual thinkers—which led to their systematic suppression. Nearly all the thinkers featured in this book, including those who were relatively fortunate and managed to avoid arrest and persecution, were silenced for years or decades, or forced to chop up their thoughts to fit the procrustean bed of the state's governing "reason."

Philosophical ideas in the Soviet Union rarely matured into well-balanced systems or rigorous and wholly consistent methods (with the notable exceptions of Bibler, Losev, Lotman, Nalimov, and Shchedrovitsky), because the state arrogated to itself the privilege of elaborating and consummating ideas in a systematic way. It fell to non-Marxist thinkers to try to dissolve this ideological rigidity in a stream of critical thinking that pointed beyond extant or even possible systems and undermined rather than consolidated them. Since the official philosophy functioned as a tool of power, it was the task and merit of nonofficial philosophy to advance anti-totalitarian modes of thinking, thus decentralizing the structure of discourse. Thought tried to free itself from subjection to ideocracy by putting down roots in authentic, concrete forms of being, such as the empirical credibility of science, the existential uniqueness of personality, faith in a living God, the spiritual integrity of humankind, the rational design of the cosmos, the symbolic meanings of culture, or the organic soul of the nation; or by challenging the master-discourse of Soviet ideology through parodic imitation and exaggeration. All of these trends: rationalist, personalist, liberal, humanistic, religious, national, culturological, postmodernist—were initially and intentionally forms of intellectual self-liberation. The internal logic of development, however, has led some of these schools of thought, especially the philosophy of national spirit, to stand as renovated or "new and improved" projects of post-Soviet fundamentalism and ideocracy. Some of these crypto-authoritarian trends, and the internal irony of their evolution, are examined in my book *Ideas against Ideocracy: Non-Marxist Thought in the Soviet Union (1953–91).*[4]

Russian intellectual history is a history of thought fighting desperately to escape the prison of an ideological system created by the strenuous and sacrificial efforts of thought itself. What makes Russian thought so remarkable is its internal tension, its struggle against itself, against its own ideational constructions and political extensions.

In the West, the field of philosophy is more or less clearly divided into ontology, the philosophy of being, and epistemology, the philosophy of knowledge. In Russia, such a division is far less relevant, since philosophy addresses a conception of being that is itself constructed by thinking. From Petr Chaadaev and then the Westernizers and Slavophiles onward, Russian philosophy placed its focus on second-order reality, the reality created by ideas. Russian philosophy may have been "derivative" and "secondary," but what it was derivative *of* was not so much imported Western thought as the ideologically fabricated and fantastical reality of Russia herself. In Russia, thought tried to confront the triumph of thought. One speculative capacity, the "intelligentsia," opposed itself to another speculative capacity, the "ideology"—but the former also created its own versions of the latter. This self-contradictory movement of thought, shattering its own foundations, is what lends Russian philosophy its unprecedented, at times "suicidal" character.

Notes

Introduction

1. "Zatem prislali greki k Vladimiru filosofa ..." ("Then the Greeks sent a philosopher to Vladimir ..."). *Povest' vremennykh let* (early twelfth century), year 986 (https://azbyka.ru/otechnik/Nestor_Letopisets/povest-vremennyh-let/2). This is not only the first mention of a philosopher in the history of the Russian language, but also a testament to the foundational role of philosophy (albeit in a very broad sense) in Russian history.
2. Boris Pasternak, *Doctor Zhivago*, trans. Richard Pevear and Larissa Volokhonsky (New York: Pantheon Books, 2010), 162–3.
3. *Filosofskii slovar'*, ed. M. M. Rozental' and P. F. Iudin (Moscow: Politizdat, 1963), 274.
4. Ivan Michurin, *Sochineniia* (Moscow: Sel'khozgiz, 1948), 2: 515.
5. The benefits and perils of ideocracy (a state ruled by ideas) as highlighted in the philosophical debate between Leo Strauss and Alexandre Kojève are discussed in my book *Ideas against Ideocracy: Non-Marxist Thought in the Soviet Union (1953–91)*.
6. Gary Saul Morson, and Caryl Emerson (eds.), *Rethinking Bakhtin: Extensions and Challenges* (Northwestern University Press, 1989), 37.
7. In his younger years, 1875–81, Vladimir Solovyov lectured at Moscow University but, characteristically, was forced to retire after he concluded a public lecture with a political statement, condemning revolutionary activities while simultaneously calling upon the tsar to pardon the terrorists who had recently assassinated his father, Alexander II.
8. Pavel Florenskii, *Sochineniia v 4-kh tomakh* (Moscow: Mysl', 1994), 1: 207.
9. Georgii Florovskii, *Puti russkogo bogosloviia* (Paris: YMCA-Press, 1988), 234–5.
10. Ibid., 236.
11. Nicholas O. Lossky, *History of Russian Philosophy* (New York: International Universities Press, 1972); V. V. Zenkovsky, *A History of Russian Philosophy*, trans. G. L. Kline (London: Routledge & Kegan Paul Ltd., 1953); Sergei A. Levitskii, *Ocherki po istorii russkoi filosofskoi i obshchestvennoi mysli* (Frankfurt/Main: Posev, 1968, 1981); Frederick C. Copleston, *Philosophy in Russia from Herzen to Lenin and Berdyaev* (Notre Dame, Ind.: University of Notre Dame Press, 1986). Even the two-volume *A History of Russian Philosophy: From the Tenth through the Twentieth Centuries* (ed. Valery A. Kuvakin), though published at the end of the twentieth century, stops at its middle, concluding with Pavel Florensky, Nikolai Lossky, and Semyon Frank.
    The same applies to practically all existing anthologies and collections of Russian philosophy. To cite a few examples: Edie, Scanlan, and Zeldin, *Russian Philosophy* concludes with a section on Russian and Soviet Marxism. Schmemann, *Ultimate Questions: An Anthology of Modern Russian Religious Thought* ends with Sergei Bulgakov; and Frank, *Iz istorii russkoi filosofskoi mysli kontsa XIX i nachala XX veka* ends with Semyon Frank (1877–1950).

12 See Herbert Marcuse, *Soviet Marxism: A Critical Analysis* (New York: Columbia University Press, 1985); J. M. Bochenski, *Soviet Russian Dialectical Materialism [Diamat]* (Dordrecht, Holland: D. Reidel, 1963); T. J. Blakeley, *Soviet Philosophy: A General Introduction to Contemporary Soviet Thought* (Kluwer Academic, 1964); Ervin Laszlo (ed.), *Philosophy in the Soviet Union. A Survey of the Mid-Sixties* (Dordrecht, Holland: Reidel, 1967); Bernard Jeu, *La philosophie soviétique et l'Occident. Essai sur les tendances et sur la signification de la philosophie soviétique contemporaine (1959–1969)* (Mercure de France, 1969); A. Callinicos, *Marxism and Philosophy* (Oxford: Oxford University Press, 1983); James P. Scanlan, *Marxism in the USSR: A Critical Survey of Current Soviet Thought* (Ithaca and London: Cornell University Press, 1985); and Helmut Dahm, Thomas Blakeley, and George L. Kline (eds.), *Philosophical Sovietology. The Pursuit of a Science* (Dordrecht, Holland: Reidel, 1987). There is an obsolete if consistent tendency in the West to take Soviet Marxism's claims to philosophical preeminence at face value, and to equate almost all postrevolutionary and non-émigré Russian thought with dialectical materialism.

13 See, e.g., Peter Seyffert, *Soviet Literary Structuralism: Background, Debate, Issues* (Columbus: Slavica, 1985), and Kline, "Recent Uncensored Soviet Philosophical Writings," devoted to three "unofficial" Russian thinkers. Several chapters on non-Marxist currents in Soviet philosophy are found in: Loren R. Graham, *Science, Philosophy, and Human Behavior in the Soviet Union* (New York: Columbia University Press, 1987); Wilhelm Goerdt, *Russische Philosophie. Zugänge und Durchblicke* (Munich: Verlag Karl Alber Freiburg, 1984), 94–112; Evert van der Zweerde, *Soviet Historiography of Philosophy: Istoriko-Filosofskaja Nauka* (Dordrecht: Kluwer Academic, 1997); and Bernard Jeu, *La philosophie soviétique et l'Occident. Essai sur les tendances et sur la signification de la philosophie soviétique contemporaine (1959–1969)* (Mercure de France, 1969).

14 V. A. Lektorskii (ed.), *Filosofiia ne konchaetsia. Iz istorii otechestvennoi filosofii. XX vek.* Kn. 2. 1960–80-e gody (Moscow: Rosspen, 1998); N. V. Motroshilova, *Otechestvennaia filosofiia 50–80-kh godov XX v. i zapadnaia mysl'* (Moscow: Akademicheskii proekt, 2012). These books contain valuable material on Russian philosophy of the period, viewed mainly through the prism of institutional history: research centers and educational programs, groups, and seminars; journals and other publications; conferences and polemics; censorship and ideological pressure; relationships among various collectives and generations; confrontations between creative philosophers and administrators and party officials; and reminiscences about leading figures and organizations (with a strong focus on the Institute of Philosophy of the USSR Academy of Sciences in Moscow). The most comprehensive research of this kind, embracing the entire Soviet epoch, is van der Zweerde, "Soviet Philosophy—the Ideology and the Handmaid." This dissertation outlines the professional fields and functions of philosophy at various stages of Soviet history and contains numerous remarkable data, including statistics, for example: "The number of professional philosophers grew from some 1,500 in 1955 to some 7,000 in 1967, and doubled to 14,000 over the following 8 years" (121).

15 http://www.rosspen.su/ru/catalog/.list/id/3026/.

16 V. A. Lektorskii (ed.), *Problemy i diskussii v filosofii Rossii vtoroi poloviny XX v.: sovremennyi vzgliad* (Moscow: Rosspen, 2014); translated as Bykova and Lektorsky, *Philosophical Thought in Russia in the Second Half of the Twentieth Century.*

17 In particular, thinkers who have distinguished themselves mostly in the fields of the history of philosophy, the philosophy of science, logic and psychology, or the study of Eastern philosophy and religion, such as Valentin Asmus, Bonifatii Kedrov, Sergei Rubinshtein, Piama Gaidenko, Aleksandr Piatigorsky, and David Zilberman, despite the considerable merit and depth of their contributions, are not considered in the book. I would emphasize that this study represents only a preliminary attempt to explore the vast, complex, and heterogeneous field of late-Soviet philosophy, investigation of which will subsequently require the joint efforts of many specialists.

I Vicissitudes of Soviet Marxism

1 Marx and Engels never used this term; it was coined only in 1887 by Joseph Dietzgen, a tanner and socialist activist who independently of them developed the theory of dialectical materialism.
2 On the course of these debates and Stalin's role in them, see David Joravsky, *Soviet Marxism and Natural Science: 1917–1932* (New York: Columbia University Press), 961; and Iegoshua Iakhot, *Podavlenie filosofii v SSSR (20–30-e gody)* (New York: Chalidze Publications, 1981), especially 59–129.
3 This essay became the most authoritative ideological source for all fields of knowledge under Stalinism. Though *A Short Course* was anonymous, the general presumption was—and remains—that the chapter on philosophy had been written by Stalin himself.
4 This work was originally written as a series of five letters, published in the newspaper *Pravda* from June 20 to August 2, 1950.
5 I. V. Stalin, *Sochineniia/Works*, ed. Robert H. McNeal (The Hoover Institution on War, Revolution, and Peace. Stanford: Stanford University Press, 1967), 3: 131. Here as throughout the book, all translations from Russian are mine unless otherwise indicated.
6 Ibid., 123.
7 Ibid., 149.
8 Ibid., 150.
9 Ibid., 151.
10 Ibid., 123.
11 Published in *Pravda* on October 3 and 4, 1952. Stalin died on March 5, 1953.
12 Stalin, *Sochineniia*, 3: 190.
13 *The Economic and Philosophic Manuscripts of 1844* was first published by the Institute of Marxism-Leninism in Moscow in the language of the original: Marx/Engels, *Gesamtausgabe*, Abt. 1, Bd. 3, 1932. The first complete Russian-language edition: K. Marks and F. Engel's, *Iz rannikh proizvedenii*, Moscow: Gosudarstvennoe izdatel'stvo politicheskoi literatury, 1956. This work was first published in English in 1959 by the Foreign Languages Publishing House (Moscow), translated by Martin Milligan.
14 Robert C. Tucker (ed.), *The Marx-Engels Reader* (New York: W. W. Norton, 1972), 70.
15 From the "Private Property and Communism" section of Marx, *Economic and Philosophic Manuscripts of 1844*.
16 For a thorough investigation of Ilyenkov's philosophy and its Soviet background (the debates of the 1920s, Deborin, Vygotsky) in English, see David Bakhurst,

Consciousness and Revolution in Soviet Philosophy: From the Bolsheviks to Evald Ilyenkov (New York: Cambridge University Press, 1991).
17 E. V. Il'enkov, *Filosofiia i kul'tura* (Moscow. Izdatel'stvo politicheskoi literatury, 1991), 286, 287.
18 Ibid., 281.
19 Il'enkov, *Filosofiia i kul'tura*, 55–6. Ilyenkov's views on dialectics are most completely stated in his last book published during his lifetime, *Dialectical Logic: Essays in Its History and Theory* (1977); and in the first published posthumously, *Leninist Dialectics and the Metaphysics of Positivism* (1982).
20 Il'enkov, *Filosofiia i kul'tura*, 309.
21 Cited from Ilyenkov, *The Dialectics of the Abstract and the Concrete in Marx's Capital*.
22 Il'enkov, *Filosofiia i kul'tura*, 261.
23 Ibid., 269.
24 Marx, *Grundrisse*; cited by Ilyenkov in *Filosofiia i kul'tura* (286).
25 Tucker, *The Marx-Engels Reader*, 109.
26 Il'enkov, *Filosofiia i kul'tura*, 393.
27 Ibid., 398.
28 Tucker, *The Marx-Engels Reader*, 74–5; cited by Ilyenkov in *Filosofiia i kul'tura*, 396.
29 Most of these children attained normal developmental/intellectual levels in Meshcheriakov's school, and four of them, under the guidance of Ilyenkov, even graduated Moscow State University and became professional psychologists.
30 Il'enkov, *Filosofiia i kul'tura*, 37.
31 Ibid., 43.
32 Cited from the introduction to ibid., 10.
33 Engels, *The Dialectics of Nature*; cited by Ilyenkov in *Filosofiia i kul'tura*, 430.
34 Ibid., 435, 431.
35 Since 1991, international Ilyenkov conferences have been held annually in various cities of Russia and the near abroad, and their proceedings have been regularly published.
36 Tucker, *The Marx-Engels Reader*, 143.
37 G. S. Batishchev, "Deiatel'nostnaia sushchnost' cheloveka kak filosofskii printsip," in *Problema cheloveka v sovremennoi filosofii*, eds. I. Balakina, B. Grigorian, S. Oduev, and L. Shershenko (Moscow: Nauka, 1969), 81. This is almost a literal repetition of Marx's famous injunction that "human activity itself" be "conceive[d] as *objective* activity" (Tucker, *The Marx-Engels Reader*, 107).
38 Batishchev, "Deiatel'nostnaia sushchnost' cheloveka kak filosofskii printsip," 86.
39 Ibid., 101.
40 Ibid., 109.
41 K. Marx, *Capital*, trans. Ben Fowkes (London: Penguin Classics, 1990), 3: 959.
42 See G. S. Batishchev, *Protivorechie kak kategoriia dialekticheskoi logiki* (Moscow: Vysshaia shkola, 1963), 64–79.
43 The "activity approach" (*deiatel'nostnyi podkhod*), an important trend in late-Soviet philosophy developed by Ilyenkov and Batishchev, is thoroughly investigated in Maidansky and Oittinen, *The Practical Essence of Man: The "Activity Approach" in Late Soviet Philosophy*.
44 Batishchev's *Introduction to the Dialectic of Creativity* (1984) was published in 1997 by the Russian Christian Humanities Institute.

45 As Engels puts it in *Anti-Dühring*: "We therefore reject every attempt to impose on us any moral dogma whatsoever as an eternal, ultimate and forever immutable ethical law on the pretext that the moral world, too, has its permanent principles which stand above history and the differences between nations" (Tucker, *The Marx-Engels Reader*, 667).

46 V. I. Lenin, *Polnoe sobranie sochinenii*. 55 vols. (Moscow: Gosudarstvennoe izdatel'stvo politicheskoi literatury, 1958–65), 41: 311.

47 Milner-Irinin began to work on his project of Marxist ethics in 1931, but Russian readers were first afforded exposure to his views only in 1987, in *Voprosy filosofii* (Questions of Philosophy) (no. 5), and even then, not without the editors' caveat that they did "not share a number of the author's positions, and above all his treatment of ethics as a strictly normative science" (Mil'ner-Irinin, "The Concept of Human Nature and Its Place in the Science of Ethics," 6–7). The full edition of his ethics, under the title of *Ethics, or the Principles of True Humanness*, came out only in 1999: Mil'ner-Irinin, *Etika, ili Printsipy istinnoi chelovechnosti*.

48 Iakov A. Mil'ner-Irinin, "The Concept of Human Nature and Its Place in the Science of Ethics." *Soviet Studies in Philosophy* 27, no. 1 (1988): 6–24.

49 Cited ibid., 24.

50 Cited ibid., 17.

51 Ibid., 24. For a classification of these positions in perestroika-era debates on the fates of Marxism, see E. N. Moshchelkov, *Sovremennye diskussii o kommunisticheskoi teorii K. Marksa i F. Engel'sa. Spetskurs* (Moscow: Izdatel'stvo MGU, 1991).

52 F. P. Shiller and M. A. Lifshits, *Marks i Engel's ob iskusstve*, ed. A. V. Lunacharskii (Moscow: Sovetskaia literatura, 1933); in English, see Mikhail Lifshitz, *The Philosophy of Art of Karl Marx*, trans. B. Ralph Winn, ed. Angel Flores (New York: Critics Group, 1938).

53 Mikhail Lifshits, *Mifologiia drevniaia i novaia* (Moscow: Iskusstvo, 1980), 261, 575.

54 Ibid., 581.

55 A. I. Burov, *Esteticheskaia sushchnost' iskusstva* (Moscow: Iskusstvo, 1956), 280.

56 Ibid., 222.

57 Ibid., 204.

58 Ibid., 286.

59 *Kratkii filosofskii slovar'*, ed. M. Rozental' and P. Iudin (Moscow: Gosudarstvennoe izdatel'stvo politicheskoi literatury, 1954), 256.

60 *Filosofskii slovar'*, 197–8.

61 As mentioned above, the Third Program of the Communist Party of the Soviet Union, adopted at the Twenty-First Party Congress, predicted that the "present generation" would see communism implemented by 1980.

62 M. A. Markov, *O prirode materii* (Moscow: Nauka, 1976), 145.

63 A. A. Liubishchev, *V zashchitu nauki. Stat'i i pis'ma, 1953–1972* (Leningrad: Nauka, 1991), 20.

64 Liubishchev was remarkable not only as a scientist and thinker, but also as someone who managed to organize his time in the most effective way possible, transforming his life into an unending service to intellectual pursuits. Daniil Granin's famous book *This Strange Life* (1974) is devoted to Liubishchev's heroic life and his art of time-management.

65 A. Bogomolov, and I. Narskii (eds.), *Sovremennaia burzhuaznaia filosofiia* (Moscow: MGU, 1972), 518.

66 N. V. Motroshilova, "Fenomenologiia," in *Sovremennaia burzhuaznaia filosofiia*, eds. A. Bogomolov and I. Narskii (Moscow: MGU, 1972), 510.
67 Bogomolov and Narskii, *Sovremennaia burzhuaznaia filosofiia*, 9.
68 Ibid., 15.
69 Ibid.
70 Iu. N. Davydov, *Iskusstvo kak sotsiologicheskii fenomen. K kharakteristike estetiko-politicheskikh vzgliadov Platona i Aristotelia* (Moscow: Nauka, 1968), 18.
71 Ibid., 279.
72 Iu. N. Davydov, *Iskusstvo i elita* (Moscow: Iskusstvo, 1966), 316.
73 See Davydov's books *Estetika nigilizma (iskusstvo i "novye levye")* and *Kritika sotsial'no-filosofskikh vozzrenii Frankfurtskoi shkoly*.
74 Iu. N. Davydov, *Begstvo ot svobody. Filosofskoe mifotvorchestvo i literaturnyi avangard* (Moscow: Khudozhestvennaia literatura, 1978), 356.
75 See Iu. N. Davydov, *Sotsiologiia kontrkul'tury (Infantilizm kak tip mirovospriiatiia i sotsial'naia bolezn'* (Moscow: Nauka, 1980), 259.
76 Davydov, *Iskusstvo i elita*, 126.
77 Davydov, *Begstvo ot svobody*, 151.
78 Iu. N. Davydov, *Etika liubvi i metafizika svoevoliia* (Moscow: Molodaia gvardiia, 1982), 258.
79 See Davydov, *Begstvo ot svobody*, 343–5.
80 Davydov, *Etika liubvi i metafizika svoevoliia*, 271.
81 See Iu. N. Davydov, "Etika i perestroika," in *Opyty. Literaturno-filosofskii ezhegodnik*, ed. Arsenii Gulyga (Moscow: Sovetskii pisatel', 1990), 21.
82 Boris Slavin, *Neokonchennaia istoriia: Besedy Mikhaila Gorbacheva s politologom Borisom Slavinym* (Moscow: OLMA, 2001), 84.
83 S. Platonov, *Posle kommunizma. Kniga ne prednaznachennaia dlia pechati. Vtoroe prishestvie. Besedy* (Moscow: Molodaia gvardiia, 1991), 61.
84 Ibid., 78.
85 Ibid., 70.
86 Ibid., 66.
87 Ibid., 142.
88 K. Marx and F. Engels, "Manifesto of the Communist Party (1848)," Ch. 2. Available electronically: https://www.marxists.org/archive/marx/works/1848/communist-manifesto/ch02.htm.
89 Platonov, *Posle kommunizma*, 130.
90 This tendency can be traced all the way back to medieval Russia, as shown in the influential works of Iurii Lotman and Boris Uspensky. "The specific trajectory of Russian culture ... is its principal polarity, expressed in its dualistic structure. In the system of Russian medievalism, the fundamental cultural values (ideological, political, religious) lie in a bipolar field of values, bisected by a sharp line and lacking any neutral axial zone" ("Rol' dual'nikh modelii v dinamike russkoi kul'tury," 220). These binary mechanisms of Russian culture are discussed more extensively in my *Irony of the Ideal*, especially xiii–xvii, 245, 251, 261–7.
91 Aleksandr Iakovlev, *Predislovie. Obval. Posleslovie* (Moscow: Novosti, 1992), 21.
92 Ibid., 54.
93 See ibid., 75.
94 Ibid., 68.

95 As chief party ideologist, Iakovlev had to conceal his views in order to attempt their implementation on the political scene; thus his critique of Marxism was publicized a year or two after that of Tsipko, although the latter, in his introduction to Iakovlev's book, recognizes his indebtedness to Iakovlev. "The time has come to say that Marxism was, from the very beginning, utopian and erroneous"—these were the words with which Iakovlev in the fall of 1988 greeted Tsipko, who had come to work under his guidance in the Central Committee of the Communist Party (Iakovlev, *Predislovie. Obval. Posleslovie*, 5). Tsipko emphasizes that in Iakovlev's book, "[f]or the first time, a Soviet scholar in Russia has written the truth about Marxism, and has told of the catastrophic consequences of the practical application of this doctrine" (ibid., 3).
96 Aleksandr Tsipko, "Protivorechiia ucheniia Karla Marksa," in *Cherez ternii* by Aleksandr Tsipko (Moscow: Progress, 1990), 67, 68, 71.
97 Cited from S. E. Kurginian, *Sed'moi stsenarii* (Moscow: Eksperimental'nyi tvorcheskii tsentr, 1992), 1: 6.
98 One of the earliest and most significant investigations of the religious underpinnings of communism and Marxism itself is Sergei Bulgakov's 1906 study *Karl Marx as a Religious Type*.
99 S. E. Kurginian, B. Autenshlus, P. Goncharov, Iu. Gromyko, I. Sundiev, V. Ovchinskii, *Postperestroika: kontseptual'naia model' razvitiia nashego obshchestva, politicheskikh partii i obshchestvennykh organizatsii* (Moscow: Politizdat, 1990), 59–60, 66.
100 Ibid., 59.
101 Kurginian, *Sed'moi stsenarii*, 3: 35, 36.
102 Ibid., 1: 328.
103 Ibid., 331.
104 Ibid., 3: 320.
105 Ibid., 3: 228, 226–7, 217, 201.
106 On Eurasianism and its late-Soviet transformations, see Epstein, *Ideas against Ideocracy: Non-Marxist Thought in the Soviet Union (1953–1991)*.
107 For a classification of these positions in perestroika-era debates on the fates of Marxism, see Moshchelkov, *Sovremennye diskussii o kommunisticheskoi teorii K. Marksa i F. Engel'sa*.

II Neo-Rationalism, Structuralism, and General Methodology

1 *The Cambridge Dictionary of Philosophy*. Robert Audi, general editor, 2nd edn. (Cambridge: Cambridge University Press, 1999), 771.
2 Viktor Shklovsky, *A Reader*, ed., trans. Alexandra Berlina (London: Bloomsbury, 2017), 280–1.
3 Ibid., 468.
4 Viktor Shklovskii, *Sobranie sochinenii v 3 tt.* (Moscow: Khudozhestvennaia literatura, 1974), 3: 516.
5 In Lévi-Strauss's example from Native American narratives, the plum tree is significant for its abundance of fruit, the apple for its deep and powerful roots.

6 Claude Lévi-Strauss, *Structural Anthropology*, trans. Monique Layton (New York: Basic Books, 1976), 167, 179.
7 V. Ia. Propp, *Fol'klor i deistvitel'nost'. Izbrannye stat'i* (Moscow: Nauka, glavnaia redaktsiia vostochnoi literatury, 1976), 151–2.
8 V. V. Ivanov, *Ocherki po istorii semiotiki v SSSR* (Moscow: Nauka, 1976), 3.
9 On the history of Soviet semiotics and structuralism, see D. M. Segal, *Aspects of Structuralism in Soviet Philology* (Tel Aviv, 1974); Peter Seyffert, *Soviet Literary Structuralism: Background, Debate, Issues* (Columbus: Slavica, 1985); Stephen Rudy, "Semiotics in the USSR," in *The Semiotic Sphere*, eds Thomas A. Sebeok and Jean Umiker-Sebeok, 555–82 (New York: Plenum Press, 1986); and A. D. Koshelev and M. L. Gasparov, *Iu. M. Lotman i Tartusko-moskovskaia semioticheskaia shkola* (Moscow: Gnozis, 1994). Rather than focusing strictly on the theoretical views and contributions of structuralists, Peter Seyffert's meticulously documented research concentrates on the social and ideological aspects of the debates between structuralists and orthodox Marxists as manifested in conference papers and critical periodicals.
10 On Lotman, see Ann Shukman, *Literature and Semiotics: A Study in the Writings of Ju. M. Lotman* (Amsterdam, New York: North-Holland, 1977); and the special issue of *Russian Literature* (5, no. 1, 1977) devoted to his work.
11 Iu. M. Lotman, *Lektsii po struktural'noi poetike. Vvedenie, teoriia stikha* (Tartu, Estonia, 1964) Brown University Slavic Reprint 5 (Providence: Brown University Press, 1968), 6.
12 Paul Lafargue, "Reminiscences of Marx" (Progress, 1972). Available electronically: https://www.marxists.org/archive/lafargue/1890/xx/marx.htm.
13 Y. Lotman and B. A. Uspensky, "On the Semiotic Mechanism of Culture," trans. George Mihaychuk, in *Critical Theory since 1965*, ed. Hazard Adams and Leroy Searle (Tallahassee: Florida State University Press, 1990), 421.
14 "Culture itself may be regarded both as the totality of messages exchanged by different senders ... and as a single message sent by the collective 'I' of humanity to itself. From this point of view, the culture of humanity is a colossal example of autocommunication" (Iu. M. Lotman, "O dvukh modeliakh kommunikatsii v sisteme kul'tury," in *Izbrannye stat'i*, ed. Iu. M. Lotman, Tallinn: Aleksandra, 1992, 87).
15 Lotman and Uspensky, "On the Semiotic Mechanism of Culture," 415–17.
16 Ju. M. Lotman, "Problems in the Typology of Culture," in *Soviet Semiotics. An Anthology*, ed. Daniel P. Lucid (Baltimore: Johns Hopkins University Press, 1988), 217.
17 Ibid., 218.
18 Ju. M. Lotman, "Primary and Secondary Communication-Modeling Systems," in *Soviet Semiotics. An Anthology*, ed. Daniel P. Lucid (Baltimore: Johns Hopkins University Press, 1988), 97.
19 Yuri M. Lotman, *Universe of the Mind. A Semiotic Theory of Culture*, trans. Ann Shukman (Introduction by Umberto Eco. Bloomington: Indiana University Press, 1990), 125.
20 "The progression in modern Russian theoretical thought from the biosphere to the logosphere and then to the semiosphere constitutes a new organicism that restructures Russian structuralism in a way paralleling post-structuralist reconsiderations of formalism, structuralism, and semiotics.... Lotman transcends the structuralist gridlock in ways that have yet to be recognized by theorists in the

West" (Amy Mandelker, "Semiotizing the Sphere: Organicist Theory in Lotman, Bakhtin, and Vernadsky," *PMLA* 109, no. 3 (1994): 390, 393).
21 Iu. M. Lotman, *Izbrannye stat'i* (Tallinn: Aleksandra, 1992), 1: 478.
22 Lotman, *Universe of the Mind*, 131.
23 Ibid., 142.
24 Ibid., 246. Lotman does, however, recognize another type of memory that "aims to preserve information about the established order and not about its violations" (ibid.). Thus, there exists the possibility of a culture without literacy and without history—"a culture before culture."
25 Lotman and Uspensky, "On the Semiotic Mechanism of Culture," 411.
26 Lotman and Uspenskii, "Binary Models in the Dynamics of Russian Culture," 33.
27 Lotman, *Universe of the Mind*, 218.
28 Ibid., 271.
29 Lotman, "O roli sluchainykh faktorov v istorii kul'tury," in *Izbrannye stat'i* by Iu. M. Lotman (Tallinn: Aleksandra, 1992), 476.
30 In the same way, jeans, which had once been work clothes, became neutral and common to all when "young people in the West rejected the mainstream culture of the twentieth century and saw their ideal in the cultural periphery" (Lotman, *Universe of the Mind*, 141).
31 Iu. M. Lotman, "O roli sluchainykh faktorov v istorii kul'tury," 475.
32 Ibid., 479.
33 Ju. M. Lotman, *Culture and Explosion*, trans. Wilma Clark, ed. Marina Grishakova (Berlin: Mouton de Gruyter, 2009), 24.
34 Ibid., 13.
35 Ibid., 28.
36 Ibid., 174.
37 Ibid. Lotman cites from the celebrated "International," the anthem of the proletariat, which was also the official anthem of the Communist Party of the USSR.
38 On the formation of this group and, more generally, the first postwar generation of Soviet philosophers, see "A Beginning Is Always Historical, i.e. Governed by Chance. Fragments from a Conversation with M. K. Mamardashvili," and A. M. Piatigorsky and V. N. Sadovnikov, "How We Studied Philosophy. Moscow University in the 1950s," *Russian Studies in Philosophy* 32, no. 4 (1994): 48–88.
39 See Shchedrovitskii, "Mesto logicheskikh i psikhologicheskikh metodov v pedagogicheskoi nauke"; and the sections "Refleksiia" and "Smysl i znachenie" in Shchedrovitskii, *Izbrannye trudy*, 485–95, 545–76.
40 V. A. Lefevr, "Nepostizhimaia effektivnost' matematiki v issledovaniiakh chelovecheskoi deiatel'nosti." *Voprosy filosofii*, no. 7 (1990): 51–4.
41 G. P. Shchedrovitskii, *Izbrannye trudy* (Moscow: Izdatel'stvo Shkoly kul'turnoi politiki, 1995), 297–8.
42 P. G. Shchedrovitskii, *Ocherki po filosofii obrazovaniia* (Moscow: Pedagogicheskii tsentr "Eksperiment," 1993), 65–6. This book is one of the most complete expositions of the school's philosophical ideas, though it focuses primarily on pedagogical issues.
43 Ibid., 110.
44 G. P. Shchedrovitskii, *Pedagogika i logika* (Moscow: Kastal', 1993), 133.
45 Shchedrovitskii, *Ocherki po filosofii obrazovaniia*, 142.
46 Ibid., 141.

47 Ibid., 66.
48 Ibid., 76.
49 Ibid., 119. This evokes Lenin's famous definition of literature, which "bourgeois" thought conceptualizes as a free activity of creative spirit, but which, from a Marxist point of view, is a "cog" in the great machine of the proletarian cause.
50 Ibid., 116.
51 Ibid., 71.
52 All these materials, including papers, archives, and bibliography, are available on the site: http://www.fondgp.ru/ (from which this motto is quoted).
53 V. A. Lefevr, "Ot psikhofiziki k modelirovaniiu dushi," *Voprosy filosofii*, no. 7 (1990): 25; see also V. Lefebvre, "The Fundamental Structures of Human Reflexion," in *The Structure of Human Reflection: The Reflexional Psychology of Vladimir Lefebvre*, ed. H. Wheeler (New York: Peter Lang, 1990), 5–70.
54 V. Lefebvre, *Algebra of Conscience. A Comparative Analysis of Western and Soviet Ethical Systems* (Dordrecht: D. Reidel, 1982), xiv–xv.
55 Ibid., 30.
56 Nalimov's main books published in English are *In the Labyrinths of Language*; *Faces of Science*; *Realms of the Unconscious*; and *Space, Time, and Life*. All were edited by Robert G. Colodny (1915–1997), a specialist in the history of science and European history.
57 V. Nalimov, *Veroiatnostnaia model' iazyka* (Moscow: Nauka, 1974); translated as *In the Labyrinths of Language*.
58 V. Nalimov, *In the Labyrinths of Language: A Mathematician's Journey* (Philadelphia: ISI Press, 1981), xv.
59 Ibid., 179.
60 Ibid., 197.
61 Ibid., 87.
62 V. Nalimov, *Space, Time, and Life: The Probabilistic Pathways of Evolution*, trans. A. V. Yarkho (Philadelphia: ISI Press, 1985), 90. Available electronically: http://garfield.library.upenn.edu/nalimov/spacetimelife.pdf.
63 Ibid., 95. "Packing" and "unpacking" are essential terms for Nalimov, referring to the increase and decrease of fuzziness. The more discrete and articulate is the language, the more unpacked is the continuum of existence. "Everything cannot but exist within what is unpacked, as the continuum is unpacked."
64 Ibid., 94.
65 Ibid., 97.
66 V. Nalimov, *Realms of the Unconscious: The Enchanted Frontier*, trans. A. V. Yarkho (Philadelphia: ISI Press, 1982), 6.
67 Ibid., 77.
68 See V. Nalimov, "On the History of Mystical Anarchism in Russia," *The International Journal of Transpersonal Studies* 20 (2001): 85–98. Available electronically: https://digitalcommons.ciis.edu/cgi/viewcontent.cgi?article=1283&context=ijts-transpersonalstudies; Aleks Moma, "Vasilii Nalimov kak gnostik." Paper delivered at the OTO Conference (St. Petersburg, 2015). Available electronically: https://sphinx-oto.ru/wp-content/uploads/2015/08/Moma_A_Vasiliy_Nalimov_kak_gnostik_doklad_2015.pdf.
69 Nalimov, *In the Labyrinths of Language*, 182. Incidentally, Nalimov believes that the probabilistic model of language suggests a new interpretation of "the stream

of consciousness," the concept introduced by the American philosopher and psychologist William James (1842–1910).
70 "In biology the most precisely given unit is the initial taxon, namely, a species. There is interspecific uncertainty. It may be very serious: there even exists a catalog for plant deformities.... Biology is more statistical than physics" (Nalimov, *Space, Time, and Life*, 90).
71 Nalimov, *Realms of the Unconscious*, 291, 292.
72 Ibid., 292.
73 This was the title of a 1988 lecture, published in Mamardashvili's collection on "My Understanding of Philosophy" (*Kak ia ponimaiu filosofiiu*, 100).
74 Ibid., 63.
75 Piatigorsky emigrated to the UK in 1974, joining the faculty of the School of Oriental and African Studies at the University of London. He continued to produce religious and philosophical studies both in Russian and English, and authored several philosophical novels, such as *The Philosophy of a Side Street* (1994).
76 Merab Mamardashvili and Aleksandr Piatigorskii, *Simvol i soznanie. Metafizicheskie rassuzhdeniia o soznanii, simvolike i iazyke* (Jerusalem: I. Maler and V. Glozman, 1982), 273.
77 Ibid., 180.
78 Merab Mamardashvili, *Kak ia ponimaiu filosofiiu*. 2nd edn (Moscow: Progress, 1992), 59.
79 Mamardashvili, *Kak ia ponimaiu filosofiiu*, 263.
80 Ibid., 332.
81 Merab Mamardashvili, *Klassicheskii i neklassicheskii idealy ratsional'nosti* (Tbilisi: Metsniereba, 1984), 67.
82 Ibid., 68.
83 Ibid., 67.
84 Ibid., 78.
85 Ibid., 69.
86 Ibid., 64.
87 Ibid., 81.
88 Mamardashvili, *Kak ia ponimaiu filosofiiu*, 56, 57.
89 Posthumous publications edited by Senokosov include *Kartezianskie razmyshleniia*; *Kantianskie variatsii*; *Strela poznaniia*; *Estetika myshleniia*; and Mamardashvili's lectures on Proust, *Psikhologicheskaia topologiia puti*.
90 Mamardashvili, *Kak ia ponimaiu filosofiiu*, 335.
91 Ibid., 337.
92 Ibid., 336.
93 On Mamardashvili's thinking in the context of transcultural theory, see Ellen Berry and Mikhail Epstein, *Transcultural Experiments: Russian and American Models of Creative Communication* (New York: Palgrave MacMillan, 1999), 82–3.
94 Mamardashvili, *Kak ia ponimaiu filosofiiu*, 50.
95 As described, for example, in a work on Mamardashvili translated into English: Diana Gasparyan, *Merab Mamardashvili's Philosophy of Consciousness* (Independent, 2012). Introduction and partial bibliography available electronically: https://www.hse.ru/pubs/share/direct/demo_document/138019057.

See also Alyssa DeBlasio, *The Filmmaker's Philosopher: Merab Mamardashvili and Russian Cinema* (Edinburgh: Edinburgh University Press, 2019).
96 The proceedings of the first conference (*Pervye filosofskie chteniia*, 1992) are published in the collection: Kruglikov, *Kongenial'nost' mysli*.
97 The foundation's website: https://mamardashvili.com/. For a bibliography of works by and (mostly) about Mamardashvili in English, see http://www.autodidactproject.org/bib/mamardashvili.html.

III The Philosophy of Personality and of Freedom

1 Prishvin's diaries were published posthumously, first only in excerpts called "forget-me-nots" (*nezabudki*)—the title of a 1968 book of his selected and thematically organized meditations; and in full only after the collapse of the Soviet Union and its censorship apparatus, in eighteen volumes (1991–2017)—about 14,000 printed pages. According to the publishers, the volume of the diaries is three times that of Prishvin's works in all other genres.
2 Mikhail Prishvin, *Nezabudki* (Moscow: Khudozhestvennaia literatura, 1968), 227.
3 Ibid., 228.
4 Ibid.
5 See the chapters on cosmism in my book *Ideas against Ideocracy: Non-Marxist Thought in the Soviet Union (1953–1991)*.
6 Mikhail Prishvin, *Sobranie sochinenii v 8 tomakh* (Moscow: Khudozhestvennaia literatura, 1986), 8: 525.
7 This thought was originally expressed by Prishvin's wife Valeriia Dmitrievna (1899–1979) in a letter to him.
8 Prishvin, *Sobranie sochinenii v 8 tomakh*, 8: 603, 645.
9 Ibid., 525.
10 Prishvin, *Nezabudki*, 234.
11 Ibid., 53.
12 Prishvin, *Sobranie sochinenii*, 8: 516.
13 Iakov Druskin, *Dnevniki*, ed. annot. L. S. Druskina (St. Petersburg: Akademicheskii proekt, 1999), 11.
14 Iakov Druskin, *Pered prinadlezhnostiami chego-libo. Dnevniki, 1963–1979* (St. Petersburg: Akademicheskii proekt, 2001), 53.
15 Ibid., 51.
16 Iakov Druskin, *Vblizi vestnikov*, ed. with a preface Genrikh Orlov (Washington, DC: H. A. Frager, 1988), 52.
17 Ibid.
18 Ibid., 119.
19 Ibid., 166.
20 Ibid., 258.
21 Ibid.
22 Ibid., 165–6.
23 Ibid., 9.
24 Ibid., 179.

25 Ibid., 169.
26 Ibid., 167–8.
27 Ibid., 173.
28 Ibid., 118.
29 Lidiia Ginzburg, *Prokhodiashchie kharaktery: Proza voennykh let. Zapiski blokadnogo cheloveka*, ed. Emily van Buskirk and Andrei Zorin (Moscow: Novoe izdatel'stvo, 2011). The second part of this book has been published in English as *Notes from the Blockade*.
30 Lidiia Ginzburg, *Chelovek za pis'mennym stolom* (Leningrad: Sovetskii pisatel', 1989), 283.
31 From Pasternak's poem "Sublime Sickness," 1923–8. http://slova.org.ru/pasternak/visokayabolezn/
32 Ginzburg, *Chelovek za pis'mennym stolom*, 463.
33 Ibid., 288.
34 Ibid., 516.
35 Ibid., 464.
36 Ibid., 287–8.
37 Grigorii Pomerants, *Sny zemli* (Long Island City, NY: Izd-vo "Poiski", 1979), 86.
38 Ibid., 87.
39 Ibid., 345.
40 Ibid., 281.
41 Ibid., 285.
42 From a talk Pomerants gave at a discussion on communism and religion at Moscow's Institute of the Countries of Asia and Africa in 1968. Cited from Roi Medvedev, ed. *Politicheskii dnevnik* (Amsterdam: The Alexander Herzen Foundation, 1975), 533.
43 Ibid., 537.
44 Pomerants, *Sny zemli*, 180.
45 See the short essay on "God and nothingness" in Pomerants, *Neopublikovannoe. Bol'shie i malye esse. Publitsistika* (Frankfurt: Posev, 1972), 188–9.
46 Pomerants, *Sny zemli*, 43.
47 Ibid., 84. Pomerants's imagery implicitly refers to Kierkegaard's likening of the (existential) faith-position to floating "out upon the deep, over seventy thousand fathoms of water" (Søren Kierkegaard, *The Living Thoughts of Kierkegaard*, ed. W. H. Auden, New York: New York Review Books, 1999, 152).
48 Solzhenitsyn is discussed in my book *Ideas against Ideocracy* (in the part "The Philosophy of National Spirit").
49 Pomerants, *Sny zemli*, 345.
50 Pomerants, *Neopublikovannoe*, 128.
51 Ibid., 148.
52 Ibid., 168. What Pomerants extols as the intelligent minority becomes for his nationalist opponents, such as Igor Shafarevich, the "minor people" (or "little nation," *malyi narod*) that undermines the healthy moral foundations of the majority, the "major people" or "great nation."
53 Ibid., 167.
54 Cited from Lyman Tower Sargent, "Camus: The Absurdity of Politics," in *The Artist and Political Vision*, ed. Benjamin R. Barber, Michael J. Gargas McGrath (London: Transaction Books, 1983), 110.

55 Pomerants, *Neopublikovannoe*, 151.
56 Ibid.
57 Pomerants, *Sny zemli*, 345.
58 Ibid., 351.
59 Ibid., 287.
60 Grigorii Pomerants, *Otkrytost' bezdne. Etiudy o Dostoevskom* (New York: Liberty, 1989), 124.
61 In particular, Pomerants blames Dostoevsky for his ardent hatred of liberals and for the same "dirty" methods of political denunciation that revolutionaries used. "It is sad to see a devil take possession of Dostoevsky himself, to see his hatred for 'devils' lead him to a kind of 'devilish' spasms, to the lampoon of Liamshin [a character of Jewish origin in *The Devils*], to the literary denunciation of Turgenev" (ibid., 104).
62 Ibid., 99.
63 Grigorii Pomerants, "V poiskakh sviatyni." *Sintaksis* (Paris), no. 27 (1990): 24.
64 Ibid.
65 Boris Khazanov, *Mif Rossiia. Opyt romanticheskoi politologii* (New York: Liberty, 1986), 108.
66 Boris Khazanov, *Idushchii po vode. Stat'i i pis'ma* (München: Strana i mir, 1985), 206.
67 Boris Khazanov, *Zapakh zvezd* (Tel-Aviv: Vremia i my, 1977), 284.
68 Khazanov, *Idushchii po vode*, 96.
69 Ibid., 97; see also 215.
70 Ibid., 96.
71 Ibid., 214.
72 One of these is the Russian Orthodox priest Sergei Zheludkov (1909–1984), whose views are discussed in my book *Ideas against Ideocracy*; another, designated by the initials Iu. A. Sh., is probably Iulii Shreider (1927–1998), a well-known Moscow philosopher and semiotician, and a member of the Catholic Church.
73 Khazanov, *Idushchii po vode*, 100.
74 Khazanov, *Zapakh zvezd*, 103; capitalization as in original.
75 Ibid.
76 Ibid., 103.
77 Ibid., 207.
78 Ibid., 241.
79 Mihajlo Mihajlov, *Underground Notes*, trans. Maria Mihajlov Ivusic and Christopher W. Ivusic (New Rochelle, NY: Caratzas Brothers, 1982), 23.
80 Ibid., 15.
81 Mihajlo Mihajlov, *Planetarnoe soznanie* (Ann Arbor: Ardis, 1982), 127. This important article "The Return of the Grand Inquisitor" was omitted in the American translation of the book. Andrei Sakharov in his *Memoirs* emphasizes his appreciation of Mihajlov's critique of Solzhenitsyn and repeats the thesis "The homeland is freedom" (*Rodina—eto svoboda*). See Andrei Sakharov, *Vospominaniia* (New York: Chekhov, 1990), 818, 821, 828.
82 Mihajlov, *Planetarnoe soznanie*, 100.
83 Mihajlov, *Underground Notes*, 68.
84 See Fyodor Dostoevsky, *The Brothers Karamazov*, trans. Richard Pevear and Larissa Volokhonsky (New York: Vintage Books, 1992), 251–2.
85 Mihajlov, *Planetarnoe soznanie*, 107.

86 Andrei Sakharov will be discussed in this part's second section, on liberalism.
87 Mihajlov, *Underground Notes*, 15.
88 Ibid., 2–3.
89 Ibid., 4.
90 Mihajlov, *Planetarnoe soznanie*, 124.
91 Mihajlov, *Underground Notes*, 176; emphasis in original.
92 Ibid., 189.
93 Ibid., 186, 187.
94 Mihajlo Mihajlov, *Abram Terts ili Begstvo iz retort* (Frankfurt/Main: Posev, 1969), 61.
95 Mihajlo Mihajlov, *Russian Themes*, trans. Maria Mihajlov (New York: Farrar, Straus and Giroux, 1968), 65.
96 Ibid.
97 This analogy was suggested by Pasternak in his poem "I like the obstinate temperament," on Stalin.
98 Boris Paramonov, "Nizkie istiny demokratii. Opyt vynuzhdennogo ponimaniia." *Grani*, no. 139 (1986): 233.
99 Ibid., 226.
100 Boris Paramonov, "Panteon. Demokratiia kak religioznaia problema." *Strana i mir* (Munich), no. 1 (1988): 63.
101 As will be discussed in the next chapter, a similar connection between democracy and polytheism is explicitly stated in the writings of Joseph Brodsky.
102 Boris Paramonov, *Konets stilia* (Moscow: Agraf, 1997), 230.
103 Ibid., 231–2.
104 Paramonov, "Nizkie istiny demokratii," 243.
105 Paramonov, "Panteon," 72–3.
106 Andrei Platonov, *Chevengur* (Paris: IMCA-Press, 1972), 217–18.
107 Boris Paramonov, "Chevengur i okrestnosti." *Kontinent* (Paris), no. 54 (1987): 340.
108 Paramonov discusses his views on the metaphysical aspects of gender and (homo)sexuality in his essay collection *Men and Women*.
109 Paramonov, "Panteon," 75.
110 Andrei Ariev, "Na chempionate po nich'im." *Russkaia mysl'* (Paris), May 14, 1993.
111 Boris Paramonov, "Slavianofil'stvo." *Grani*, no. 135 (1985): 257.
112 Ibid., 246.
113 Joseph Brodsky, "Uncommon Visage. The Nobel Lecture," in *On Grief and Reason: Essays* by Joseph Brodsky (New York: Farrar, Straus and Giroux, 1995), 46.
114 Ibid., 49.
115 Joseph Brodsky, *Less than One. Selected Essays* (New York: Farrar, Straus and Giroux, 1986), 435.
116 Ibid., 410–11.
117 Ibid., 385.
118 Incidentally, the theologian and art historian Evgenii Barabanov (b. 1943) participated in both collections—a sign that the liberal and conservative wings of the dissident movement still had areas of overlap in the mid-1970s.
119 Roman Redlikh, *Solidarnost' i svoboda* (Frankfurt a.M.: Posev, 1984), 269–70.
120 Ibid., 271.
121 See Vadim Belotserkovskii, *Svoboda, vlast' i sobstvennost'* (Achberg, 1977), 108.

122 A. S. Yesenin-Volpin, *A Leaf of Spring*, trans. George Reavey (New York: Frederick A. Praeger, 1961), 111. Also available electronically: http://webct.biz/yesseninvolpin/phil-treatise.html.
123 Ibid., 121.
124 See ibid., 163.
125 Ibid., 147.
126 Ibid., 145.
127 Ibid., 165.
128 Ibid., 117.
129 Ibid., 139.
130 Ibid., 113, 169.
131 Ibid., 113.
132 Ibid., 129.
133 Esenin-Volpin's other treatise "On the Logic of the Moral Sciences" was published in samizdat in 1970 and later included in the most complete edition of his works in various disciplines and genres (including logic, mathematics, theory of modalities, poetry, and law): Esenin-Vol'pin, *Filosofiia. Logika. Poeziia. Zashchita prav cheloveka.*
134 Arkadii Belinkov, "Strana rabov, strana gospod ..." *Novyi kolokol. Literaturno-publitsisticheskii sbornik* (London), no. 1 (1972), 355.
135 Andrei Amalrik, *Will the Soviet Union Survive Until 1984?* (New York and Evanston: Harper and Row, 1970), 34.
136 Arkadii Belinkov, *Iurii Tynianov* (Moscow: Sovetskii pisatel', 1960), 64.
137 Arkadii Belinkov, *Sdacha i gibel' sovetskogo intelligenta. Iurii Olesha*, ed. N. Belinkova (Madrid: Ediciones Castilla, 1976), 562.
138 Belinkov, "Strana rabov, strana gospod ... ," 353.
139 Ibid., 363.
140 Ibid., 342–3.
141 Ibid., 365.
142 Amalrik, *Will the Soviet Union Survive Until 1984?*, 5.
143 Ibid., 33, 34.
144 Ibid., 35.
145 Ibid., 36.
146 Andrei Amal'rik, *SSSR i Zapad v odnoi lodke* (London: Overseas Publications Interchange, 1978), 93.
147 Amalrik, *Will the Soviet Union Survive Until 1984?*, 41–2.
148 Ibid., 64–5.
149 Ibid., 65.
150 Andrei Sakharov, *Trevoga i nadezhda* (Moscow: Inter-Verso, 1990), 59.
151 Ibid., 41–2.
152 Ibid., 40.
153 Ibid., 42.
154 Andrei Sakharov, *My Country and the World*, trans. Guy V. Daniels (New York: Vintage Books, 1975), 91.
155 Sakharov, *Trevoga i nadezhda*, 177.
156 Andrei Sakharov, "On Aleksandr Solzhenitsyn's 'Letter to the Soviet Leaders,'" in *The Political, Social and Religious Thought of Russian "Samizdat": An Anthology*,

ed. Michael Meerson-Aksenov and Boris Shragin, trans. Nicholas Lupinin (Belmont: Nordland, 1977), 297.
157 Ibid., 297–8.
158 See Solzhenitsyn's response to Sakharov's criticism, "Sakharov i kritika 'Pis'ma vozhdiam,'" 196.
159 Sakharov, "On Aleksandr Solzhenitsyn's 'Letter to the Soviet Leaders,'" 300.
160 Ibid., 301. The history of the Solzhenitsyn-Sakharov polemic may be summarized by the following principal texts listed in the Bibliography: (1) Solzhenitsyn, "Pis'mo vozhdiam Sovetskogo Soiuza" (1973); (2) Sakharov, "On Aleksandr Solzhenitsyn's 'Letter to the Soviet Leaders'" (April 1974); (3) Solzhenitsyn, "Sakharov i kritika 'Pis'ma vozhdiam,'" (November 1974); (4) Solzhenitsyn, *Bodalsia telenok s dubom* (1975); (5) Sakharov, *Vospominaniia* (1990), 549–62.
161 Sakharov, *My Country and the World*, 89.
162 Sakharov, *Trevoga i nadezhda*, 84.
163 Ibid.
164 Andrei Sakharov, "Nobel Lecture: Peace, Progress, Human Rights." December 11, 1975. Available electronically: https://www.nobelprize.org/nobel_prizes/peace/laureates/1975/sakharov-lecture.html.
165 Sakharov, *Vospominaniia*, 13.
166 N. Ia. Eidel'man, *Pushkin i dekabristy. Iz istorii vzaimootnoshenii* (Moscow: Khudozhestvennaia literatura, 1979), 444.
167 N. Ia. Eidel'man, *Gran' vekov. Politicheskaia bor'ba v Rossii. Konets XVIII–nachalo XIX stoletiia* (Moscow: Mysl', 1982), 346–7.
168 Eidel'man, *Pushkin i dekabristy*, 404. Characteristically, even in his early book on Herzen, Eidelman showed that Herzen evaluated "the figures of the past both according to their objective role in the fight for liberation and according to their subjective world, the degree of their inner emancipation" (N. Ia. Eidel'man, *Gertsen protiv samoderzhaviia. Sekretnaia politicheskaia istoriia Rossii XVIII–XIX vekov i Vol'naia pechat'* (Moscow: Mysl', 1973), 103). The latter factor became ever more important for Eidelman himself and for the intelligentsia of his generation as the political hopes and aspirations of Khrushchev's Thaw gave way to the moribund "stagnation" of the late Brezhnev period.
169 Eidel'man, *Pushkin i dekabristy*, 404–5.
170 N. Ia. Eidel'man, *Pushkin. Istoriia i sovremennost' v khudozhestvennom soznanii poeta. Monografiia* (Moscow: Sovetsky pisatel', 1984), 363.
171 Aleksandr Ianov, *Russkaia ideia i 2000-yi god* (New York: Liberty, 1988), 116–17.
172 L. M. Batkin, *Vozobnovlenie istorii. Razmyshleniia o politike i kul'ture* (Moscow: Moskovskii rabochii, 1991), 290.

IV Culturology, or, the Philosophy of Culture

1 Herder's *Ideas on the Philosophy of the History of Mankind* (1784–91) can be considered the first systematic treatise on the philosophy of culture grounded in organicist or holistic interpretive methods.
2 The term "culturology" (German *Kulturologie*) was first proposed by the distinguished German chemist and Nobel laureate Wilhelm Ostwald in 1915 in his

address "The System of the Sciences" at the Rice Institute in Houston, Texas. (See also W. Ostwald, *Energetische Grundlagen der Kulturwissenschaft* [Leipzig, 1909].) In Anglophone social sciences, the concept of *culturology* was developed by the American anthropologist Leslie A. White in his influential 1949 study *The Science of Culture*. For White, culturology should be distinguished both from psychology and sociology, as the former deals not with individuals and society considered separately, but with the objective products of their interaction. He provides an example: "Psychology presents the man of genius and demonstrates his effect upon society. Sociology shows how society conditions the life of the exceptionally gifted person. Culturology explains both the great man and society and the relationship between them" (*The Science of Culture*, 197). For a brief history of the term and concept, see ibid., 410–12. Overall, Soviet culturology, following in the footsteps of the prerevolutionary Russian thinkers Nikolai Danilevsky and Konstantin Leontiev, relied more on German than American theoretical approaches to culture.

3 N. Ia. Danilevskii, *Rossiia i Evropa* (Moscow: Kniga, 1991), 471–2.
4 Nikolai Berdiaev, *Sobranie sochinenii* (Paris: YMCA-Press), 4: 556.
5 One of the first Soviet scholars to begin developing culturology as an integrative discipline was the Armenian philosopher Eduard Markarian, who (e.g., in *Essays on the Theory of Culture* [1969]) viewed culture from a Marxist perspective, in particular, as the method by which human activity organizes itself and adapts to the external environment.
6 Mikhail Bakhtin, *Speech Genres and Other Late Essays*, ed. Caryl Emerson and Michael Holquist, trans. Vern W. McGee (Austin: University of Texas Press, 1986), 135.
7 Ibid., 2.
8 A. F. Losev, *Istoriia antichnoi estetiki. Poslednie veka* (Moscow: Iskusstvo, 1988), 2: 379.
9 A. F. Losev, *Ocherki antichnogo simvolizma i mifologii* (Moscow: Izdanie avtora, 1930), 1: 690, 693.
10 A valuable comparison of the two thinkers and their parallel fates is offered by Caryl Emerson in her article "On the Generation That Squandered Its Philosophers (Losev, Bakhtin, and Classical Thought as Equipment for Living)."
11 Seminal works on Bakhtin, to mention only books and monographs, include Todorov, *Mikhail Bakhtin: The Dialogical Principle*; Clark and Holquist, *Mikhail Bakhtin*; Morson, *Bakhtin: Essays and Dialogues on His Work*; Morson and Emerson, *Rethinking Bakhtin: Extensions and Challenges*; Morson and Emerson, *Mikhail Bakhtin: Creation of a Prosaics*; Emerson, *The First Hundred Years of Mikhail Bakhtin*; Bibler, *Mikhail Mikhailovich Bakhtin, ili poetika kul'tury*; Pechey, *Mikhail Bakhtin: The Word in the World*; and Isupov, *M. M. Bakhtin: Pro et Contra*. The full bibliography would include thousands of publications in dozens of languages.
12 Averintsev's critique of Bakhtin will be discussed in the chapter on Averintsev.
13 See Caryl Emerson, "On Mikhail Bakhtin and Human Studies (with Continual Reference to Moscow and Sheffield)." *Russian Journal of Communication* 8, no. 2 (2017): 119–41.
14 Bakhtin, *Speech Genres and Other Late Essays*, 78.
15 Ibid., 79.
16 Ibid., 2.
17 Mikhail Bakhtin, *Literaturno-kriticheskie stat'i* (Moscow: Khudozhestvennaia literatura, 1986), 478, 484.

18 Bakhtin, *Speech Genres and Other Late Essays*, 136.
19 Bakhtin, *Literaturno-kriticheskie stat'i*, 478.
20 Bakhtin, *Speech Genres and Other Late Essays*, 169.
21 Ibid., 136-7.
22 Dale E. Peterson, "Response and Call: The African American Dialogue with Bakhtin." *American Literature* 65, no. 4 (1993): 762.
23 Bakhtin, *Literaturno-kriticheskie stat'i*, 523.
24 Ibid., 509.
25 Ibid., 424.
26 Ibid.
27 Ibid., 516.
28 Bakhtin, *Speech Genres and Other Late Essays*, 7.
29 Ibid., 6.
30 Ibid., 7.
31 Ibid., 152.
32 Ibid., 148-9.
33 Ibid., 148.
34 Ibid., 137.
35 Nicholas O. Lossky, *History of Russian Philosophy* (New York: International Universities Press, 1972), 292-6; V. V. Zenkovsky, *A History of Russian Philosophy*, trans. G. L. Kline (London: Routledge & Kegan Paul, 1953), 2: 833-9. Losev is one of the most prolific Russian thinkers, the author of approximately five hundred published works, including over thirty books. Only a small portion of Losev's shorter essays have been translated into English; see *Soviet Studies in Literature* 20 (1984), nos. 2-3 (special issue on A. F. Losev's ninetieth birthday, including a list of Losev publications for the period 1916-83).
36 Of all Losev's books, the only one available in English is *The Dialectics of Myth*.
37 A. F. Losev, *Filosofiia. Mifologiia. Kul'tura* (Moscow, Politizdat, 1991), 169.
38 Ibid., 170.
39 A. F. Losev, "Imiaslavie" (1918), *Voprosy filosofii*, no. 9 (1993): 56; capitalization as in original.
40 Losev, *Filosofiia. Mifologiia. Kul'tura*, 78.
41 Ibid., 79.
42 Ibid., 112.
43 Ibid., 113-14.
44 Ibid., 473.
45 Ibid., 498.
46 A. F. Losev, *Istoriia antichnoi estetiki. Sofisty. Sokrat. Platon* (Moscow: Iskusstvo, 1969), 5-6.
47 Ibid., 502.
48 Ibid., 150.
49 A. F. Losev, *Vladimir Solov'ev i ego vremia* (Moscow: Progress, 1990), 625-6.
50 Ibid., 625.
51 A. F. Losev, *Strast' k dialektike. Literaturnye razmyshleniia filosofa* (Moscow: Sovetskii pisatel', 1990), 316.
52 S. S. Averintsev, "'Mirovozzrencheskii stil'': podstupy k iavleniiu Loseva," *Voprosy filosofii*, no. 9 (1993): 21, 22.

53 Olga Freidenberg, *Image and Concept: Mythopoetic Roots of Literature*, ed. and annot. Nina Braginskaia and Kevin Moss, trans. Kevin Moss (London: Routledge, 1997), 26. The legacy of Olga Freidenberg, as well as that of Iakov Golosovker, has been researched, and certain of their works that never saw print during their lifetimes have been first published, by the philologist-classicist and cultural historian Nina Braginskaia, who also co-edited the English translation of Freidenberg's book.
54 Ibid., 42.
55 Written in 1925–8 (published only in 1991), this novel is considered by a number of researchers to have been a source of inspiration and imitation for Mikhail Bulgakov's *The Master and Margarita* (1928–40), with Golosovker himself serving as the prototype of the Master.
56 Ia. E. Golosovker, *Logika mifa* (Moscow: Nauka (Glavnaia redaktsiia vostochnoi literatury), 1987), 9.
57 Ibid., 153.
58 Ibid., 47.
59 Ibid., 119.
60 Ibid., 190.
61 Ia. E. Golosovker, *Dostoevskii i Kant* (Moscow: Izdatel'stvo akademii nauk SSSR, 1963).
62 Golosovker, *Logika mifa*, 195.
63 D. S. Likhachev, *Poetika drevnerusskoi literatury* (Leningrad: Khudozhestvennaia literatura, 1971), 96.
64 Ibid., 96.
65 Solzhenitsyn's story "Matrena's House" (1963) and Vasilii Belov's novella *That's How Things Are* (1966) gave momentum to "village prose."
66 D. S. Likhachev, *Proshloe—budushchemu. Stat'i i ocherki* (Leningrad: Nauka, 1985), 50.
67 D. S. Likhachev, *Zemlia rodnaia* (Moscow: Prosveshchenie, 1983), 54.
68 Ibid., 55.
69 Ibid., 57.
70 D. S. Likhachev, *Poetika drevnerusskoi literatury* (Leningrad: Khudozhestvennaia literatura, 1971), 405.
71 D. S. Likhachev, "Drevnerusskaia literatura i sovremennost'," *Russkaia literatura*, no. 4 (1978): 25.
72 Likhachev, *Poetika drevnerusskoi literatury*, 411.
73 Ibid.
74 D. S. Likhachev, *O filologii* (Moscow: Vysshaia shkola, 1989), 28.
75 Ibid., 204.
76 Ibid., 206.
77 Ibid., 207.
78 N. I. Konrad, *Zapad i vostok. Stat'i* (Moscow: Glavnaia redaktsiia vostochnoi literatury, 1972), 311.
79 Ibid., 493. The preferred contemporary transliteration of this term is *jinbun-kagaku* (literally "human science"). I am grateful to Prof. Mitsuyoshi Numano of the University of Tokyo for this information.
80 Ibid., 454.
81 Ibid., 485.

82. Vladimir Bibler, *Ot naukoucheniia—k logike kul'tury. Dva filosofskikh vvedeniia v dvadtsat' pervyi vek* (Moscow: Izdatel'stvo politicheskoi literatury, 1991), 292. In the title of this book (*From the Doctrine of Science to the Logic of Culture*), Bibler uses Fichte's term *Wissenschaftslehre*.
83. Ibid., 358.
84. Ibid., 312.
85. Vladimir Bibler, "Byt' filosofom." Available electronically: https://www.bibler.ru/bim_ng_byt_f.php
86. Bibler, *Ot naukoucheniia—k logike kul'tury*, 396; italics and question marks in original.
87. Ibid., 37.
88. Vladimir Bibler, "Iz 'Zametok vprok,'" *Voprosy filosofii*, no. 6 (1991): 37.
89. Bibler, *Ot naukoucheniia—k logike kul'tury*, 301.
90. Ibid., 391.
91. Bibler, "Iz 'Zametok vprok,'" 39.
92. Ibid., 40.
93. See https://www.bibler.ru/index.html, https://www.bibler.ru/arche1.html, and https://www.bibler.ru/arche7.html.
94. Vladimir Bibler, "The Foundations of the School of the Dialogue of Cultures Program," *Journal of Russian and East European Psychology* 47, no. 1 (2009): 34–60.
95. In the 2000s, Kiev's Dukh i litera Press issued a four-volume edition of Sergei Averintsev's collected works, including the volume *Sophia-Logos: A Dictionary* (2005), which contains Averintsev's encyclopedia articles on philosophical and theological issues and his works on the concept of wisdom. Other of the volumes contain his works on cultural and religious history, aesthetics, and poetics, and his translations from the Old and New Testaments and Eastern Church Fathers.
96. S. S. Averintsev, "Grecheskaia 'literatura' i blizhnevostochnaia 'slovesnost.' Dva tvorcheskikh printsipa," in *Religiia i literatura* by S. S. Averintsev (Ann Arbor: Hermitage, 1981), 9.
97. S. S. Averintsev, *Poetika rannevizantiiskoi literatury* (Moscow: Nauka, Glavnaia redaktsiia vostochnoi literatury, 1977), 31.
98. From Augustini's *De vera religione*; cited ibid., 37.
99. Averintsev, *Poetika rannevizantiiskoi literatury*, 38.
100. S. S. Averintsev, "'Morfologiia kul'tury' Osval'da Shpenglera," in *Religiia i literatura* by S. S. Averintsev (Ann Arbor: Hermitage, 1981), 86.
101. Averintsev, *Poetika rannevizantiiskoi literatury*, 238.
102. T. S. Eliot, *Selected Prose of T. S. Eliot*, ed. Frank Kermode (London: Faber, 1984), 60–1.
103. Averintsev, *Poetika rannevizantiiskoi literatury*, 269.
104. S. S. Averintsev, "Pravoslavie," in *Filosofskaia entsiklopediia*, ed. F. V. Konstantinov (Moscow: Sovetskaia entsiklopediia, 1967), 333–4.
105. Averintsev, *Poetika rannevizantiiskoi literatury*, 63.
106. Ibid., 157.
107. Viktor Krivulin, "Konets epokhi Ryb." *Novoe russkoe slovo* (New York), February 17, 1995, 36.
108. S. S. Averintsev, *Ot beregov Bosfora do beregov Evfrata* (Moscow: Izd. Nauka, 1987), 49.

109 S. S. Averintsev, "Vizantiia i Rus': dva tipa dukhovnosti. Stat'ia pervaia," *Novyi mir*, no. 7 (1988): 212.
110 S. S. Averintsev, "Zhak Mariten, neotomizm, katolicheskaia teologiia iskusstva," in *Religiia i literatura* by S. S. Averintsev (Ann Arbor: Hermitage, 1981), 129.
111 S. S. Averintsev, "Spasenie," in *Filosofskaia entsiklopediia*, ed. F. V. Konstantinov (Moscow: Sovetskaia entsiklopediia, 1970), 108.
112 Averintsev, *Poetika rannevizantiiskoi literatury*, 57.
113 S. S. Averintsev, "Vizantiia i Rus': dva tipa dukhovnosti. Stat´ia vtoraia," *Novyi mir*, no. 9 (1988): 235.
114 Ibid., 234–5.
115 Ibid., 235.
116 "Razdelennoe khristianstvo." (An interview with Sergei Averintsev in Rome). *Russkaia mysl'* (Paris), no. 3964 (January 29, 1993).
117 S. S. Averintsev, "Bakhtin, smekh, khristianskaia kul'tura," *Rossiia* (Venice, Italy) 6 (1988): 124.
118 Ibid., 127.
119 Ibid., 122.
120 G. D. Gachev, *Soderzhatel'nost' khudozhestvennykh form (Epos. Lirika. Drama)* (Moscow: Prosveshchenie, 1968), 19.
121 Ibid., 20.
122 Ibid., 162.
123 G. D. Gachev, *Natsional'nye obrazy mira* (Moscow: Sovetskii pisatel', 1988), 438.
124 As e.g., in his 1993 book *Images of India: An Experiment in Existential Culturology*.
125 G. D. Gachev, *Zhiznemysli* (Moscow: Pravda, 1989), 23.
126 G. D. Gachev, *Kniga udivlenii, ili Estestvoznanie glazami gumanitariia, ili Obrazy v nauke* (Moscow: Pedagogika, 1991), 212–13.
127 Ibid., 218.
128 Ibid., 23.
129 Gachev, *Natsional'nye obrazy mira*, 439.
130 Gachev, *Kniga udivlenii*, 18.
131 Ibid., 26–7.
132 Gachev, *Natsional'nye obrazy mira*, 431.
133 In such works of Gaston Bachelard as *Water and Dreams*, *The Psychoanalysis of Fire*, *Air and Dreams*, and *Earth and Reveries of Will*. Despite striking similarities, Gachev never refers to Bachelard. In general, Gachev was uninterested in twentieth-century Western thought and ignored contemporary authors, adhering to a mostly Soviet philosophical curriculum and focusing on classics like Descartes, Spinoza, Kant, and Hegel.
134 Gachev, *Kniga udivlenii*, 25.
135 Gachev, *Natsional'nye obrazy mira*, 436.
136 G. D. Gachev, *Russkaia duma. Portrety russkikh myslitelei* (Moscow: Novosti, 1991), 144.
137 Ibid., 149.
138 There is a certain affinity between Gachev's and Ilya Kabakov's visions of Russian negation, although in the latter, this vision is pushed to the extreme of conceptualism, whereas Gachev balances it with more materialistic, even paganistic, elements of Russian culture, as shaped by earthly and airy cosmic determinants.

139 Cited from Jean-Francois Lyotard, *Why Philosophize?* (Cambridge: Polity Press, 2013), 50.
140 Gachev, *Russkaia duma*, 430.
141 Gachev, *Kniga udivlenii*, 7.
142 Ibid., 44.
143 Ibid., 258.
144 Discussed in the last part of my book *Ideas against Ideocracy: Non-Marxist Thought in the Soviet Union (1953–1991)*.

Conclusion

1 Aron Gurevich, *Kategorii srednevekovoi kul'tury* (Moscow: Iskusstvo, 1972).
2 L. M. Batkin, *Ital'ianskoe vozrozhdenie v poiskakh individual'nosti* (Moscow: Nauka, 1989).
3 The best introduction to the vast and diverse field of contemporary Russian culturology at its most advanced level is ROSSPEN's 2007 encyclopedia *Kul'turologiia: entsiklopediia*.
4 This book, to be published by Bloomsbury Academic Press, is devoted to four other major trends of thought: nationalism and Eurasianism; Orthodox Christianity; cosmism, esoterism, and universalism; and postmodernism and conceptualism. The concluding sections of this book (forthcoming in 2020) provide a general perspective on the development of all eight trends.

Bibliography

Amalrik, Andrei. *Will the Soviet Union Survive Until 1984?* New York and Evanston: Harper & Row, 1970.
Amal'rik, Andrei. *SSSR i Zapad v odnoi lodke*. London: Overseas Publications Interchange, 1978.
Ariev, Andrei. "Na chempionate po nich'im." *Russkaia mysl'* (Paris), May 14, 1993.
Averintsev, S. S. "Bakhtin, smekh, khristianskaia kul'tura." *Rossiia* (Venice, Italy) 6 (1988): 119–30.
Averintsev, S. S. "Grecheskaia 'literatura' i blizhnevostochnaia 'slovesnost'.' Dva tvorcheskikh printsipa." In *Religiia i literatura* by S. S. Averintsev, 5–34. Ann Arbor: Hermitage, 1981.
Averintsev, S. S. "'Mirovozzrencheskii stil': podstupy k iavleniiu Loseva." *Voprosy filosofii*, no. 9 (1993): 16–22.
Averintsev, S. S. "'Morfologiia kul'tury' Osval'da Shpenglera." In *Religiia i literatura* by S. S. Averintsev, 68–90. Ann Arbor: Hermitage, 1981.
Averintsev, S. S. *Ot beregov Bosfora do beregov Evfrata*. Moscow: Izd. Nauka, 1987.
Averintsev, S. S. *Poetika rannevizantiiskoi literatury*. Moscow: Nauka, Glavnaia redaktsiia vostochnoi literatury, 1977.
Averintsev, S. S. "Pravoslavie." In *Filosofskaia entsiklopediia*, ed. F. V. Konstantinov, 4: 333–6. Moscow: Sovetskaia entsiklopediia, 1967.
Averintsev, S. S. "Spasenie." In *Filosofskaia entsiklopediia*, ed. F. V. Konstantinov, 5: 107–8. Moscow: Sovetskaia entsiklopediia, 1970.
Averintsev, S. S. "Vizantiia i Rus': dva tipa dukhovnosti. Stat'ia pervaia." *Novyi mir*, no. 7 (1988): 210–20.
Averintsev, S. S. "Vizantiia i Rus': dva tipa dukhovnosti. Stat'ia vtoraia." *Novyi mir*, no. 9 (1988): 227–40.
Averintsev, S. S. "Zhak Mariten, neotomizm, katolicheskaia teologiia iskusstva." In *Religiia i literatura* by S. S. Averintsev, 121–38. Ann Arbor: Hermitage, 1981.
Bachelard, Gaston. *Air and Dreams: An Essay on the Imagination of Movement*. Trans. Edith R. Farrell and C. Frederick Farrell. Dallas: Dallas Institute Publications, 2011.
Bachelard, Gaston. *Earth and Reveries of Will: An Essay on the Imagination of Matter*. Trans. Kenneth Haltmann. Dallas: Dallas Institute of Humanities and Culture, 2002.
Bachelard, Gaston. *The Psychoanalysis of Fire*. Trans. Alan C. M. Ross. Boston: Beacon Press, 1968.
Bachelard, Gaston. *Water and Dreams: An Essay on the Imagination of Matter*. Trans. Edith R. Farrell. Dallas: The Pegasus Foundation, 1983.
Bakhurst, David. *Consciousness and Revolution in Soviet Philosophy: From the Bolsheviks to Evald Ilyenkov*. New York: Cambridge University Press, 1991.
Bakhtin, Mikhail. *Literaturno-kriticheskie stat'i*. Moscow: Khudozhestvennaia literatura, 1986.
Bakhtin, Mikhail. *Speech Genres and Other Late Essays*. Ed. Caryl Emerson and Michael Holquist. Trans. Vern W. McGee. Austin: University of Texas Press, 1986.

Batkin, L. M. *Ital'ianskoe vozrozhdenie v poiskakh individual'nosti.* Moscow: Nauka, 1989.

Batkin, L. M. *Vozobnovlenie istorii. Razmyshleniia o politike i kul'ture.* Moscow: Moskovskii rabochii, 1991.

Batishchev, G. S. "Deiatel'nostnaia sushchnost' cheloveka kak filosofskii printsip." In *Problema cheloveka v sovremennoi filosofii*, ed. I. Balakina, B. Grigorian, S. Oduev, and L. Shershenko, 73–144. Moscow: Nauka, 1969.

Batishchev, G. S. *Protivorechie kak kategoriia dialekticheskoi logiki.* Moscow: Vysshaia shkola, 1963.

Batishchev, G. S. *Vvedenie v dialektiku tvorchestva.* St. Petersburg: Russkii khristianskii gumanitarnyi institut, 1997. Available electronically: http://marxistphilosophy.org/SovPhil/Batishchev97.html.

Belinkov, Arkadii. *Iurii Tynianov.* Moscow: Sovetskii pisatel', 1960.

Belinkov, Arkadii. *Sdacha i gibel' sovetskogo intelligenta. Iurii Olesha.* Ed. N. Belinkova. Madrid: Ediciones Castilla, 1976.

Belinkov, Arkadii. "Strana rabov, strana gospod …" *Novyi kolokol. Literaturno-publitsisticheskii sbornik* (London), no. 1 (1972).

Belotserkovskii, Vadim. *Svoboda, vlast' i sobstvennost'.* Achberg, 1977.

Berdiaev, Nikolai. *Sobranie sochinenii.* Paris: YMCA-Press.

Berry, Ellen, and Mikhail Epstein. *Transcultural Experiments: Russian and American Models of Creative Communication.* New York: Palgrave MacMillan, 1999.

Bibler, Vladimir. "Byt' filosofom." Available electronically: https://www.bibler.ru/bim_ng_byt_f.php

Bibler, Vladimir. "The Foundations of the School of the Dialogue of Cultures Program." *Journal of Russian and East European Psychology* 47, no. 1 (2009): 34–60.

Bibler, Vladimir. "Iz 'Zametok vprok'" *Voprosy filosofii*, no. 6 (1991): 15–45.

Bibler, Vladimir. *Mikhail Mikhailovich Bakhtin, ili poetika kul'tury.* Moscow: Progress, 1991.

Bibler, Vladimir. *Ot naukoucheniia—k logike kul'tury. Dva filosofskikh vvedeniia v dvadtsat' pervyi vek.* Moscow: Izdatel'stvo politicheskoi literatury, 1991.

Blakeley, T. J. *Soviet Philosophy: A General Introduction to Contemporary Soviet Thought.* Kluwer Academic, 1964.

Bochenski, J. M. *Soviet Russian Dialectical Materialism [Diamat].* Dordrecht, Holland: D. Reidel, 1963.

Bogomolov, A., and I. Narskii, eds. *Sovremennaia burzhuaznaia filosofiia.* Moscow: MGU, 1972.

Brodsky, Joseph. *Less Than One. Selected Essays.* New York: Farrar, Straus and Giroux, 1986.

Brodsky, Joseph. "Uncommon Visage. The Nobel Lecture." In *On Grief and Reason: Essays* by Joseph Brodsky, 44–58. New York: Farrar, Straus and Giroux, 1995.

Bulgakov, Sergei. *Karl Marx as a Religious Type.* Trans. Luba Barna. Belmont, MA: Nordland, 1979.

Burov, A. I. *Esteticheskaia sushchnost' iskusstva.* Moscow: Iskusstvo, 1956.

Bykova, Marina F., and Vladislav Lektorsky, eds. *Philosophical Thought in Russia in the Second Half of the Twentieth Century: A Contemporary View from Russia and Abroad.* London, New York: Bloomsbury Academic, 2019.

Callinicos, A. *Marxism and Philosophy.* Oxford: Oxford University Press, 1983.

The Cambridge Dictionary of Philosophy. Robert Audi, general editor, 2nd ed. Cambridge: Cambridge University Press, 1999.
Clark, Katerina, and Michael Holquist. *Mikhail Bakhtin.* Cambridge, MA: Harvard University Press, 1984.
Copleston, Frederick C. *Philosophy in Russia from Herzen to Lenin and Berdyaev.* Notre Dame, IN: University of Notre Dame Press, 1986.
Dahm, Helmut, Thomas Blakeley, and George L. Kline, eds. *Philosophical Sovietology: The Pursuit of a Science.* Dordrecht, Holland: Reidel, 1987.
Danilevskii, N. Ia. *Rossiia i Evropa.* Moscow: Kniga, 1991.
Davydov, Iu. N. *Begstvo ot svobody. Filosofskoe mifotvorchestvo i literaturnyi avangard.* Moscow: Khudozhestvennaia literatura, 1978.
Davydov, Iu. N. *Estetika nigilizma (iskusstvo i "novye levye").* Moscow: Iskusstvo, 1975.
Davydov, Iu. N. "Etika i perestroika." In *Opyty. Literaturno-filosofskii ezhegodnik,* ed. Arsenii Gulyga. Moscow: Sovetskii pisatel', 1990.
Davydov, Iu. N. *Etika liubvi i metafizika svoevoliia.* Moscow: Molodaia gvardiia, 1982.
Davydov, Iu. N. *Iskusstvo i elita.* Moscow: Iskusstvo, 1966.
Davydov, Iu. N. *Iskusstvo kak sotsiologicheskii fenomen. K kharakteristike estetiko-politicheskikh vzgliadov Platona i Aristotelia.* Moscow: Nauka, 1968.
Davydov, Iu. N. *Kritika sotsial'no-filosofskikh vozzrenii Frankfurtskoi shkoly.* Moscow: Nauka, 1977.
Davydov, Iu. N. *Sotsiologiia kontrkul'tury (Infantilizm kak tip mirovospriiatiia i sotsial'naia bolezn'.* Moscow: Nauka, 1980.
DeBlasio, Alyssa. *The Filmmaker's Philosopher: Merab Mamardashvili and Russian Cinema.* Edinburgh: Edinburgh University Press, 2019.
Dostoevsky, Fyodor. *The Brothers Karamazov.* Trans. Richard Pevear and Larissa Volokhonsky. New York: Vintage Books, 1992.
Druskin, Iakov. *Dnevniki.* Ed. and annot. L. S. Druskina. St. Petersburg: Akademicheskii proekt, 1999.
Druskin, Iakov. *Lestnitsa Iakova. Esse, traktaty, pis'ma.* Ed. L. S. Druskina. St. Petersburg: Akademicheskii proekt, 2004.
Druskin, Iakov. *Pered prinadlezhnostiami chego-libo. Dnevniki, 1963–1979.* St. Petersburg: Akademicheskii proekt, 2001.
Druskin, Iakov. *Vblizi vestnikov.* Ed., with a preface, by Genrikh Orlov. Washington, DC: H. A. Frager, 1988.
Edie, J. M., J. P. Scanlan, and M.-B. Zeldin, eds. *Russian Philosophy.* With the collaboration of G. L. Kline. 3 vols. Chicago: Quadrangle Books, 1965.
Eidel'man, N. Ia. *Gertsen protiv samoderzhaviia. Sekretnaia politicheskaia istoriia Rossii XVIII–XIX vekov i Vol'naia pechat'.* Moscow: Mysl', 1973.
Eidel'man, N. Ia. *Gran' vekov. Politicheskaia bor'ba v Rossii. Konets XVIII–nachalo XIX stoletiia.* Moscow: Mysl', 1982.
Eidel'man, N. Ia. *Pushkin i dekabristy. Iz istorii vzaimootnoshenii.* Moscow: Khudozhestvennaia literatura, 1979.
Eidel'man, N. Ia. *Pushkin. Istoriia i sovremennost'v khudozhestvennom soznanii poeta. Monografiia.* Moscow: Sovetsky pisatel', 1984.
Eidel'man, N. Ia. *Pushkin. Iz biografii i tvorchestva. 1826–1837.* Moscow: Khudozhestvennaia literatura, 1987.
Eliot, T. S. *Selected Prose of T. S. Eliot.* Ed. Frank Kermode. London: Faber, 1984.

Emerson, Caryl. *The First Hundred Years of Mikhail Bakhtin*. Princeton: Princeton University Press, 1998.
Emerson, Caryl. "On the Generation That Squandered Its Philosophers (Losev, Bakhtin, and Classical Thought as Equipment for Living)." *Studies in East European Thought* 56, nos. 2/3 (2004): 95–117.
Emerson, Caryl. "On Mikhail Bakhtin and Human Studies (with Continual Reference to Moscow and Sheffield)." *Russian Journal of Communication* 8, no. 2 (2017): 119–41.
Engels, Friedrich. *The Dialectics of Nature*. Available electronically: https://www.marxists.org/archive/marx/works/1883/don/index.htm
Epstein, Mikhail. *The Irony of the Ideal: Paradoxes of Russian Literature*. Trans. A. S. Brown. Boston: Academic Studies Press, 2017.
Esenin-Vol'pin, A. S. *Filosofiia. Logika. Poeziia. Zashchita prav cheloveka*. Moscow: RGGU, 1999.
Filosofskii slovar'. Ed. M. M. Rozental' and P. F. Iudin. Moscow: Politizdat, 1963.
Florenskii, Pavel. *Sochineniia v 4-kh tomakh*. Moscow: Mysl', 1994.
Florovskii, G. *Puti russkogo bogosloviia*. Paris: YMCA-Press, 1988.
Frank S. L., ed. *Iz istorii russkoi filosofskoi mysli kontsa XIX i nachala XX veka. Antologiia*. Inter-Language Literary Associates: Washington-New York, 1965.
Freidenberg, Olga. *Image and Concept: Mythopoetic Roots of Literature*. Ed. and annot. Nina Braginskaia and Kevin Moss. Trans. Kevin Moss. London: Routledge, 1997.
Gachev, G. D. *Kniga udivlenii, ili Estestvoznanie glazami gumanitariia, ili Obrazy v nauke*. Moscow: Pedagogika, 1991.
Gachev, G. D. *Natsional'nye obrazy mira*. Moscow: Sovetskii pisatel', 1988.
Gachev, G. D. *Russkaia duma. Portrety russkikh myslitelei*. Moscow: Novosti, 1991.
Gachev, G. D. *Soderzhatel'nost' khudozhestvennykh form (Epos. Lirika. Drama)*. Moscow: Prosveshchenie, 1968.
Gachev, G. D. *Zhiznemysli*. Moscow: Pravda, 1989.
Gasparyan, Diana. *Merab Mamardashvili's Philosophy of Consciousness*. Independent Publisher, 2012. Introduction and partial bibliography available electronically: https://www.hse.ru/pubs/share/direct/demo_document/138019057.
Ginzburg, Lidiia. *Chelovek za pis'mennym stolom*. Leningrad: Sovetskii pisatel', 1989.
Ginzburg, Lidiia. *Prokhodiashchie kharaktery: Proza voennykh let. Zapiski blokadnogo cheloveka*. Ed. Emily van Buskirk and Andrei Zorin. Moscow: Novoe izdatel'stvo, 2011.
Ginzburg, Lidiia. *Notes from the Blockade*. Trans. Alan Myers. London: Random House UK, 2016.
Goerdt, Wilhelm. *Russische Philosophie. Zugänge und Durchblicke*. Munich: Verlag Karl Alber Freiburg, 1984.
Golosovker, Ia. E. *Dostoevskii i Kant*. Moscow: Izdatel'stvo akademii nauk SSSR, 1963.
Golosovker, Ia. E. *Logika mifa*. Moscow: Nauka (Glavnaia redaktsiia vostochnoi literatury), 1987.
Graham, Loren R. *Science, Philosophy, and Human Behavior in the Soviet Union*. New York: Columbia University Press, 1987.
Gurevich, Aron. *Kategorii srednevekovoi kul'tury*. Moscow: Iskusstvo, 1972.
Iakhot, Iegoshua. *Podavlenie filosofii v SSSR (20–30-e gody)*. New York: Chalidze, 1981.
Iakovlev, Aleksandr. *Predislovie. Obval. Posleslovie*. Moscow: Novosti, 1992.
Ianov, Aleksandr. *Russkaia ideia i 2000-yi god*. New York: Liberty, 1988.

Ilyenkov, E. V. *Dialectical Logic. Essays in Its History and Theory.* Trans. H. Campbell Creighton. Moscow: Progress, 1977.
Ilyenkov, E. V. *The Dialectics of the Abstract and the Concrete in Marx's Capital.* Trans. Sergei Kuzyakov. Available electronically: https://www.marxists.org/archive/ilyenkov/works/abstract/index.htm.
Ilyenkov, E. V. *Leninist Dialectics and the Metaphysics of Positivism.* London: New Park Publications, 1982.
Il'enkov, E. V. *Filosofiia i kul'tura.* Moscow. Izdatel'stvo politicheskoi literatury, 1991.
Isupov, K. G., ed. *M. M. Bakhtin: Pro et Contra.* Moscow: Russkii Khristianskii gumanitarnyi universitet, 2002.
Ivanov, V. V. *Ocherki po istorii semiotiki v SSSR.* Moscow: Nauka, 1976.
Jeu, Bernard. *La philosophie soviétique et l'Occident. Essai sur les tendances et sur la signification de la philosophie soviétique contemporaine (1959–1969).* Mercure de France, 1969.
Joravsky, David. *Soviet Marxism and Natural Science: 1917–1932.* New York: Columbia University Press, 1961.
Kierkegaard, Søren. *The Living Thoughts of Kierkegaard.* Ed. W. H. Auden. New York: New York Review Books, 1999.
Khazanov, Boris. *Idushchii po vode. Stat'i i pis'ma.* München: Strana i mir, 1985.
Khazanov, Boris. *Mif Rossiia. Opyt romanticheskoi politologii.* New York: Liberty, 1986.
Khazanov, Boris. *Zapakh zvezd.* Tel-Aviv: Vremia i my, 1977.
Kline, George L. "Recent Uncensored Soviet Philosophical Writings." In *Dissent in the USSR. Politics, Ideology, and People,* ed. Rudolf L. Tokes, 158–90. Baltimore: Johns Hopkins University Press, 1975.
Konrad, N. I. *Zapad i vostok. Stat'i.* Moscow: Glavnaia redaktsiia vostochnoi literatury, 1972.
Koshelev, A. D., and M. L. Gasparov. *Iu. M. Lotman i Tartusko-moskovskaia semioticheskaia shkola.* Moscow: Gnozis, 1994.
Kratkii filosofskii slovar'. Ed. M. Rozental' and P. Iudin. Moscow: Gosudarstvennoe izdatel'stvo politicheskoi literatury, 1954.
Krivulin, Viktor. "Konets epokhi Ryb." *Novoe russkoe slovo* (New York), February 17, 1995.
Kruglikov, V. A., ed. *Kongenial'nost' mysli: o filosofe Merabe Mamardashvili.* Moscow: Progress, 1999.
Kul'turologiia: entsiklopediia. Editor in chief: S. Ia. Levit. Moscow: ROSSPEN, 2007.
Kurginian, S. E. *Sed'moi stsenarii.* Moscow: Eksperimental'nyi tvorcheskii tsentr, 1992.
Kurginian, S. E., B. Autenshlus, P. Goncharov, Iu. Gromyko, I. Sundiev, and V. Ovchinskii. *Postperestroika: kontseptual'naia model' razvitiia nashego obshchestva, politicheskikh partii i obshchestvennykh organizatsii.* Moscow: Politizdat, 1990.
Kuvakin, Valery A., ed. *A History of Russian Philosophy: From the Tenth through the Twentieth Centuries.* Buffalo, NY: Prometheus Books, 1994.
Lafargue, Paul. "Reminiscences of Marx." Progress, 1972. Available electronically: https://www.marxists.org/archive/lafargue/1890/xx/marx.htm.
Laszlo, Ervin, ed. *Philosophy in the Soviet Union. A Survey of the Mid-Sixties.* Dordrecht, Holland: Reidel, 1967.
Lefebvre, V. *Algebra of Conscience. A Comparative Analysis of Western and Soviet Ethical Systems.* Dordrecht, Boston, London: D. Reidel, 1982.

Lefebvre, V. "The Fundamental Structures of Human Reflexion." In *The Structure of Human Reflection: The Reflexional Psychology of Vladimir Lefebvre*, ed. H. Wheeler, 5–70. New York: Peter Lang, 1990.
Lefevr, V. A. "Nepostizhimaia effektivnost' matematiki v issledovaniiakh chelovecheskoi deiatel'nosti." *Voprosy filosofii*, no. 7 (1990): 51–4.
Lefevr, V. A. "Ot psikhofiziki k modelirovaniiu dushi." *Voprosy filosofii*, no. 7 (1990): 25–31.
Lektorskii, V. A., ed. *Filosofiia ne konchaetsia. Iz istorii otechestvennoi filosofii. XX vek.* Kn. 2. 1960–80-e gody. Moscow: Rosspen, 1998.
Lektorskii, V. A., ed. *Problemy i diskussii v filosofii Rossii vtoroi poloviny XX v.: sovremennyi vzgliad.* Moscow: Rosspen, 2014.
Lenin, V. I. *Polnoe sobranie sochinenii.* 55 vols. Moscow: Gosudarstvennoe izdatel'stvo politicheskoi literatury, 1958–65.
Lévi-Strauss, Claude. *Structural Anthropology.* Trans. Monique Layton. New York. Basic Books, 1976.
Levitskii, S. A. *Ocherki po istorii russkoi filosofskoi i obshchestvennoi mysli.* Frankfurt/Main: Posev, 1968, 1981.
Lifshits, Mikhail. *Mifologiia drevniaia i novaia.* Moscow: Iskusstvo, 1980.
Lifshitz, Mikhail. *The Philosophy of Art of Karl Marx.* Trans. Ralph B. Winn. Ed. Angel Flores. New York: Critics Group, 1938.
Likhachev, D. S. "Drevnerusskaia literatura i sovremennost'." *Russkaia literatura*, no. 4 (1978): 25–31.
Likhachev, D. S. *O filologii.* Moscow: Vysshaia shkola, 1989.
Likhachev, D. S. *Poetika drevnerusskoi literatury.* Leningrad: Khudozhestvennaia literatura, 1971.
Likhachev, D. S. *Proshloe—budushchemu. Stat'i i ocherki.* Leningrad: Nauka, 1985.
Likhachev, D. S. *Zemlia rodnaia.* Moscow: Prosveshchenie, 1983.
Liubishchev, A. A. *V zashchitu nauki. Stat'i i pis'ma, 1953–1972.* Leningrad: Nauka, 1991.
Losev, A. F. *The Dialectics of Myth.* Trans. Vladimir Marchenkov. London: Routledge, 2014.
Losev, A. F. *Filosofiia. Mifologiia. Kul'tura.* Moscow, Politizdat, 1991.
Losev, A. F. "Imiaslavie" (1918). *Voprosy filosofii*, no. 9 (1993): 52–60.
Losev, A. F. *Istoriia antichnoi estetiki. Poslednie veka.* Moscow: Iskusstvo, 1988.
Losev, A. F. *Istoriia antichnoi estetiki. Sofisty. Sokrat. Platon.* Moscow: Iskusstvo, 1969.
Losev, A. F. *Ocherki antichnogo simvolizma i mifologii.* Moscow: Izdanie avtora, 1930.
Losev, A. F. *Strast' k dialektike. Literaturnye razmyshleniia filosofa.* Moscow: Sovetskii pisatel', 1990.
Losev, A. F. *Vladimir Solov'ev i ego vremia.* Moscow: Progress, 1990.
Lossky, Nicholas O. *History of Russian Philosophy.* New York: International Universities Press, 1972.
Lotman, Iu. M. *Izbrannye stat'i.* Tallinn: Aleksandra, 1992.
Lotman, Iu. M. *Lektsii po struktural'noi poetike. Vvedenie, teoriia stikha* (Tartu, Estonia, 1964), Brown University Slavic Reprint 5. Providence: Brown University Press, 1968.
Lotman, Iu. M. "O dvukh modeliakh kommunikatsii v sisteme kul'tury." In *Izbrannye stat'i* by Iu. M. Lotman, 1: 76–89. Tallinn: Aleksandra, 1992.
Lotman, Iu. M. "O roli sluchainykh faktorov v istorii kul'tury." In *Izbrannye stat'i* by Iu. M. Lotman, 1: 472–9. Tallinn: Aleksandra, 1992.

Lotman, Iu. M., and B. A. Uspenskii. "Binary Models in the Dynamics of Russian Culture (to the End of the 18th Century)." In *The Semiotics of Russian Cultural History*, ed. A. D. Nakhimovsky and A. S. Nakhimovsky, 30–66. Ithaca: Cornell University Press, 1985.

Lotman, Iu. M., and B. A. Uspenskii. "Rol' dual'nikh modelii v dinamike russkoi kul'tury (do kontsa XVIII veka). In *Izbrannye trudy* by B. A. Uspenskii. Moscow: Gnosis, 1994.

Lotman, Ju. M. *Culture and Explosion*. Trans. Wilma Clark. Ed. Marina Grishakova. Berlin: Mouton de Gruyter, 2009.

Lotman, Ju. M. "Primary and Secondary Communication-Modeling Systems." In *Soviet Semiotics: An Anthology*, ed. Daniel P. Lucid, 95–8. Baltimore and London: Johns Hopkins University Press, 1988.

Lotman, Ju. M. "Problems in the Typology of Culture." In *Soviet Semiotics: An Anthology*, ed. Daniel P. Lucid, 213–21. Baltimore and London: Johns Hopkins University Press, 1988.

Lotman, Yuri M. *Universe of the Mind: A Semiotic Theory of Culture*. Trans. Ann Shukman. Introduction by Umberto Eco. Bloomington: Indiana University Press, 1990.

Lotman, Y., and B. A. Uspensky. "On the Semiotic Mechanism of Culture." Trans. George Mihaychuk. In *Critical Theory since 1965*, ed. Hazard Adams and Leroy Searle, 410–22. Tallahassee: Florida State University Press, 1990.

Lyotard, Jean-Francois. *Why Philosophize?* Cambridge: Polity Press, 2013.

Maidansky, Andrey, and Vesa Oittinen, eds. *The Practical Essence of Man: The "Activity Approach" in Late Soviet Philosophy*. Brill, 2015.

Mamardashvili, Merab. *Estetika myshleniia*. Moscow: Moskovskaia shkola politicheskikh issledovanii, 2000.

Mamardashvili, Merab. *Kak ia ponimaiu filosofiiu*. 2nd ed. Moscow: Progress, 1992.

Mamardashvili, Merab. *Kantianskie variatsii*. Moscow: Agraf, 2002.

Mamardashvili, Merab. *Kartezianskie razmyshleniia*. Ed. Iu. P. Senokosov. Moscow: Progress, 1993.

Mamardashvili, Merab. *Klassicheskii i neklassicheskii idealy ratsional'nosti*. Tbilisi: Metsniereba, 1984.

Mamardashvili, Merab. *Psikhologicheskaia topologiia puti*. Moscow: Ad Marginem, 1995.

Mamardashvili, Merab. *Strela poznaniia*. Moscow: Taideks, 2004.

Mamardashvili, Merab, and Aleksandr Piatigorskii. *Simvol i soznanie. Metafizicheskie rassuzhdeniia o soznanii, simvolike i iazyke*. Jerusalem: I. Maler and V. Glozman, 1982.

Mandelker, Amy. "Semiotizing the Sphere: Organicist Theory in Lotman, Bakhtin, and Vernadsky." *PMLA* 109, no. 3 (1994): 385–96.

Marcuse, Herbert. *Soviet Marxism: A Critical Analysis*. New York: Columbia University Press, 1985.

Markov, M. A. *O prirode materii*. Moscow: Nauka, 1976.

Marx, K. *Capital*. Trans. Ben Fowkes. London: Penguin Classics, 1990.

Marx, K. *Economic and Philosophic Manuscripts of 1844*. Trans. Martin Mulligan. Available electronically: https://www.marxists.org/archive/marx/works/1844/manuscripts/preface.htm.

Marx, K. *Grundrisse: Foundations of the Critique of Political Economy*. Trans. Martin Nicolaus. Penguin Books, New Left Review, 1973. Available electronically: https://www.marxists.org/archive/marx/works/1857/grundrisse/index.htm.

Marx, K., and F. Engels. "Manifesto of the Communist Party (1848)." Ch. 2. Available electronically: https://www.marxists.org/archive/marx/works/1848/communist-manifesto/ch02.htm.
Medvedev, Roi. ed. *Politicheskii_dnevnik*. Amsterdam: The Alexander Herzen Foundation, 1975.
Michurin, Ivan. *Sochineniia*. Moscow: Sel'khozgiz, 1948.
Mihajlov, Mihajlo. *Abram Terts ili Begstvo iz retorty*. Frankfurt/Main: Posev, 1969.
Mihajlov, Mihajlo. *Planetarnoe soznanie*. Ann Arbor: Ardis, 1982.
Mihajlov, Mihajlo. *Russian Themes*. Trans. Maria Mihajlov. New York: Farrar, Straus and Giroux, 1968.
Mihajlov, Mihajlo. *Underground Notes*. Trans. Maria Mihajlov Ivusic and Christopher W. Ivusic. New Rochelle, NY: Caratzas Brothers, 1982.
Mil'ner-Irinin, Iakov A. "The Concept of Human Nature and Its Place in the Science of Ethics." *Soviet Studies in Philosophy* 27, no. 1 (1988): 6–24.
Mil'ner-Irinin, Iakov A. *Etika, ili Printsipy istinnoi chelovechnosti*. Moscow: Nauka, 1999.
Moma, Aleks. "Vasilii Nalimov kak gnostik." Paper delivered at the OTO Conference (St. Petersburg, 2015). Available electronically: https://sphinx-oto.ru/wp-content/uploads/2015/08/Moma_A_Vasiliy_Nalimov_kak_gnostik_doklad_2015.pdf.
Morson, Gary Saul, ed. *Bakhtin: Essays and Dialogues on His Work*. University of Chicago Press, 1986.
Morson, Gary Saul, and Caryl Emerson, eds. *Rethinking Bakhtin: Extensions and Challenges*. Evanston: Northwestern University Press, 1989.
Morson, Gary Saul, and Caryl Emerson. *Mikhail Bakhtin: Creation of a Prosaics*. Stanford University Press, 1990.
Moshchelkov, E. N. *Sovremennye diskussii o kommunisticheskoi teorii K. Marksa i F. Engel'sa. Spetskurs*. Moscow: Izdatel'stvo MGU, 1991.
Motroshilova, N. V. "Fenomenologiia." In *Sovremennaia burzhuaznaia filosofiia*, ed. A. Bogomolov and I. Narskii, 211–80. Moscow: MGU, 1972.
Motroshilova, N. V. *Otechestvennaia filosofia 50–80-kh godov XX v. i zapadnaia mysl'*. Moscow: Akademicheskii proekt, 2012.
Nalimov, V. *Faces of Science*. Philadelphia: ISI Press, 1981.
Nalimov, V. *In the Labyrinths of Language: A Mathematician's Journey*. Philadelphia: ISI Press, 1981.
Nalimov, V. "On the History of Mystical Anarchism in Russia." *The International Journal of Transpersonal Studies* 20 (2001): 85–98. Available electronically: https://digitalcommons.ciis.edu/cgi/viewcontent.cgi?article=1283&context=ijts-transpersonalstudies.
Nalimov, V. *Realms of the Unconscious: The Enchanted Frontier*. Trans. A. V. Yarkho. Philadelphia: ISI Press, 1982.
Nalimov, V. *Space, Time, and Life: The Probabilistic Pathways of Evolution*. Trans. A. V. Yarkho. Philadelphia: ISI Press, 1985. Available electronically: http://garfield.library.upenn.edu/nalimov/spacetimelife.pdf.
Nalimov, V. *Veroiatnostnaia model' iazyka*. Moscow: Nauka, 1974.
Ostwald, W. *Energetische Grundlagen der Kulturwissenschaft*. Leipzig, 1909.
Paramonov, Boris. "Chevengur i okrestnosti." *Kontinent* (Paris), no. 54 (1987): 332–72.
Paramonov, Boris. *Konets stilia*. Moscow: Agraf, 1997.
Paramonov, Boris. *Muzhchiny i zhenshchiny*. Moscow: AST, 2009.

Paramonov, Boris. "Nizkie istiny demokratii. Opyt vynuzhdennogo ponimaniia." *Grani*, no. 139 (1986): 224–51.
Paramonov, Boris. "Panteon. Demokratiia kak religioznaia problema." *Strana i mir* (Munich), no. 1 (1988): 60–74.
Paramonov, Boris. "Slavianofil'stvo." *Grani*, no. 135 (1985): 190–259.
Pasternak, Boris. *Doctor Zhivago*. Trans. Richard Pevear and Larissa Volokhonsky. New York: Pantheon Books, 2010.
Pechey, Graham. *Mikhail Bakhtin: The Word in the World*. London: Routledge, 2007.
Peterson, Dale E. "Response and Call: The African American Dialogue With Bakhtin." *American Literature* 65, no. 4 (1993): 761–75.
Platonov, Andrei. *Chevengur*. Paris: IMCA-Press, 1972.
Platonov, S. *Posle kommunizma. Kniga ne prednaznachennaia dlia pechati. Vtoroe prishestvie. Besedy*. Moscow: Molodaia gvardiia, 1991.
Pomerants, Grigorii. *Neopublikovannoe. Bol'shie i malye esse. Publitsistika*. Frankfurt: Posev, 1972.
Pomerants, Grigorii. *Otkrytost' bezdne. Etiudy o Dostoevskom*. New York: Liberty Publishing House, 1989.
Pomerants, Grigorii. *Sny zemli*. Long Island City, NY: Izd-vo "Poiski," 1979.
Pomerants, Grigorii. "V poiskakh sviatyni." *Sintaksis* (Paris), no. 27 (1990): 19–24.
Prishvin, Mikhail. *Nezabudki*. Moscow: Khudozhestvennaia literatura, 1968.
Prishvin, Mikhail. *Sobranie sochinenii v 8 tomakh*. Moscow: Khudozhestvennaia literatura, 1986.
Propp, V. Ia. *Fol'klor i deistvitel'nost'. Izbrannye stat'i*. Moscow, Nauka, glavnaia redaktsiia vostochnoi literatury, 1976.
Redlikh, Roman. *Solidarnost' i svoboda*. Frankfurt a.M.: Posev, 1984.
Rudy, Stephen. "Semiotics in the USSR." In *The Semiotic Sphere*, ed. Thomas A. Sebeok and Jean Umiker-Sebeok, 555–82. New York and London: Plenum Press, 1986.
Sakharov, Andrei. *My Country and the World*. Trans. Guy V. Daniels. New York: Vintage Books, 1975.
Sakharov, Andrei. "Nobel Lecture: Peace, Progress, Human Rights." December 11, 1975. Available electronically: https://www.nobelprize.org/nobel_prizes/peace/laureates/1975/sakharov-lecture.html.
Sakharov, Andrei. "On Aleksandr Solzhenitsyn's 'Letter to the Soviet Leaders.'" In *The Political, Social and Religious Thought of Russian "Samizdat": An Anthology*, ed. Michael Meerson-Aksenov and Boris Shragin, 291–301. Trans. Nicholas Lupinin. Belmont (Mass.): Nordland, 1977.
Sakharov, Andrei. *Trevoga i nadezhda*. Moscow: Inter-Verso, 1990.
Sakharov, Andrei. *Vospominaniia*. New York: Chekhov, 1990.
Sargent, Lyman Tower. "Camus: The Absurdity of Politics." In *The Artist and Political Vision*, ed. Benjamin R. Barber and Michael J. Gargas McGrath, 87–116. London: Transaction Books, 1983.
Scanlan, James P. *Marxism in the USSR: A Critical Survey of Current Soviet Thought*. Ithaca and London: Cornell University Press, 1985.
Schmemann, Alexander, ed. *Ultimate Questions: An Anthology of Modern Russian Religious Thought*. Crestwood, NY: Saint Vladimir's Seminary Press, 1977.
Segal, D. M. *Aspects of Structuralism in Soviet Philology*. Tel Aviv: Tel Aviv University, 1974.

Seyffert, Peter. *Soviet Literary Structuralism: Background, Debate, Issues.* Columbus: Slavica, 1985.

Shchedrovitskii, G. P. *Izbrannye trudy.* Moscow: Izdatel'stvo Shkoly kul'turnoi politiki, 1995.

Shchedrovitskii, G. P. "Mesto logicheskikh i psikhologicheskikh metodov v pedagogicheskoi nauke." *Voprosy filosofii,* no. 7 (1964): 35–49.

Shchedrovitskii, G. P. *Pedagogika i logika.* Moscow: Kastal', 1993.

Shchedrovitskii, P. G. *Ocherki po filosofii obrazovaniia.* Moscow: Pedagogicheskii tsentr "Eksperiment," 1993.

Shiller, F. P., and M. A. Lifshits. *Marks i Engel's ob iskusstve.* Ed. A. V. Lunacharskogo. Moscow: Sovetskaia literatura, 1933.

Shklovskii, Viktor. *Sobranie sochinenii v 3 tt.* Moscow: Khudozhestvennaia literatura, 1974.

Shklovsky, Viktor. *A Reader.* Ed. and trans. Alexandra Berlina. London, New York: Bloomsbury, 2017.

Shukman, Ann. *Literature and Semiotics: A Study in the Writings of Ju. M. Lotman.* Amsterdam, New York, Oxford: North-Holland, 1977.

Slavin, Boris. *Neokonchennaia istoriia: Besedy Mikhaila Gorbacheva s politologom Borisom Slavinym.* Moscow: OLMA, 2001.

Solzhenitsyn, Aleksandr. *Bodalsia telenok s dubom.* Paris: YMCA-Press, 1975.

Solzhenitsyn, Aleksandr. "Pis'mo vozhdiam Sovetskogo Soiuza." Available electronically: http://www.lib.ru/PROZA/SOLZHENICYN/s_letter.txt.

Solzhenitsyn, Aleksandr. "Sakharov i kritika 'Pis'ma vozhdiam.'" In *Sobranie sochinenii* by Aleksandr Solzhenitsyn, 9: 193–200. Vermont-Paris: YMCA-Press, 1981.

Stalin, I. V. *Sochineniia/ Works.* Ed. Robert H. McNeal. The Hoover Institution on War, Revolution, and Peace. Stanford: Stanford University Press, 1967.

Todorov, Tzvetan. *Mikhail Bakhtin: The Dialogical Principle.* Trans. Wlad Godzich. University of Minnesota Press, 1984.

Tsipko, Aleksandr. "Protivorechiia ucheniia Karla Marksa." In *Cherez ternii* by Aleksandr Tsipko, 60–83. Moscow: Progress, 1990.

Tucker, Robert C., ed. *The Marx-Engels Reader.* New York: W. W. Norton, 1972.

van der Zweerde, Evert. *Soviet Historiography of Philosophy: Istoriko-Filosofskaja Nauka.* Dordrecht and Boston: Kluwer Academic, 1997.

van der Zweerde, Evert. "Soviet Philosophy—the Ideology and the Handmaid: A Historical and Critical Analysis of Soviet Philosophy, with a Case-Study into Soviet History of Philosophy." PhD diss., Radboud University Nijmegen, 1994. Available electronically: https://repository.ubn.ru.nl/bitstream/handle/2066/145891/mmubn000001_191196266.pdf.

White, Leslie A. *The Science of Culture: A Study of Man and Civilization.* New York: Farrar, Straus and Cudahy, 1949.

Yesenin-Volpin, A. S. *A Leaf of Spring.* Trans. George Reavey. New York: Frederick A. Praeger, 1961. Also available electronically: http://webct.biz/yesseninvolpin/phil-treatise.html.

Zenkovsky, V. V. *A History of Russian Philosophy.* Trans. G. L. Kline. London: Routledge & Kegan Paul, 1953.

Appendix

Original Russian and Other Foreign-Language Titles

Amalrik, Andrei

Will the Soviet Union Survive until 1984?—*Prosushchestvuet li Sovetskii Soiuz do 1984 goda?*
"Ideology in Soviet Society"—"Ideologiia v sovetskom obshchestve"

Averintsev, Sergei

The Poetics of Early Byzantine Literature—*Poetika rannevizantiiskoi literatury*
Sophia-Logos: A Dictionary—*Sofiia-Logos. Slovar'*

Bakhtin, Mikhail

The Formal Method in Literary Scholarship—*Formal'nyi metod v literaturovedenii*
Freudianism: A Critical Sketch—*Freidizm. Kriticheskii ocherk*
"From Notes Made in 1970–1971"—"Iz zapisei 1970–1971 gg."
Marxism and the Philosophy of Language—*Marksizm i filosofiia iazyka*
"On the Philosophical Bases of Scholarship in the Humanities"—"K filosofskim osnovam gumanitarnykh nauk"
"The Problem of Speech Genres"—"Problema rechevykh zhanrov"
"The Problem of the Text in Linguistics, Philology, and Other Human Sciences: An Experiment in Philosophical Analysis"—"Problema teksta v lingvistike, filologii i drugikh gumanitarnykh naukakh. Opyt filosofskogo analiza"
"Toward a Methodology for the Human Sciences"—"K metodologii gumanitarnykh nauk"

Batishchev, Genrikh

Introduction to the Dialectic of Creativity—*Vvedenie v dialektiku tvorchestva*

Belinkov, Arkadii

Anti-Fascist Novel—Antifashistskii roman
A Draft of Feelings. An Anti-Soviet Novel—Chernovik chuvstv. Antisovetskii roman
The Surrender and Demise of a Soviet Intelligent—Sdacha i gibel' sovetskogo intelligenta

Belotserkovsky, Vadim

Freedom, Power, and Property—Svoboda, vlast' i sobstvennost'

Belov, Vasilii

That's How Things Are—Privychnoe delo

Berdiaev, Nikolai

The Russian Idea—Russkaia ideia

Bibler, Vladimir

Conceptions—Zamysly
Mikhail Bakhtin, or The Poetics of Culture—Mikhail Mikhailovich Bakhtin, ili Poetika kul'tury
Thinking as Creativity—Myshlenie kak tvorchestvo

Bulgakov, Mikhail

The Master and Margarita—Master i Margarita

Bulgakov, Sergei

Karl Marx as a Religious Type—Karl Marks kak religioznyi tip

Burov, Aleksandr

The Aesthetic Essence of Art—Esteticheskaia sushchnost' iskusstva
The Concise Philosophical Dictionary—Kratkii filosofskii slovar'
Contemporary Bourgeois Philosophy—Sovremennaia burzhuaznaia filosofiia
Context—Kontekst

Danilevsky, Nikolai

Russia and Europe—Rossiia i Evropa

Davydov, Iurii

Art and the Elite—Iskusstvo i elita
Art as a Sociological Phenomenon: Toward a Characterization of Aesthetic-Political Views in Plato and Aristotle—Iskusstvo kak sotsiologicheskii fenomen. K kharakteristike estetiko-politicheskikh vzgliadov Platona i Aristotelia
The Ethics of Love and the Metaphysics of Self-Will—Etika liubvi i metafizika svoevoliia

Dostoevsky, Fedor

The Brothers Karamazov—Brat'ia Karamazovy
Crime and Punishment—Prestuplenie i nakazanie
The Devils—Besy
The Diary of a Writer—Dnevnik pisatelia
The Idiot—Idiot

Druskin, Iakov

Before Accessories of Something—Pered prinadlezhnostiami chego-libo
Diaries—Dnevniki
Jacob's Ladder. Essays, Treatises, and Letters—Lestnitsa Iakova. Esse, traktaty, pis'ma
Near the Messengers—Vblizi vestnikov
"The Vision of Non-Vision"—"Videnie nevideniia"

Eidelman, Natan

Pushkin and the Decembrists—Pushkin i dekabristy
Pushkin: History and the Present in the Artistic Consciousness of the Poet—Pushkin. Istoriia i sovremennost' v khudozhestvennom soznanii poeta

Engels, Friedrich

The Dialectics of Nature—Dialektik der Natur

Esenin-Volpin, Aleksandr

"A Free Philosophical Treatise, or an Instantaneous Exposition of My Philosophical Views"—"Svobodnyi filosofskii traktat, ili Mgnovennoe izlozhenie moikh filosofskikh vzgliadov"
"On the Logic of the Moral Sciences"—"O logike nravstvennykh nauk"

Freidenberg, Olga

Image and Concept—*Obraz i poniatie*
The Poetics of Plot and Genre (The Period of Ancient Literature)—*Poetika siuzheta i zhanra (period antichnoi literatury)*

Gachev, Georgii

The Accelerated Development of Literature—*Uskorennoe razvitie literatury*
"The American Image of the World, or, America through the Eyes of a Person Who Has Never Seen It"—"Amerikanskii obraz mira, ili Amerika glazami cheloveka, kotoryi ee ne videl"
The Content of Artistic Forms—*Soderzhatel'nost' khudozhestvennykh form*
Images of India: An Experiment in Existential Culturology—*Obrazy Indii: opyt ekzistentsial'noi kul'turologii*

Ginzburg, Lidiia

On the Literary Hero—*O literaturnom geroe*
On Lyricism—*O lirike*
On Psychological Prose—*O psikhologicheskoi proze*
The Thought That Has Traced a Circle—*Mysl', opisavshaia krug*

Golosovker, Iakov

Burned Novel—*Sozhzhennyi roman*
A Great Romanticist—*Velikii romantik*
The Imaginative Absolute—*Imaginativnyi absoliut*
The Indestructible Inscription—*Zapis' neistrebimaia*
The Logic of Ancient Myth—*Logika antichnogo mifa*

Granin, Daniil

This Strange Life—Eta strannaia zhizn'

Hegel, G. W. F.

Lectures on the History of Philosophy—Vorlesungen über die Geschichte der Philosophie
The Science of Logic—Wissenschaft der Logik

Heidegger, Martin

Being and Time—Sein und Zeit

Herder, Johann Gottfried

Ideas on the Philosophy of the History of Mankind—Ideen zur Philosophie der Geschichte der Menschheit

Herzen, Aleksandr

My Past and Thoughts—Byloe i dumy

Hesse, Hermann

The Glass Bead Game—Das Glasperlenspiel

Ianov, Aleksandr

The Slavophiles and Konstantin Leontiev: The Degeneration of Russian Nationalism 1839-1891—Slavianofily i Konstantin Leont'ev. Vyrozhdenie russkogo natsionalizma. 1839-1891.

Ilyenkov, Evald

"*The Cosmology of Spirit. A Philosophical and Poetical Phantasmagoria Relying on the Principles of Dialectical Materialism*"—"*Kosmologiia dukha.*

Filosofsko-poeticheskaia fantasmagoriia, opiraiushchaiasia na printsipy dialekticheskogo materializma"
Dialectical Logic. Essays in Its History and Theory—Dialekticheskaia logika: Ocherki istorii i teorii
The Dialectics of the Abstract and Concrete in Marx's "Capital"—Dialektika abstraktnogo i konkretnogo v 'Kapitale' Marksa
Of Idols and Ideals—Ob idolakh i idealakh
Leninist Dialectics and the Metaphysics of Positivism—Leninskaia dialektika i metafizika pozitivizma

Kant, Immanuel

Critique of Pure Reason—Kritik der reinen Vernunft

Konrad, Nikolai

"On the Meaning of History"—"O znachenii istorii"
West and East—Zapad i vostok

Lafargue, Paul

"Reminiscences of Marx"—"Souvenirs sur Marx"
Landmarks—Vekhi

Lenin, Vladimir

Materialism and Empirio-Criticism—Materializm i empiriokrititsizm
"On the Significance of Militant Materialism"—"O znachenii voinstvuiushchego materializma"
Philosophical Notebooks—Filosofskie tetradi
"Toward the Question of Dialectics"—"K voprosu o dialektike"

Lévi-Strauss, Claude

Structural Anthropology—Anthropologie structurale
"Structure and Form: Reflections on a Work by Vladimir Propp"—"La structure et la forme. Réflexions sur un ouvrage de Vladimir Propp"

Levitsky, Sergei

The Tragedy of Freedom—Tragediia svobody

Lifshits, Mikhail

Marx and Engels on Art—Marks i Engel's ob iskusstve
"Why I Am Not a Modernist"—"Pochemu ia ne modernist?"

Likhachev, Dmitrii

"The Future of Literature as an Object of Investigation"—"Budushchee literatury kak predmet izucheniia"
The Poetics of Old Russian Literature—Poetika drevnerusskoi literatury

Liubishchev, Aleksandr

The Lines of Plato and Democritus in the History of Culture—Linii Platona i Demokrita v istorii kul'tury
Science and Religion—Nauka i religiia

Losev, Aleksei

The Aesthetics of the Renaissance—Estetika vozrozhdeniia
Ancient Cosmos and Contemporary Science—Antichnyi kosmos i sovremennaia nauka
The Critique of Platonism in Aristotle—Kritika platonizma u Aristotelia
The Dialectics of Artistic Form—Dialektika khudozhestvennoi formy
The Dialectics of Myth—Dialektika mifa
The Dialectics of Number in Plotinus—Dialektika chisla u Plotina
"Eros in Plato"—"Eros u Platona"
The History of Ancient Aesthetics—Istoriia antichnoi estetiki
Music as an Object of Logic—Muzyka kak predmet logiki
Outlines of Ancient Symbolism and Mythology—Ocherki antichnogo simvolizma i mifologii
The Philosophy of the Name—Filosofiia imeni
Vladimir Solovyov and His Time—Vladimir Solov'ev i ego vremia

Lotman, Iurii

Culture and Explosion—Kul'tura i vzryv
Lectures on Structuralist Poetics—Lektsii po struktural'noi poetike

Lucretius

"On the Nature of Things"—"De rerum natura"

Mamardashvili, Merab

Classical and Nonclassical Ideals of Rationality—Klassicheskii i neklassicheskii idealy ratsional'nosti

Markarian, Eduard

Essays on the Theory of Culture—Ocherki teorii kul'tury

Markov, Moisei

On the Nature of Matter—O prirode materii

Marx, Karl

Capital—Das Kapital
Economic and Philosophic Manuscripts of 1844—Ökonomisch-philosophische Manuskripte aus dem Jahre 1844
Theses on Feuerbach—Thesen über Feuerbach

Marx, Karl, and Friedrich Engels

The German Ideology—Die deutsche Ideologie

Mihajlov, Mihajlo

Global Consciousness—Planetarnoe soznanie
Moscow Summer—Moskovskoe leto
"The Mystical Experience of Captivity"—"Misticheskii opyt nevoli"
"The Return of the Grand Inquisitor"—"Vozvrashchenie velikogo Inkvizitora"

Russian Themes—Russkie temy
Unscientific Thoughts—Nenauchnye mysli

Nalimov, Vasilii

The Probabilistic Model of Language—Veroiatnostnaia model' iazyka

Nietzsche, Freidrich

Thus Spake Zarathustra—Also sprach Zarathustra

Paramonov, Boris

Men and Women—Muzhchiny i zhenshchiny
"Pantheon"—"Panteon"
"Shit"—"Govno"

Pasternak, Boris

"I Like the Obstinate Temperament"—"Mne po dushe stroptivyi norov"
"Sublime Sickness"—"Vysokaia bolezn'"

People's Labor Union of Russian Solidarists—Narodno-trudovoi soiuz russkikh solidaristov

Philosophical Encyclopedia—Filosofskaia entsiklopediia
The Philosophy of Russia in the Second Half of the Twentieth Century—Filosofiia Rossii vtoroi poloviny XX veka

Piatigorsky, Aleksandr

The Philosophy of a Side Street—Filosofiia odnogo pereulka

Platonov, S.

After Communism—Posle kommunizma

Pomerants, Grigorii

"The Person from Nowhere"—"Chelovek niotkuda"

Propp, Vladimir

The Historical Roots of the Fairy Tale—Istoricheskie korni volshebnoi skazki
Morphology of the Fairy Tale—Morfologiia volshebnoi skazki
Russian Agrarian Feasts (An Experiment in Historical-Ethnographic Investigation)—
  Russkie agrarnye prazdniki (Opyt istoriko-etnograficheskogo issledovaniia)
The Russian Heroic Epic—Russkii geroicheskii epos

Redlikh, Roman

Solidarity and Freedom—Solidarnost' i svoboda

Sakharov, Andrei

Memoirs—Vospominaniia
"Memorandum"—"Memorandum"
My Country and the World—O strane i mire
"Reflections on Progress, Peaceful Coexistence, and Intellectual Freedom"—
  "Razmyshleniia o progresse, mirnom sosushchestvovanii i intellektual'noi svobode"

Sartre, Jean-Paul

Being and Nothingness—L'Être et le néant
Self-Awareness—Samosoznanie

Shchedrovitsky, G. P.

Pedagogy and Logic—Pedagogika i logika

Solovyov, Vladimir

Critique of Abstract Principles—Kritika otvlechennykh nachal

Solzhenitsyn, Aleksandr

The Gulag Archipelago—Arkhipelag GULAG
"Letter to the Soviet Leaders"—"Pis'mo vozhdiam Sovetskogo Soiuza"
"Matrena's House"—Matrenin dvor

Solzhenitsyn, Aleksandr, et al.

From Under the Rubble—Iz-pod glyb

Spengler, Oswald

The Decline of the West—Der Untergang des Abendlandes

Stalin, Iosif

The Economic Problems of Socialism in the USSR—Ekonomicheskie problemy sotsializma v SSSR
Marxism and Questions of Linguistics—Marksizm i voprosy iazykoznaniia
"On Dialectical and Historical Materialism"—"O dialekticheskom i istoricheskom materializme"
A Short Course in the History of the All-Union Communist Party (Bolsheviks)—Kratkii kurs istorii VKP(b)
The Tale of Bygone Years—Povest' vremennykh let

Tolstoy, Lev

War and Peace—Voina i mir

Tynianov, Iurii

The Death of Vazir-Mukhtar—Smert' Vazir-Mukhtara
Kiukhlia—Kukhlia

Name Index

Notes: References to figures are in italicized text.
Page numbers in bold refer to the pages specifically devoted to the given author.

Adashev, Aleksei 170
Adorno, Theodor W. 1, 53, 58, 59
Aitmatov, Chingiz 223
Akhmadulina, Bella 7
Akhutin, Anatolii 205
Aksakov, Ivan and Konstantin 6
Aksenov, Vasilii 151
Aksenov, Viktor 62
Alekseev, N. G. 93
Althusser, Louis 75, 97, 104
Amalrik, Andrei 151, **158–62**, 167, 234
Anaxagoras 222
Andreev, Daniil 6
Aquinas, St. Thomas 206
Aristotle 55, 57, 58, 105, 186, 188, 207, 208, 218
Augustine, St. 123, 212, 213
Averintsev, Sergei 7, 8, 176, 177, 179, 192, 198, 203, *211*, **211–22**, 233, 257 n.95

Bachelard, Gaston 228, 258 n.133
Bacon, Francis 167
Bagaturiia, Georgii 64
Bakhtin, Mikhail 5, 7, 8, 11, 13, 87, 121, 122, 127, 176, 177, *178*, **178–85**, 189, 191, 196, 197, 198, 201, 205, 208, **209–10**, 212, **220–2**, 223, 224, 233, 234, 254 n.11
Barabanov, Evgenii 142, 251 n.118
Barth, Karl 136
Barthes, Roland 35
Batishchev, Genrikh 25, 26, **35–40**, 43, 56
Batiushkov, Konstantin 7
Batkin, Leonid 172, 173, 205, 231
Baumgarten, Alexander 188
Belinkov, Arkadii 152, **158–62**, 234
Belinsky, Vissarion 6, 43, 127, 171
Belotserkovsky, Vadim **155**

Belov, Vasilii 148
Belyi, Andrei 72
Benjamin, Walter 118
Berdiaev, Nikolai 1, 3, 6, 7, 8, 11, 17, 35, 114, 133, 142, 145, 146, 147, 153, 176, 185, 234
Bibikhin, Vladimir 211
Bibler, Vladimir 8, 97, 176, 203, *204*, **204–11**, 233, 234
Bitov, Andrei 149
Blok, Aleksandr 190
Boehme, Jacob 103
Bohr, Niels 98–9
Böll, Heinrich 129
Bonhoeffer, Dietrich 136
Borev, Iurii 47
Borodai, Iurii 35
Brezhnev, Leonid 3, 21, 23, 61–2, 66, 71, 98, 136, 158, 165, 170, 179
Brodsky, Joseph 6, **148–51**, 234
Buber, Martin 121, 129, 184
Bukharin, Nikolai 18, 61, 170, 192
Bulgakov, Mikhail 179
Bulgakov, Sergei 6, 7, 153, 185
Burov, Aleksandr **45–7**
Butenko, Aleskandr 61

Camus, Albert 11, 52, 55, 59, 131, 135
Cantor, Georg 205
Cassirer, Ernst 193
Catherine the Great 2
Chaadaev, Petr 5, 6, 127, 158, 235
Chalidze, Valerii 151
Chardin, Teilhard de 34
Chernyshev, Sergei 62
Chernyshevsky, Nikolai 43
Chukovskaia, Lidiia 151
Collingwood, R. G. 89

Copleston, Frederick 7
Curtius, Ernst Robert 198

Daniel, Iulii 151
Danilevsky, Nikolai 176
Davydov, Iurii 35, 47, **54–60**
DeBlasio, Alyssa 8
Deborin, Abram 18, 35
Democritus 53
Derrida, Jacques 13, 52, 87, 180–1, 184, 206
Descartes, René 27, 77, 101, 105, 106, 107, 108, 116, 206, 208, 226
Dominic of Caleruega 129
Dostoevsky, Fedor 1, 5, 6, 11, 55, 59, 60, 80, 114, 121, 132–3, 138, 141, 152, 171, 179, 196, 225, 230
Druskin, Iakov 13, 114, **118–23**, *119*, 124, 125, 132, 133, 136, 172, 225
Dubrovsky, D. I. 32

Eidelman, Natan **167–71**, 253 n.168
Eikhenbaum, Boris 78, 124
Eliot, T. S. 215
Emerson, Caryl 5, 254 n.10
Engels, Friedrich 18, 19, 22, 23, 34, 48, 53, 55, 62, 68, 189
Esenin-Volpin, Aleksandr 79, 151, 152, **156–8**, 234, 252 nn.122, 133
Etkind, Efim 151
Evola, Giulio 11
Evtushenko, Evgenii 7

Fedorov, Nikolai 5, 8, 12, 55, 74, 117, 146, 147
Fedotov, Georgii 133, 142, 153
Feuerbach, Ludwig Andreas 24, 27, 33, 53, 107
Fichte, Johann Gottlieb 26, 27, 36, 68, 207
Florensky, Pavel 5, 6, 7, 11, 45, 176, 185, 222
Florovsky, Georgii 6, 7
Foucault, Michel 54, 181
Frank, Semyon 6, 8, 17, 142, 153–4
Freidenberg, Olga 7, **192–4**, 223, 256 n.53

Gachev, Georgii 13, 26, 35, 176, 204, **222–30**, *223*, 258 nn.133, 138
Galich, Aleksandr 151

Genisaretsky, Oleg 93–4
Ginzburg, Aleksandr 151
Ginzburg, Lidiia 114, **123–6**, *124*, 136, 211, 225, 249 n.29
Goethe, Johann Wolfgang von 176
Goldentrikht, Semyon 47
Golitsyn, Vasilii 170
Golosovker, Iakov 7, **192–7**, *194*, 227, 234
Gorbachev, Mikhail 61, 62, 66, 69, 70, 71, 75, 92, 110, 162
Gorbanevskaia, Natalia 151
Gorky, Maksim 72
Griboedov, Aleksandr 7, 159
Gromyko, Iu. B. 93
Grushin, Boris 92
Gulyga, Arsenii **54–60**
Gurevich, Aron 205, 231

Hall, Stuart 232
Hegel, G. W. F. 2, 3, 18, 24, 26, 27, 29, 30, 35, 40, 42, 43, 47, 53, 54, 64, 67–8, 79, 94, 114, 138, 155, 184, 185, 190, 207, 209, 210, 224, 225
Heidegger, M. 27, 52, 53, 114, 115, 225
Heraclitus 53, 85, 229
Herder, Johann Gottfried 176
Herzen, Aleksandr 5, 6, 124, 127, 168, 171
Hesse, Hermann 11, 35, 74, 217, 231
Hoggart, Richard 232
Humboldt, Wilhelm von 176
Husserl, Edmund 27, 51–2, 109, 123, 186, 225

Iakobson, S. G. 93
Iakovlev, Aleksandr 61, **65–9**, 75, 243 n.95
Ianov, Aleksandr **167–71**
Ignatius, St. 129
Ilyenkov, Evald 25, 26, *27*, **27–35**, 36, 43, 47, 56, 103, 108, 109, 224, 234
Ilyin, Ivan 17
Ivan the Terrible 159, 170, 220
Ivanov, Viacheslav V. 81, 83, 181, 217

Jakobson, Roman 78, 81
James, William 145, 228
Jaspers, Karl 52, 114, 121, 124

Kafka, Franz 131
Kant, Immanuel 2, 18, 26, 27–8, 41, 42–3, 46, 54, 57, 90, 106, 176, 183, 184, 196, 213, 226, 227
Kantor, Karl 47
Kapustin, Mikhail 61
Kharms, Daniil 119
Khazanov, Boris **133–6**, 139, 234
Khlebnikov, Velimir 12
Khomiakov, Aleksei 6
Khrushchev, Nikita 21, 23, 26, 35, 48, 61, 136, 168, 170
Kierkegaard, Soren 11, 51, 52, 53, 107, 114, 137, 141, 248 n.47
Kireevsky, Ivan 11, 51, 52, 53, 107, 114, 137, 141
Kolmogorov, Andrei 82
Konrad, Nikolai **197–8, 202–4**, 234
Kopelev, Lev 151, 153
Korzhavin, Naum 151
Kozhinov, Vadim 181, 182
Krivorukov, Viktor 62
Krivulin, Viktor 217
Kuhn, Thomas 181
Kurginian, Sergei 69, 70, **71–5**
Kushner, Aleksandr 149

Lafargue, Paul 84
Laruelle, Marlène 8
Latsis, Otto 61
Lefebvre, Vladimir 13, 93, **97–9**
Lektorsky, Vladislav 8
Lenin, Vladimir 17, 18, 19–20, 30, 35, 39, 40–1, 43, 48, 51, 53, 57, 61, 63, 73, 84, 159
Leontiev, Konstantin 5, 176
Lévi-Strauss, Claude 54
Levitsky, Sergei **153–4**
Lifshits, Mikhail **43–5**
Likhachev, Dmitrii **197–202**, 203–4, 234
Lipavsky, Leonid 119, 122
Lisichkin, Gennadii 61
Liubishchev, Aleksandr **51**, 241 n.64
Losev, Aleksei 7, 8, 103, 176, 177, 178, **185–92**, *186*, 193, 196, 197, 201, 212, 214, 215, 233, 234, 255 n.35
Lossky, Nikolai 7, 17, 153, 185
Lossky, Vladimir 7

Lotman, Iurii 7, 8, 77, 79, **83–92**, *84*, 97, 102–3, 105, 181, 208, 229, 234, 244 n.20
Louth, Andrew 8
Luther, Martin 123

Malinovsky, A. A. 32
Mamardashvili, Merab 7, 8, 26, 35, 43, 77, 87, 92, **103–11**, *104*, 247 n.95
Mandelshtam, Osip 217
Mann, Thomas 11, 206, 217, 230
Mao Zedong 221
Marcuse, Herbert 53, 54, 55, 58
Maritain, Jacque 218
Markarian, Eduard 254 n.5
Markov, Moisei 50
Marr, Naum 19
Marr, Nikolai 193
Marx, Karl 3, 9, 18, 19, 23–4, 26, 28, 32, 38, 42, 43, 56, 60, 63, 64, 65, 67, 68, 69, 75, 96, 103, 125, 156, 209
Medvedev, Pavel 179
Meerson-Aksenov, Mikhail 142, 153
Meletinsky, Eleazar 83
Melville, Herman 228
Men, Aleksandr 8, 152
Merezhkovsky, Dmitrii 6, 8, 176
Meshcheriakov, Aleksandr 32
Michurin, Ivan 4
Mihajlov, Mihajlo **136–42**, 250 n.81
Mikhailov, Feliks 35
Milner-Irinin, Iakov **40–3**, **241 n.47**
Mirandola, Pico de 202
Morozov, Pavlik 41
Morson, Gary 5
Moses 135
Moskaeva, A. I. 93
Mounier, Emmanuel 114, 141

Nalimov, Vasilii 77, **99–103**, 157, 234, 246 nn.56, 63, 68, 69
Nedoshivin, G. A. 47
Nekrasov, Viktor 151
Nepomniashchaia, N. I. 93
Nicholas I 170
Nietzsche, Friedrich Wilhelm 27, 34, 36, 53, 55, 58, 74, 107, 192, 195, 196, 205, 207, 225
Nikon, Patriarch 144

Okudzhava, Bulat 7, 151
Olesha, Iurii 159
Orwell, George 139, 160
Ovsiannikov, Mikhail 47

Palievsky, Petr 181, 182
Pantin, Igor 64
Pantina, N. S. 93
Paramonov, Boris 13, **142–8**
Pascal, Blaise 114, 135
Pasternak, Boris 3, 6, 12, 125, 193
Pazhitnov, Leonid 47
Pechenev, Vadim 64
Peirce, Charles 53, 81, 228
Peter the Great 158, 170
Peterson, Dale 182
Piatigorsky, Aleksandr 105–6, 247 n.75
Picasso, Pablo Ruiz 44
Plato 22–3, 27, 30, 55, 57, 58, 94, 105, 106, 108, 122, 145, 177, 185, 188, 191, 192, 206, 208, 217, 222, 225, 227
Platonov, Andrei 72, 145, 221
Platonov, S. **60–5**
Plekhanov, Georgii 72
Plimak, Evgenii 64
Plotinus 188
Pomerants, Grigorii 9, **126–33**, *127*, 136, 139, 142, 153, 220, 234, 249 nn.47, 52, 250 n.61
Popov, S. V. 93
Pospelov, Gennadii 47
Prishvin, Mikhail 6, 7, 13, 114, *115*, **115–18**, 124, 125, 133, 136, 225
Propp, Vladimir 78, 79, **80–1**
Proudhon, Pierre 68
Pseudo-Dionysius the Areopagite 20–1, 214
Pushkin, Aleksandr 7, 82, 141, 159, 168–9

Rabelais, Francois 179, 189
Rabinovich, Vadim 205
Rasputin, Valentin 148
Ratushinskaia, Irina 151
Redlikh, Roman 153, 154, 155
Roerich, Nicholas 12, 40
Rozanov, Vasilii 6, 7, 11, 114, 133, 142, 146, 147, 148, 152, 225
Rozin, V. M. 93–4
Russell, Bertrand 44, 93

Said, Edward 202
St. Augustine 123, 212, 213
St. Ignatius 129
Sakharov, Andrei 139, 142, 151, 156, **162–7**, *163*, 172, 234, 253 n.160
Sartre, Jean-Paul 25, 27, 52, 55, 59, 105, 114, 115, 123, 134, 225
Saussure, Ferdinand de 81, 180
Scheler, Max 183
Schelling, Friedrich Wilhelm Joseph 54–5, 185, 197
Schlegel, Friedrich 1, 197
Schopenhauer, Arthur 27, 36, 53, 55, 58, 107
Schweitzer, Albert 118
Senokosov, Iurii 110
Shaff, Adam 27–8
Shchedrovitsky, Georgii 26, 35, 77, **92–7**, *93*, 103, 234
Shcheglov, Iurii 83
Shestov, Lev 6, 7, 11, 114, 133, 141, 145, 147
Shklovsky, Igor 49–50
Shklovsky, Viktor 7, **78–9**, 81, 122
Shpet, Gustav 7, 103
Shragin, Boris 47, 153
Simmel, Georg 176
Siniavsky, Andrei 6, 9, 13, 140, 151, 158
Sira, Ben 216
Skriabin, Aleksandr 190
Socrates 70, 103, 105
Solovyov, Vladimir 5, 53, 55, 114, 146, 147, 154, 185, 190–1, 219, 222
Solzhenitsyn, Aleksandr 6, 9, 12, 44–5, 129–30, 131–2, 138–9, 140, 142, 144–5, 151, 153, 164–6, 170, 253 n.160
Spengler, Oswald 11, 35, 58, 176, 184, 191, 192, 196, 205–6, 214–15, 228, 232
Spinoza, Baruch 27, 141, 207
Stalin, Iosif 9, 18–19, **19–23**, 26, 75
Stankevich, Nikolai 6
Steiner, Rudolf 72
Stolovich, Leonid 47

Tagore, Rabindranath 129
Terts, Abram 6, 9, 13, 140, 151, 158
Tillich, Paul 136
Timofeev, Lev 151

Tolstoy, Lev 5, 6, 33, 55, 59, 78, 118, 143, 199, 223
Toporov, Vladimir 83
Trubetskoi, Evgenii 154
Trubetskoi, Nikolai 73
Tsiolkovsky, Konstantin 7, 12
Tsipko, Aleksandr 61, 68
Twain, Mark 228
Tynianov, Iurii 78, 158–9

Uspensky, Boris 83, 88

Venclova, Tomas 151
Vernadsky, Vladimir 7, 12, 87
Veselovsky, Aleksandr 193
Vladimir, Prince 1–2
Voinovich, Vladimir 151
Voloshinov, Valentin 179

Voznesensky, Andrei 7
Vvedensky, Aleksandr 119
Vygotsky, Lev 7
Vysheslavtsev, Boris 7

Wagner, Wilhelm Richard 57, 58, 59, 72, 190
Whitman, Walt 228–9
Williams, Raymond 232
Windelband, Wilhelm 176

Yeltsin, Boris 92
Young, George 8

Zenkovsky, Vasilii 7, 185
Zholkovsky, Aleksandr 83
Zhukovsky, Vasilii 7
Zinoviev, Aleksandr 6, 92

Subject Index

Notes: References to notes comprise the page number plus the note number e.g. 245 n.21 refers to note 21 on page 245.
Page numbers in bold refer to the pages specifically devoted to the given subject.

Absolute, the 59, 195, 215, 218
    absolute beginning 206
    absolute idealism 209
    absolute power 150
    see also autocracy
    absolute spirit 24, 53, 94, 197, 207, 224, 226
    absolute totalitarianism 139
    absolute truth 127–8, 130, 132, 147
    absolute values 132
absolutism 40, 42, 45, 46, 53, 109, 129–30
    ethical 54
    moral 59–60
absolutist monarchy 166
absolutization
    of abstract concepts 187
    of culture 231, 232
absurdity 39, 44, 51, 52, 123, 131, 134–5
acceleration 223
act and action 94
activity **35–40**, 94, 97, 243 nn.37, 43
    thought-activity **93–6**
aesthetic elitism 57–8
aesthetic knowledge 57–8
aesthetics 5, 8, **43–7**, 57, 177, 213, 218
    of equivalence 86
    Losev on 188–91
    of the New Left 55
    Soviet 198
agnostic existentialism 145
agnosticism 144, 145
Alexandrianism 215
alienation 24, 25, 27–8, 29, 43, 52–3, 56
    of knowledge from the object 57–8
    overcoming of 62, 107
    and philosophy of human activity 36, 38, 39
    of Russian intelligentsia 159
    self-alienation 26, 67–8, 224
all-encompassing unity 154, 222
Americanism 147
anarchism 101, 154, 157, 158
anthropology, anthropologism 54, 183
    anthropological communism 24–5
    anthropological idealism 42
    anthropological religion 43
    anthropotechnics 95–6
antinomies 26, 39, 136, **196**, 219
Antiquity 177, 188–9
antisocial escapism 58
anti-Soviet activity 133
anti-utopianism 56
apriorism 226, 227
arche 87, 205, 206
art 57–9, 149–51, 218
    artistic creativity 47, 57, 89, 118, 149, 184
    artistic culture 57
    artistic freedom 149
    artistic modernism 44
    artistic work 44, 90, 143, 175, 223, 224, 230
assimilation 32, 53, 61, 96, 131, 173
atheism 49, 125, 135–6, 141, 150, 153, 165, 218
    and classical liberalism 171
    mass 142
    Mihajlov on 138, 139, 141
    Voltarian 169
attention 118
author 184–5
authoritarianism 128, 129, 130, 132, 171, 220
autocommunication 85, 244 n.14

autocracy
    "autocracy—Orthodoxy—nationality" 2
    in prerevolutionary Russia 130
    Russian 150, 160, 165, 168, 169, 170
    Solzhenitsyn's 138

Bakhtinianism 181, 182
behaviorism 52
being 213
    and thinking 106, 107, 207-8, 225
Big Bang theory 49
biology 51, 102, 247 n.70
Black Hundred nationalism 171
bodhisattva, Buddhist 129
Bolshevik Revolution 2, 3, 52, 61, 62, 73, 103, 114, 159, 170, 222
Bolshevism 3, 18, 22, 23, 61, 107
    aggressive policies of 153
    ideocracy of 130
    and religion 146
    repentance of 159
    sublimated homosexuality in 145, 146, 147
border theology 136
boundary (in culture) 87, 181, 182
bourgeois individualism 10, 52
"bourgeois mechanicism" 18
bourgeois philosophy 36, **51-4**
bourgeois utilitarianism 52
Brothers Karamazov, The 1, 121, 152, 196
Buddhism 12, 13, 73, 100-1, 102, 129, 202
    bodhisattva 129
    Buddhist enlightenment 105
    Zen 127, 128
bureaucratic socialism 38
bureaucratism 38, 41
Byzantium 1-2, 4, 150, 214, 217, 219, 231-2
    and culturology 212, 214-15, 216, 217, 219

Calvinism 144
capitalism 58, 63, 71, 74, 144-5, 155, 163, 164
    Batishchev on 38
    capitalist civilisation 147
    capitalist democracy 145, 155
    capitalist political economy 62
    capitalist revolution, against absolutist monarchy 166
    capitalist society 10, 52, 58, 64, 67, 138, 164
    capitalist system 22, 68, 108, 155, 164
    capitalist technocracy 139
    communism as negation of 63-4
    convergence with socialism 163, 164
    Davydov on 58
    Marx on 68-9, 108
    and Marxist moralism 57
    Paramonov on 143-5
Capital 24, 28, 42, 103
carnival, carnivalesque 179-80, 189, **220-2**
Cartesian *cogito* 105, 108, 116, 206
Cartesian dualism 107
China 160, 202
Chinari 118-19, 122
Christianity 60, 88, 141, 150, 191, **215-16**
    and art **218**
    Averintsev on **215-16**
    and carnivalesque 179-80
    and church 123
    and dialectical materialism 188
    Dostoevsky's 152
    Druskin's conversion to 120
    as existential loneliness 144
    as intercultural mediator **215-16**
    and nationalism 161
    Orthodox 2, 12, 40, 73, 74, 150, 192, 216
    Orthodoxy vs Catholicism 216, 219-20
    Paramonov on 142, 144, 146, 148
    and personalism 128, 133
    and Russian statehood **219**
church 123, 141, 152
CIS (Commonwealth of Independent States) 162
civil war 3, 92
class(es)
    bourgeois 2
    and culture 175
    and nationality **19-23**
    class categories of traditional Marxism 9
    class consciousness 69
    class determinism 59
    class ideology 21
    class structure 50
    class struggle 19, 23, 24, 45, 74

class theory 21
class values 41, 61
  dominant 40, 41, 57
  kulaks as a 3
  and language **20**, **21–2**
  Lenin's doctrine **19–20**
  lower 161
  Marx on **21**, 66, 69
  middle 73, 161
  and post-Stalinist Marxism 25
  social 2
  and universal human values **25–6**
  upper 88
  working 38, 130
cogito, Cartesian 105, 108, 116, 206
collectivism 4, 13, 40–1, 55, 63, 164, 231
  as alienation 67
  "closest collectives" 155
  and general methodology 96
  and individualism 117, 156
  and knowledge 74
  moral values of 130
  religious 148
collectivist subjectivity 43, 72
Commonwealth of Independent States (CIS) 162
communism
  and fascism 107
  mystical neo- 69–75
  post- 62, 74
  as religion 69–75
Communist Manifesto 23–4
Communist Party 4, 18, 22, 23, 64, 71
  Third Program of 21, 22, 26
  Twentieth Congress of 23
conceptualism 13
Confucianism 202
consciousness 10, 25, 39, 51, 75, 85, **103–11**
  and activism 36
  aesthetic 47, 200
  bourgeois 44
  class 69
  collectivist 193
  false 75
  human 62, 75, 106, 108, 116, 196, 200, 201
  and individualism 150

and language 100
Mamardashvili on **103–11**
and meditation 102
of the other 185
planetary 136–42
priority of matter over 62
religious 5, 136, 217
Russian 7
self- 32, 68, 209, 210
social 4, 25, 30, 62, 219
and subjectivism 36
theory of **103–11**
and translation 87
see also self-consciousness
conservatism 88, 127, 133, **152–3**, 170, 217, 230
  conservative dissidentism 145
  conservative ritualism 132
  romantic 170
constructive dialectics 185–6
consumerism 58
contingency 89–90
convergence, between capitalism and communism/socialism 64, 139, 156, 163, 164, 165
corporeality 133, 189, 190
cosmic evolution 34–5
cosmism 8, 12, 117
cosmology 49, 188, 226
cosmopolitanism 54, 202
"cosmo-psycho-logos" 228
counterculture, of younger generation 58
creativity 5, 40, 45, 46, **89–90**, 118, 126
  artistic 47, 57
  in behavior 118
  cultural 195
  freedom as condition for 154
  spiritual 146
culture **85–6**, **175–8**
  artistic 57
  Brodsky on 150
  bourgeois 44, 91
  cultural diversity 175, 177, 201, 222–30
  cultural dynamics 91–2
  cultural forms 96, 213–15
  cultural studies 52, 185, 186, 205, 232–3
  cultural synthesis 216–19
  in culturology 175–8

definition 175–8, 205–6, 244 n.14
diversity of **222–30**
ecology of culture 199, 200
and explosion 91–2, 103
and imagination **192–7**
Lotman on 85, 87–8, 91
and myth **192–7**
phenomenology of **185–92**
philosophy of *see* culturology
and politics 212, 232–3
Russian 142, 143, 148
Soviet 93, 110
Stalin on 20
typology of 85–6, 88
Western 172
culturology **11**, 13, 14, 172, **175–230**,
   231–3, 253 nn.1, 2, 259 n.3
vs cultural studies 232–3
two procedures in research 177–8
cybernetics 10, 48, 49, 52, 103

Darwinism 48, 51
deaf-blind children, education of 32–3
death **34**
   of author 184
   "corpse" metaphor 188
Decembrists 2, 21, 159, 168–9, 170
defamiliarization (*ostranenie*) 24, 78, 122
   self-defamiliarization 125
   see also estrangement
democracy 92, 150, 152, 153, 155, 161, 170,
   220
   democratic socialism 138
   liberalism and science in political
      thought **164, 165, 166**
   personal freedom and planetary
      consciousness 137, 138, 140, 142
   personalism, pluralism, and spiritual
      universalism 130, 132
   privacy as the ultimate value 149, 150
   religious justification of 144–5, 150
   sexual liberation against nationalism
      144, 145, 147
   vs theocracy 220
Devils, The 133, 171, 250 n.61
dialectical idealism **185–92**
dialectical materialism 3, 4, **18–19**, 25, 56,
   61, 64, 79, 187–8, 239 n.1

and historical materialism 4, 8, 18, 20,
   56, 233
philosophy of science **48, 49, 50–1**
renewal of dialectics 27, 30–1, 32, 33
technology and nature **48, 49, 50–1**
dialectics 18, 25, **27–35**, 46, 50, 66, 177,
   185, **190**
   constructive 185–6
   Frankfurt School 39
   Hegelian 35, 53, 79
   Losev on 187, 188, 190, 191
   Marxist 38, 184
   renewal of **27–35**
dialogical logic **204–11**
   dia-logic **207–9**
dialogism **178–85, 206–11**
   in Bakhtin and Bibler 209–10
   dialogic imagination 183
   and structuralism 180–1
diamat *see* dialectical materialism
diary (philosophical) 115–26, 225
difference 117
disputes and controversies
   Averintsev vs Bakhtin 220–2
   Averinttev vs Spengler 214–15
   Bakhtin vs Spengler 184
   Bibler vs Hegel 209
   Mihajlov vs Solzhenitsyn 138–9
   Paramonov vs Solzhenitsyn 144–5
   Pomerants vs Dostoevsky 133,
      250 n.61
   Pomerants vs Solzhenitsyn 130–2
   Sakharov vs Solzhenitsyn 164–6
dissidentism, dissident movement 145, 151,
   162, 164, 169
   conservative 145
dissident scholars, liberal 158–62
distinctivism 38–9
diversity of cultures 175, 177, 201, 222–30
dualism
   Cartesian 107
   in Russian culture 65, 91, 242 n.90

East and West 150, 202–4
Eastern Orthodoxy 105, 215–16
eccentricity 151
eclecticism 45, 74, 182, 201
ecology, of culture 199, 200

Economic and Philosophic Manuscripts of 1844 9–10, 23, 61, 67
economic determinism 21, 64, 75, 214
Economic Problems of Socialism in the USSR, The 22
ecumenism 129
eidos 186–7, 189, 190, 191, 192, 196
  and meaning-image (smysloobraz) 196
elitism 57–8, 63–4
émigré thought/émigrés 147, **153–6**
empire 162
empiricism 28–9, 30, 36, 152, 172
emptiness 102, 105, 120, 122, 134, 213, 229
Enlightenment, the 2, 44, 53, 86, 114, 172, 211
enlightenment, Buddhist 105, 108
epistemology 28, 49, 100, 101, 195, 235
essentialism 67–8
estrangement 24, 122
eternal recurrence 167
ethics 33, **40–3**, 46, 49, 54–60, **98–9**, 116–17, 118, 143–5, 156, 198, **210**, **216–19**
  ethical absolutism 54
  and art and cultural synthesis 216–19
  and democracy 143–4
  Marxist **41–2**, **43**, 241 n.47
  and pedagogy 210–11
  renewal of **40–3**
  ethical skepticism 69
etiquette, literary 198, 199
Eurasianism 8, 11, 72, 73–4, 75, 170, 243 n.106
Eurocentrism 173, 202–3
European Enlightenment 44
evolutionism 101
  synthetic theory of 51
excluded middle 157, 195
existentialism 9, 11, 31, **52**, 104, 106–7, 120–3, 152
  agnostic 145, 147
  and antinomies 39
  atheistic 134
  Bakhtinian 180, 181, 184
  and bourgeois individualism 52
  Camusian 55, 131
  existential culturology 225
  French 25, 55, 131, 134
  and idealism 54
  Pomerantsian 131, 220
  religious **118–23**, 133, 171
  in Russian thought **114–15**
  Sartrean 55, 134
  Shestovian 145, 147
  and personalism **114–15**
  and structuralism 78
  existential transcendence 126
  see also personalism
explosion (in culture) 91–2, 103

fact (in history) 88–9
faith, religious 1, 46, 60, 134, 138, 153
fanaticism 127, 129, 135, 165, 218
fate 189
feedback 66–7
fetishism 31, 38
filosofiia, definition of 5
Five Year Plans 22
Formal School/formalism 10, **78–81**, 83, 180, 182, 244 n.20
Frankfurt School 39, 53, 55, 58
freedom 11, 24, 38, 52, 68, 70, 96, 97, 123, 139, 161
  and Cartesian dualism 107
  cognitive 106
  Davydov on 59–60
  in émigré thought **153–6**
  free will 123
  and Kant's antinomies 196
  kingdom of 63
  Lotman and Nalimov on 86, 90, 102
  Mamardashvili on 110
  and necessity 154
  paradoxes of 171–3
  philosophy of personality and 113–73
  Platonov on 64–5
  and solidarity 153–6
  Shchedrovitsky on 96
  see also liberalism, personal freedom
French
  Enlightenment 53
  existentialism 25, 55, 131, 134
  image of the world 228
  Revolution 21, 70, 91
friend, friendship 118

game (organizational) **95**
"general line" 116
general methodology 10, **92–7**
  and Marxism 96–7
general'naia liniia (general party line) 116
genre **181**, 193, 210, **223–4**
  speech genres 180–1
German
  Enlightenment 172
  idealism 43, 54–5, 195, 197
glasnost 14, 55, **60–5**, 66, 68
Gnosticism 146
God-builders movement 72
Grand Inquisitor, in Dostoevsky 138, 196
grassroots ideology 11, 59
grassroots turn, in Marxism **54–60**
Great Canon 45
Great Depression 63
"Great Tradition" 12
Guernica 44
Gulag 101, 129, 158, 195

Hegelian idealism 3, 35, 42, 94, 114, 209
hermeneutics 11, 67, 201, **212–13**
heroic pessimism 135
histmat *see* historical materialism
historians, liberal 167–71
historical determinism 36, 62, 63, 65, 75, 96
historical materialism 3, 4, 8, 18–19, 56, 66, 67, 233
  and Orthodox Marxism 62, 65
  and renewal of ethics 40, 42, 43
  and Stalin's later thinking 20, 22
  see also dialectical materialism
historicism 79, **123–6**, 149–50, 197–204
history 160, **167–71**, 203
  four approaches to 169–70
  and personality **124–6, 150**
  and philosophy 1–4
  philosophy of 150
  Russian 1–4, 160, 169–70
  and semiotics **88–9**
history of philosophy 8, 18, 53, 106, 142, 190, 239 n.17
holism 28, 230
"Holy Russia" 219
Homo Sovieticus 69

human activity 8, 10, 24, 25, **35–40**, 46, 56, 94, 96, 97, 104, 143, 240 n.37
human values, universal 26, 203
humanism, humanness, humankind 10, 12, **23–6**, 60, 63, 64, 70–1, 72, 144, 153, 185, **197–204**, 218, 219
  "humanistic revolution" 38
  universal, panhuman values 26, 41, 203
humanities 5, 10, 11, 77, 81–2, 100, 102, 119, **178–85**, 200–1
  Bakhtin on methodology of 11, 82, **178–85**, 201
  Japanese 203
  Russian 81, 92, 176, 194, 201–2
  Soviet 61, 83, 158, 192
  specificity of 183–4
  against "vulgar sociologism" 22
  see also culturology
Husserlianism 52
hyperreality 13

I, ego, self 121, 156
  egocentrism 200
  self-defamiliarization 125
idea 94, 157, 190–1, 235
  ideas against ideocracy 13, 14, 235, 259 n.4
  see also ideocracy
ideal 30, 157
idealism 32, 36, 40, 50, 53, 114, 185–92
  absolute 209
  of action 96
  anthropological 42
  and Bolshevism 146
  bourgeois 17, 18
  dialectical 185–92
  German 43, 54–5, 68, 195, 197
  Hegelian 3, 35, 42, 94, 114, 209
  Ilyenkov on 28–9, 30
  Menshevist 18
  militant 51
  objective 22–3, 30, 31, 42
  philosophical 95
  physical 18
  physiological 32
  Platonic 94, 108
  schools of 54
  and Silver Age religious philosophy 146

294 Subject Index

Sophiological 190–1
of thought 96
transcendental 68, 94
see also realism
ideocracy 4, 13, 130, 234, 235
see also idea
imagination 40, 47, 55, 65, 67, 155, **195–6**
Bachelard's theory of 228
deduction of the 226–7
dialogic 183
German 227
Russian 143, 161
"immanent epiphany" 118
impersonality 150
infantilism 58
integrity
in culturology 177, 178
of human nature 199, 234
moral 60, 140, 163
of an object 186–7, 189, 190, 191, 192, 196
national 9, 19–20, 21, 130
intelligentsia 2–3, 54, 110, **130–1**, 133, **159, 168**, 169, 190
and ideocracy 235
and narod (people) 130
post-Stalin 196
Russian 2, 151, 153, 158, 159, 212, 216, 235
self-reflective 199
Soviet 7, 125, 128, 168–9, 217, 231
interdisciplinarity 227, 233
internationalism 40, 69, 137–8, 141, 164, 165
irony 127, 185
irreducibility 51, 106–7, 232
Islam 72, 74, 150

Japan
humanities in 203
Zen in 128
Jews 131, 133–6
Judeophilia/Judeophobia 147

Kantianism 42–3, 106
neo-Kantianism 18, 183, 184

labor 63
language 19–22, 29–30, 36, 82, 90–1, 100

computerized 82–3
and consciousness 100
and culturology 232
meta- 227–8
and neopositivism 52
philosophical 225
poetic function of 81
probabilistic methods for studying **99–103**
and reality 90–1
semiotics of 83–4, 86–7
and speech 180
and speech utterances 180–1
see also linguistics
laughter 179, 220–1
leftism 55, 58, 166
Leninism 10, 18
see also Marxism-Leninism
"Letter to the Soviet Leaders" 164–5
liberal dissident scholars **158–62**
liberal historians **167–71**
liberalism 11, 14, 26, 132, 133, **151–73**
and personalism **151–3**
political 136
in political thought 162–7
pure 154, 155
and religion/religiosity 139, 142, 145, **152–3**
Russian **152**, 158, 160, 162
Russian and Western 166
and science
secular 139, **152**
and social atomism 154
Soviet 151, 152, 156, 158
linguistics 5, 19–20, 22, 75, 82
see also language
literature 149–51, 158–60, 168–9, 217
novel 181, 183
village prose 148, 199
literary etiquette 198, 199
living-thinking **222–30**
logic 195, 207
dia-logic 207
of paradox 208–9
logocentrism 143
Logos 20–1, 85, 184, 221, 228

Manichaeism 74
Marxism 9–10, 25, **17–75**, 106–7

criticism of Marxism **65–9**
Mamardashvili on 106–7
Marxist aesthetics 49
"Marxist eschatology" 33
Marxist epistemology 49
Marxist ethics 41–2, 43, 49, 241 n.47
Marxist methodology 50, 92
Marxist moralism 57
Marxist ontology 49
Marxist psychology 32
Western 75
Marxism-Leninism 7, 132, 161, 197, 233
master/slave relationship 189
materialism
   Losev on 187–8
   vulgar 31
   see also dialectical materialism, historical materialism
materialist scholasticism 6, 191
meaning-image (*smysloobraz*) 196–7, 227
   and eidos 196
"Menshevist idealism" 18
messenger (*vestnik*), in Druskin 122–3
metaphysics 70, 187, 190, 206
   physical 108, 109
metaphor 193–4, 226
methodology
   of Averintsev 214
   of Gachev 222
   general 10, **92–9**
   of the humanities 177, **178–85**, 201, 202
   Marxist 50, 56
   Marxist-Leninist 4
   of the natural sciences 18
   methodological tolerance 201
Middle Ages 85, 179, 189, 198, 221
   and Christianity and culture 209, 212, 213
mode of production 67, 69, 71, 189, 207
modernism 45
modernity 137, 209, 226
monism/monistic systems 40, 156, 158, 201
monotheism 101, 102, 135, 142, 150
morality 40–1, 143, 148, 154, 162, 196, 210
   collectivist 74, 116
   moralism, Marxist 57
   moralistic turn in Marxism 55, **56–7, 58, 59, 60**

Paramonov on 143
of religion 128, 161
Moscow Logical Circle/Moscow Methodological Circle 10, 92, 97, 245 n.38
multiculturalism 110, 172
mysticism 101–3
   mystical anarchism 101
   mystical communism/neo-communism **69–75**
myth 143, 144, 147, 164, 165, 168, **192–7**
   definition of 187
   and national cultures 229
mythology 44, 60, 80, 83, 136, 165–6, 185
   dialectical materialism as 187–8
   Losev on 190

name 187
narod (people) 2, 130, 131
nation, nationality **19–23**
   national images of the world 227–9
      American 228–9
      French 228–9
   national character and spirit 11–12, 229
nationalism 9, 21, 23, 26, 54, 60, 69, 75, 127, 138, 147–8
   Black Hundred 171
   and conservatism 152–5, 160
   Georgian 110–11
   and internationalism 138
   isolationist 171
   Khazanov on 134
   liberal 171
   Mihajlov on 137, 138, **142**
   national socialism 170, 171
   neo-Stalinist 161
   Paramonov on **148**
   radical 151
   religious 139, 153
   romantic 170
   Russian 150, 151, 165, 169
   sexual liberation against **142–8**
   Soviet 161, 169
   and totalitarianism 130
natural sciences 11, 17, 18, 48, 51, 52, 176, 183, 201, 208, 226
nature **48–51, 99–103, 115–18**
naturists and socialists (in aesthetics) 47

Nazi Germany/Nazism 4, 21, 124, 149, 152, 153, 218
neo-communism **69–75**
neofascism 9, 12, 170
neopositivism 52, 54
neo-rationalism 10, **77–112**, 83, 96, 108
   see also rationalism
New Left movement 55, 58
Nietzscheanism 192
nihilism 55, 58, 136
nominalism 28–9
nothingness 52, 105, 125, 129, 167, 229
   see also emptiness

objective idealism 22–3, 30, 31, 42
objective reality 37–8, 47, 51, 72
objectivism and subjectivism 36, 37
objectivity 11, 22, 31, 36–7, 108–9
October Revolution 2, 3, 52, 61, 62, 73, 103, 114, 159, 170, 222
Oedipus complex 229
Old Believers 144
Old Bolsheviks 140
one-party system 164
ontology
   Marxist 49
   probabilistic 100, 101
onto-practice 95–6
Orestes complex 229
organizational-activity games 95
orientalism 202
Orthodox Christianity 2, 12, 40, 72, 73, 74, 142, 143, 150, 192
Orthodox Church 153, 189
orthodox Marxism 20, 22, 44, 45, 49, 60–5, 108–9, 176
outsidedness, being beyond (*vnenakhodimost'*) 183–4

paradox 88, 96, 98, 100, 103, 125–6, 135, 137, 143, 147, 154, 156, 165, 168, 171–3, 181, 184, 205, **208–9**, 213, 233
party politics 26, 45
peasantry 118, 130, 168
   kulaks 3
pedagogy 32–3, 95–6, 97, 210–11

People's Labor Union of Russian Solidarists 153
perestroika 14, 49, 60–1, 65, 66, 98, 110, 162, 170–1, 224
   and mystical neo-communism 69, 71, 75, 77
personal freedom **136–42**, 151, 153, 161, 162, 169
   see also freedom, liberalism
personalism 11, 13, 14, 36, **113–50**, 182, 183, 230, 234
   critical 126
   and existentialism **114–15**
   Russian-Jewish **133–6**
   religious 129, 142, 171, 172
   see also existentialism
personality 31, **115–18**
   cult of 41, 161
   and society
pessimism, heroic 135
phenomenology 11, 52, 54, **103–11**, 184, **185–92**
philology **197–204**
   definition of 201
philosophy
   philosophical anthropology 8, 180, 183
   philosophical awakenings 6–7, 103
   philosophical diary 115–16, 225
   and *filosofiia* **4–6**
   as liberation 233–4
   and philosophers' fate 234
   and poetry 7
   and Russian history 1–4
   of science 8, 48–51, 97
   specifics of Russian philosophy **1–6**, **234–5**
   studies of Russian philosophy 7–9, 237 nn.11–14
   Western 53–4, 106
planetary consciousness **136–42**
pleasure principle 58
pluralism 11, 44–5, 63, **126–33**, 144, 145, 150, **156–8**
pochvennichestvo 11, 59
poetics 8, 83, 87, 191, 205
   poetics of culture 205
poetry 6, 7, 81, 82, 100, 215

Politburo 4, 61, 66
politics
   political conservatism 152
   and culture 212, 232-3
   political thought **162-7**
   political utopianism 231
polytheism 142, 144, **150-1**
postcapitalist economic system 63
postcommunism 62, 74
   postcommunist Marxism/post-Marxist communism 10
postmodernism 13, 183, 230
Postperestroika 69-70
post-Stalin era
   intelligentsia 196
   Marxism 25
   major trends of Russian thought in 9-14
post-structuralism 90-2, 102-3, 180, 184, 185, 102, 103, 180, 184-5, 206
pragmatism 52, 54, 72, 145, 233
precapitalism 172
privacy 67, **148-51**
   and eccentricity 151
probabilistic ontology 100-1
probabilistic philosophy 77, **99-103**
progress 166-7, 203
Protestant Reformation 144, 145, 171
psychoanalysis 36, 44, 102, 143, 144, 192-3
psychology **32**, 96, 97, 131
Puritanism 145

quantum mechanics 48, 49, 99, 100

rationalism, rationality 44, 78-111, 114, 143, 152, 172, 177, 192-3
   nonclassical, postclassical 107-9
   see also neo-rationalism
realism 28-9, 44, 47, 132, 198
   see also idealism, materialism
reality 37
reflection, theory of 39, 84
reflective analysis 93, **97-9**
relationships, social 28, 58, 62, 67, 192
relativism 29, 78, 182
relativity, theory of 48, 49, 70, 120
religion 10, 17, 33, 55, 69, 128
   annihilation of 212
   anthropological 43
   apophatic 119-20
   Bolshevism as 146
   communism as 69, 70, 71, 72
   and democracy 145
   definition of 128
   ecumenism 129
   Khazanov on 133-6, 139
   Marxism as 72
   Mihajlov on 139, 141
   and nondemocratic institutions 150
   nondenominational 128
   Paramonov on 144, 145, 147
   polytheism 142, 144, 150-1
   Protestantism 144-5
   and sexuality 146-8
   and the state 219-20
religiosity 128, 129, 141, 142, 144, 145, 148, **151-3**, 167
religious
   belief, faith 1, 4, 46, 60, 67, 123, 134, 138, 153
   conservatism 133
   denominationalism 141
   existentialism **118-23**, 133, 171
   fanaticism 135
   liberalism 139, 142, 145, **152-3**
   moralism 59
   personalism 129, 142, 171, 172
   pluralism 144, 145
   romanticism 165
   values 132, 171, 204
Renaissance 172, 189, 198, **202-3**, 231
   Italian 172, 231
repression 41, 44, 57, 58, 130, 140, 143, 145, 179
   purges 179, 221
revolution, theory of 59
romanticism 165, 170, 172, 197
   neoromanticism 170
   and structuralism 197
Russia
   Russian Empire 2, 147, 162
   "Russian eschatological postcommunism" 74
   Russian Hegelianism 185
   "Russian ideology" 160-1

Russian intelligentsia 2, 151, 153, 158, 159, 212, 216, 235
Russian-Jewish personalism **133–6**
Russian Orthodoxy 45, 55, 94, 138, 142, 150, 187
Russian religious moralism 59
Russian Revolution 19, 65, 91, 145, 189, 192
Russian Structuralism **81–3**, 244 n.20
Russian Westernism 158, 172

science **48–51, 69–75, 162–7**, 226
science, philosophy of 8, **48–51**, 97
scientific socialism 68
Second World War 19, 33, 48, 197–8, 231
sectarianism 218
secularism, secular liberalism 139, 152, **219–20**
self-alienation 26, 67–8, 224
self-consciousness 32, 68, 97, 104–5, 209, 210
   see also consciousness
semantic vacuum 100, 101
semantics 193, 194
semiosphere **86–8**, 102
semiotics 10, **85–9**, 92, 97, 208, 244 n.9
   semiotic codes 88–9, 90, 102, 181
   and history 88–9
   see also structuralism
sexuality, sexual liberation 133, **146–8**
silence 102, 121, 184–5
Silver Age 6, 8, 146–7, 191, 212
skepticism 29, 59–60, 126, 141, 145, 152, **156–8**
Slavophilism 11, 148, 165, 230
   neo-Slavophilism 11, 130, 217–18, 230
   Slavophilic "totalism" 53
slavery 123, 188–9, 192
sobornost' (togetherness) 142
social
   anthropology 24–5
   atomism 154
   class, Russian intelligentsia as 2
   democracy 61, 64, 72
   determinism 36, 107
   relationships 28, 58, 62, 67, 192
socialism 7, 10, 22–3, 25, 62, 63
   bureaucratic 38
   convergence with capitalism 163, 164
   democratic 138
   developed 3
   and elitism 64
   English 139
   humanism of 72
   national 170, 171
   scientific 68
   Stalinist 36
   utopian 68
socialist realism 44, 47, 132
societalists (in aesthetics) 47
socio-anthropological method 231
socioeconomic determinism 214
solidarity, solidarism 64, 66, 114, 131, **153–6**
   middle way, third position 155
Sophiology 190–1
Soviet
   Academy of Sciences 41, 197
   aesthetics 45, 198
   culturology 191, 212, 231, 232–3
   intelligentsia 7, 125, 128, 168–9, 217, 231
   Marxism 3, 9–10, 17–75, 79, 161, 170, 233
   see also USSR
Soviet Union *see* USSR (Union of Soviet Socialist Republics)
Sovietology 8, 154
spirit, spiritualism 75, 134, 140
   spiritual freedom 138, 159–60
   spiritual universalism **126–33**
Stalinist
   socialism 36
   totalitarianism 164
structuralism 10, 11, 36, 38, 44, 52, 54, **77–92**, 102, 172, 175, 176, 180, 244 nn.9, 20
   Bakhtin on 180–1, 182
   classical 87, 88, 89
   and culturology 176
   from formalism to **78–81**
   and literary forms 201
   post- 90–1, 103, 180, 184, 185, 206
   premises and features of Russian **81–3**

Subject Index

and post-structuralism 90–1
and semiotic systems 102–3
theoretical 92
Western 35
see also semiotics
surrealism 192
symbol 105–6
Symbolism 192, 205, 216
systematic thought-activity **93–6**
systems theory 10, 97

Tale of Bygone Years, The 1–2
Taoism 13, 100–1, 102, 128
Tartu-Moscow semiotic school 10, 83
technology **48–51**
text, textuality 85, 181–2
   vs code 85
   pan-textuality 13
"tertium non datur" 157, 195
Thaw 23, 25, 26, 35, 61
theology 20, 72, 73, 136
Theses on Feuerbach 36, 107
thinking and being 106, 107, **207–9**
   thinking-living (*zhiznemyslie*) 222–30
Third Program, of Communist Party 21, 22, 26
"third things", in Mamardashvili 108, 109
Thomism 45, 52, 54
thought-activity theory **93–6**
thought-image (*mysleobraz*) 227
time 149
togetherness (*sobornost'*) 142
tolerance 201
   repressive 45
totality, Slavophilic 53
totalitarianism 140, 150, 153, 160, 218, 221, 231
   absolute 139
   Ginzburg on 126
   and liberalism in political thought 164, 165, 166
   logic and "removal of opposites" 18, 165–6
   and nationalism 130, 145, 146, 148
   and personal freedom/planetary consciousness 137, 138, 139, 140, 141, 142
   and science in political thought 164, 165, 166
   and sexual liberation 145, 146, 148
   Soviet 68
transcendence 110
   existential 125–6
   and immanence 125–6
transduction, in Bibler 207
truth 53, 45
typology of cultures 85–6
Twentieth Congress, of Communist Party 23

understanding 105, 109
Union of Soviet Socialist Republics *see* USSR
unity 55
universe 34, 50, 100, 137, 167
universalism 12, 126–33
   universal human values 26, 203
USSR (Union of Soviet Socialist Republics) 81
   atheism in 139
   collective self-government in 155
   communism in 41, 70
   culture/culturology in 176, 232
   disintegration of 162
   formalist methodology in 78
   religion in 212
   socialism in 61
   see also Soviet
utopia **69–75**
utopianism 56, 65, 75, 142, 218
   anti- 56
   political 231
   scientific 36
   and socialism 56
   violent 217

voluntarism 36, 58, 68, 74
vulgar materialism 30, 31
vulgar sociologism 22, 57, 193

Wandering Jew/Wandering Russian 147
War and Peace 223–4
West and East 150, 202–4
Westernism 158, 165, **151–73**

late-Soviet **171–3**
  paradoxes of 171–3
Western philosophy 53–4, 106
working class 38, 130

World War II 19, 33, 48, 197–8, 231

Zen Buddhism 127, 128
Zoroastrianism 74

www.ingramcontent.com/pod-product-compliance
Lightning Source LLC
Chambersburg PA
CBHW070017010526
44117CB00011B/1614